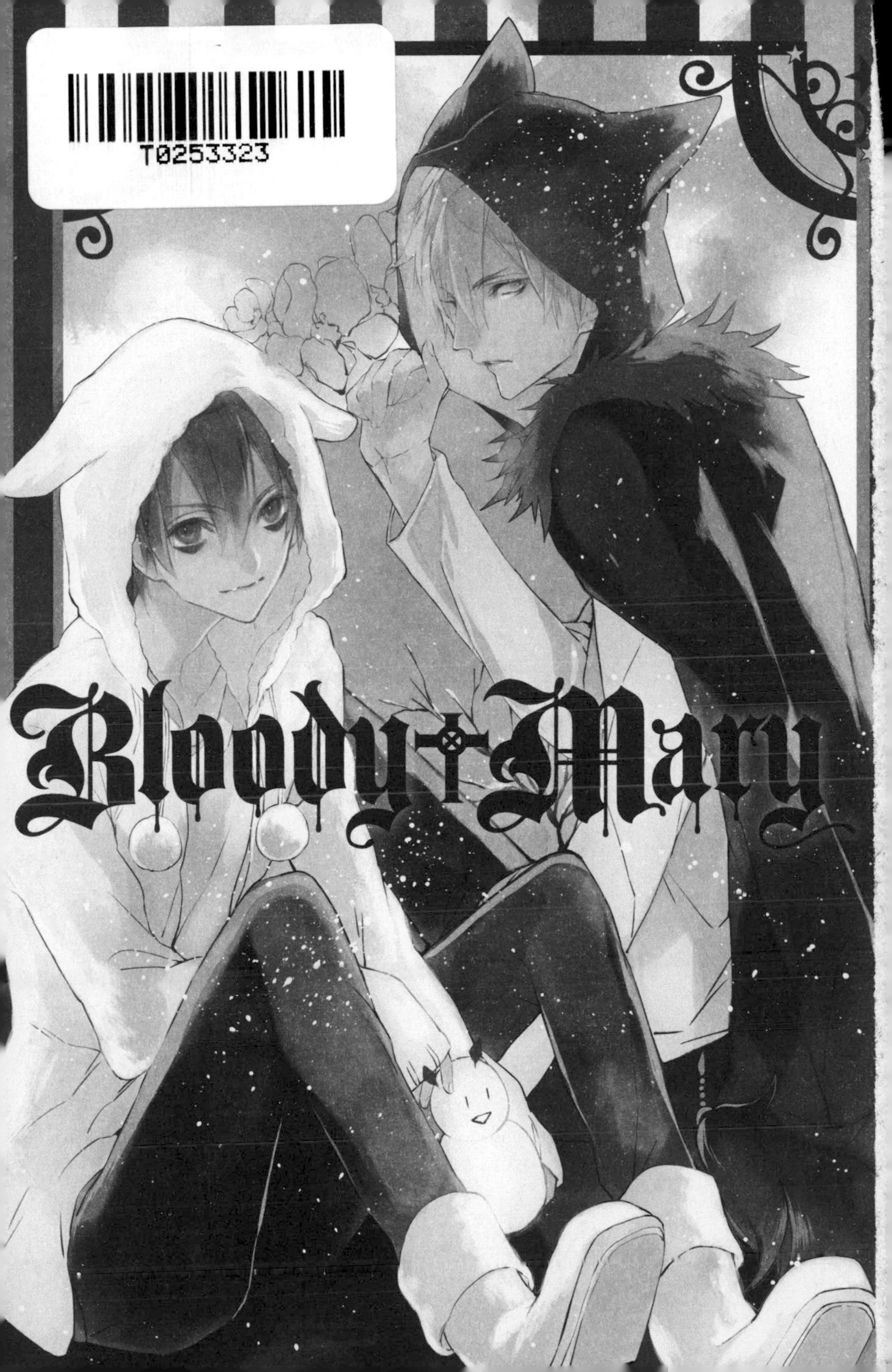
Bloody+Mary

Bloody † Mary

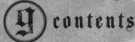

contents

BLOOD ✛ 33 The Wheels of Fate
007

BLOOD ✛ 34 Soul Fragment
036

BLOOD ✛ 35 Atonement
073

BLOOD ✛ 36 Mary and "Mary"
117

A Colloquy on the Bedroom: Follow-Up
160

Postscript
161

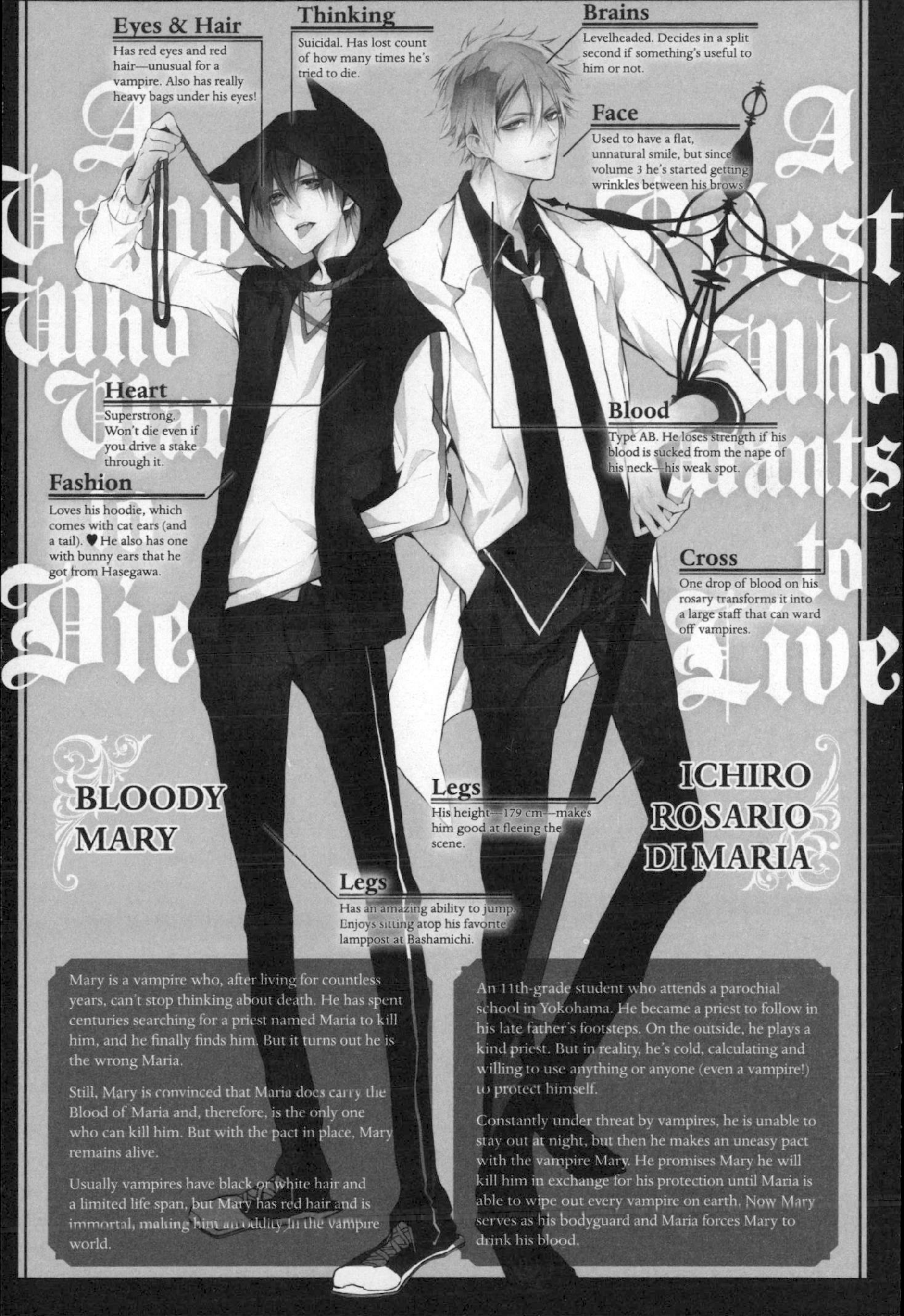

Eyes & Hair
Has red eyes and red hair—unusual for a vampire. Also has really heavy bags under his eyes!
Thinking
Suicidal. Has lost count of how many times he's tried to die.
Brains
Levelheaded. Decides in a split second if something's useful to him or not.
Face
Used to have a flat, unnatural smile, but since volume 3 he's started getting wrinkles between his brows.
Heart
Superstrong. Won't die even if you drive a stake through it.
Fashion
Loves his hoodie, which comes with cat ears (and a tail). ♥ He also has one with bunny ears that he got from Hasegawa.
Blood
Type AB. He loses strength if his blood is sucked from the nape of his neck—his weak spot.
Cross
One drop of blood on his rosary transforms it into a large staff that can ward off vampires.
BLOODY MARY
ICHIRO ROSARIO DI MARIA
Legs
His height—179 cm—makes him good at fleeing the scene.
Legs
Has an amazing ability to jump. Enjoys sitting atop his favorite lamppost at Bashamichi.

Mary is a vampire who, after living for countless years, can't stop thinking about death. He has spent centuries searching for a priest named Maria to kill him, and he finally finds him. But it turns out he is the wrong Maria.

Still, Mary is convinced that Maria does carry the Blood of Maria and, therefore, is the only one who can kill him. But with the pact in place, Mary remains alive.

Usually vampires have black or white hair and a limited life span, but Mary has red hair and is immortal, making him an oddity in the vampire world.

An 11th-grade student who attends a parochial school in Yokohama. He became a priest to follow in his late father's footsteps. On the outside, he plays a kind priest. But in reality, he's cold, calculating and willing to use anything or anyone (even a vampire!) to protect himself.

Constantly under threat by vampires, he is unable to stay out at night, but then he makes an uneasy pact with the vampire Mary. He promises Mary he will kill him in exchange for his protection until Maria is able to wipe out every vampire on earth. Now Mary serves as his bodyguard and Maria forces Mary to drink his blood.

"MARY"

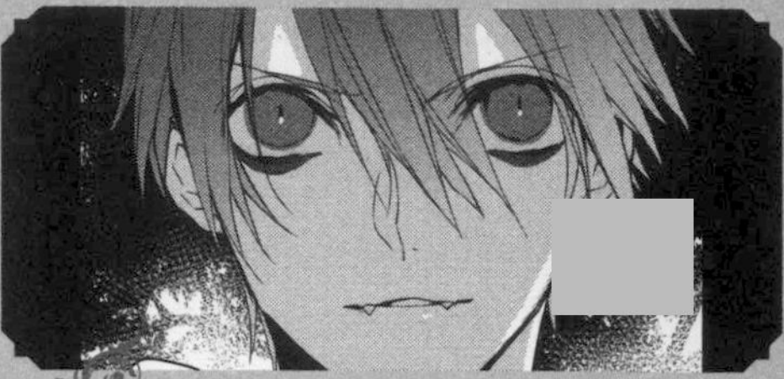

Mary's twin brother, who went by the name "Mary" when he was human. His reason for becoming a vampire will finally be revealed...! When you find out, you'll no doubt come to love the nonmasochist "Mary" as much as Mary!

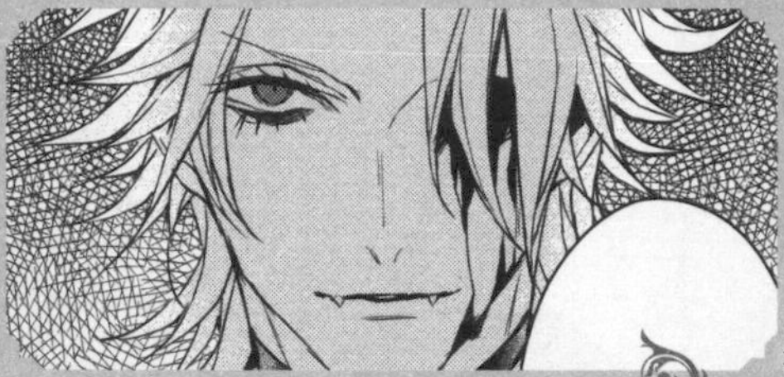

ALDILA

Because of his crazy infatuation with Bloody Eye, he offered up his own left eye for her. Clearly, this guy is reckless. Learn more about him on page 162! This volume will explain why Madam Eye needed his left eye in the first place.

BLOODY EYE

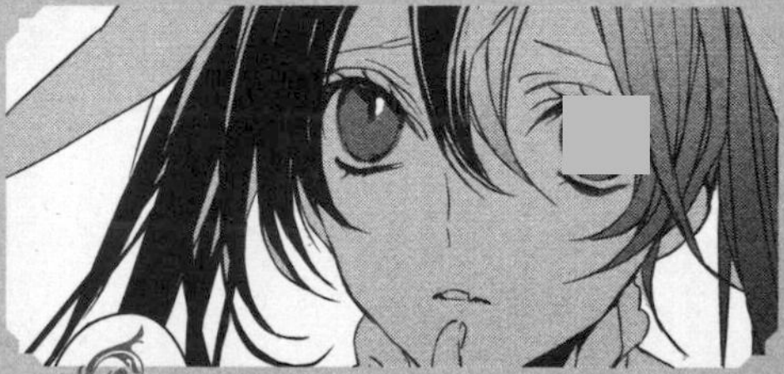

Up to now, Lady Hydra has been the most powerful heroine in the story, but now there's a new powerful vampire heroine to deal with. She is "You-know-who" (as referred to by the trio).

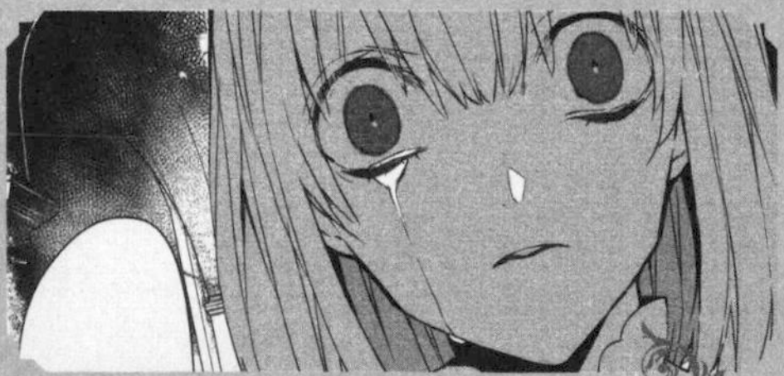

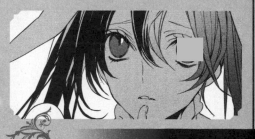

HYDRA

Despite her long life, Lady Hydra is surprisingly naive. She has tried to forget the human girl-child whom she was so charmed by and to pursue a new love. But now that same girl (Bloody Eye) is harassing her again.

\ Even a masochist could understand it A recap of volume 8 in 2-3 minutes! /

Mary finally remembers his forgotten past!

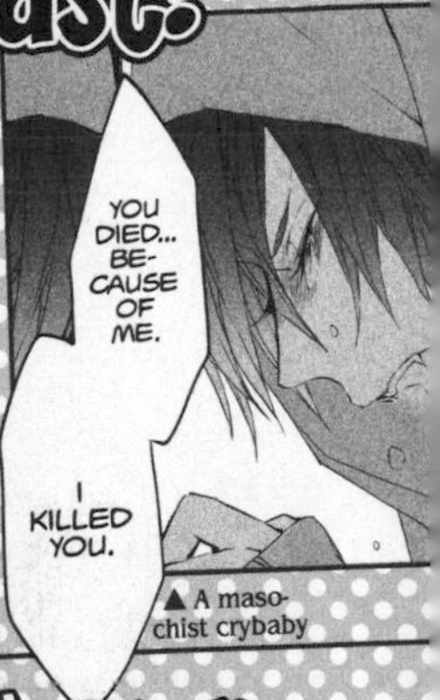
YOU DIED... BE-CAUSE OF ME.
I KILLED YOU.
▲ A masochist crybaby

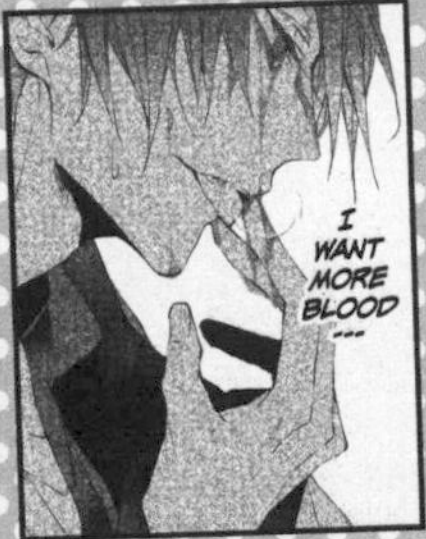
I WANT MORE BLOOD...
▲ A sadist on a rampage

...And yet, his memory was from when he was human and he killed "Mary" (the nonmasochist). This grave revelation weighs on him, and he flees reality, which allows "Mary" to surface in his place.

As for "Mary"... On one hand, it's good that he's finally come forth, but there's something crazed about him! He's become more and more bloodthirsty... "Mary" is bad news!

Lady Hydra's Situation

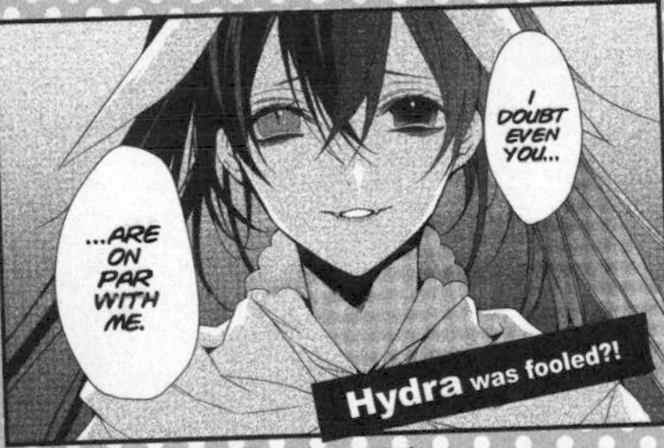
I DOUBT EVEN YOU...
...ARE ON PAR WITH ME.
Hydra was fooled?!
▲ The girl who totally duped Lady Hydra

A human girl promised her they'd always be together. But she was only manipulating Hydra in order to save herself from an incurable disease! It was "Mary" (the nonmasochist) who saved her broken heart, and ever since then she's only loved "Mary." "I swear I won't let you go!" says Lady Hydra.

And what's up with Maria?!

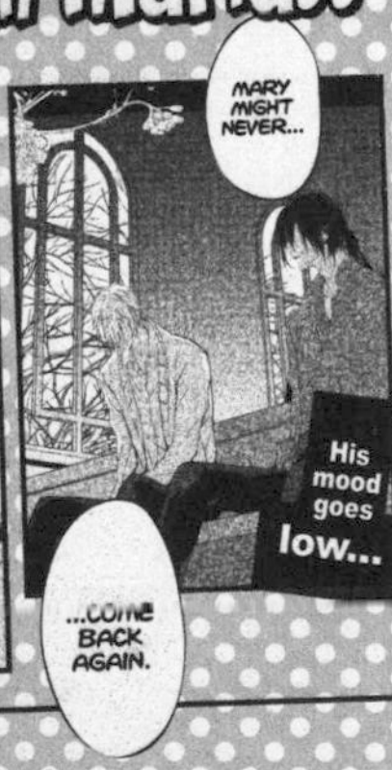
MARY MIGHT NEVER...
...COME BACK AGAIN.
His mood goes low...

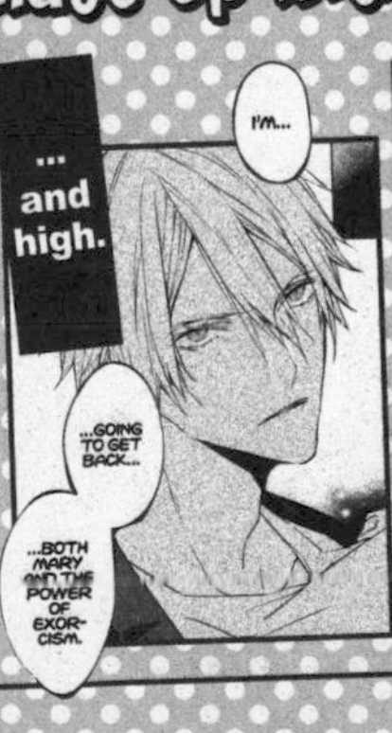
I'M...
... and high.
...GOING TO GET BACK...
...BOTH MARY AND THE POWER OF EXOR-CISM.

He broods about all that but is currently determined to get back masochist Mary, who has disappeared.

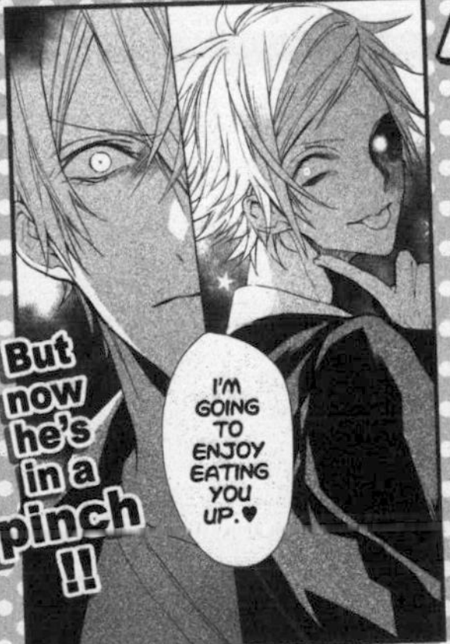
I'M GOING TO ENJOY EATING YOU UP.♥
But now he's in a pinch!!

Bloody✝Mary

Bloody Mary is in danger of being a typical "romance story"...!

I WOULDN'T REALLY MIND...

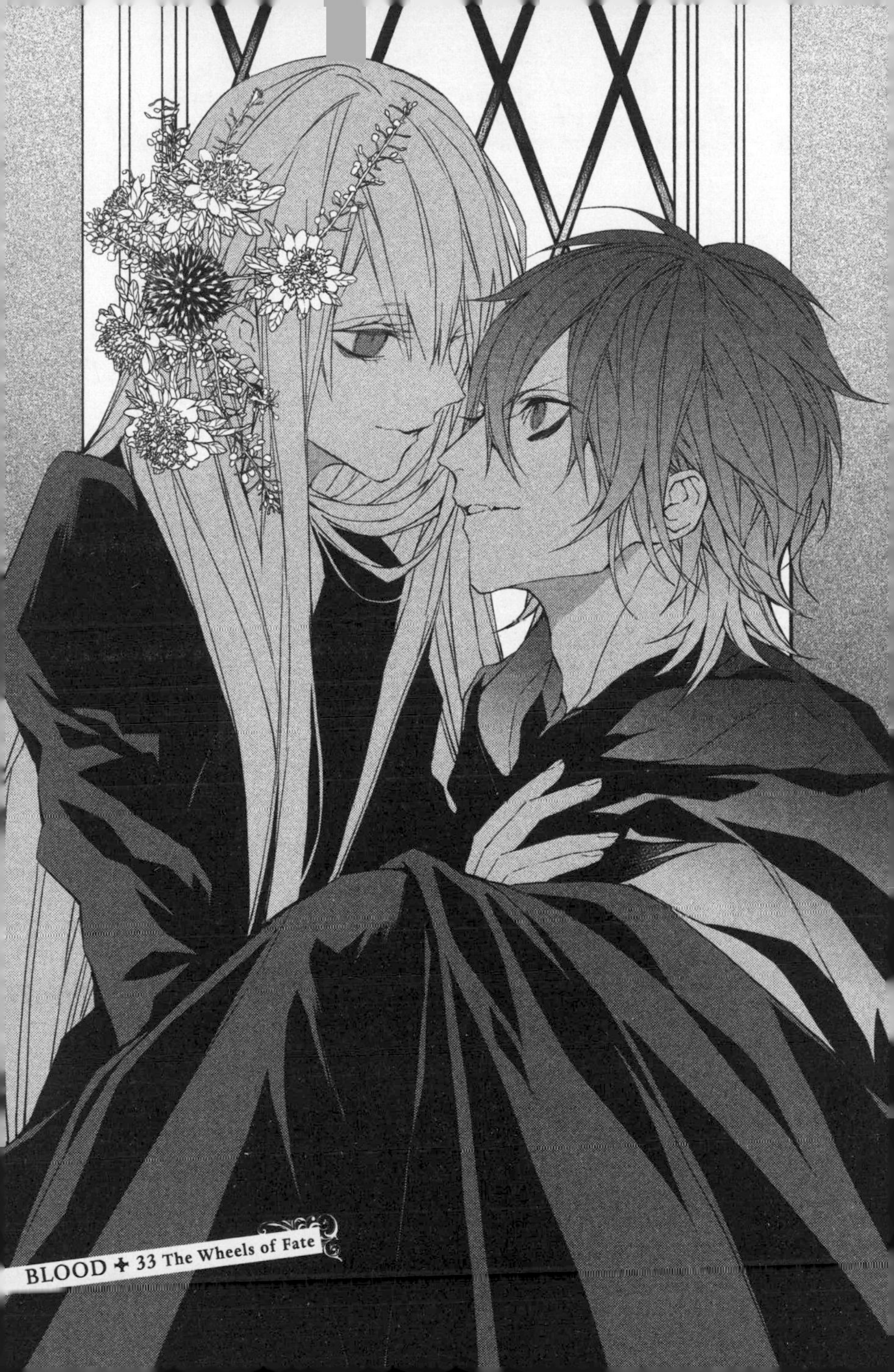
BLOOD ✢ 33 The Wheels of Fate

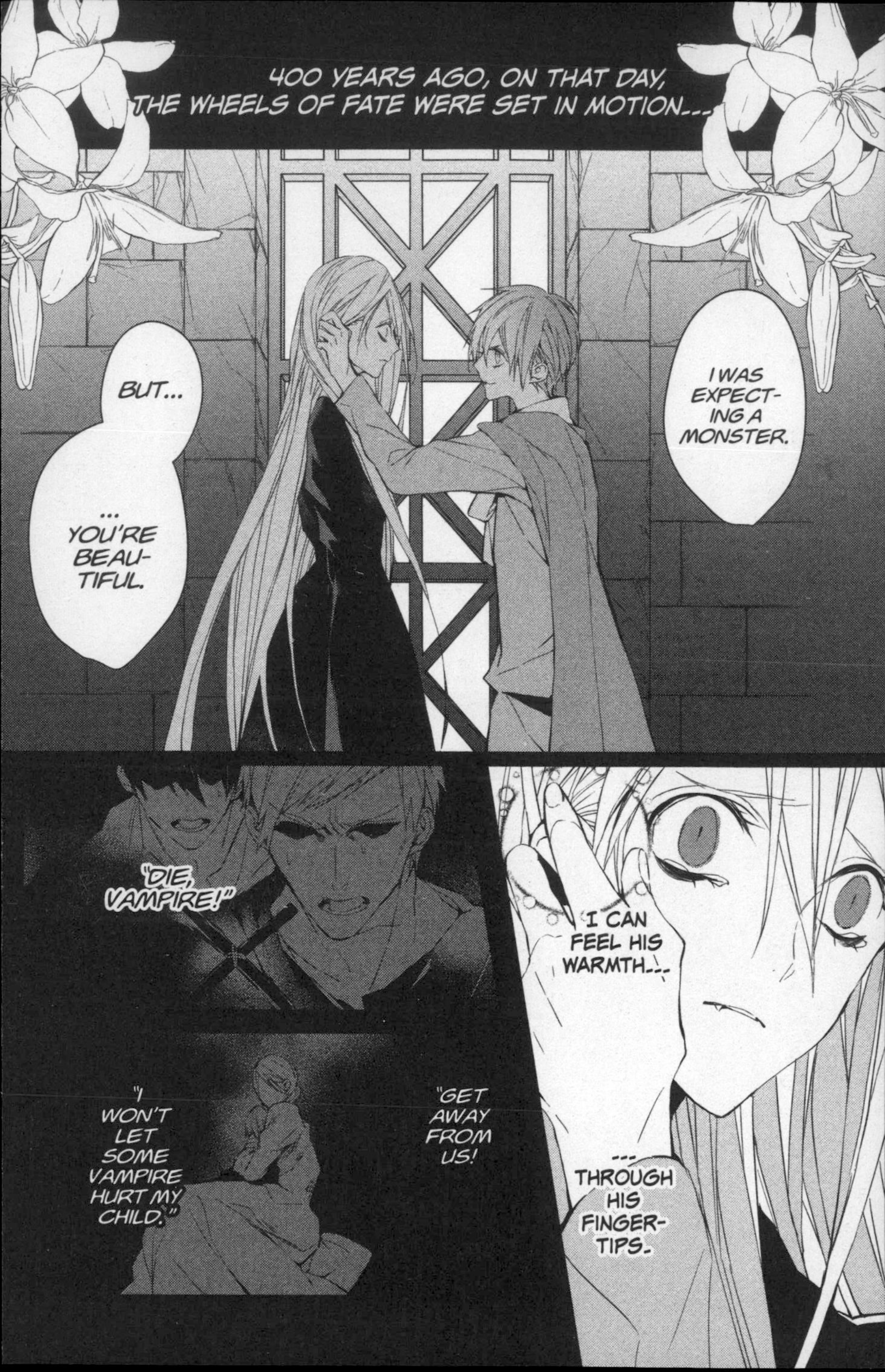
400 YEARS AGO, ON THAT DAY, THE WHEELS OF FATE WERE SET IN MOTION...
I WAS EXPECTING A MONSTER.
BUT...
...YOU'RE BEAUTIFUL.
I CAN FEEL HIS WARMTH...
...THROUGH HIS FINGERTIPS.
"DIE, VAMPIRE!"
"GET AWAY FROM US!
I WON'T LET SOME VAMPIRE HURT MY CHILD."

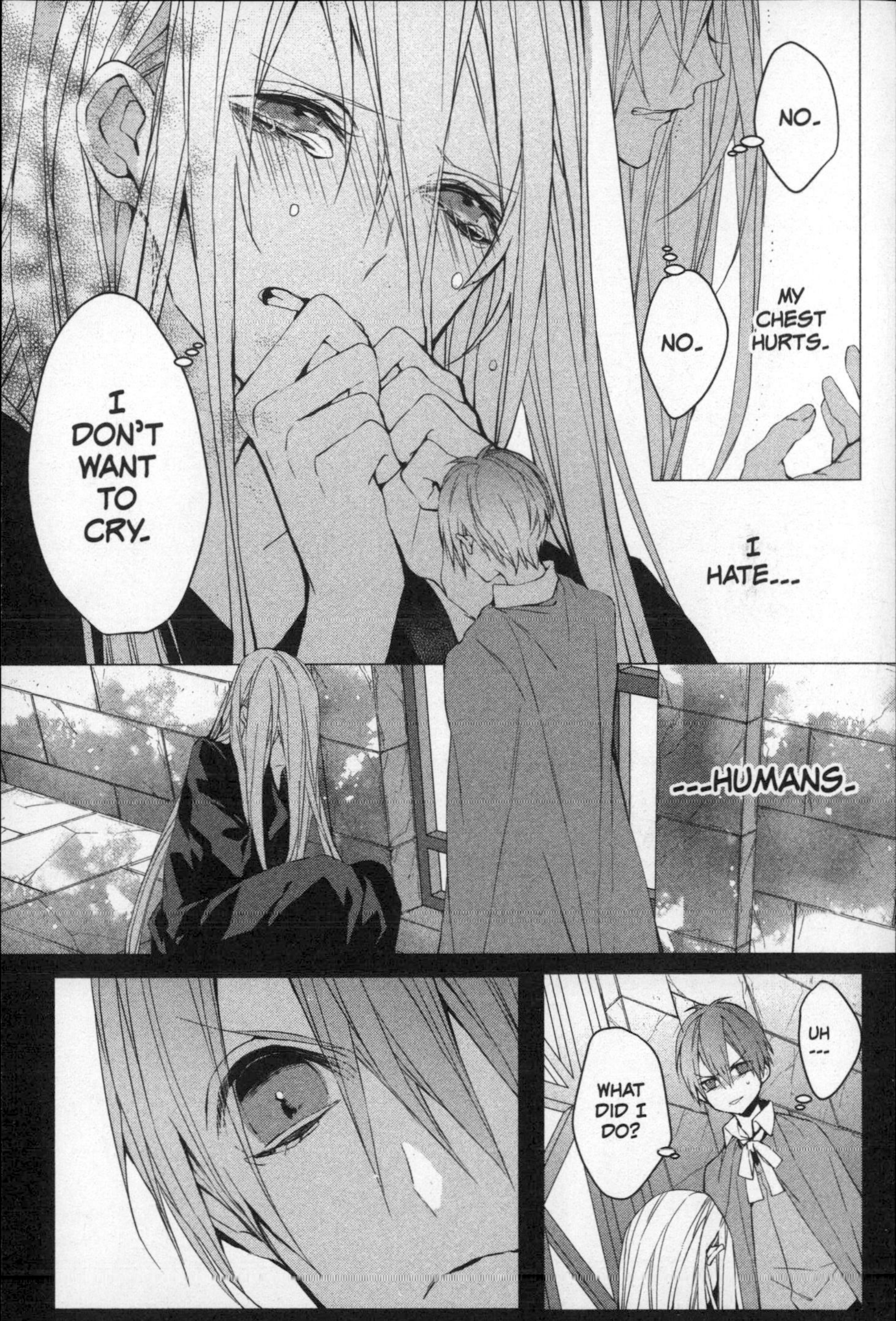
NO.
MY CHEST HURTS.
NO.
I DON'T WANT TO CRY.
I HATE...
...HUMANS.
UH...
WHAT DID I DO?

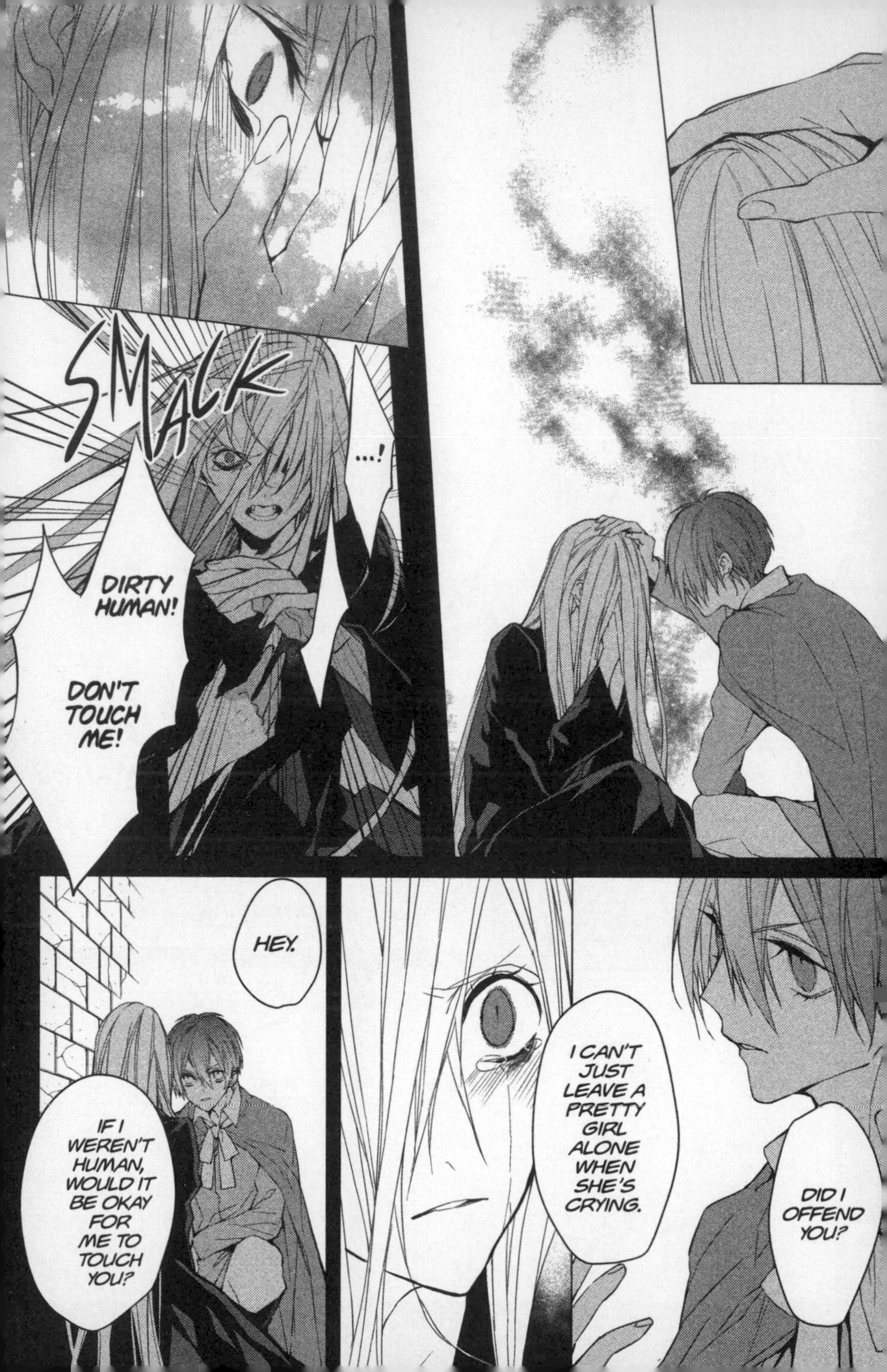
SMACK
...!
DIRTY HUMAN!
DON'T TOUCH ME!
DID I OFFEND YOU?
I CAN'T JUST LEAVE A PRETTY GIRL ALONE WHEN SHE'S CRYING.
HEY.
IF I WEREN'T HUMAN, WOULD IT BE OKAY FOR ME TO TOUCH YOU?

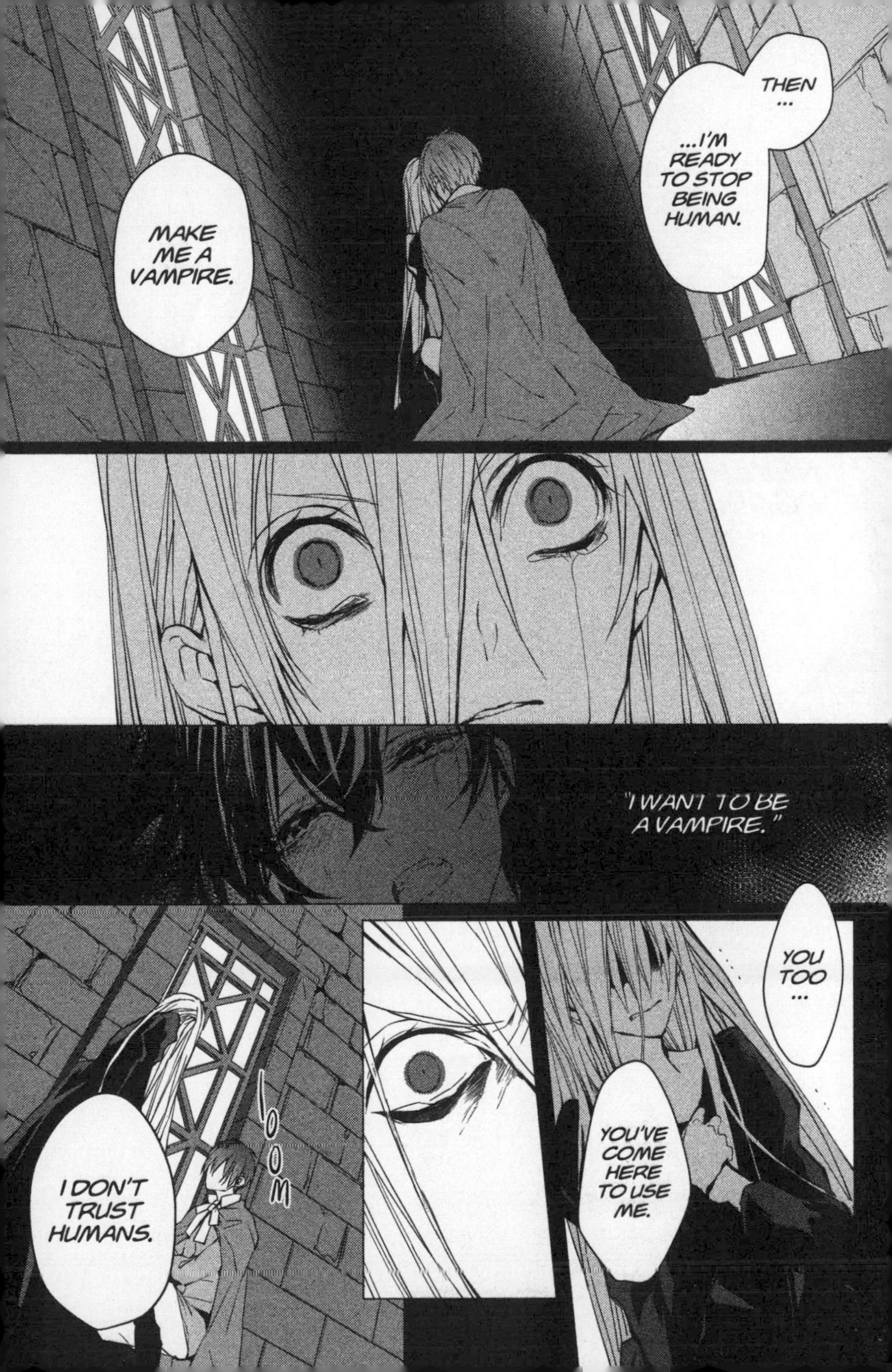
THEN ...
...I'M READY TO STOP BEING HUMAN.
MAKE ME A VAMPIRE.
"I WANT TO BE A VAMPIRE."
YOU TOO ...
YOU'VE COME HERE TO USE ME.
I DON'T TRUST HUMANS.

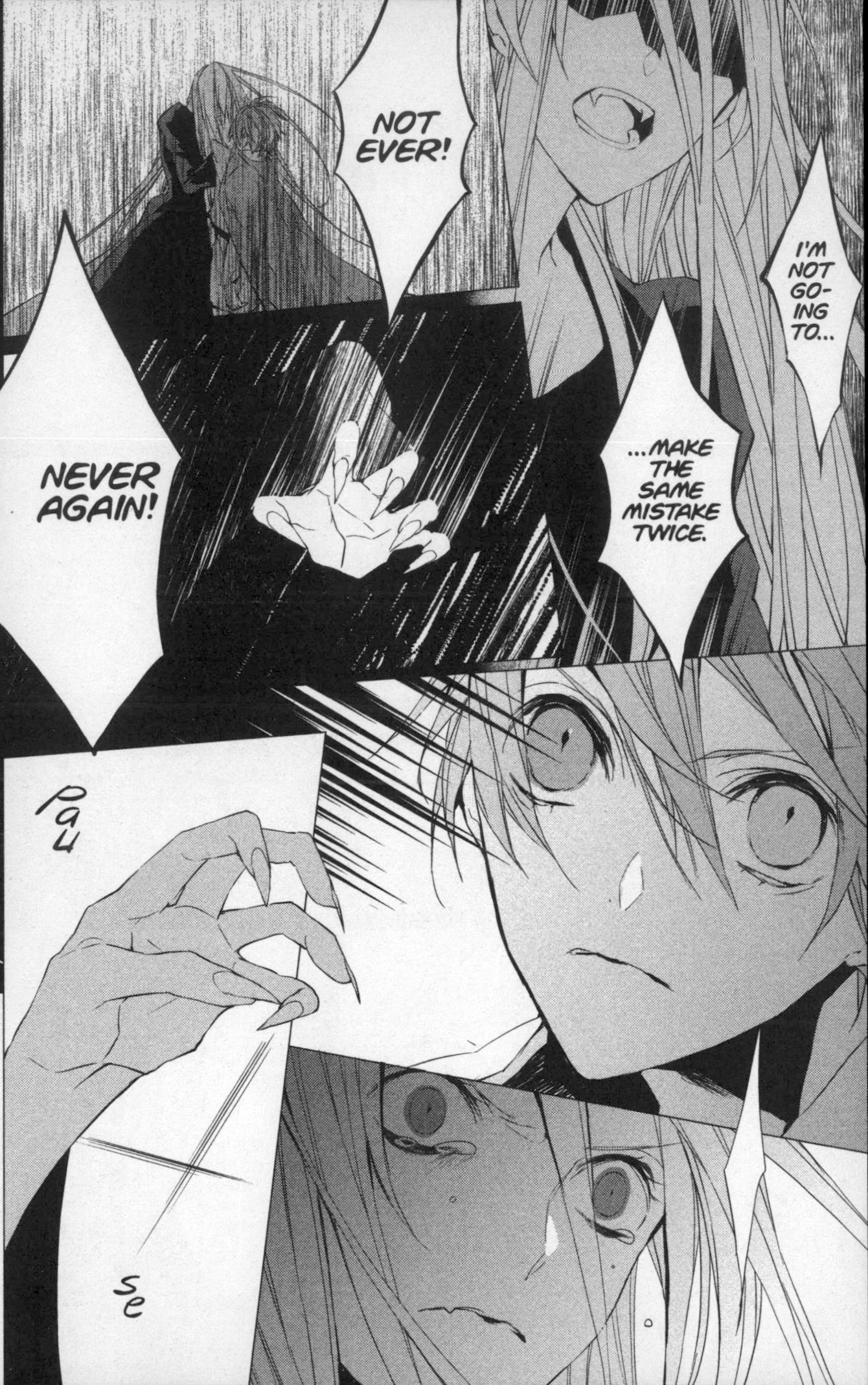
I'M NOT GO-ING TO...
...MAKE THE SAME MISTAKE TWICE.
NOT EVER!
NEVER AGAIN!
Pau
se

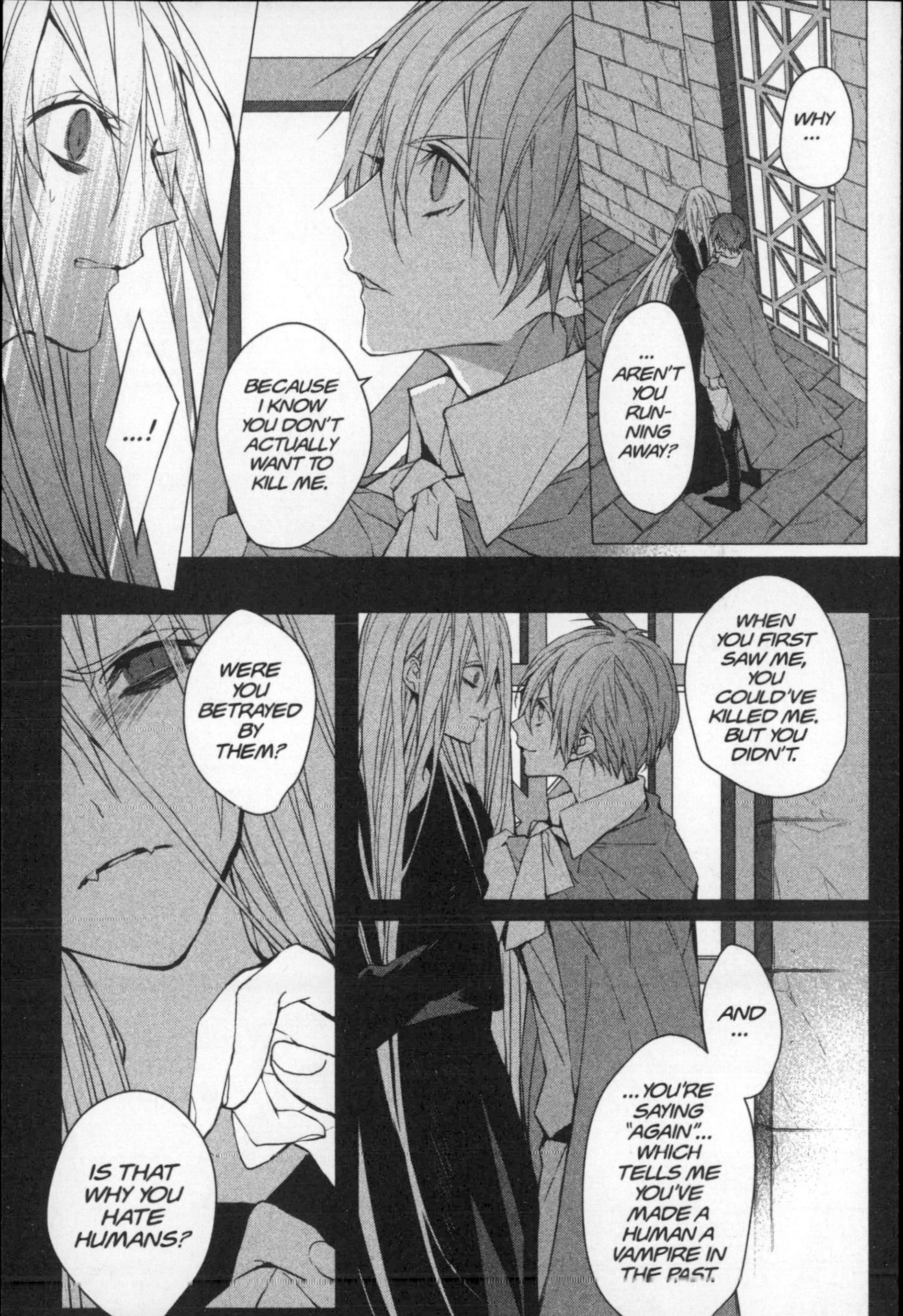
WHY ...
... AREN'T YOU RUN-NING AWAY?
BECAUSE I KNOW YOU DON'T ACTUALLY WANT TO KILL ME.
...!
WHEN YOU FIRST SAW ME, YOU COULD'VE KILLED ME. BUT YOU DIDN'T.
AND ...
...YOU'RE SAYING "AGAIN"... WHICH TELLS ME YOU'VE MADE A HUMAN A VAMPIRE IN THE PAST.
WERE YOU BETRAYED BY THEM?
IS THAT WHY YOU HATE HUMANS?

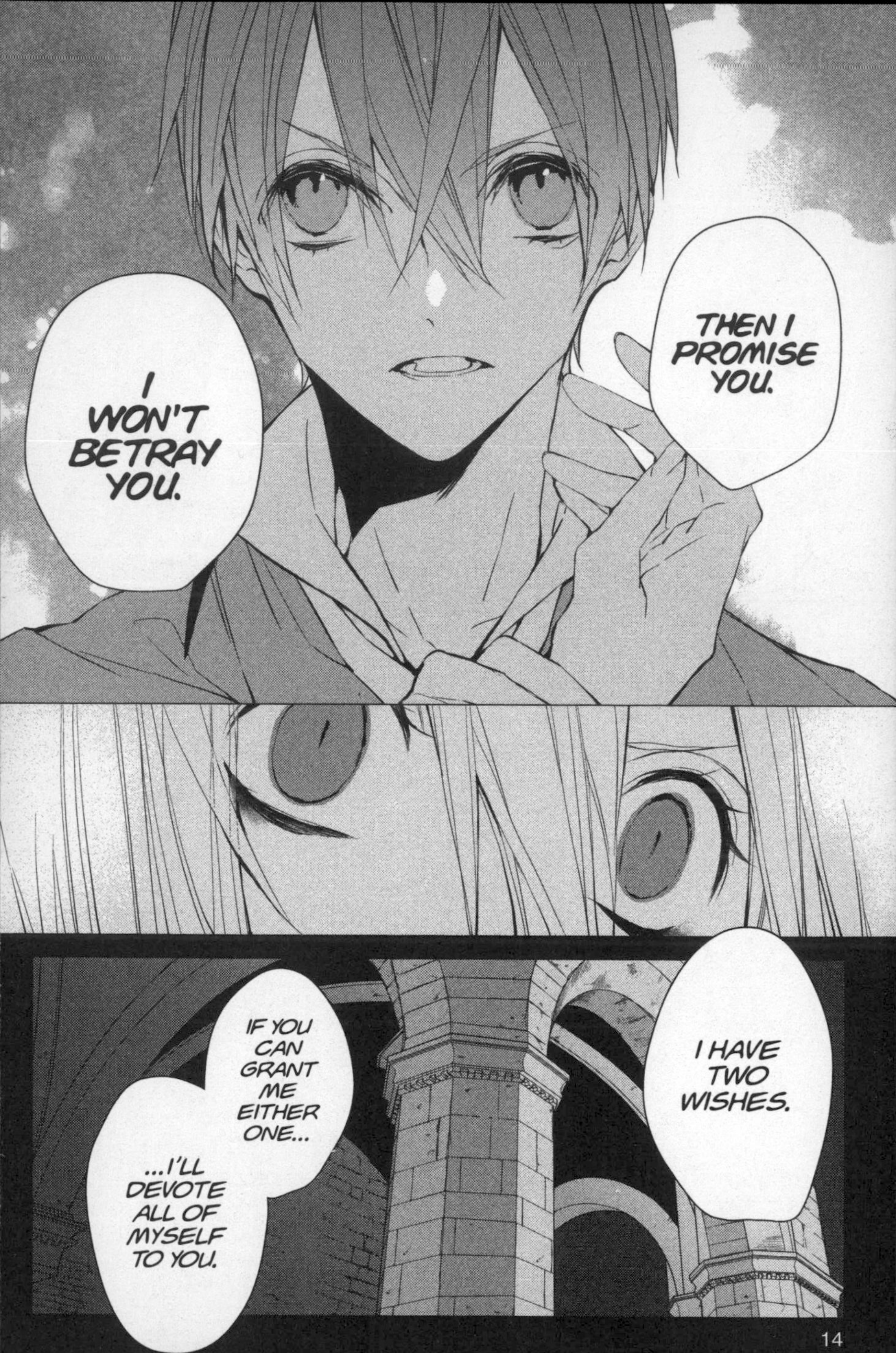
THEN I PROMISE YOU.
I WON'T BETRAY YOU.
I HAVE TWO WISHES.
IF YOU CAN GRANT ME EITHER ONE...
...I'LL DEVOTE ALL OF MYSELF TO YOU.

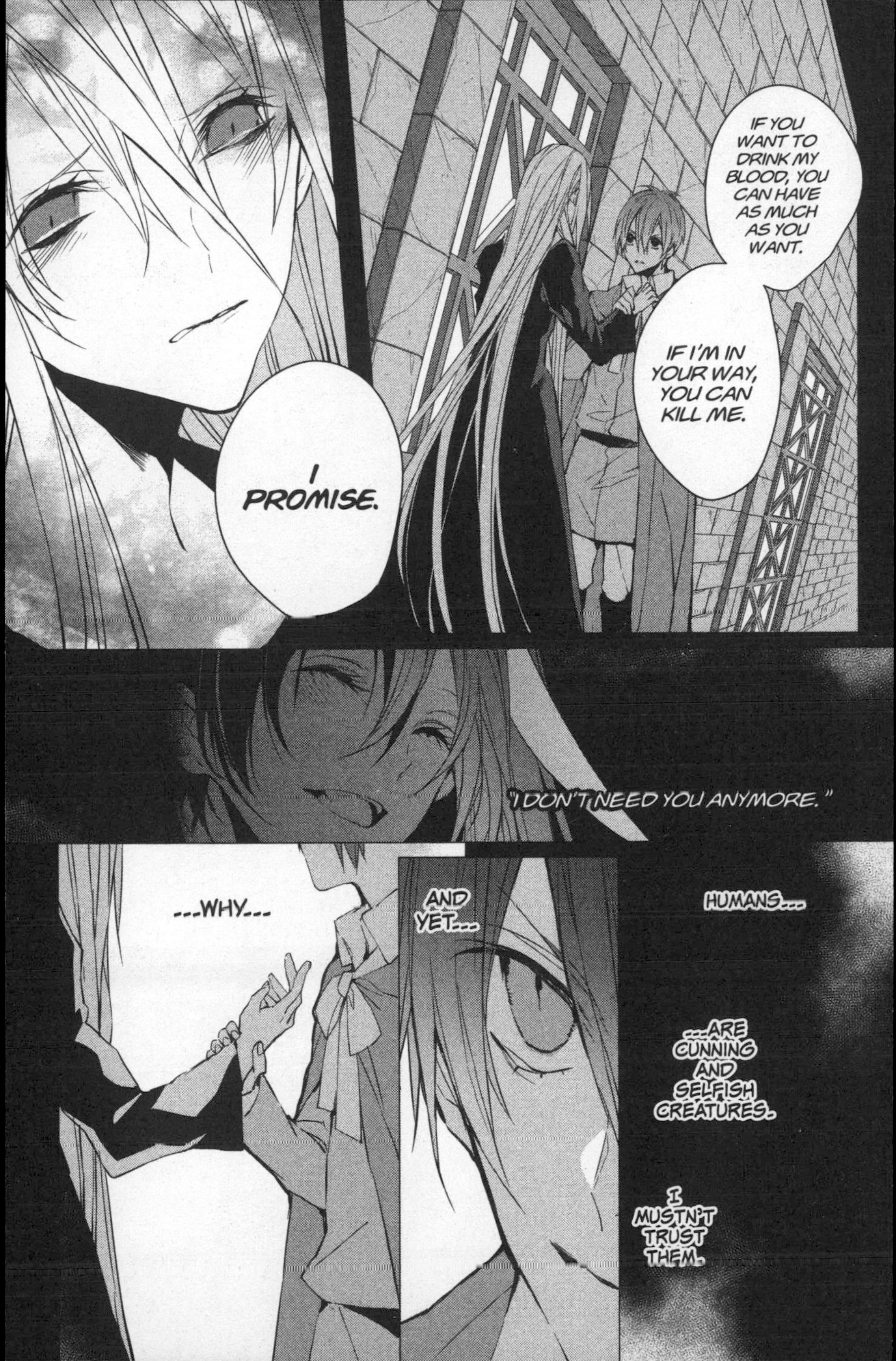
IF YOU WANT TO DRINK MY BLOOD, YOU CAN HAVE AS MUCH AS YOU WANT.
IF I'M IN YOUR WAY, YOU CAN KILL ME.
I PROMISE.
"I DON'T NEED YOU ANYMORE."
HUMANS...
...ARE CUNNING AND SELFISH CREATURES.
I MUSTN'T TRUST THEM.
AND YET...
...WHY...

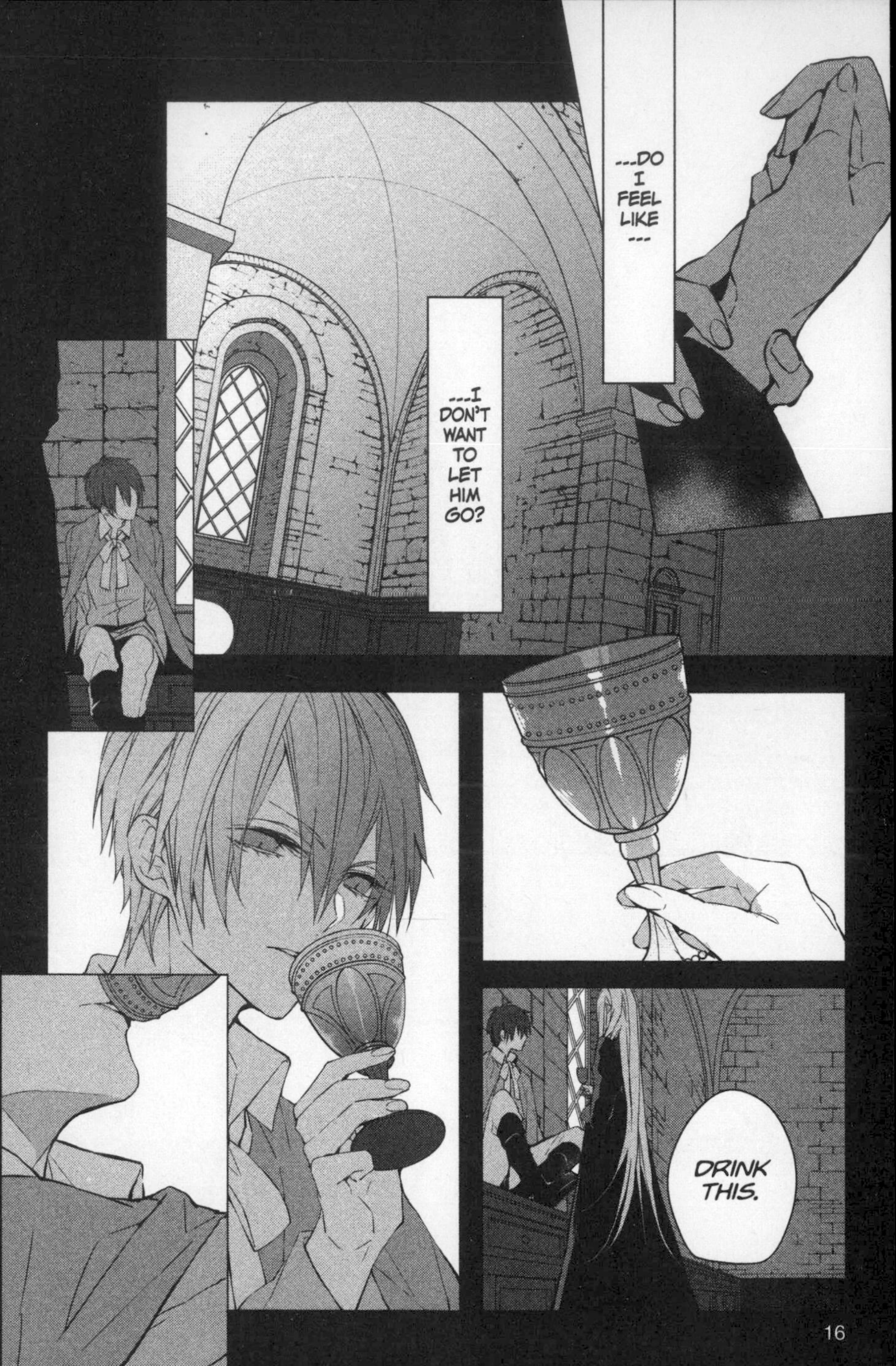
---DO I FEEL LIKE ---
---I DON'T WANT TO LET HIM GO?
DRINK THIS.

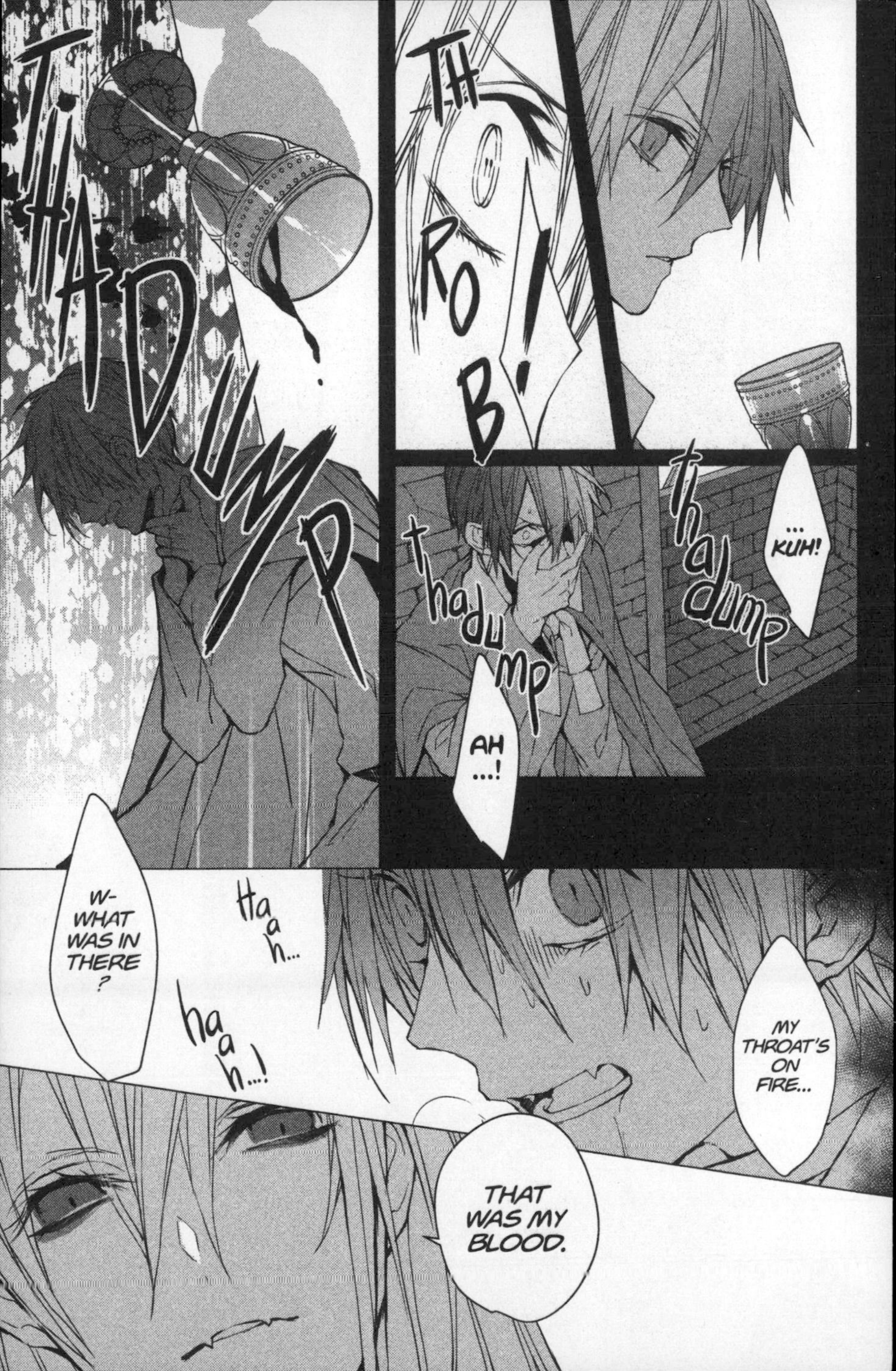
THROB!
...KUH!
thadump
thadump
AH ...!
THADUMP
MY THROAT'S ON FIRE...
Haah...
haah...!
W-WHAT WAS IN THERE?
THAT WAS MY BLOOD.

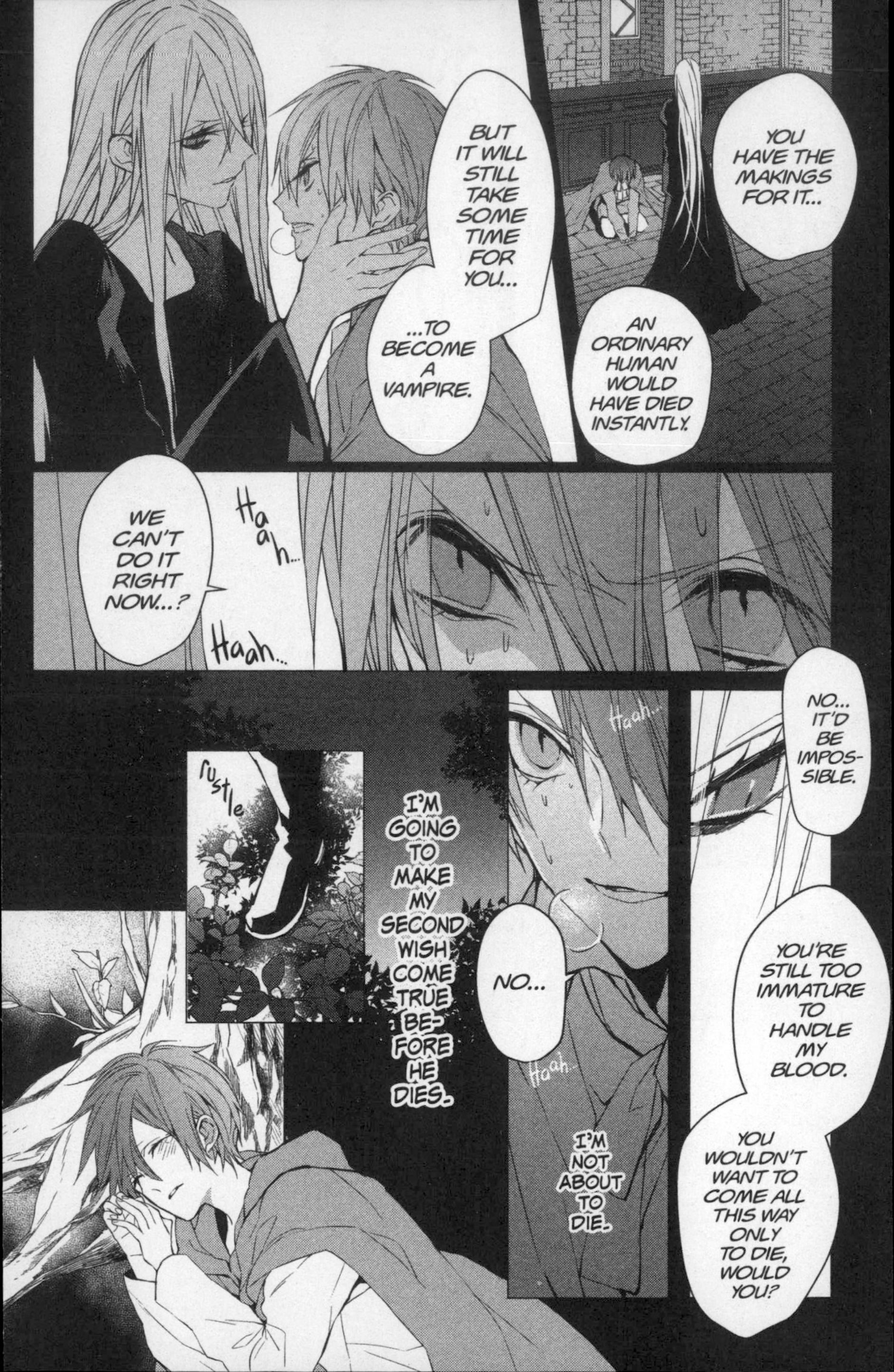
YOU HAVE THE MAKINGS FOR IT...
AN ORDINARY HUMAN WOULD HAVE DIED INSTANTLY.
BUT IT WILL STILL TAKE SOME TIME FOR YOU...
...TO BECOME A VAMPIRE.
Haah...
WE CAN'T DO IT RIGHT NOW...?
Haah...
NO... IT'D BE IMPOSSIBLE.
YOU'RE STILL TOO IMMATURE TO HANDLE MY BLOOD.
YOU WOULDN'T WANT TO COME ALL THIS WAY ONLY TO DIE, WOULD YOU?
Haah...
NO...
Haah...
I'M NOT ABOUT TO DIE.
I'M GOING TO MAKE MY SECOND WISH COME TRUE BEFORE HE DIES.
rustle

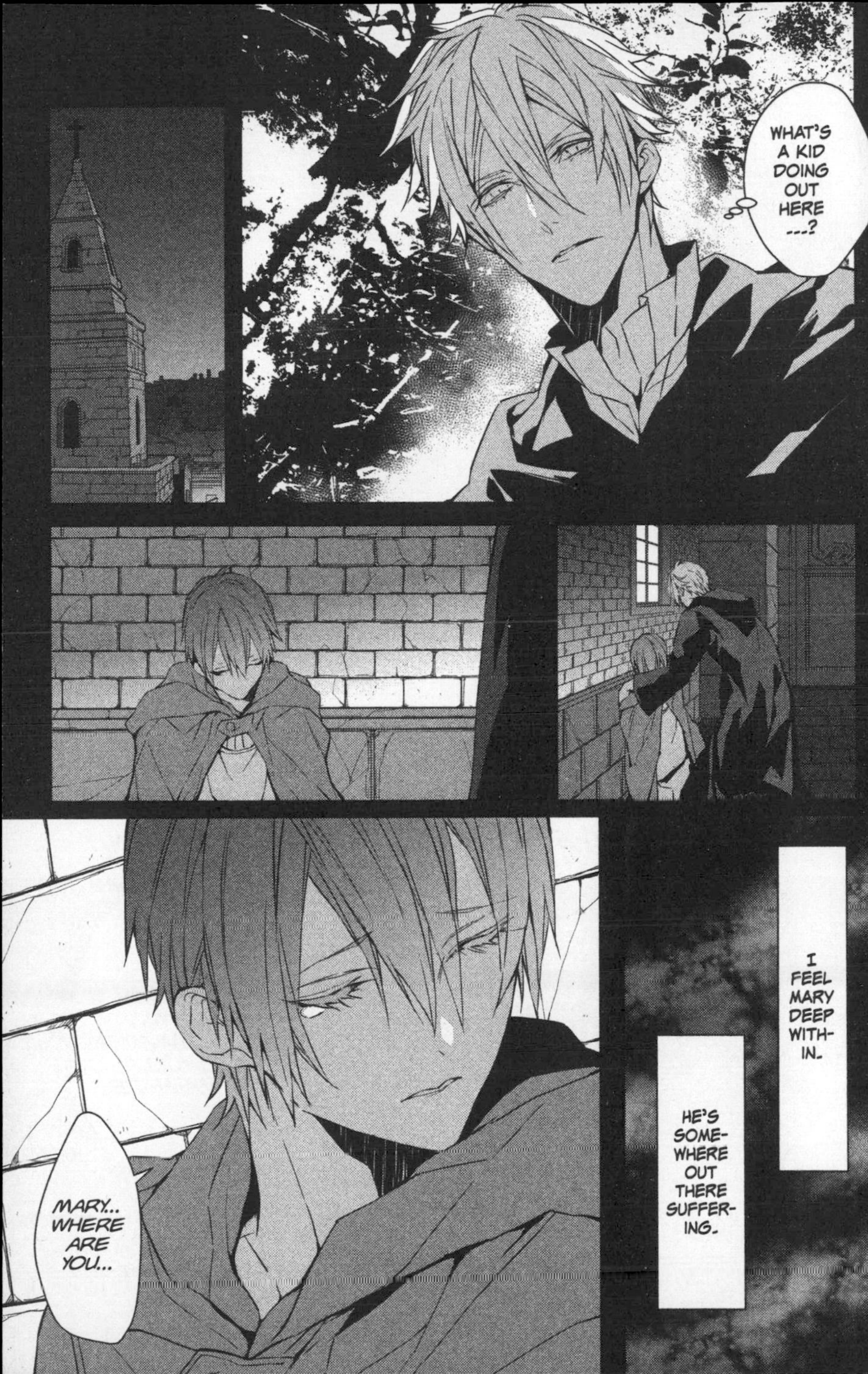
WHAT'S A KID DOING OUT HERE ---?
I FEEL MARY DEEP WITHIN.
HE'S SOMEWHERE OUT THERE SUFFERING.
MARY... WHERE ARE YOU...

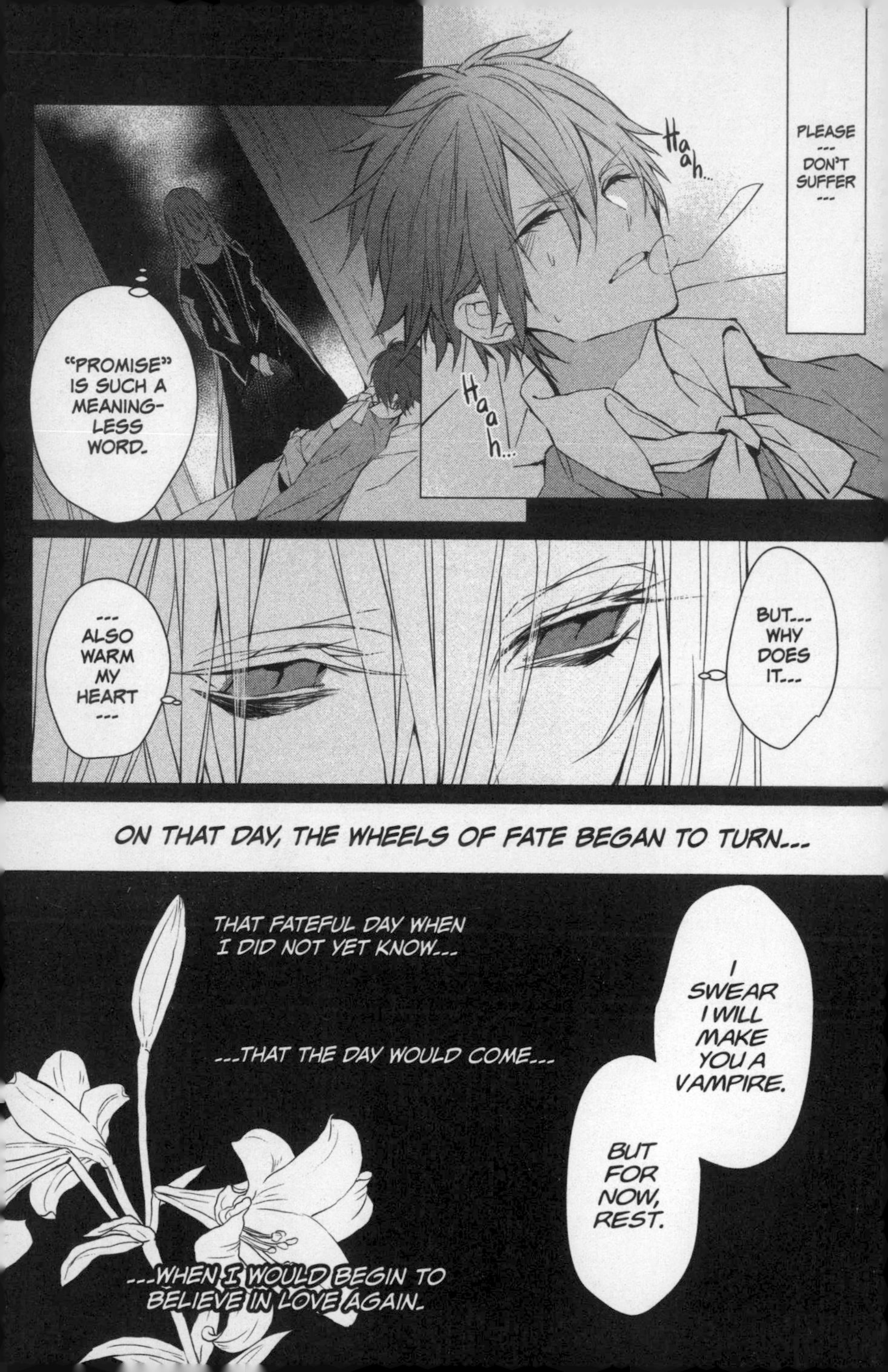
PLEASE --- DON'T SUFFER ---
Haah...
Haah...
"PROMISE" IS SUCH A MEANINGLESS WORD.
BUT--- WHY DOES IT---
--- ALSO WARM MY HEART ---
ON THAT DAY, THE WHEELS OF FATE BEGAN TO TURN---
I SWEAR I WILL MAKE YOU A VAMPIRE.
BUT FOR NOW, REST.
THAT FATEFUL DAY WHEN I DID NOT YET KNOW---
---THAT THE DAY WOULD COME---
---WHEN I WOULD BEGIN TO BELIEVE IN LOVE AGAIN.

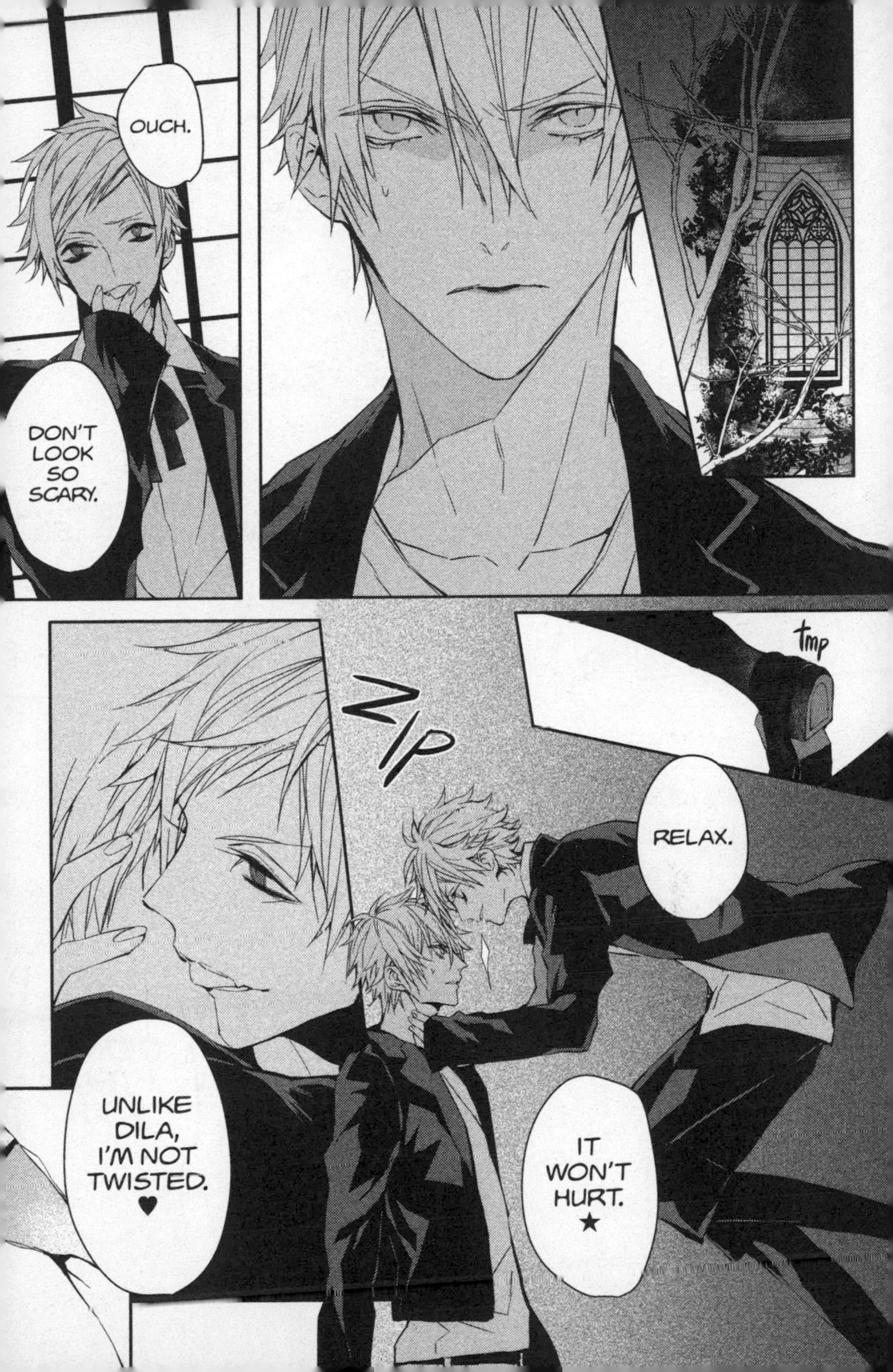
OUCH.
DON'T LOOK SO SCARY.
tmp
RELAX.
ZIP
IT WON'T HURT. ★
UNLIKE DILA, I'M NOT TWISTED. ♥

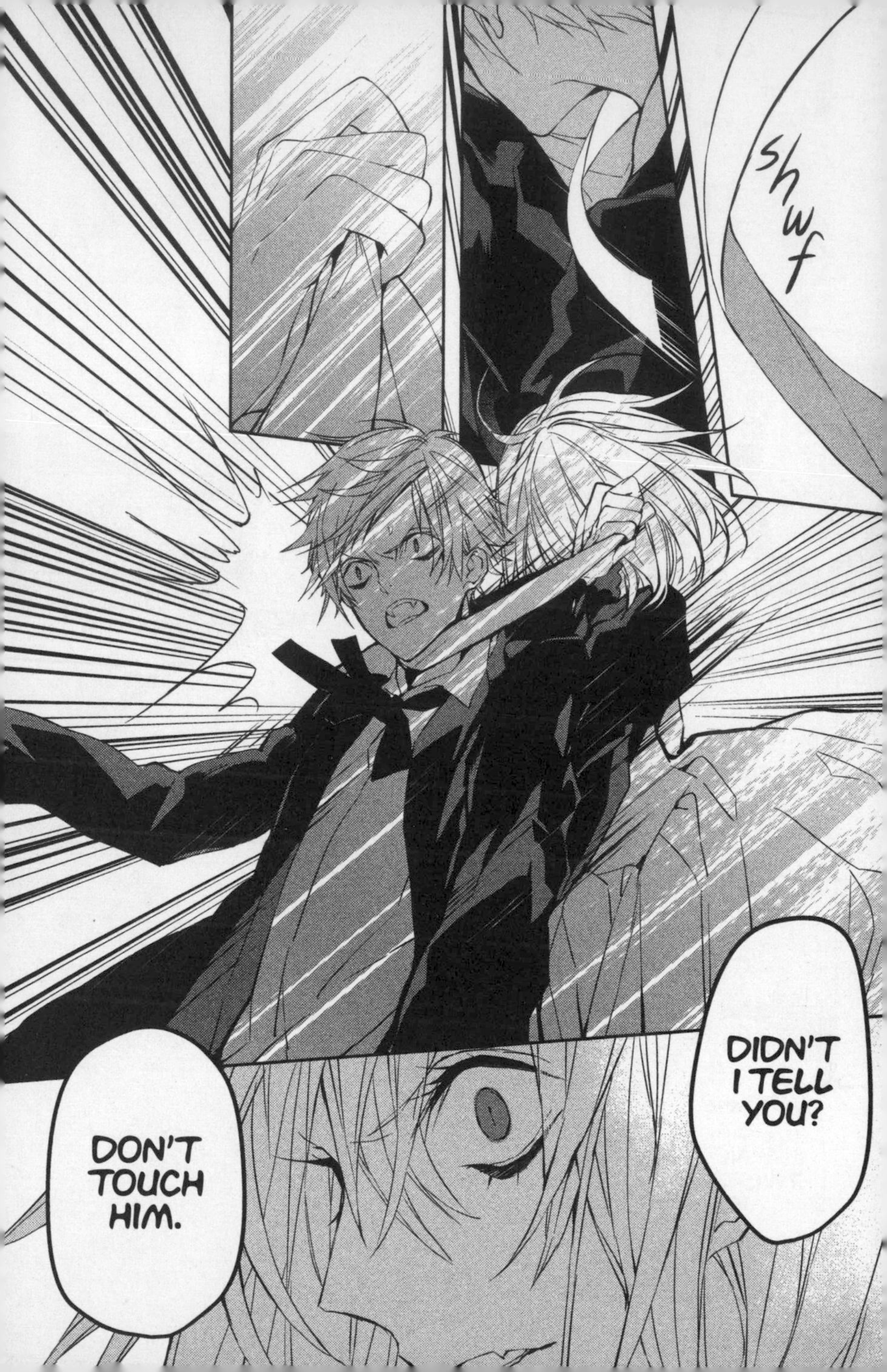
shwf
DIDN'T I TELL YOU?
DON'T TOUCH HIM.

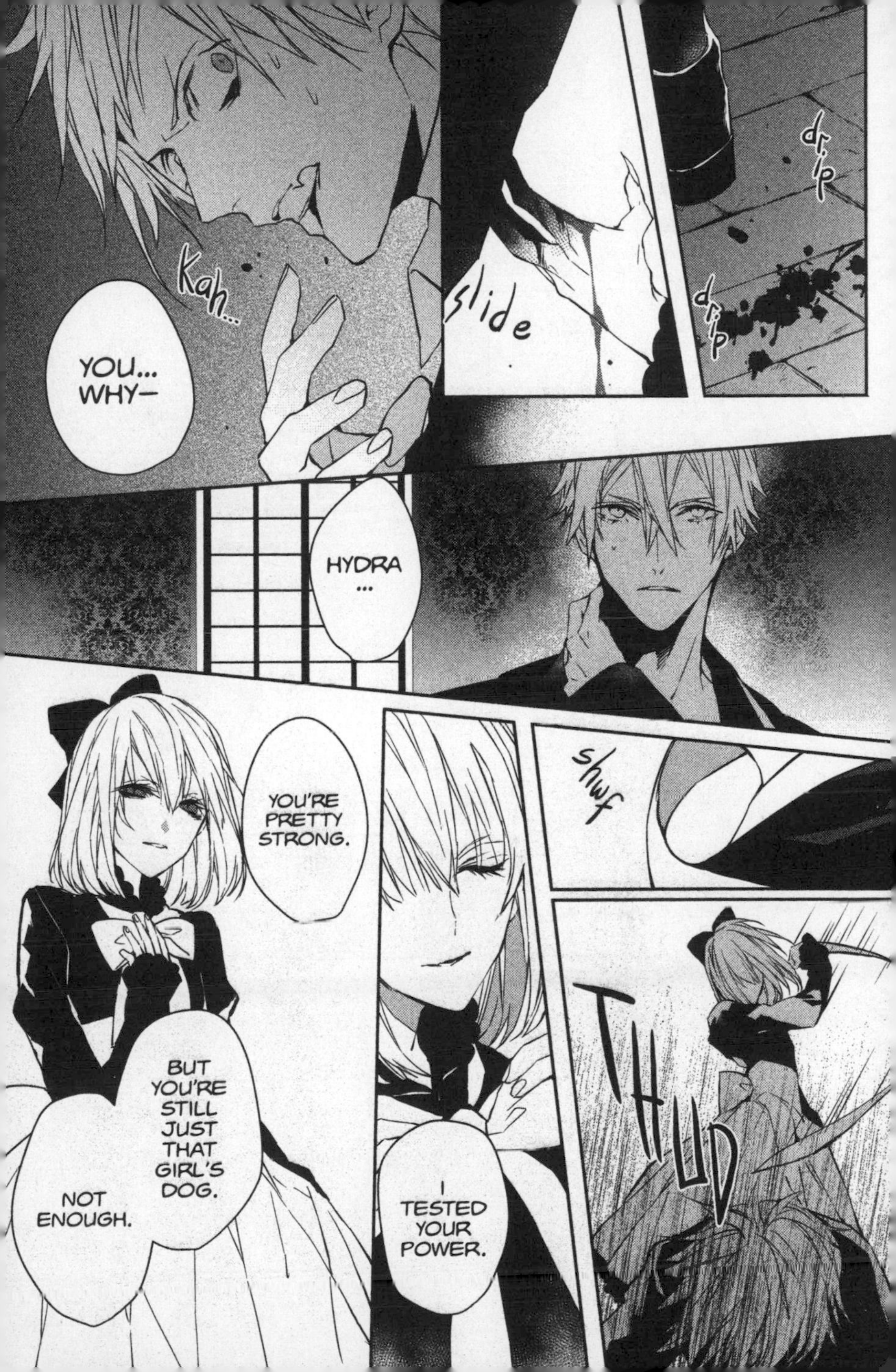
drip
drip
slide
Kah...
YOU... WHY—
HYDRA ...
shwf
THUD
I TESTED YOUR POWER.
YOU'RE PRETTY STRONG.
BUT YOU'RE STILL JUST THAT GIRL'S DOG.
NOT ENOUGH.

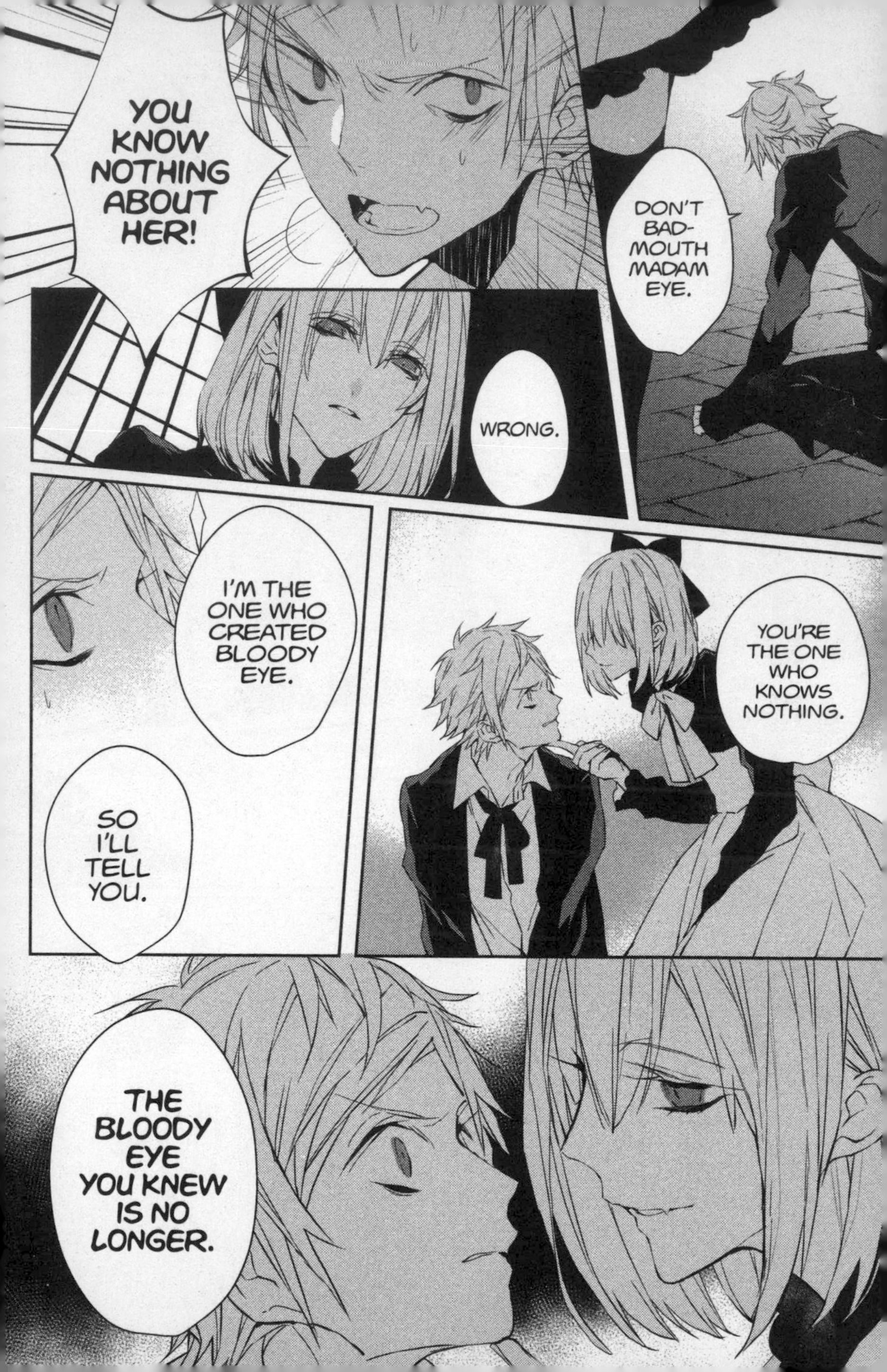
DON'T BAD-MOUTH MADAM EYE.
YOU KNOW NOTHING ABOUT HER!
WRONG.
YOU'RE THE ONE WHO KNOWS NOTHING.
I'M THE ONE WHO CREATED BLOODY EYE.
SO I'LL TELL YOU.
THE BLOODY EYE YOU KNEW IS NO LONGER.

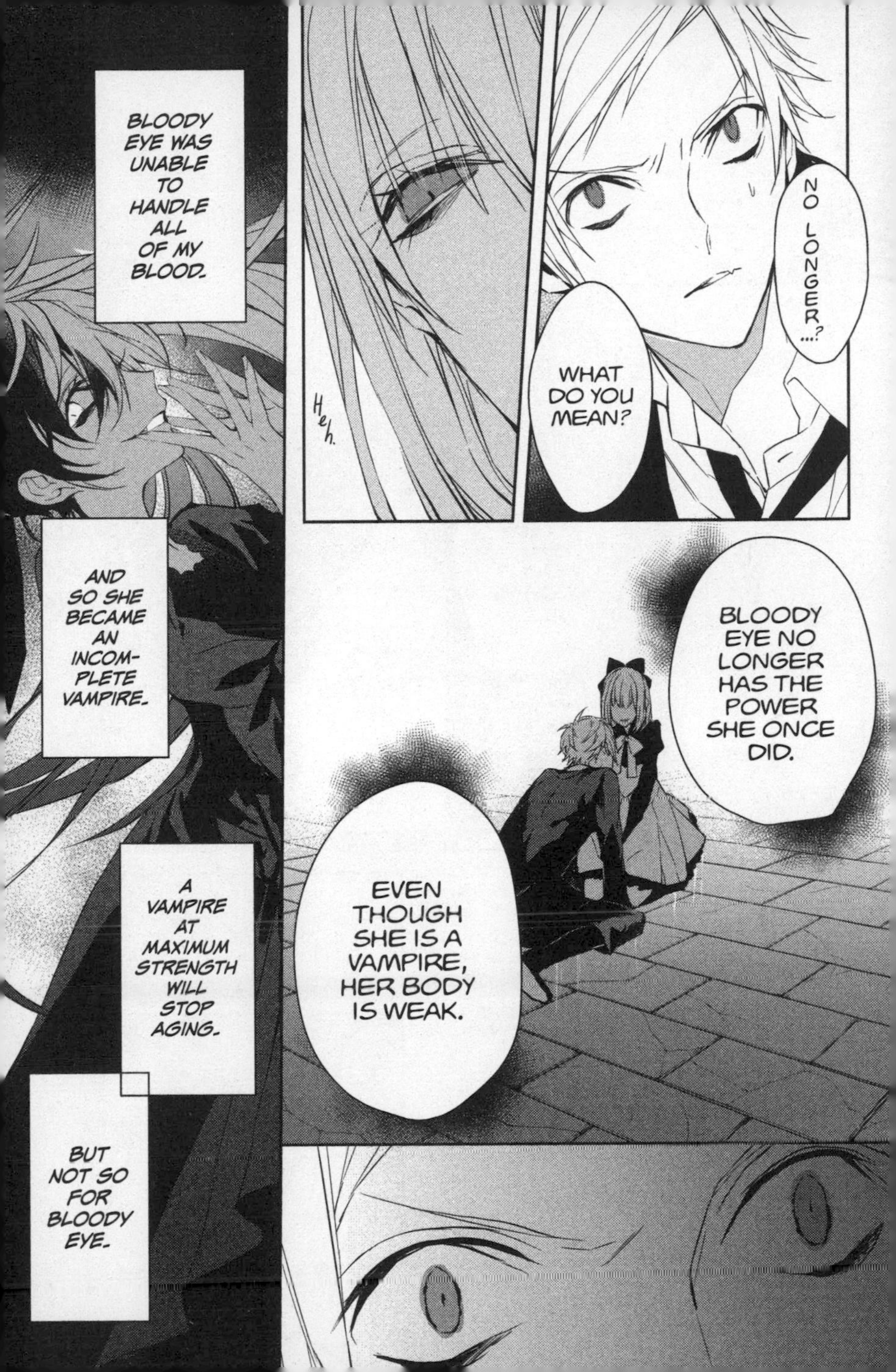
NO LONGER...?
WHAT DO YOU MEAN?
Heh.
BLOODY EYE NO LONGER HAS THE POWER SHE ONCE DID.
EVEN THOUGH SHE IS A VAMPIRE, HER BODY IS WEAK.
BLOODY EYE WAS UNABLE TO HANDLE ALL OF MY BLOOD.
AND SO SHE BECAME AN INCOMPLETE VAMPIRE.
A VAMPIRE AT MAXIMUM STRENGTH WILL STOP AGING.
BUT NOT SO FOR BLOODY EYE.

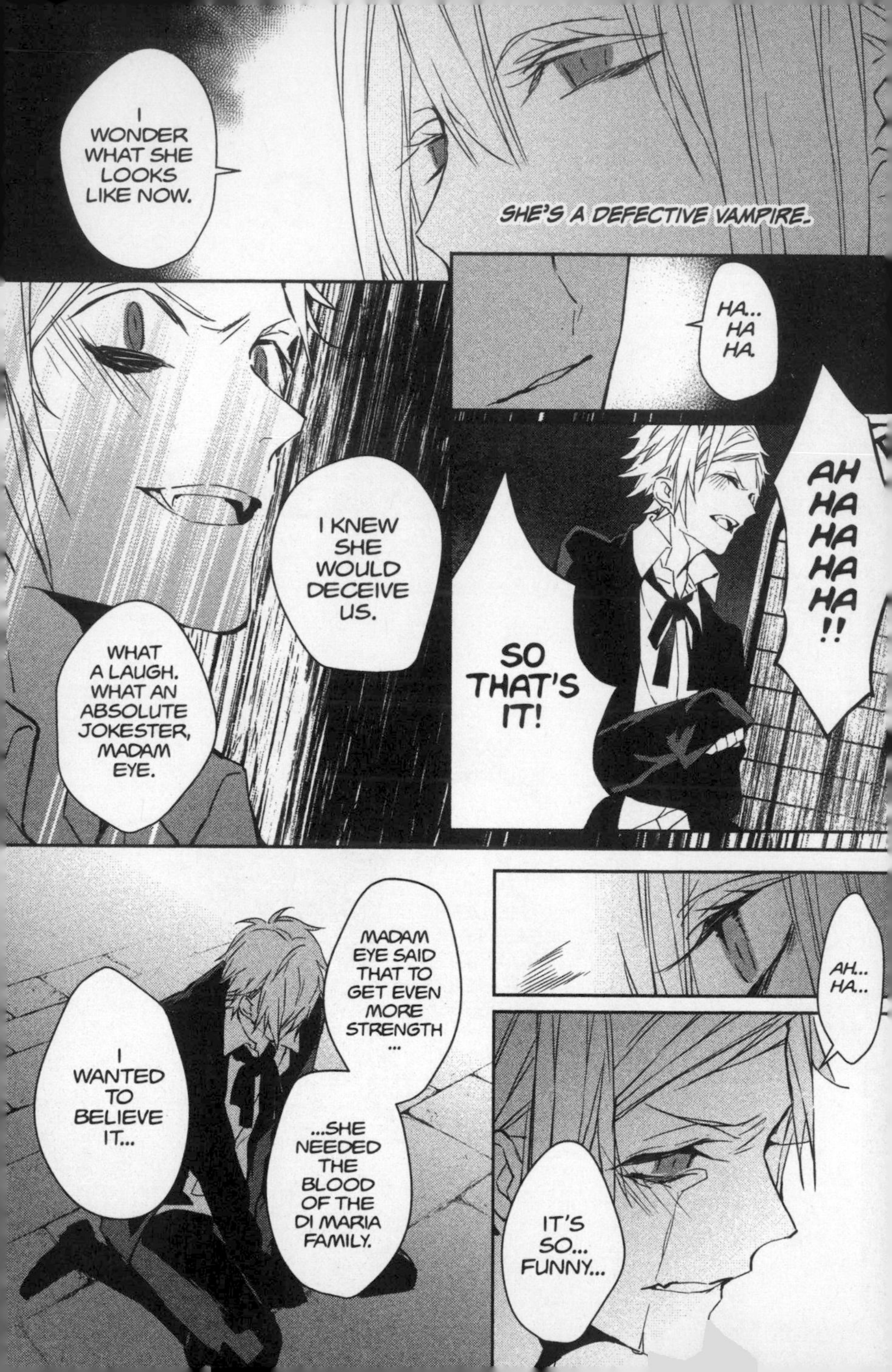
SHE'S A DEFECTIVE VAMPIRE.
I WONDER WHAT SHE LOOKS LIKE NOW.
HA... HA HA.
AH HA HA HA HA!!
SO THAT'S IT!
I KNEW SHE WOULD DECEIVE US.
WHAT A LAUGH. WHAT AN ABSOLUTE JOKESTER, MADAM EYE.
AH... HA...
IT'S SO... FUNNY...
MADAM EYE SAID THAT TO GET EVEN MORE STRENGTH...
...SHE NEEDED THE BLOOD OF THE DI MARIA FAMILY.
I WANTED TO BELIEVE IT...

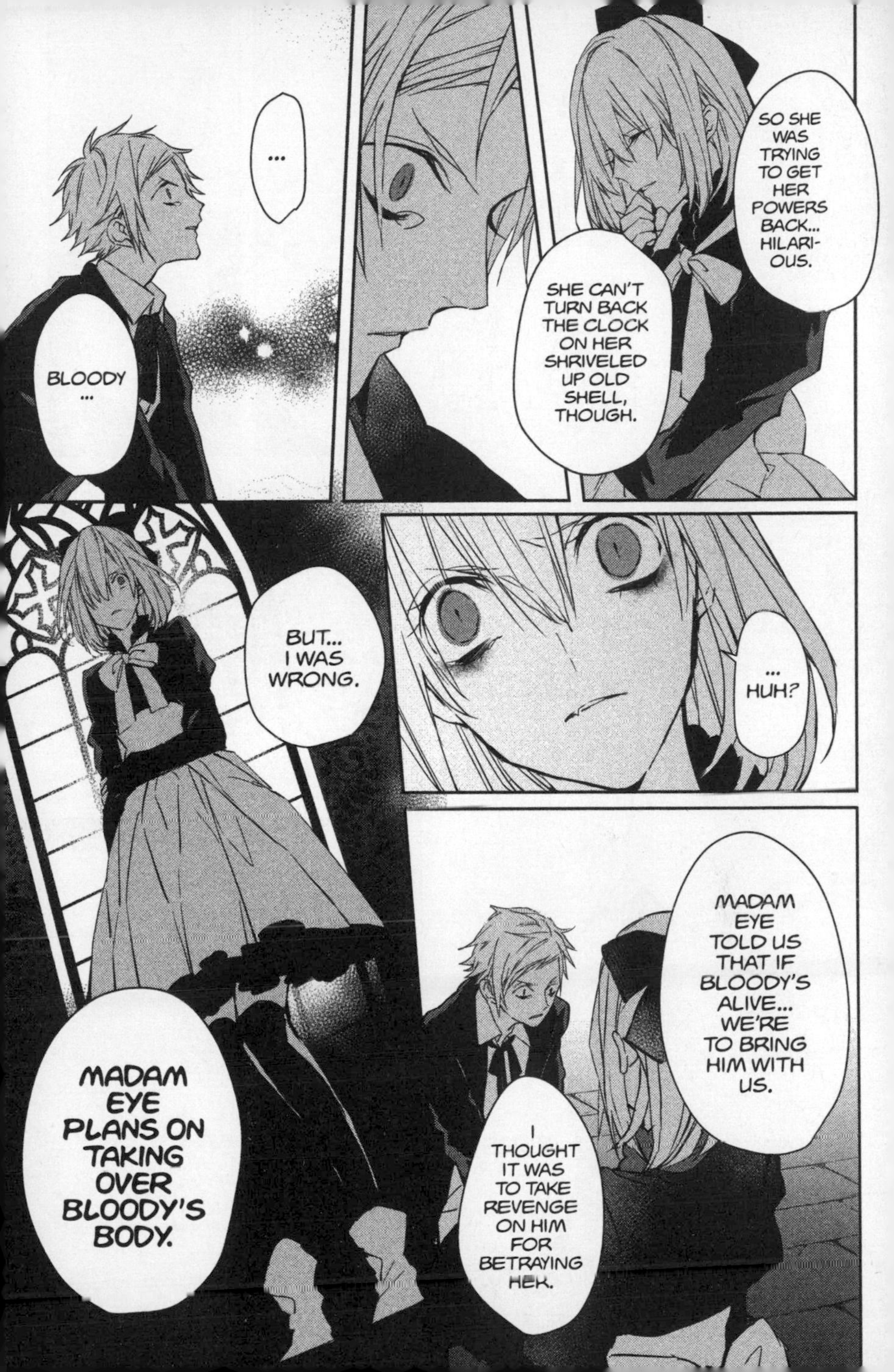
SO SHE WAS TRYING TO GET HER POWERS BACK... HILARIOUS.
SHE CAN'T TURN BACK THE CLOCK ON HER SHRIVELED UP OLD SHELL, THOUGH.
...
BLOODY ...
... HUH?
MADAM EYE TOLD US THAT IF BLOODY'S ALIVE... WE'RE TO BRING HIM WITH US.
I THOUGHT IT WAS TO TAKE REVENGE ON HIM FOR BETRAYING HER.
BUT... I WAS WRONG.
MADAM EYE PLANS ON TAKING OVER BLOODY'S BODY.

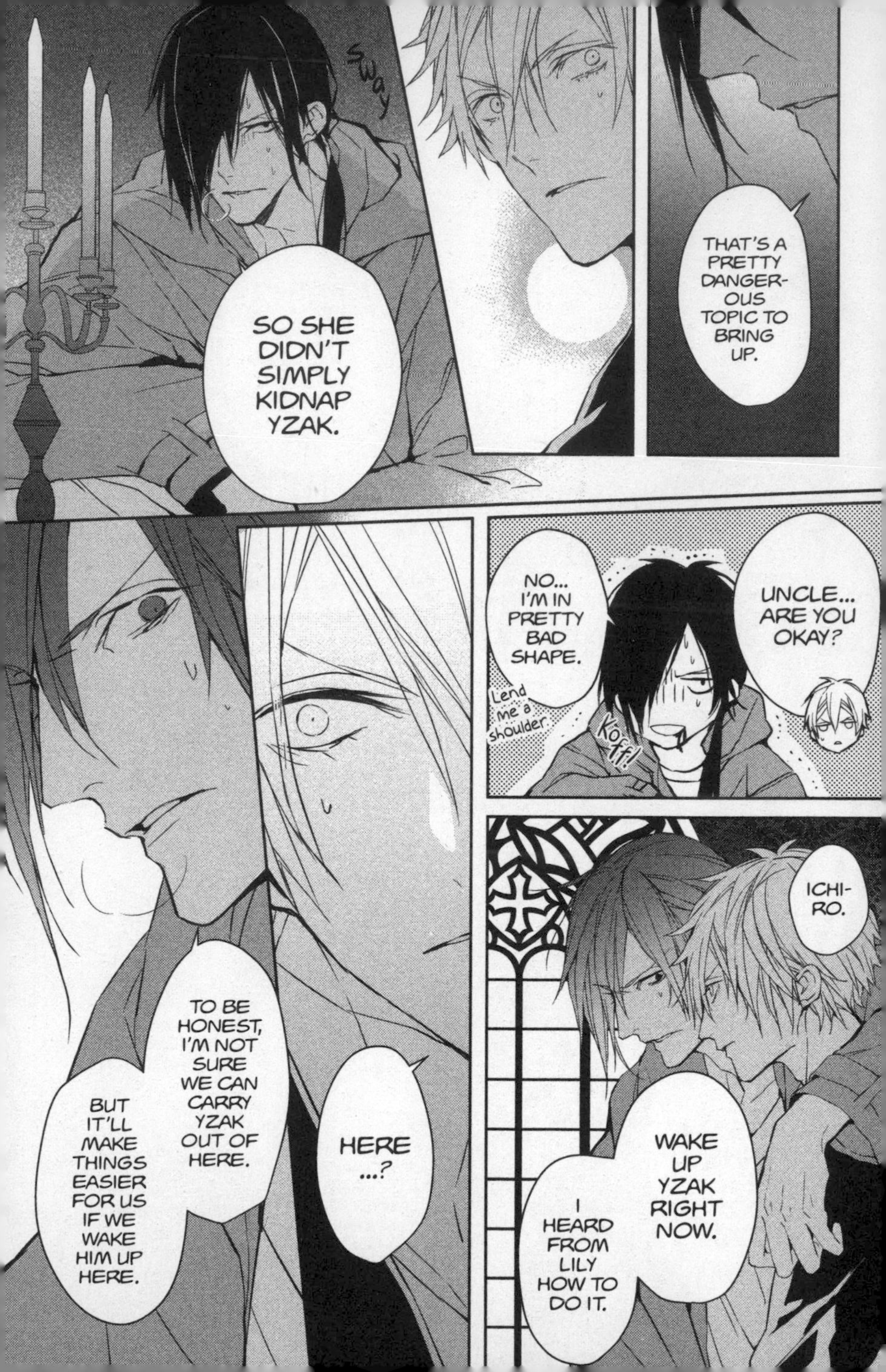
THAT'S A PRETTY DANGEROUS TOPIC TO BRING UP.
SWAY
SO SHE DIDN'T SIMPLY KIDNAP YZAK.
UNCLE... ARE YOU OKAY?
NO... I'M IN PRETTY BAD SHAPE.
Lend me a shoulder.
Koff!
ICHIRO.
WAKE UP YZAK RIGHT NOW.
I HEARD FROM LILY HOW TO DO IT.
HERE...?
TO BE HONEST, I'M NOT SURE WE CAN CARRY YZAK OUT OF HERE.
BUT IT'LL MAKE THINGS EASIER FOR US IF WE WAKE HIM UP HERE.

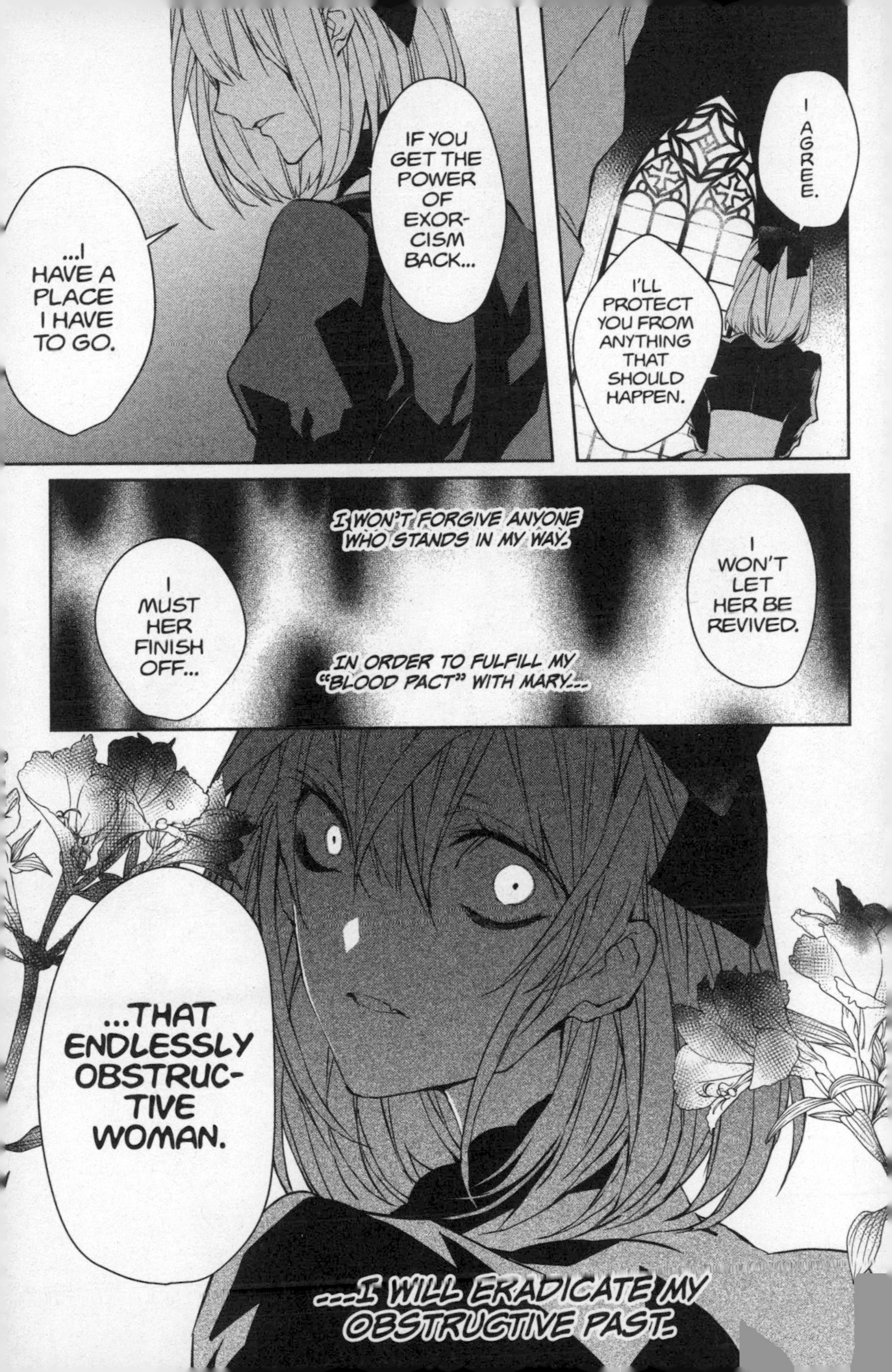
I AGREE.
I'LL PROTECT YOU FROM ANYTHING THAT SHOULD HAPPEN.
IF YOU GET THE POWER OF EXORCISM BACK...
...I HAVE A PLACE I HAVE TO GO.
I WON'T LET HER BE REVIVED.
I WON'T FORGIVE ANYONE WHO STANDS IN MY WAY.
IN ORDER TO FULFILL MY "BLOOD PACT" WITH MARY...
I MUST HER FINISH OFF...
...THAT ENDLESSLY OBSTRUCTIVE WOMAN.
...I WILL ERADICATE MY OBSTRUCTIVE PAST.

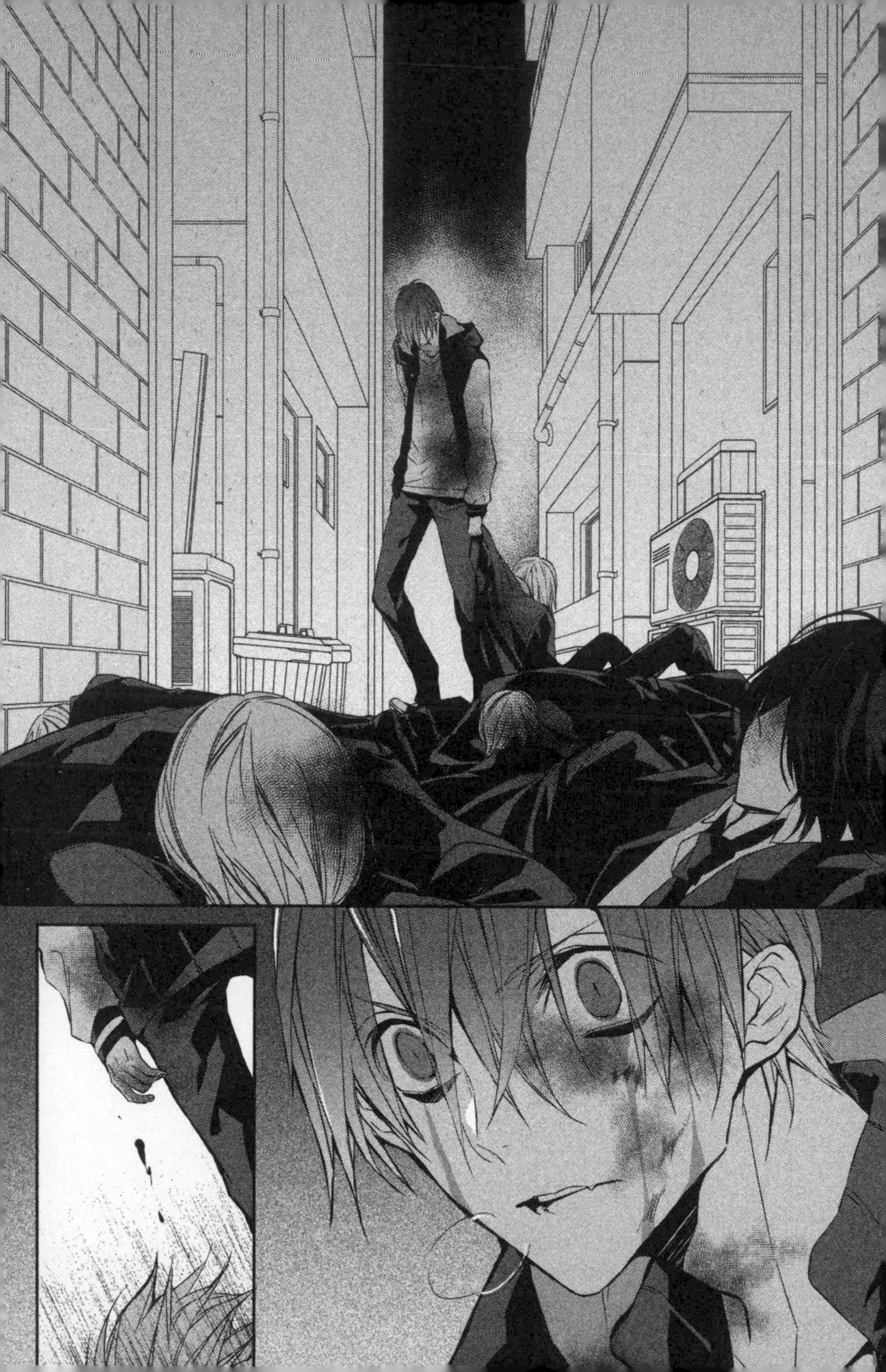

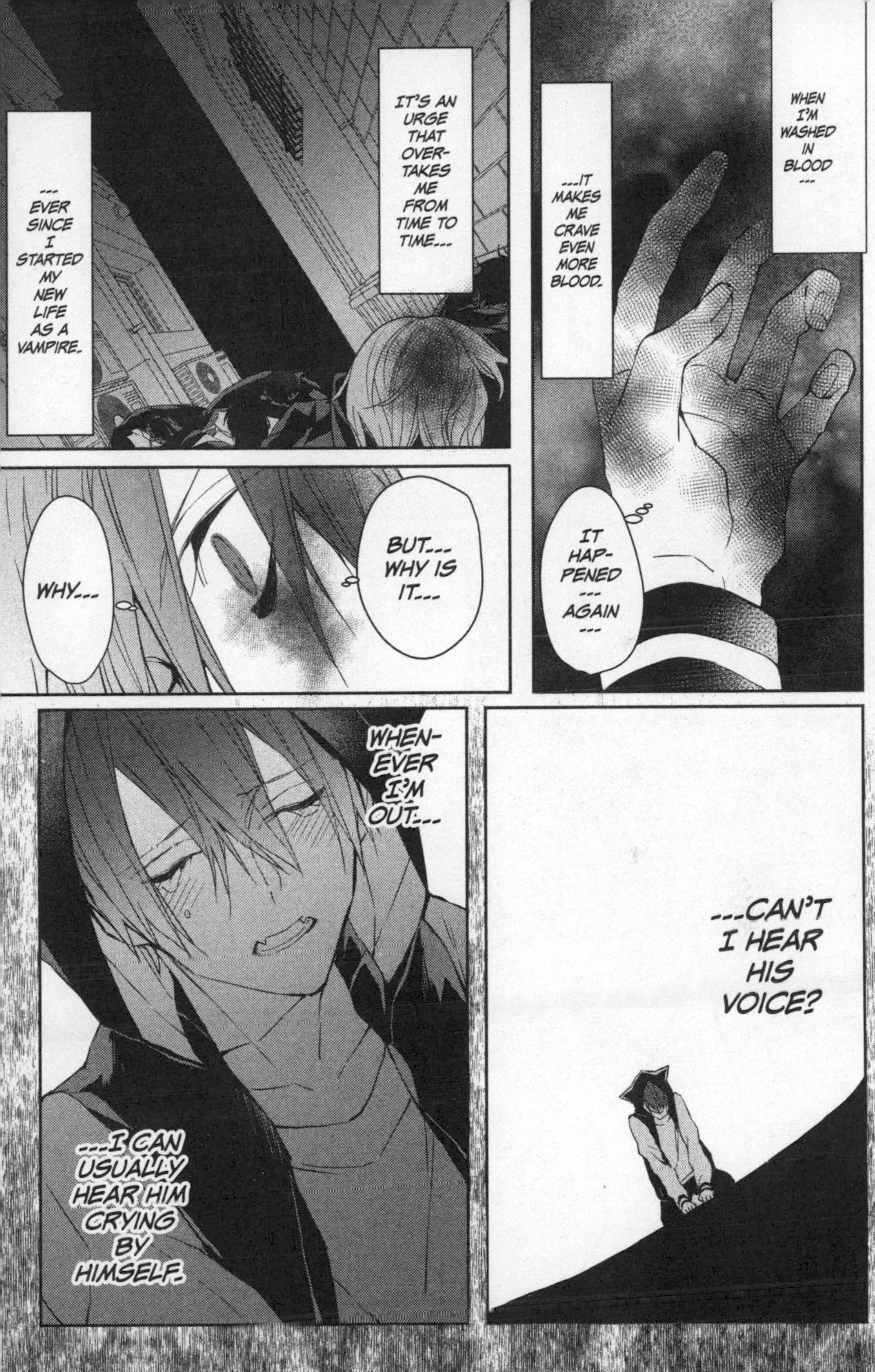
WHEN I'M WASHED IN BLOOD...
...IT MAKES ME CRAVE EVEN MORE BLOOD.
IT HAPPENED... AGAIN...
IT'S AN URGE THAT OVER-TAKES ME FROM TIME TO TIME...
...EVER SINCE I STARTED MY NEW LIFE AS A VAMPIRE.
BUT... WHY IS IT...
WHY...
...CAN'T I HEAR HIS VOICE?
WHEN-EVER I'M OUT...
...I CAN USUALLY HEAR HIM CRYING BY HIMSELF.

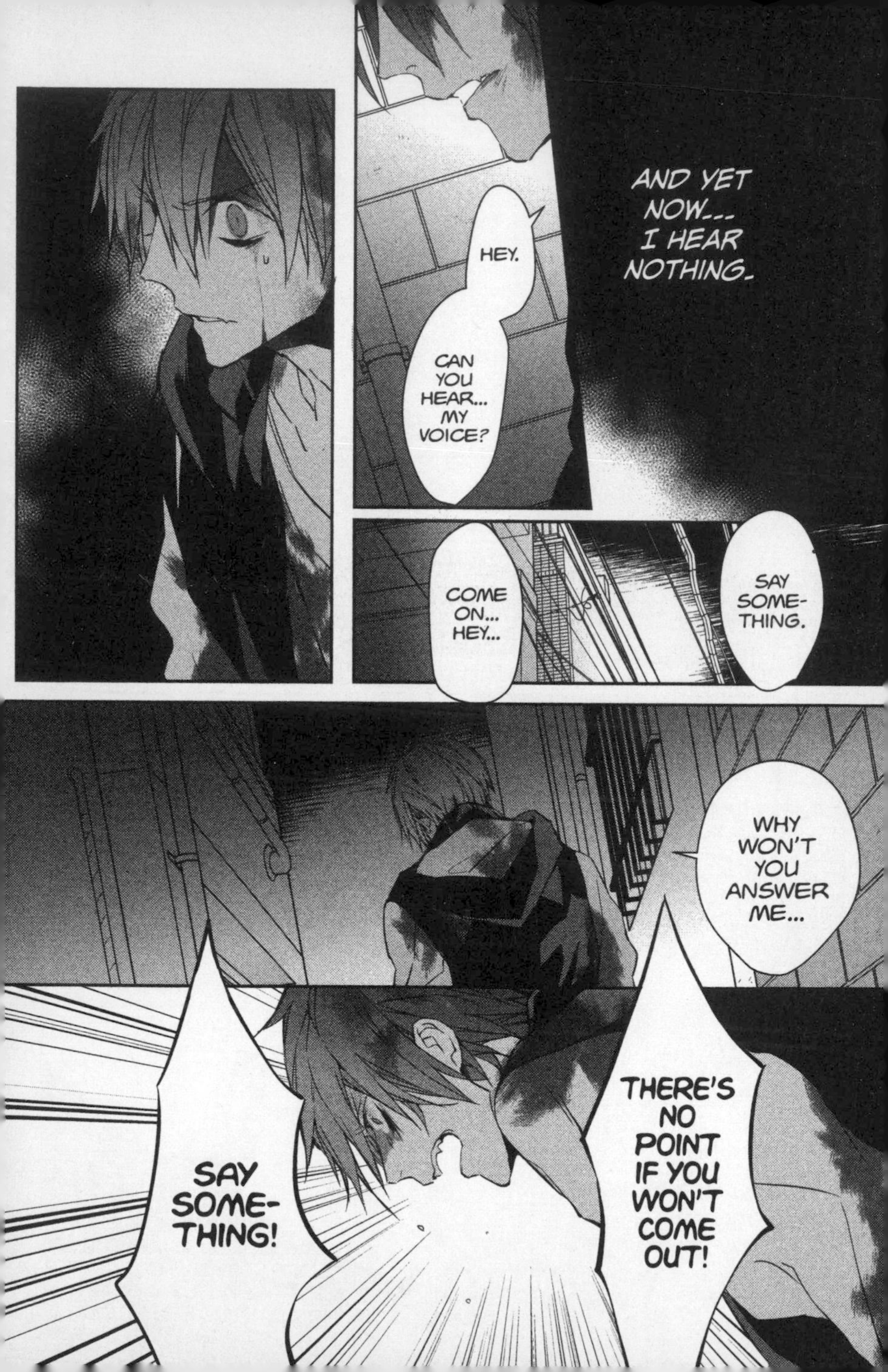
AND YET NOW... I HEAR NOTHING.
HEY.
CAN YOU HEAR... MY VOICE?
SAY SOME-THING.
COME ON... HEY...
WHY WON'T YOU ANSWER ME...
THERE'S NO POINT IF YOU WON'T COME OUT!
SAY SOME-THING!

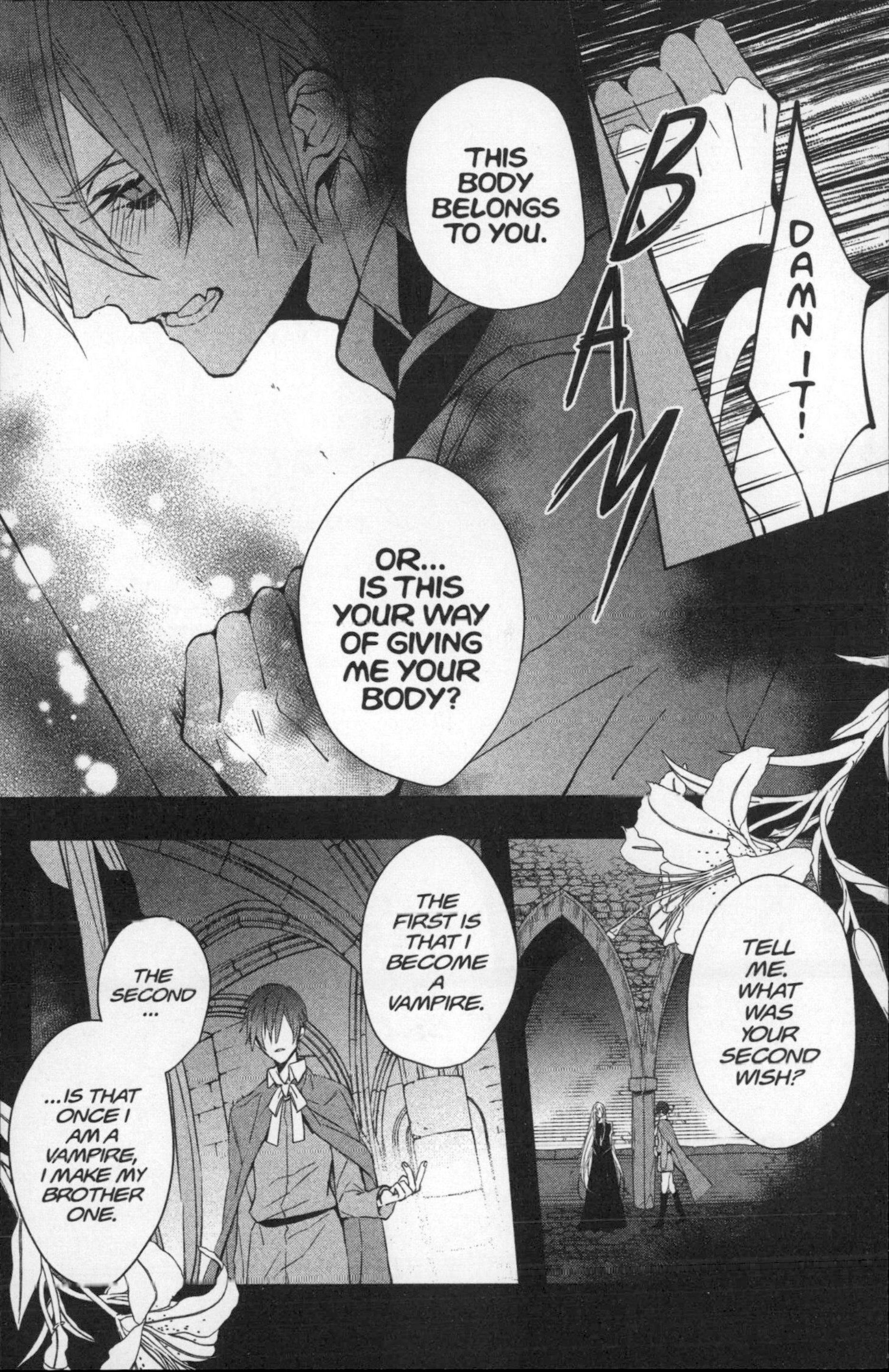
BAM
DAMN IT!
THIS BODY BELONGS TO YOU.
OR... IS THIS YOUR WAY OF GIVING ME YOUR BODY?
TELL ME. WHAT WAS YOUR SECOND WISH?
THE FIRST IS THAT I BECOME A VAMPIRE.
THE SECOND...
...IS THAT ONCE I AM A VAMPIRE, I MAKE MY BROTHER ONE.

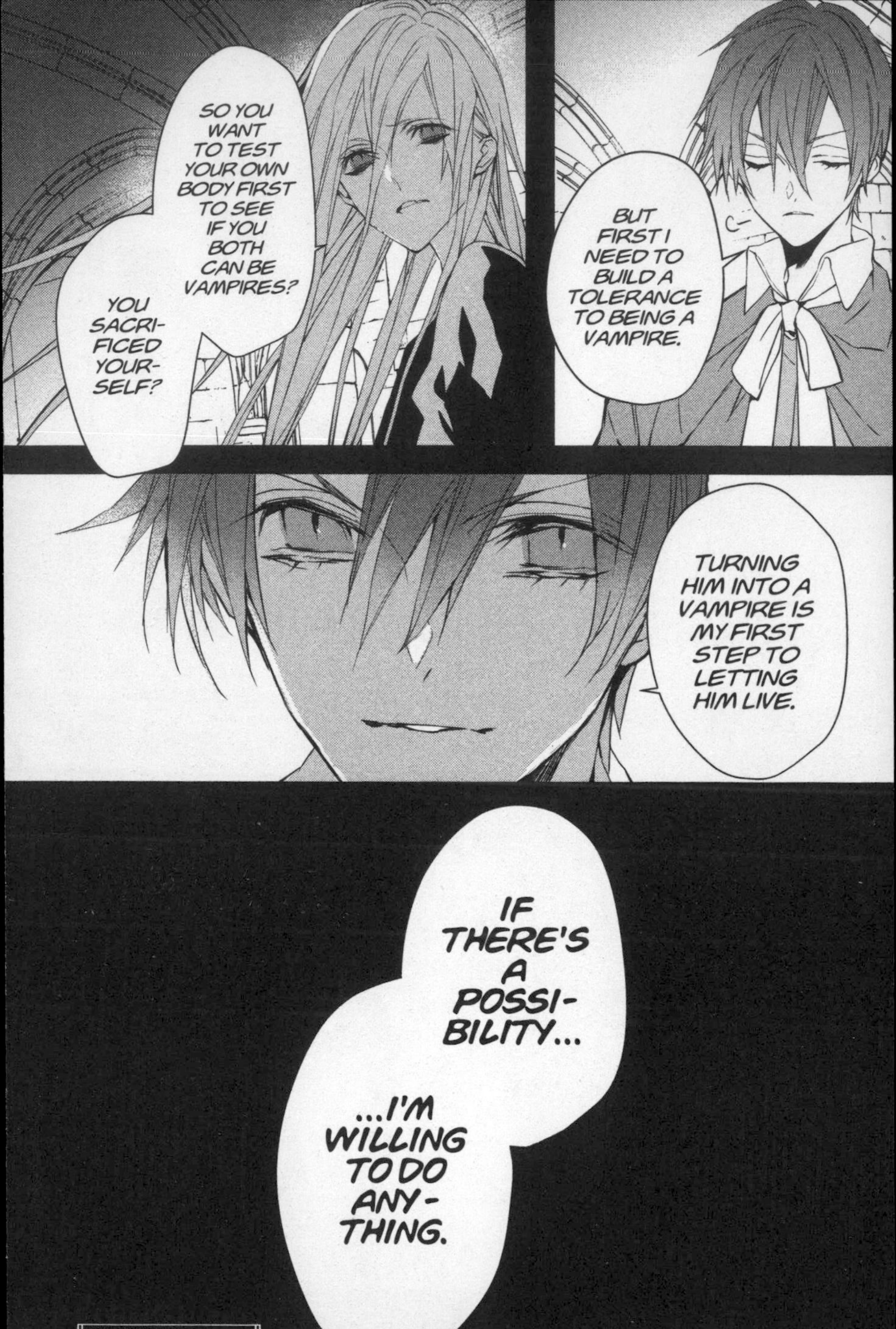
BUT FIRST I NEED TO BUILD A TOLERANCE TO BEING A VAMPIRE.
SO YOU WANT TO TEST YOUR OWN BODY FIRST TO SEE IF YOU BOTH CAN BE VAMPIRES?
YOU SACRI-FICED YOUR-SELF?
TURNING HIM INTO A VAMPIRE IS MY FIRST STEP TO LETTING HIM LIVE.
IF THERE'S A POSSI-BILITY...
...I'M WILLING TO DO ANY-THING.

BLOOD ✦ 33 end

Bloody+Mary

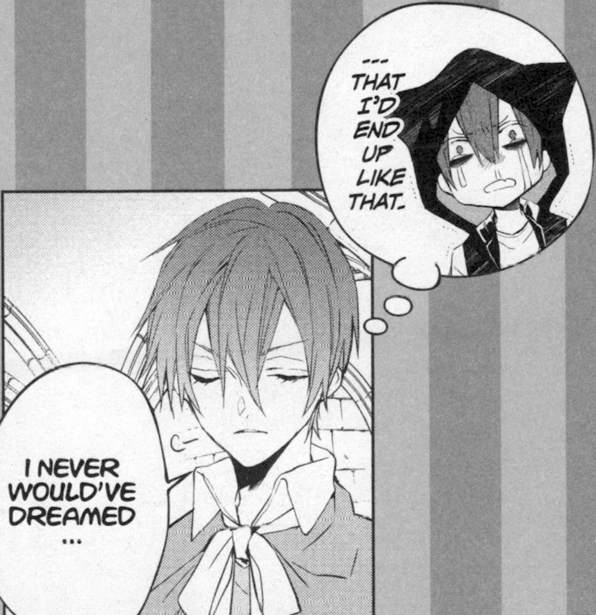
I NEVER WOULD'VE DREAMED ...
---THAT I'D END UP LIKE THAT.

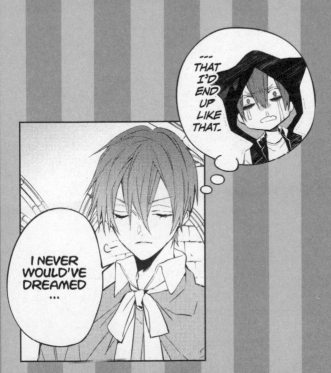

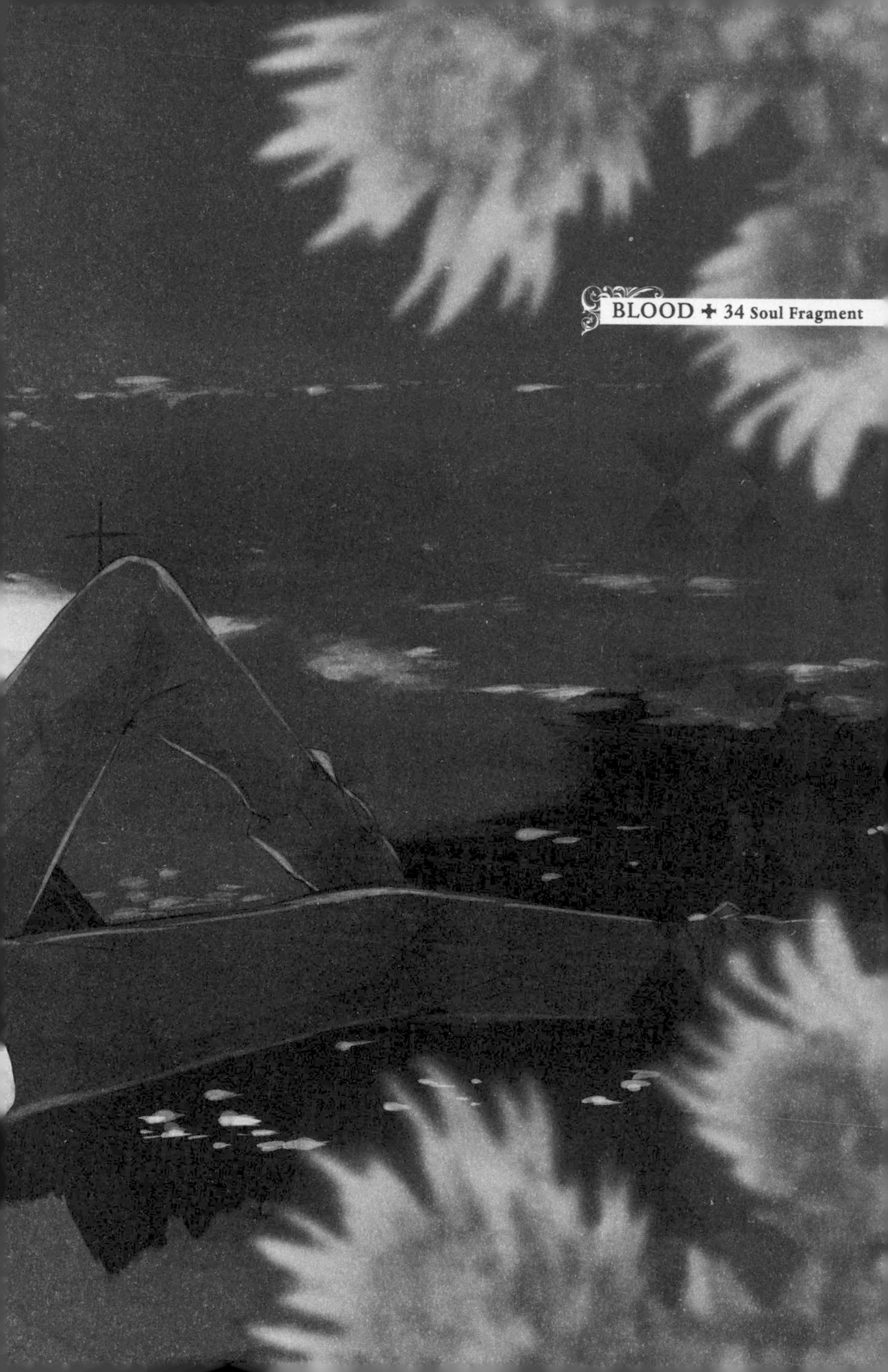
BLOOD ✣ 34 Soul Fragment

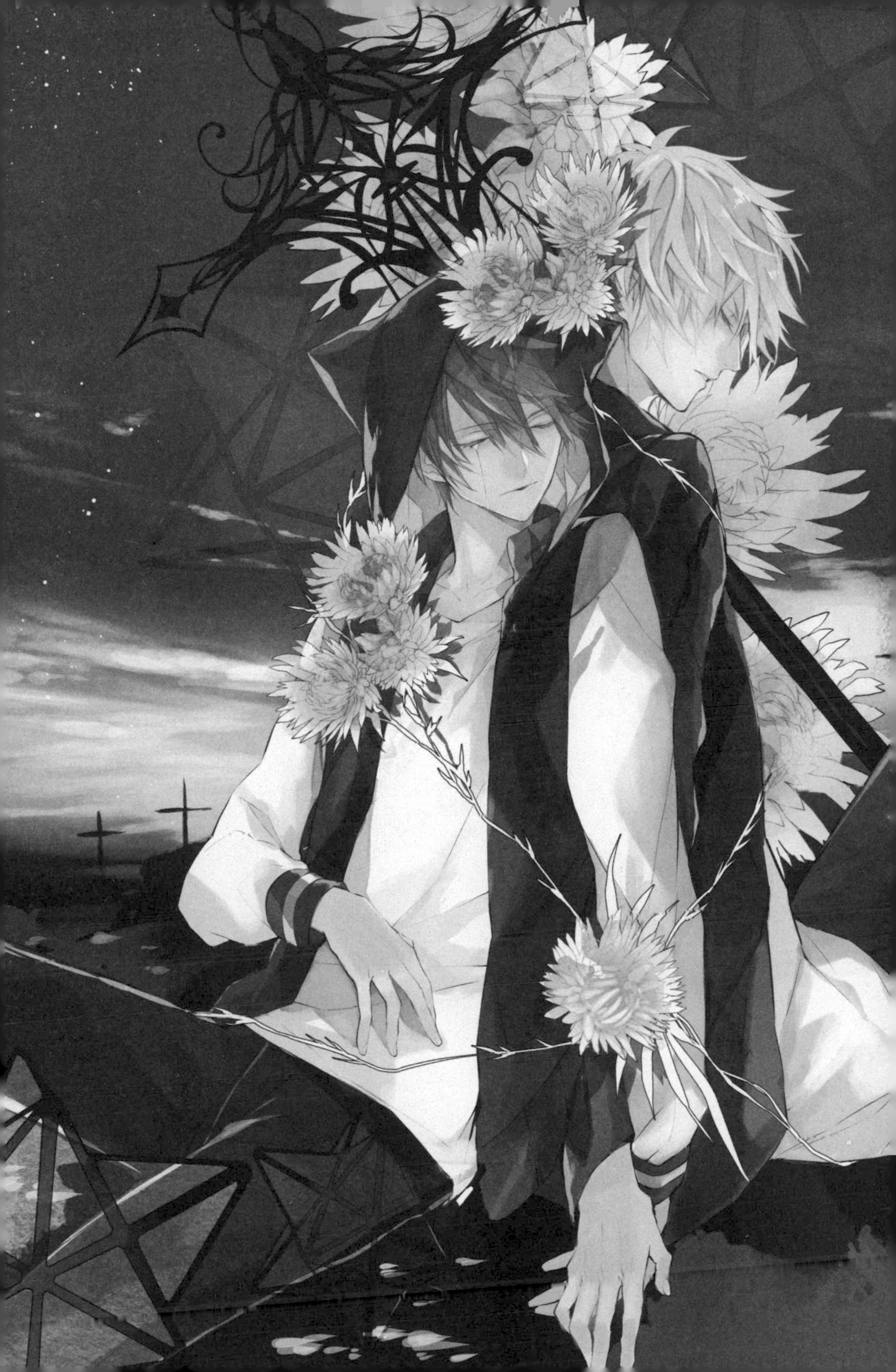

Bloody+Mary

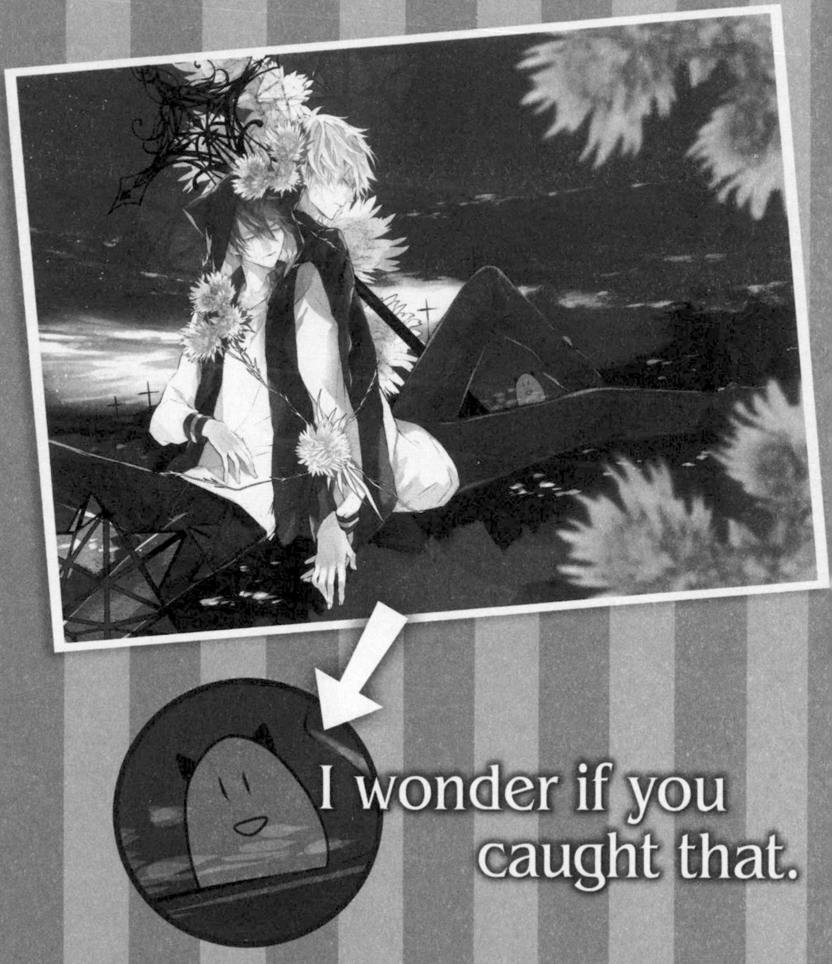

I wonder if you caught that.

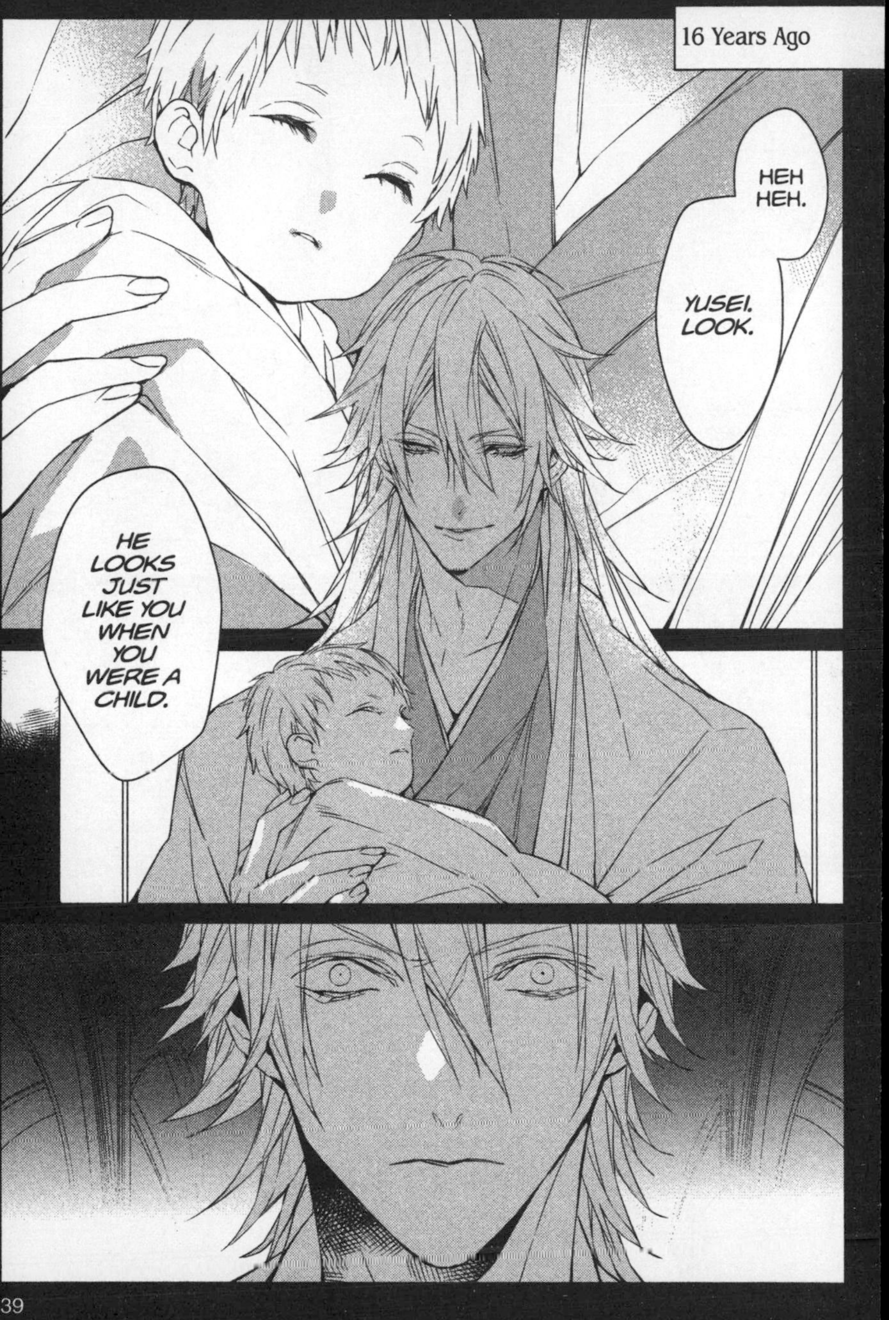
16 Years Ago
HEH HEH.
YUSEI. LOOK.
HE LOOKS JUST LIKE YOU WHEN YOU WERE A CHILD.

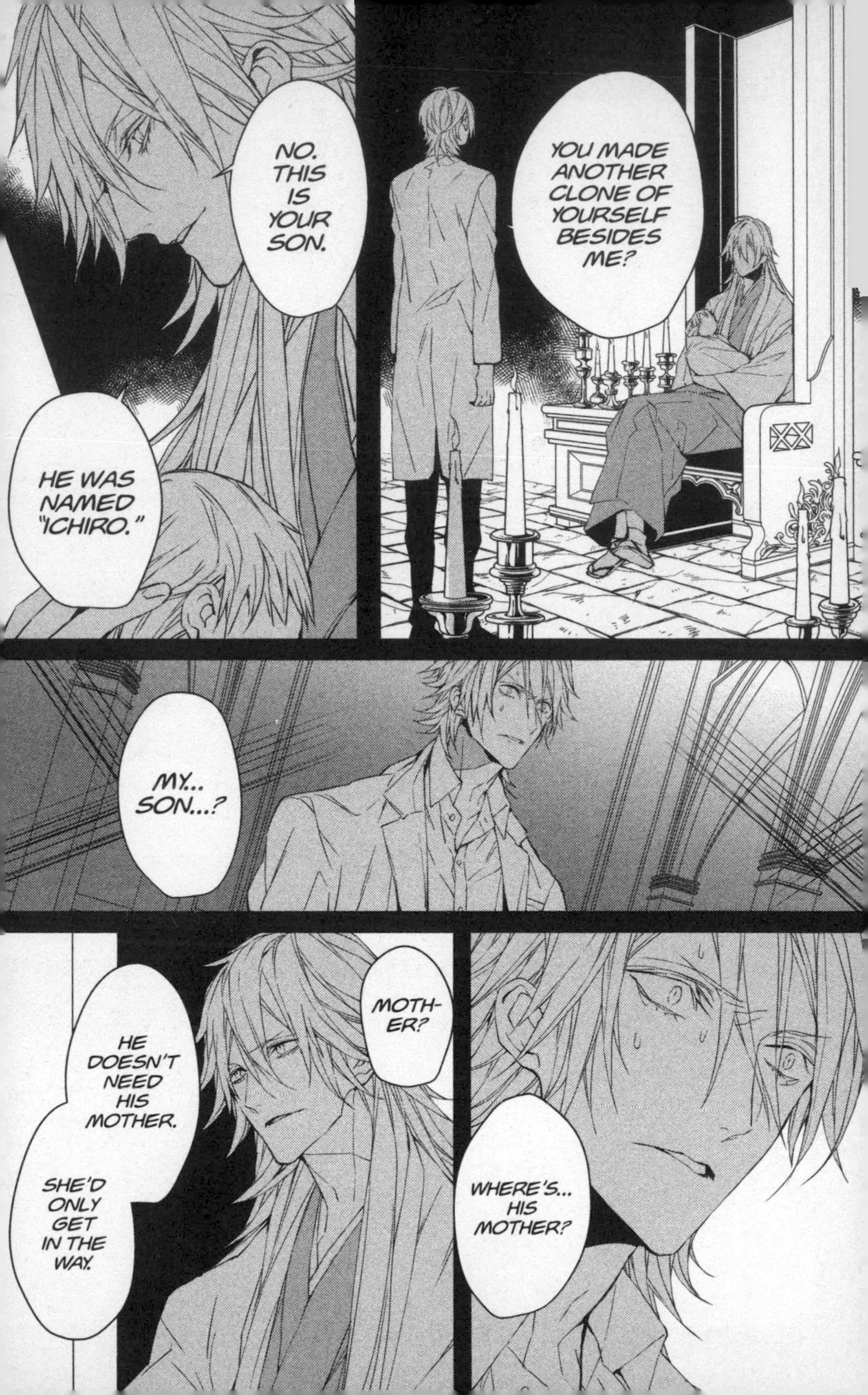
YOU MADE ANOTHER CLONE OF YOURSELF BESIDES ME?
NO. THIS IS YOUR SON.
HE WAS NAMED "ICHIRO."
MY... SON...?
WHERE'S... HIS MOTHER?
MOTHER?
HE DOESN'T NEED HIS MOTHER.
SHE'D ONLY GET IN THE WAY.

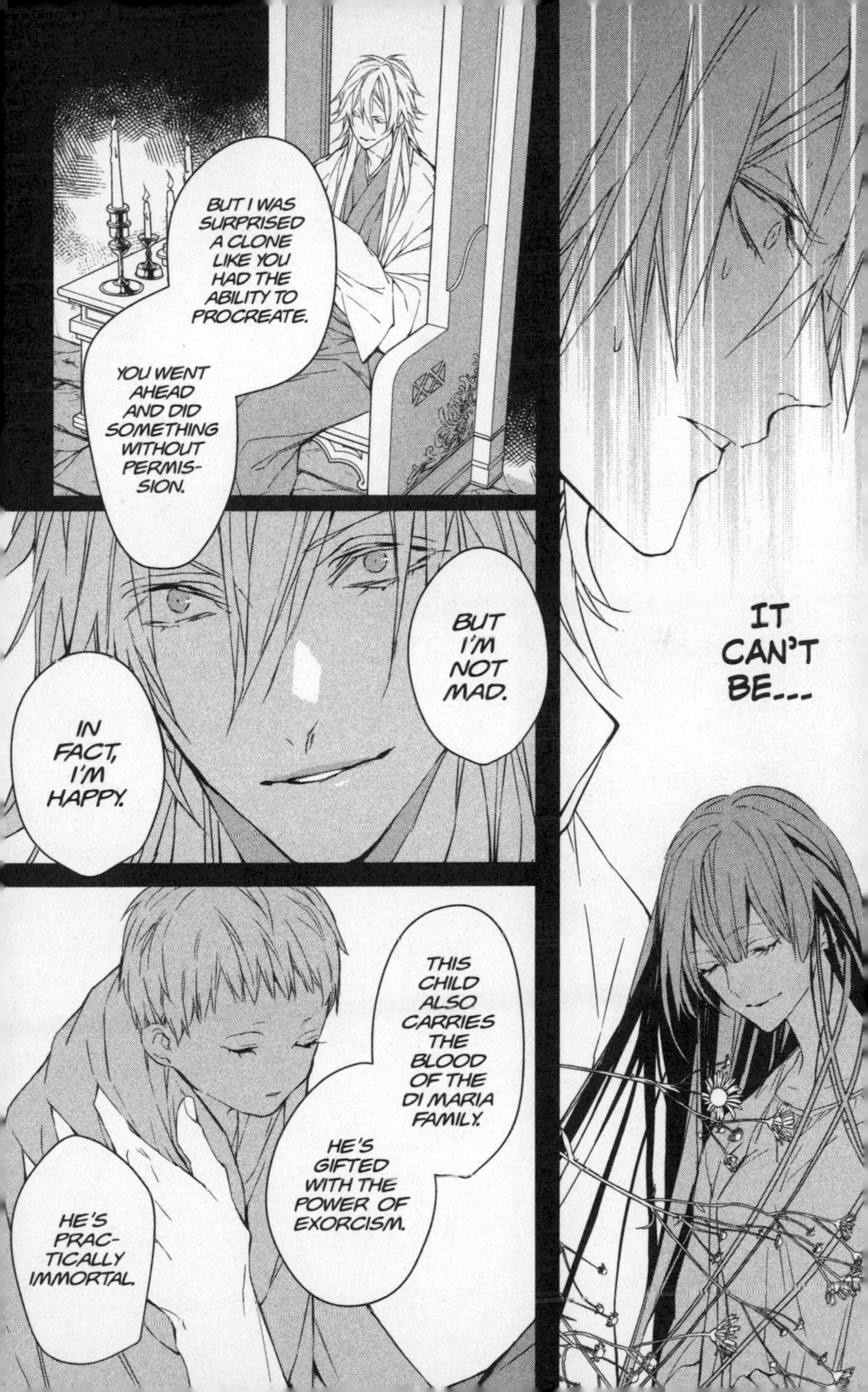
IT CAN'T BE...
BUT I WAS SURPRISED A CLONE LIKE YOU HAD THE ABILITY TO PROCREATE.
YOU WENT AHEAD AND DID SOMETHING WITHOUT PERMIS-SION.
BUT I'M NOT MAD.
IN FACT, I'M HAPPY.
THIS CHILD ALSO CARRIES THE BLOOD OF THE DI MARIA FAMILY.
HE'S GIFTED WITH THE POWER OF EXORCISM.
HE'S PRAC-TICALLY IMMORTAL.

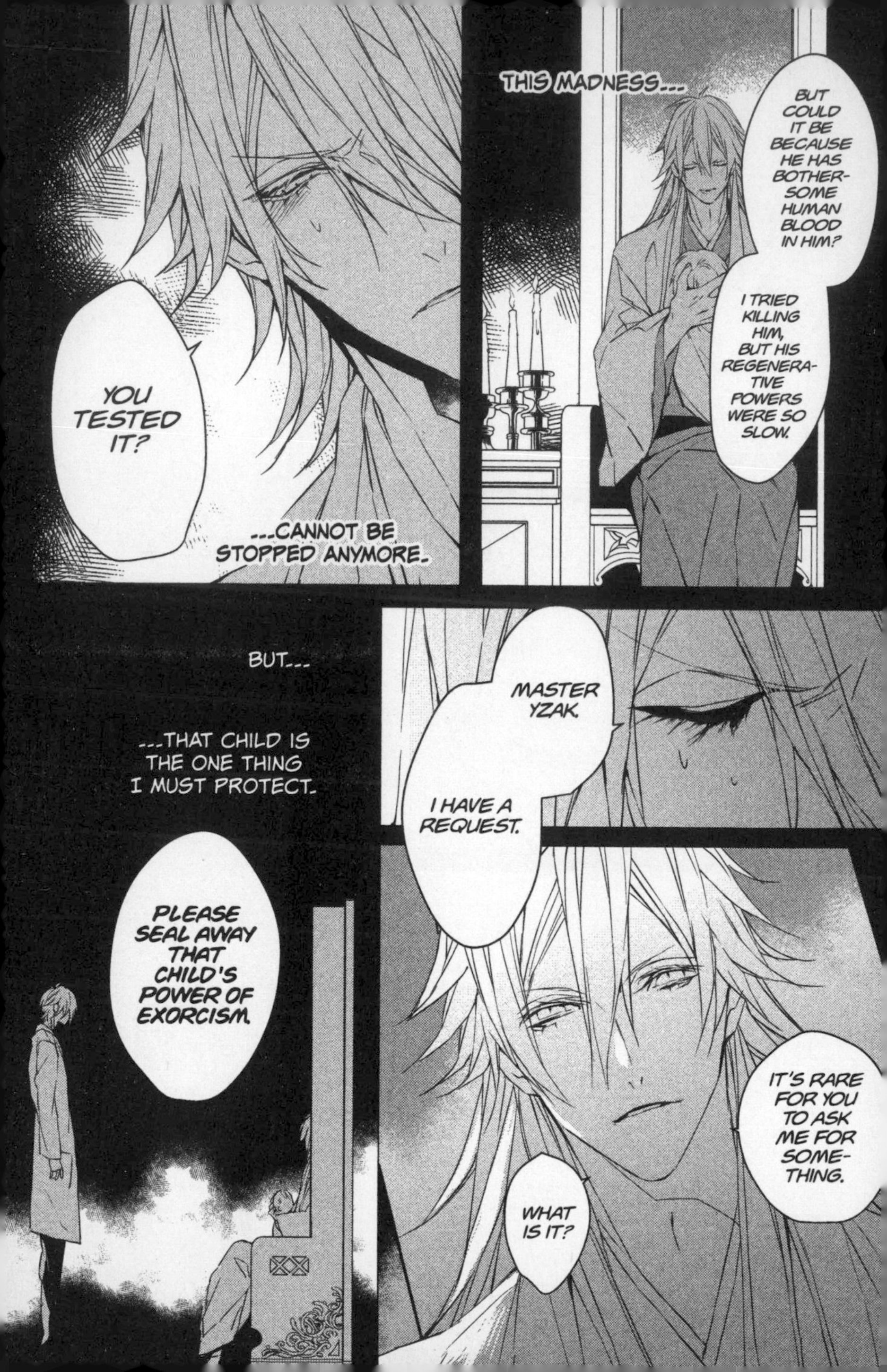
THIS MADNESS...
BUT COULD IT BE BECAUSE HE HAS BOTHER-SOME HUMAN BLOOD IN HIM?
I TRIED KILLING HIM, BUT HIS REGENERA-TIVE POWERS WERE SO SLOW.
YOU TESTED IT?
...CANNOT BE STOPPED ANYMORE.
MASTER YZAK.
I HAVE A REQUEST.
IT'S RARE FOR YOU TO ASK ME FOR SOME-THING.
WHAT IS IT?
BUT...
...THAT CHILD IS THE ONE THING I MUST PROTECT.
PLEASE SEAL AWAY THAT CHILD'S POWER OF EXORCISM.

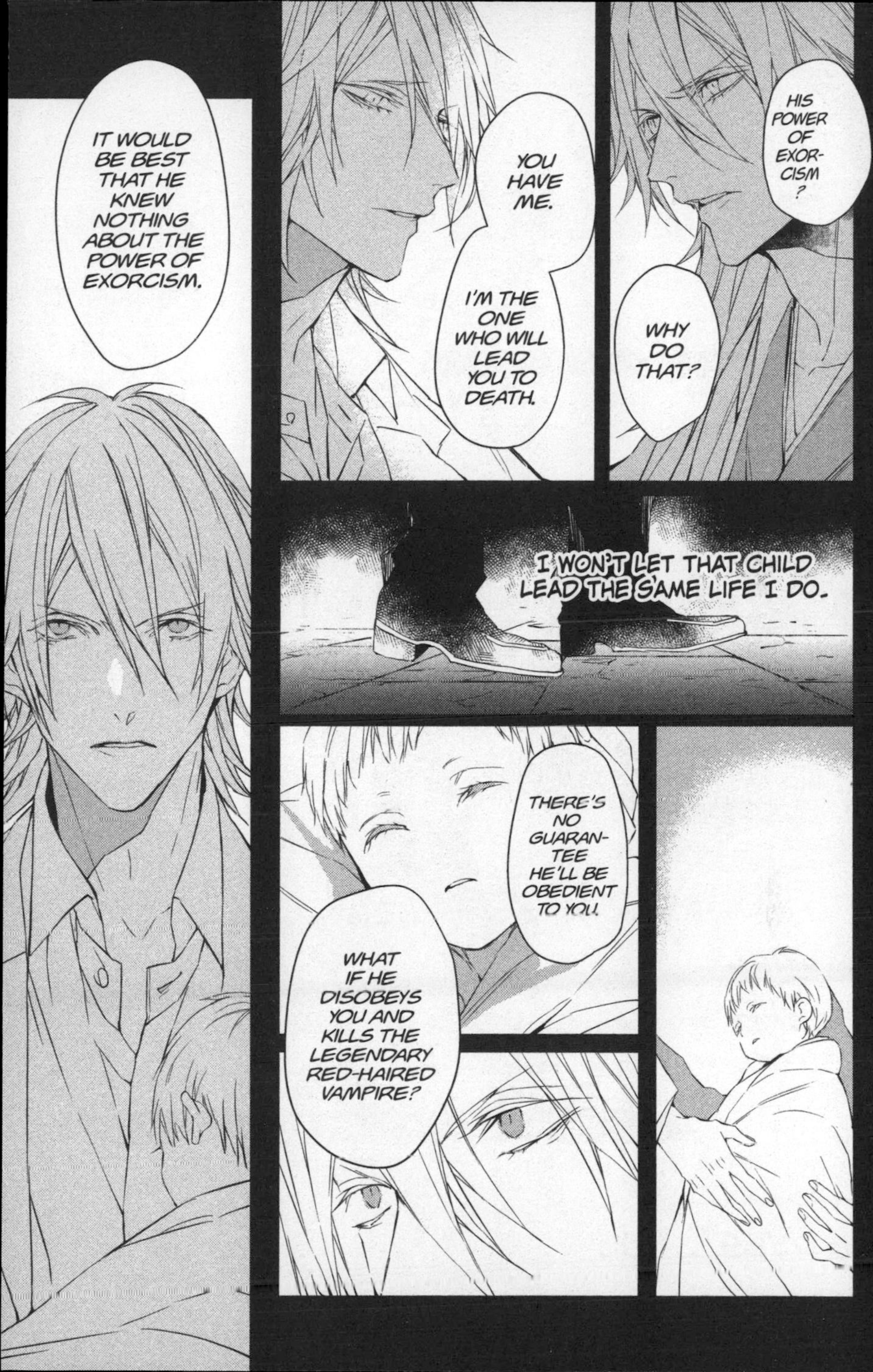
HIS POWER OF EXOR-CISM?
WHY DO THAT?
YOU HAVE ME.
I'M THE ONE WHO WILL LEAD YOU TO DEATH.
I WON'T LET THAT CHILD LEAD THE SAME LIFE I DO.
THERE'S NO GUARAN-TEE HE'LL BE OBEDIENT TO YOU.
WHAT IF HE DISOBEYS YOU AND KILLS THE LEGENDARY RED-HAIRED VAMPIRE?
IT WOULD BE BEST THAT HE KNEW NOTHING ABOUT THE POWER OF EXORCISM.

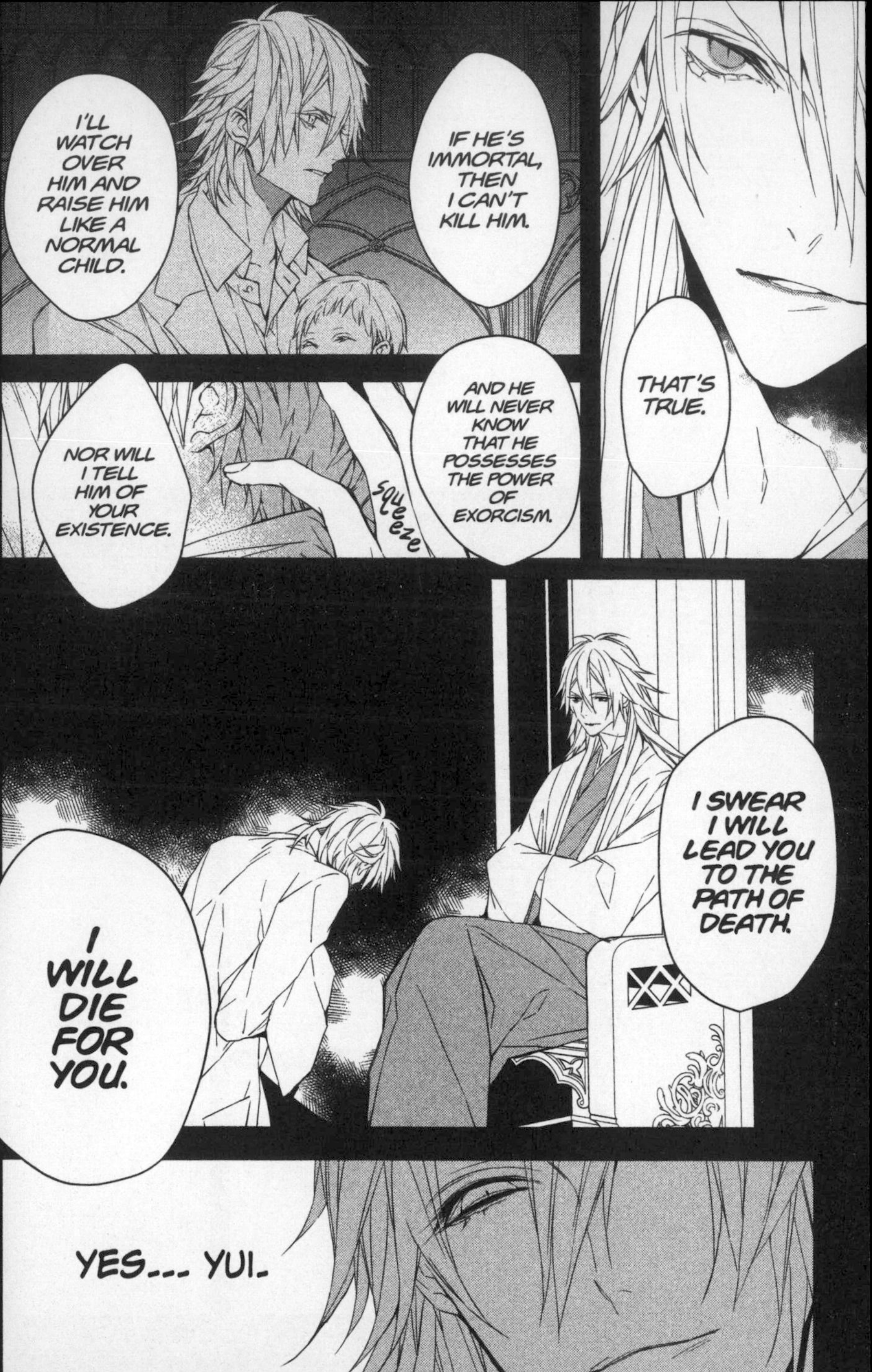
THAT'S TRUE.
IF HE'S IMMORTAL, THEN I CAN'T KILL HIM.
I'LL WATCH OVER HIM AND RAISE HIM LIKE A NORMAL CHILD.
AND HE WILL NEVER KNOW THAT HE POSSESSES THE POWER OF EXORCISM.
squeeze
NOR WILL I TELL HIM OF YOUR EXISTENCE.
I SWEAR I WILL LEAD YOU TO THE PATH OF DEATH.
I WILL DIE FOR YOU.
YES... YUI.

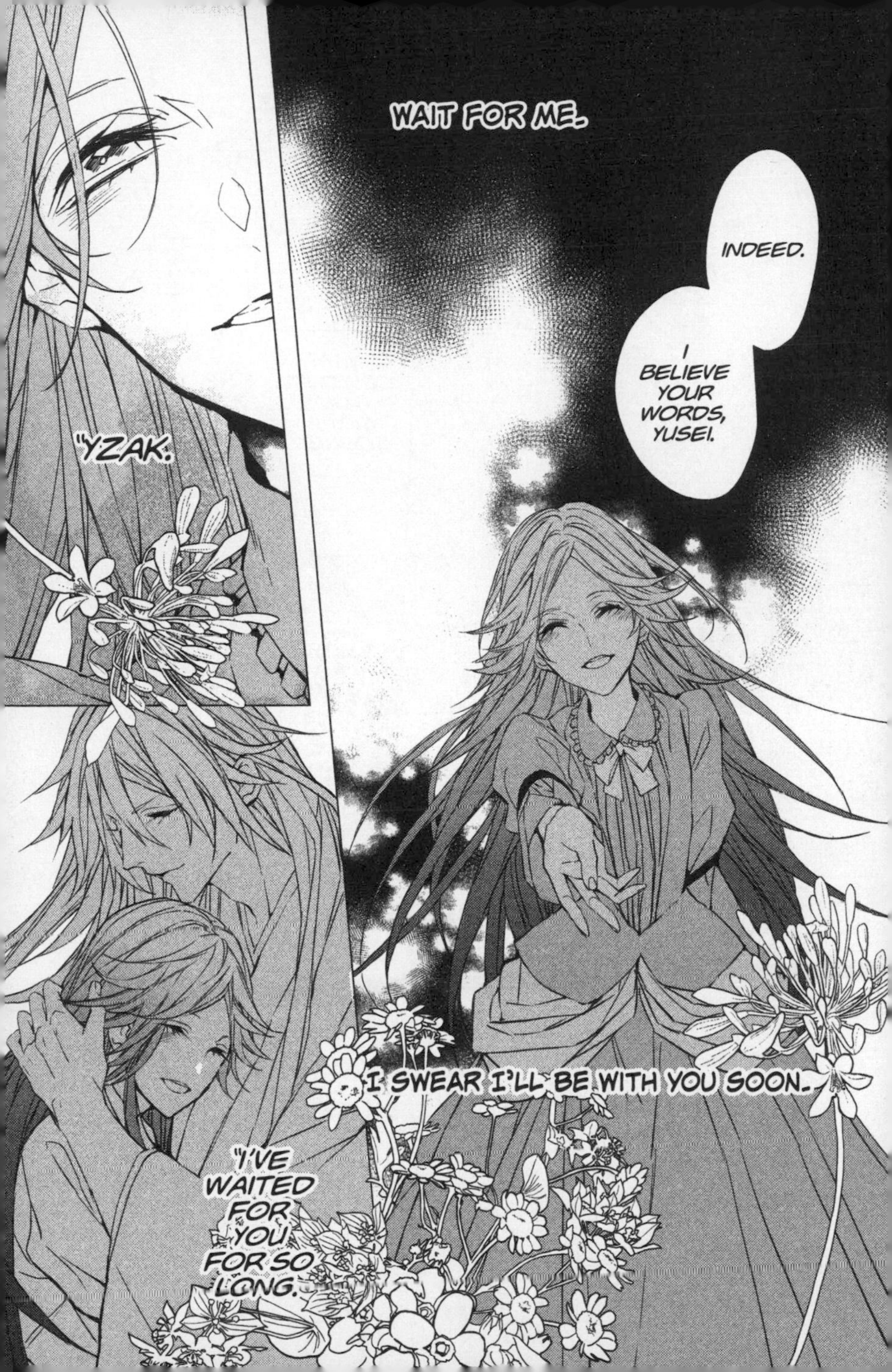
WAIT FOR ME.
INDEED.
I BELIEVE YOUR WORDS, YUSEI.
"YZAK.
I SWEAR I'LL BE WITH YOU SOON.
"I'VE WAITED FOR YOU FOR SO LONG.

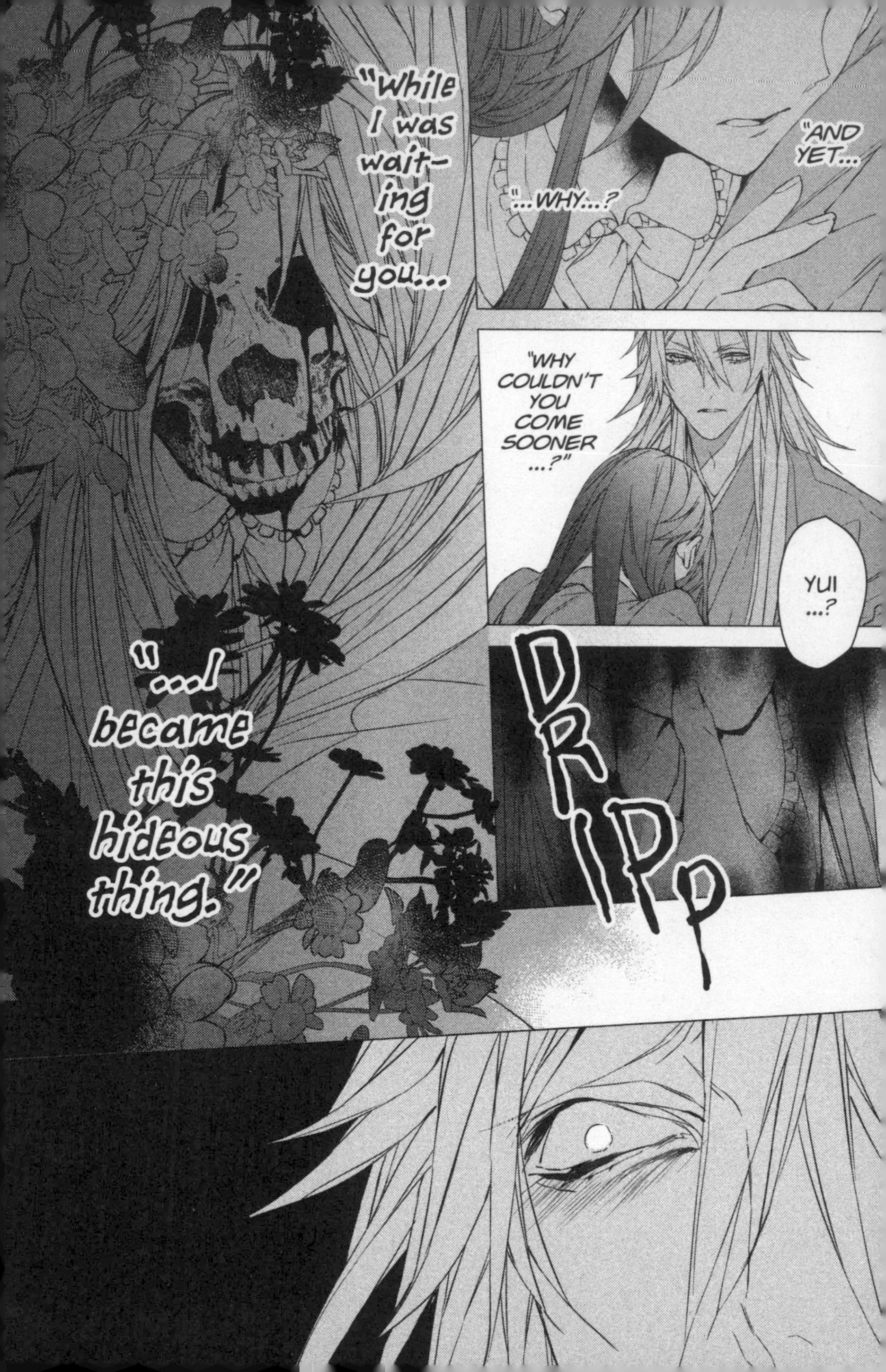
"AND YET...
"...WHY...?
"WHY COULDN'T YOU COME SOONER ...?"
YUI ...?
DRIPP
"While I was wait-ing for you...
"...I became this hideous thing."

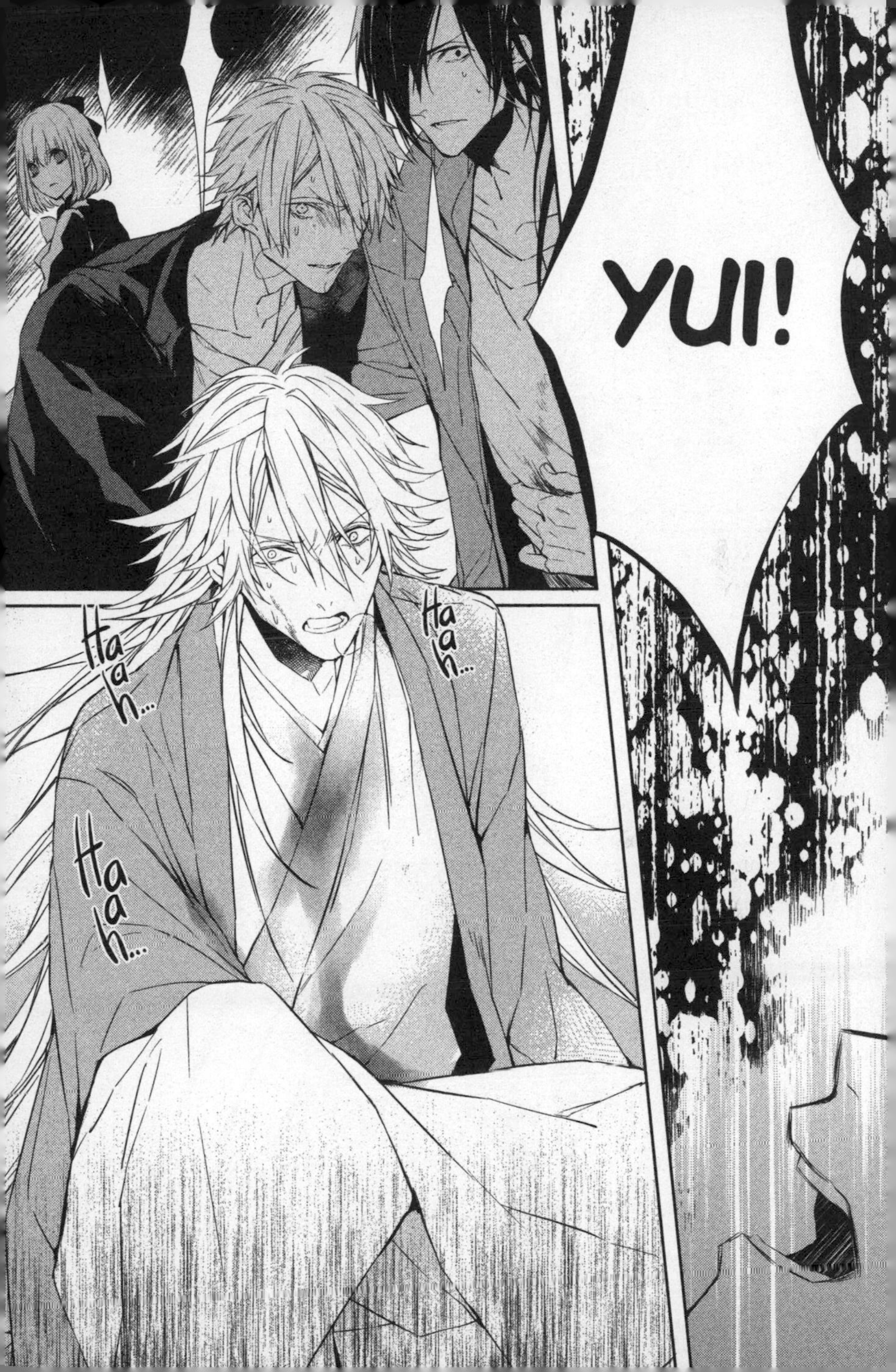
YUI!
Haah...
Haah...
Haah...

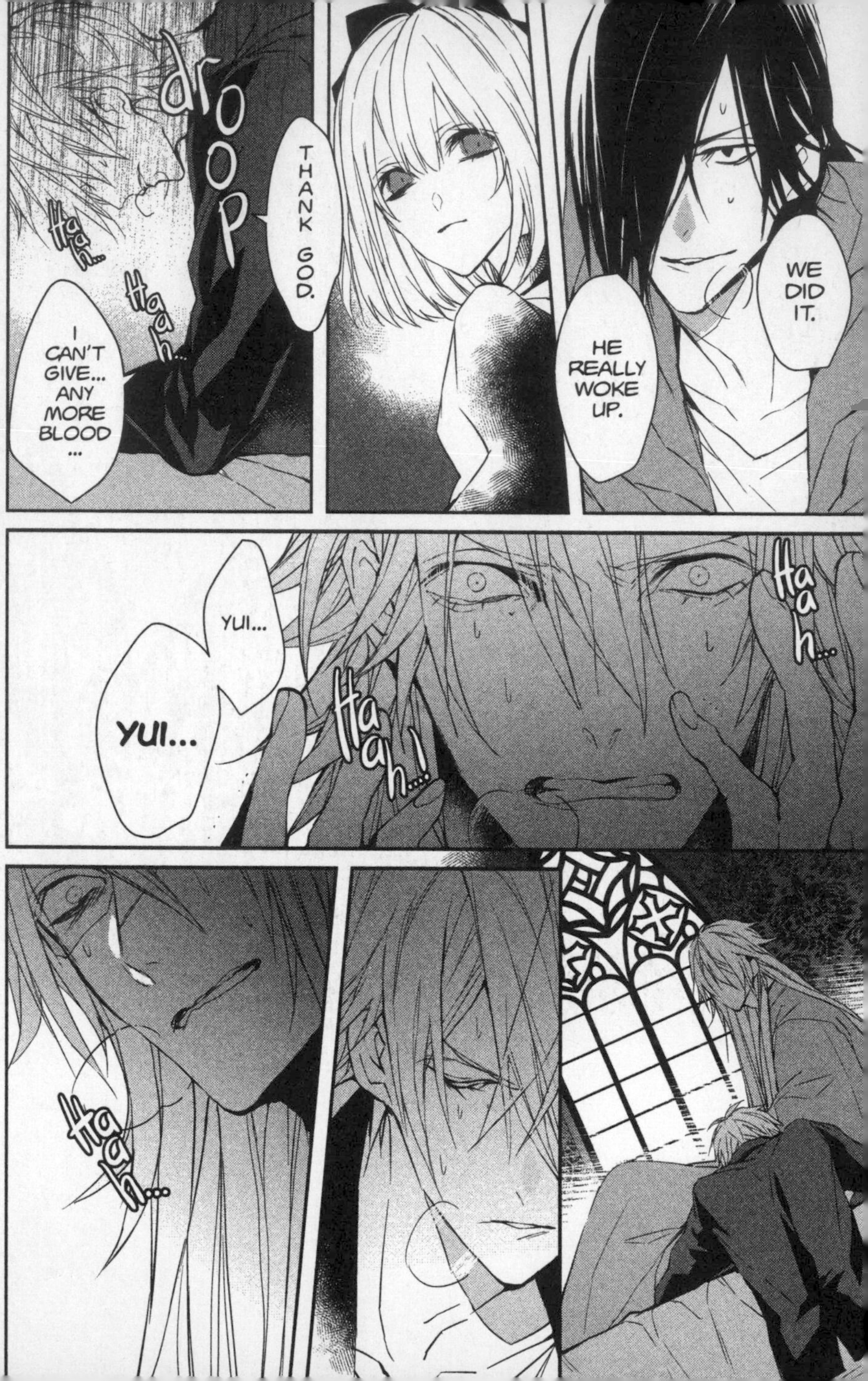
WE DID IT.
HE REALLY WOKE UP.
THANK GOD.
droop
Haah...
Haah...
I CAN'T GIVE... ANY MORE BLOOD...
Haah...
Haah...!
YUI...
YUI...
Haah...

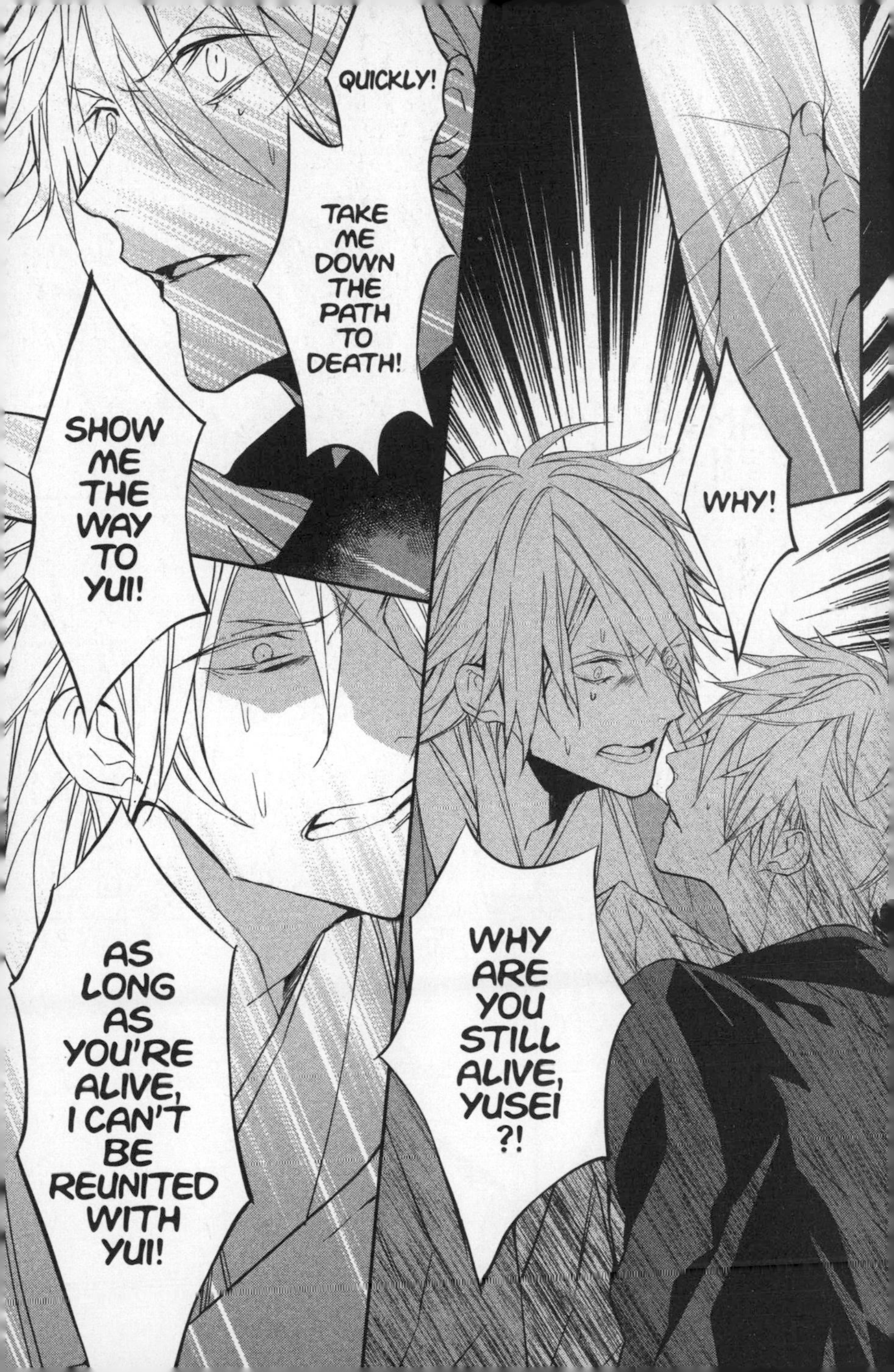
WHY!
WHY ARE YOU STILL ALIVE, YUSEI ?!
QUICKLY!
TAKE ME DOWN THE PATH TO DEATH!
SHOW ME THE WAY TO YUI!
AS LONG AS YOU'RE ALIVE, I CAN'T BE REUNITED WITH YUI!

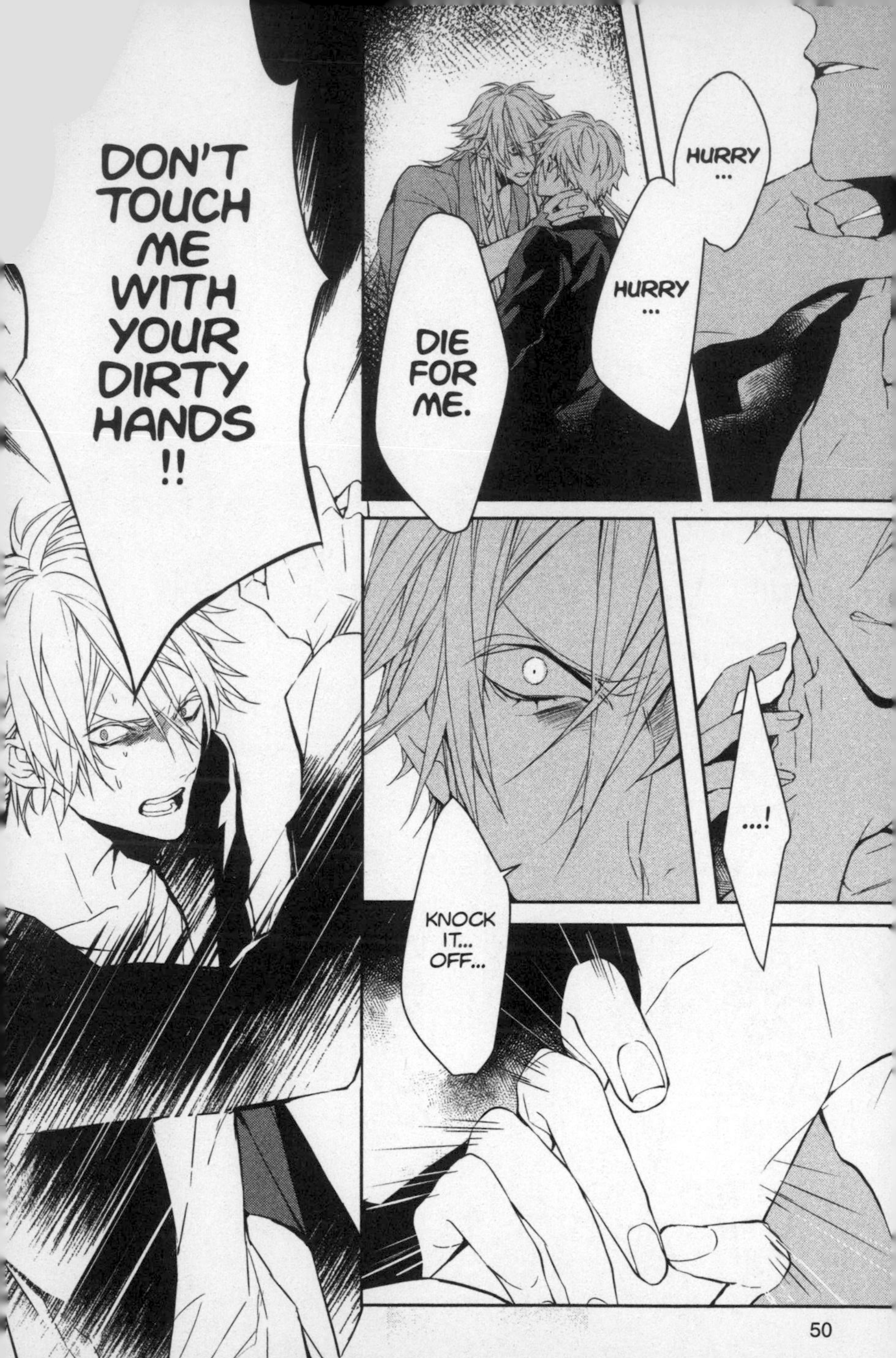
HURRY...
HURRY...
DIE FOR ME.
...!
KNOCK IT... OFF...
DON'T TOUCH ME WITH YOUR DIRTY HANDS!!

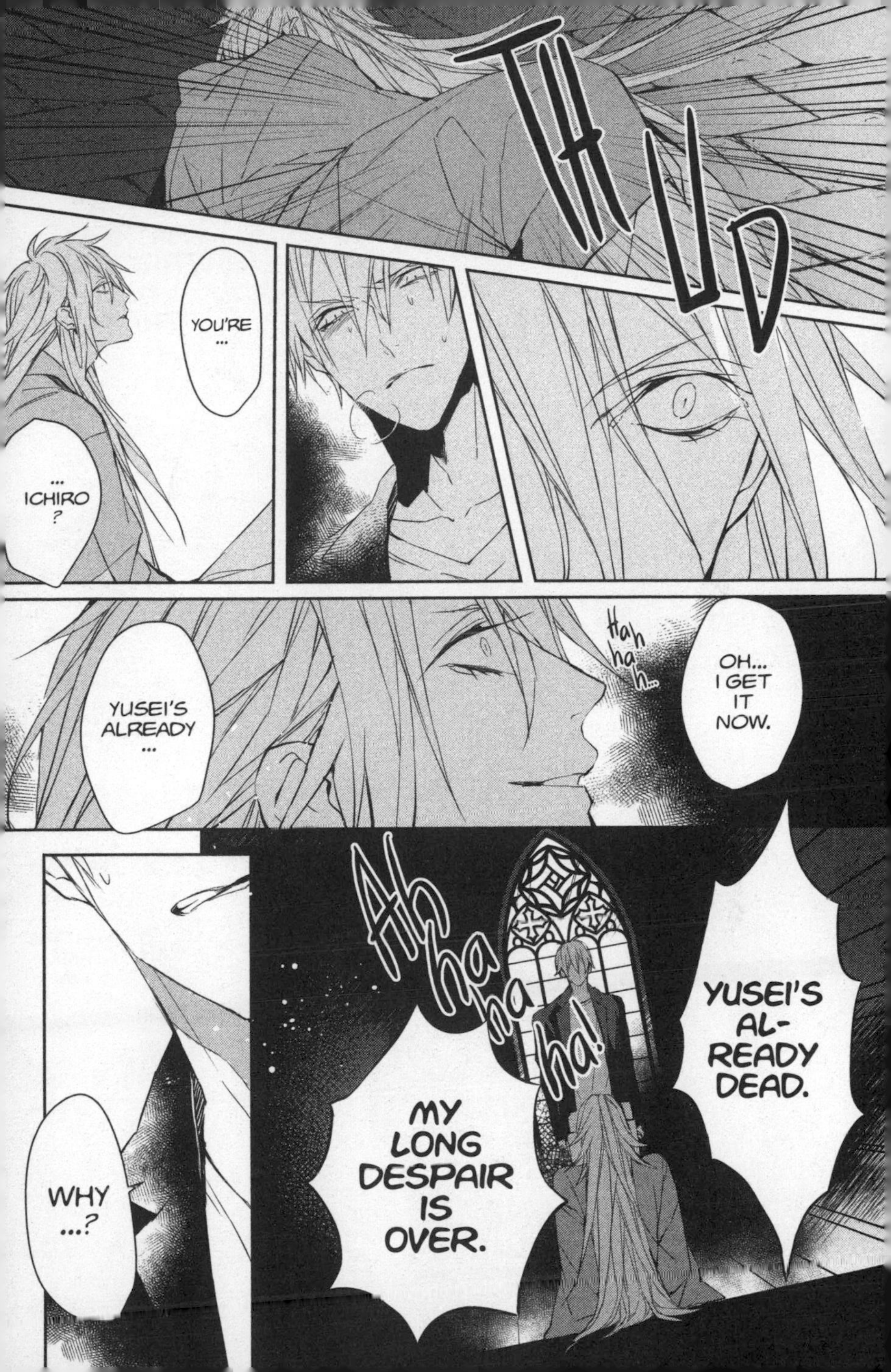
THUD
YOU'RE ...
... ICHIRO ?
Hah hah h...
OH... I GET IT NOW.
YUSEI'S ALREADY ...
YUSEI'S AL-READY DEAD.
Ah ha ha ha!
MY LONG DESPAIR IS OVER.
WHY ...?

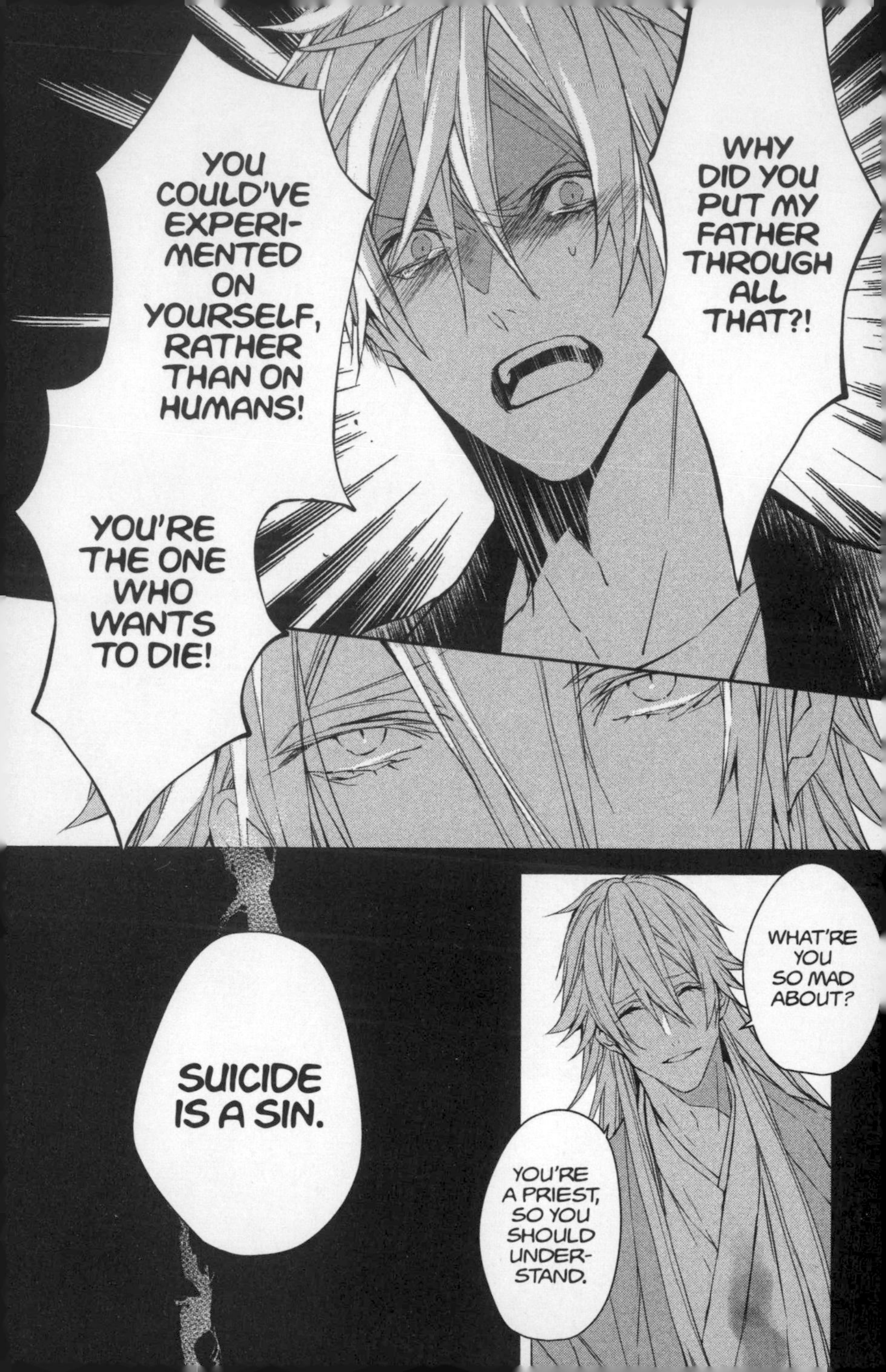
WHY DID YOU PUT MY FATHER THROUGH ALL THAT?!
YOU COULD'VE EXPERIMENTED ON YOURSELF, RATHER THAN ON HUMANS!
YOU'RE THE ONE WHO WANTS TO DIE!
WHAT'RE YOU SO MAD ABOUT?
YOU'RE A PRIEST, SO YOU SHOULD UNDERSTAND.
SUICIDE IS A SIN.

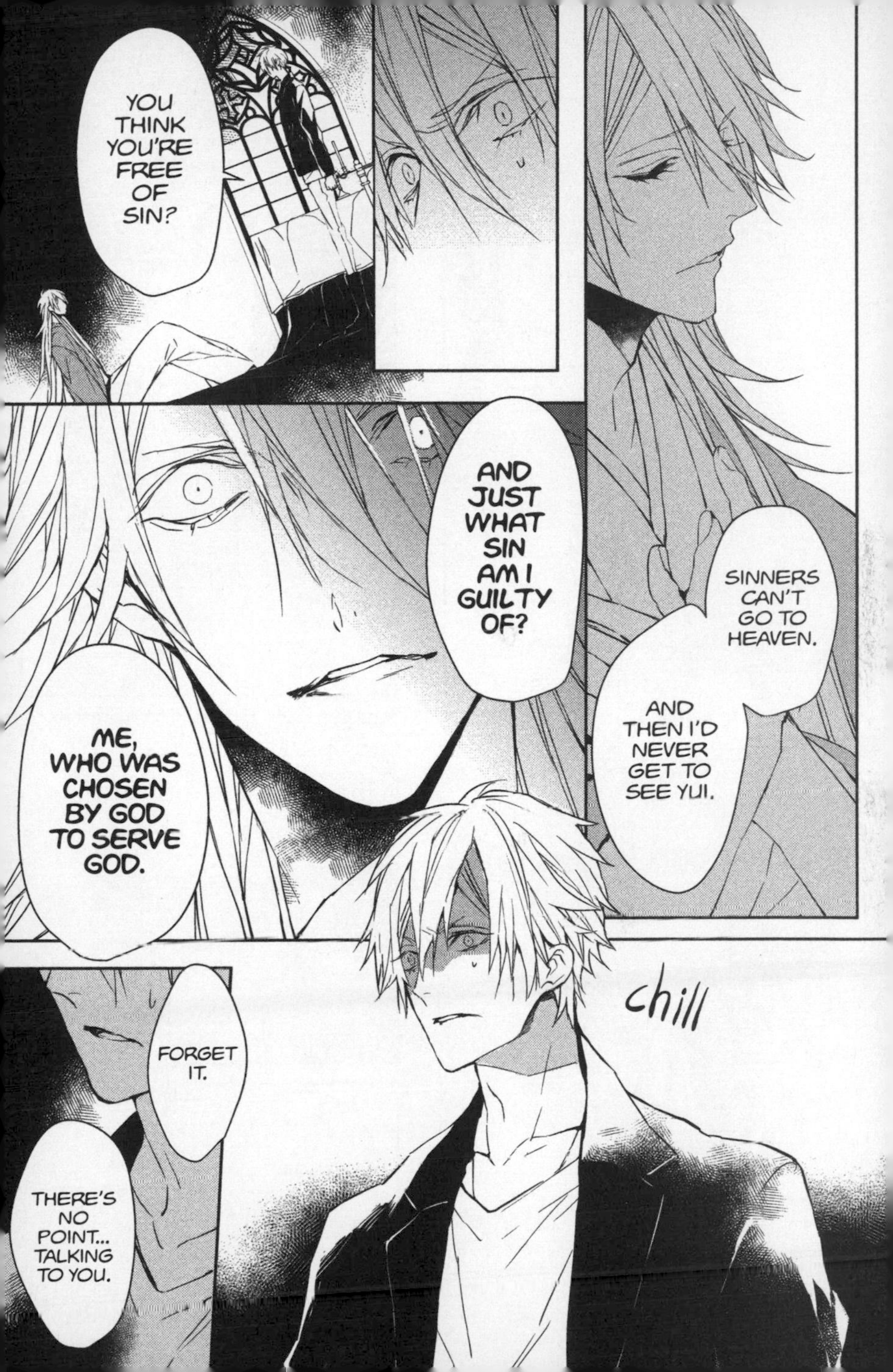
YOU THINK YOU'RE FREE OF SIN?
SINNERS CAN'T GO TO HEAVEN.
AND THEN I'D NEVER GET TO SEE YUI.
AND JUST WHAT SIN AM I GUILTY OF?
ME, WHO WAS CHOSEN BY GOD TO SERVE GOD.
chill
FORGET IT.
THERE'S NO POINT... TALKING TO YOU.

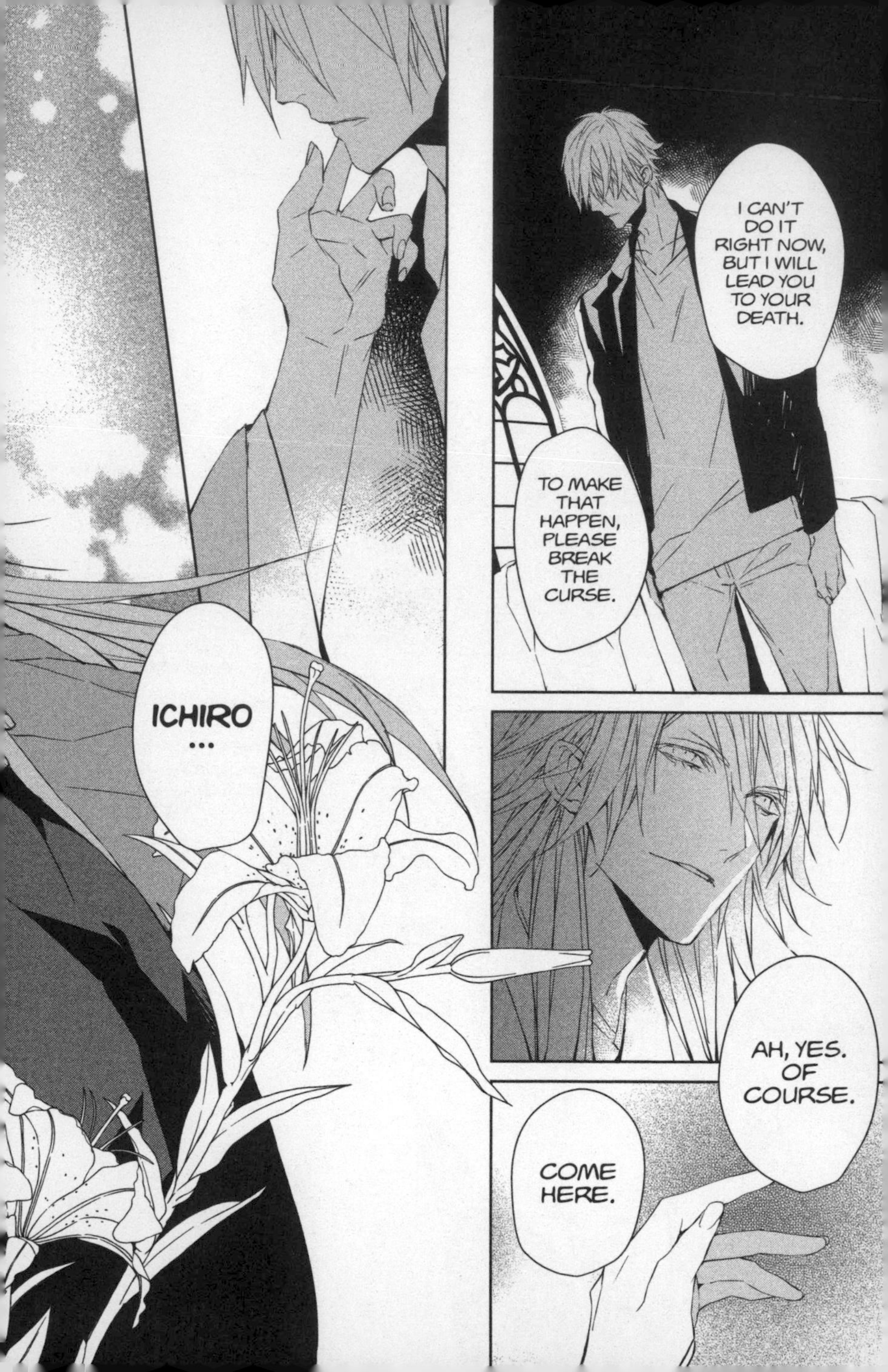
I CAN'T DO IT RIGHT NOW, BUT I WILL LEAD YOU TO YOUR DEATH.
TO MAKE THAT HAPPEN, PLEASE BREAK THE CURSE.
AH, YES. OF COURSE.
COME HERE.
ICHIRO...

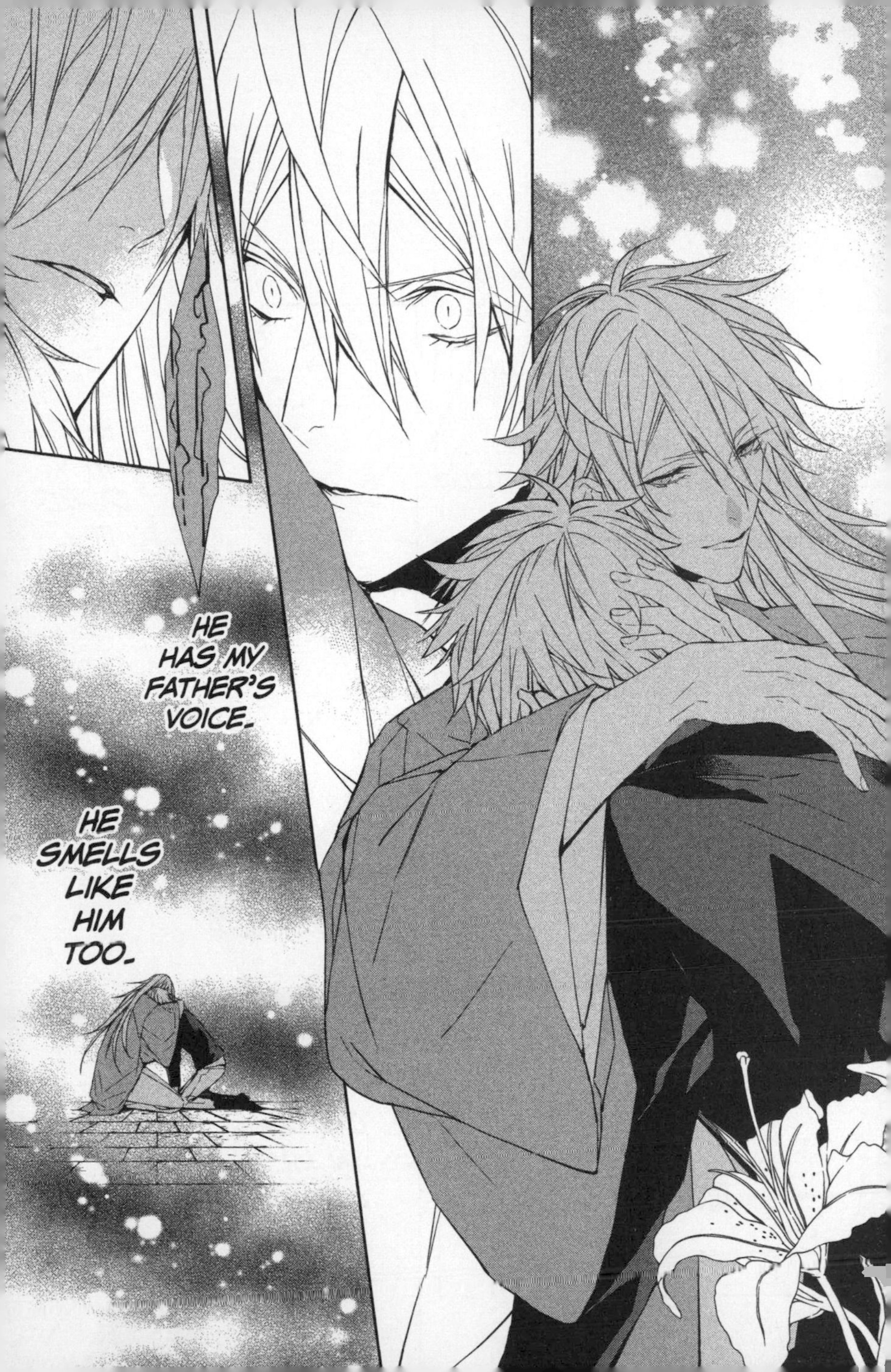
HE HAS MY FATHER'S VOICE.
HE SMELLS LIKE HIM TOO.

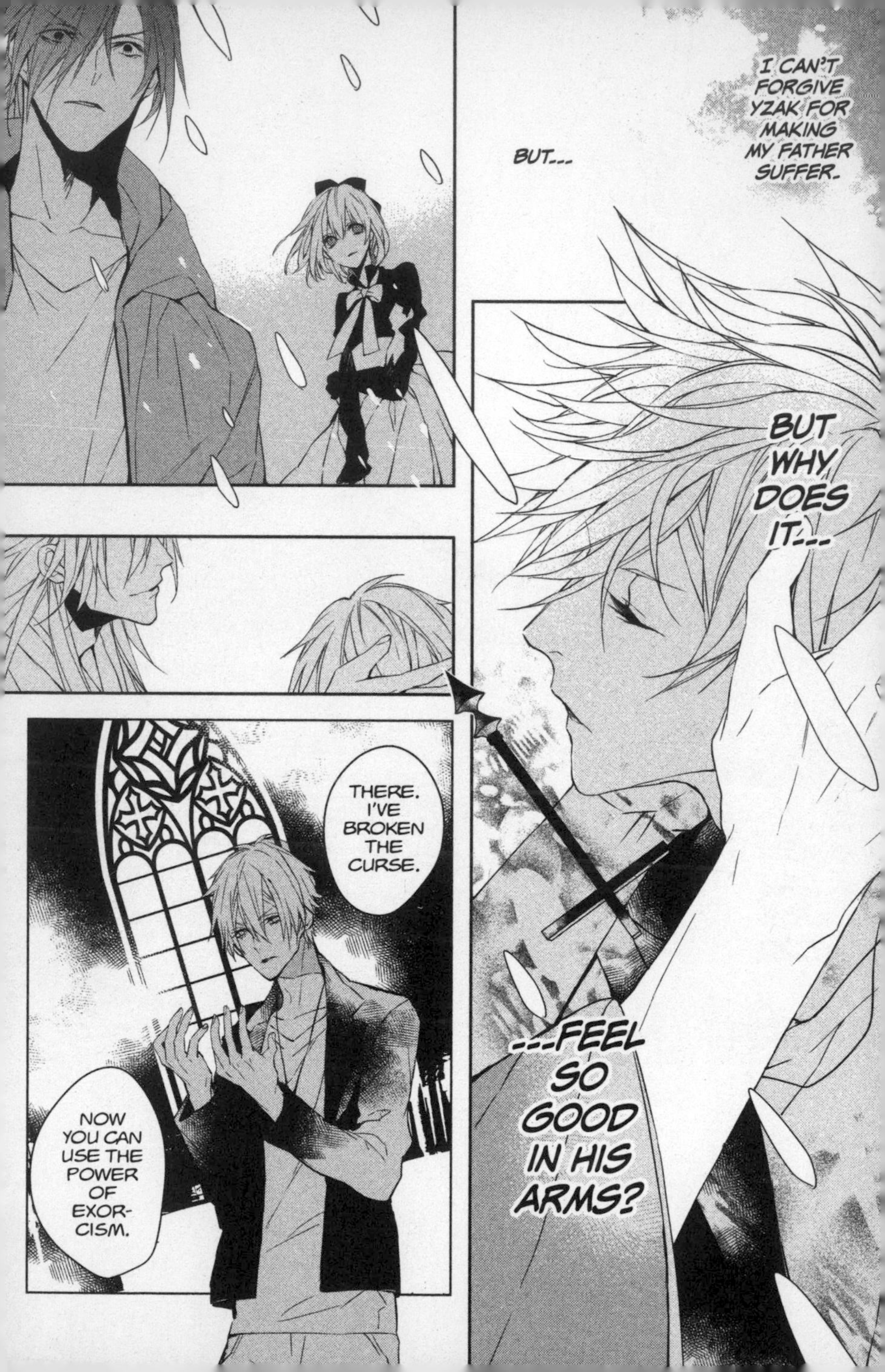
I CAN'T FORGIVE YZAK FOR MAKING MY FATHER SUFFER.
BUT...
BUT WHY DOES IT...
...FEEL SO GOOD IN HIS ARMS?
THERE. I'VE BROKEN THE CURSE.
NOW YOU CAN USE THE POWER OF EXORCISM.

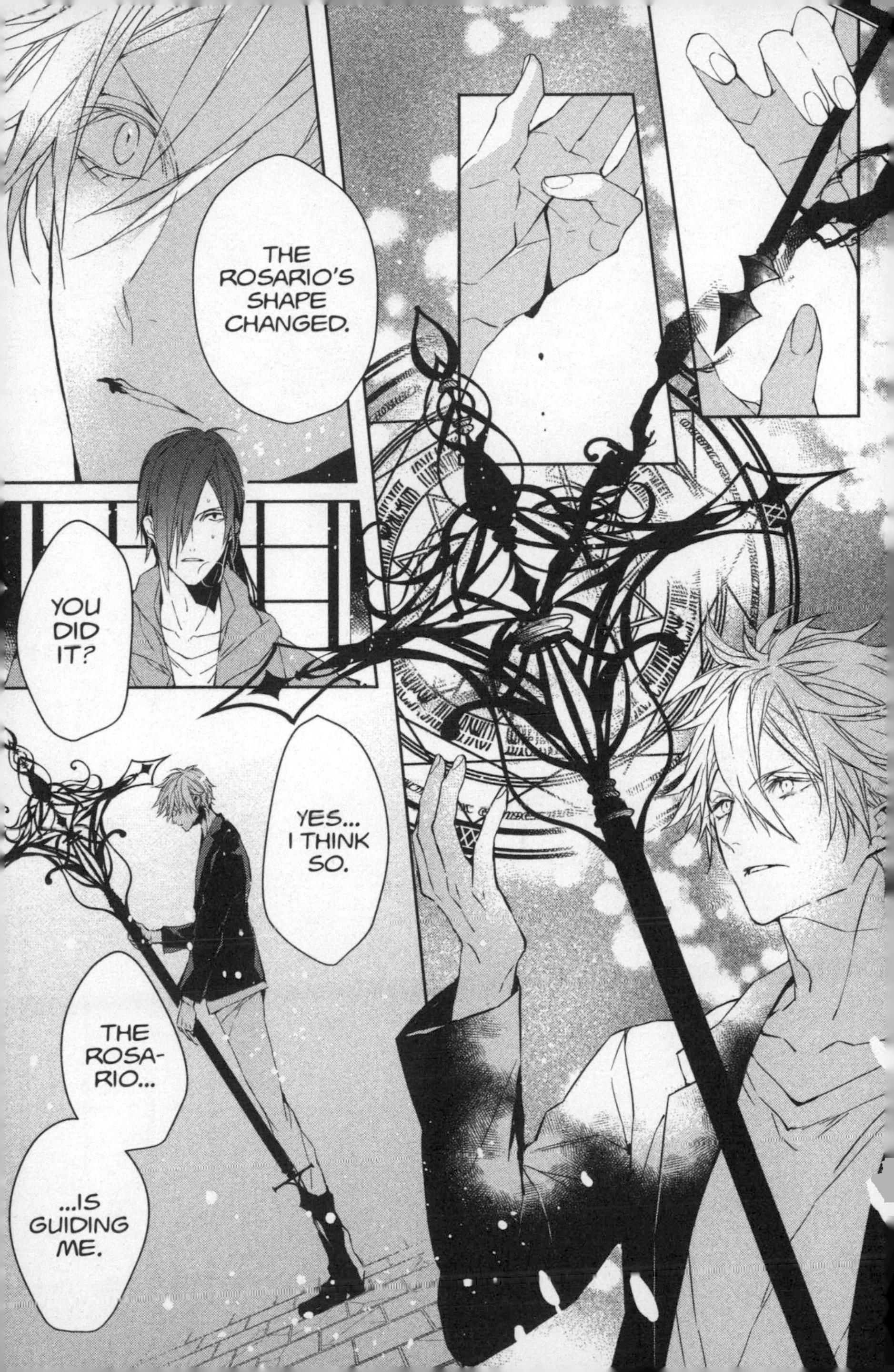
THE ROSARIO'S SHAPE CHANGED.
YOU DID IT?
YES... I THINK SO.
THE ROSA-RIO...
...IS GUIDING ME.

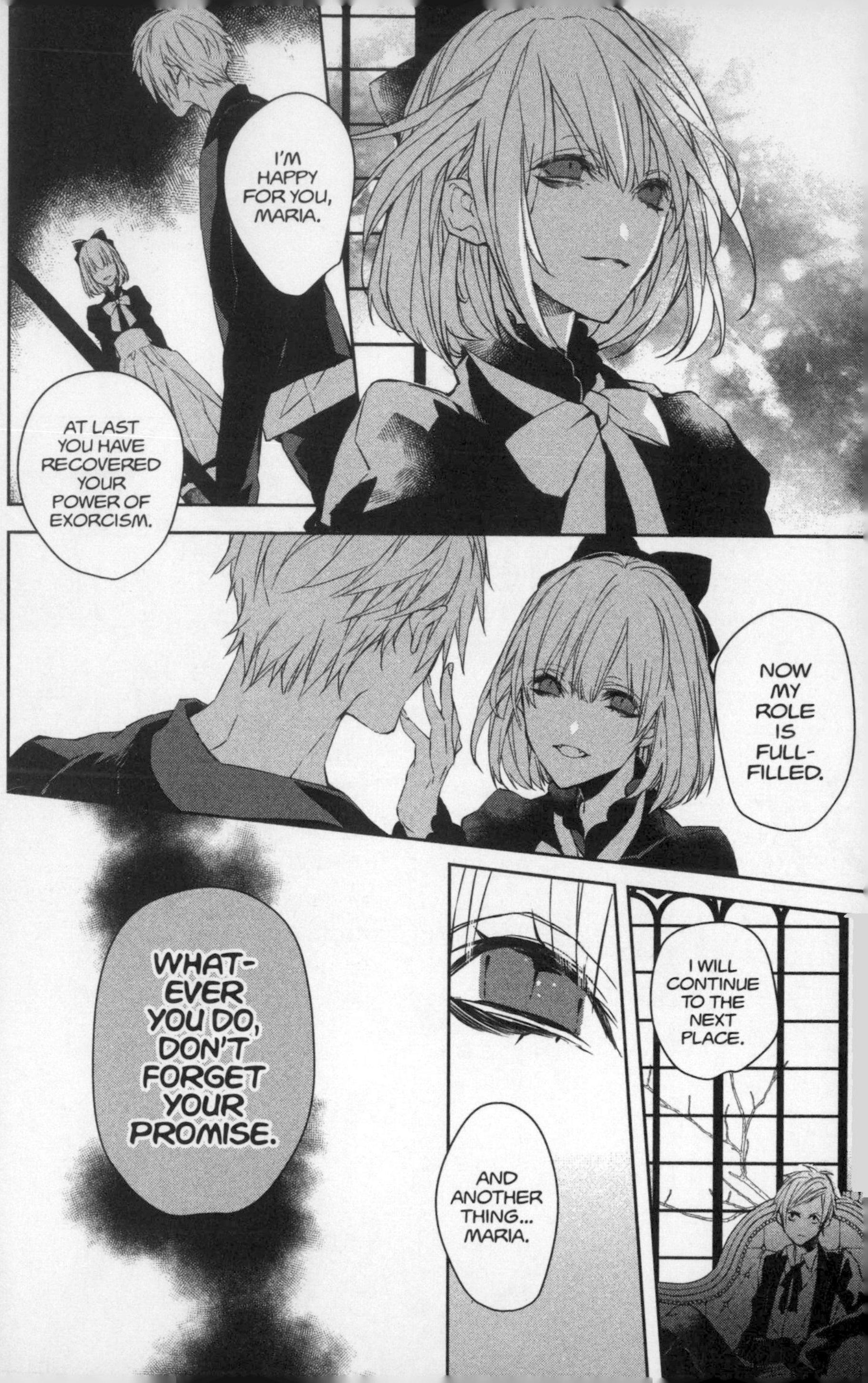
I'M HAPPY FOR YOU, MARIA.
AT LAST YOU HAVE RECOVERED YOUR POWER OF EXORCISM.
NOW MY ROLE IS FULL-FILLED.
I WILL CONTINUE TO THE NEXT PLACE.
AND ANOTHER THING... MARIA.
WHAT-EVER YOU DO, DON'T FORGET YOUR PROMISE.

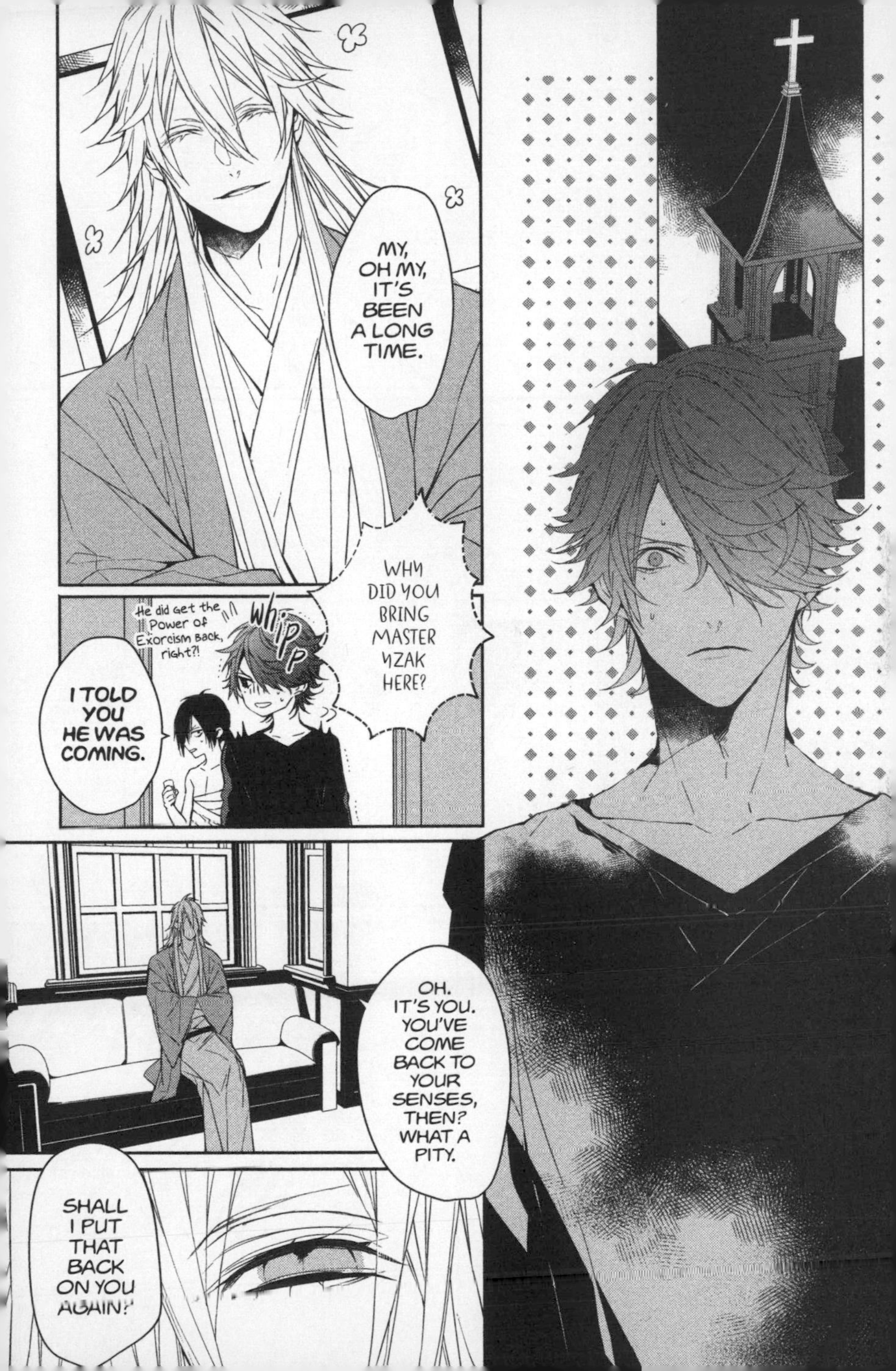
OH. IT'S YOU. YOU'VE COME BACK TO YOUR SENSES, THEN? WHAT A PITY.
MY, OH MY, IT'S BEEN A LONG TIME.
WHY DID YOU BRING MASTER YZAK HERE?
whipp
He did get the Power of Exorcism back, right?!
I TOLD YOU HE WAS COMING.
SHALL I PUT THAT BACK ON YOU AGAIN?

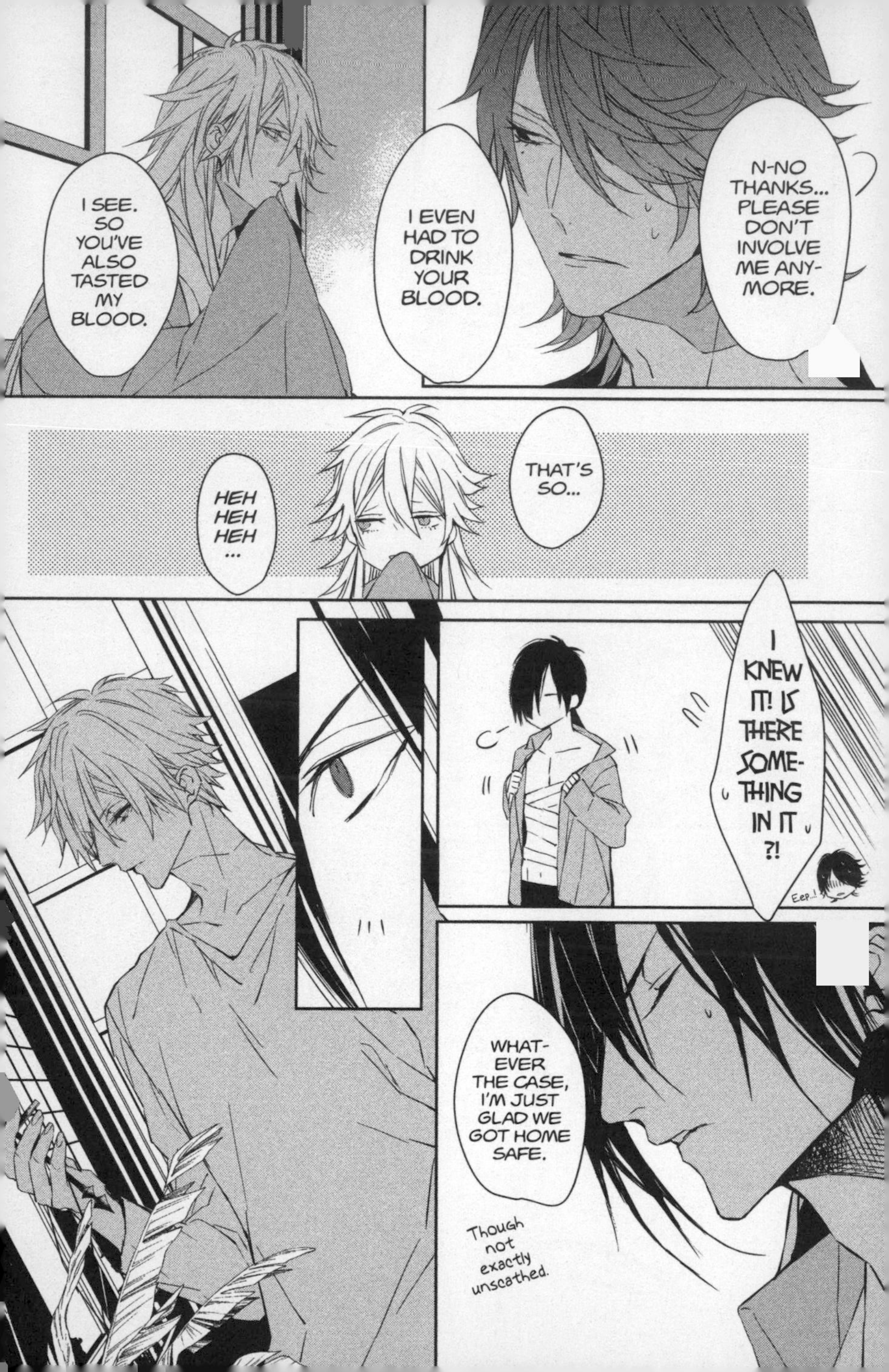
N-NO THANKS... PLEASE DON'T INVOLVE ME ANY-MORE.
I EVEN HAD TO DRINK YOUR BLOOD.
I SEE. SO YOU'VE ALSO TASTED MY BLOOD.
THAT'S SO...
HEH HEH HEH...
I KNEW IT! IS THERE SOME-THING IN IT?!
Eep..!
WHAT-EVER THE CASE, I'M JUST GLAD WE GOT HOME SAFE.
Though not exactly unscathed.

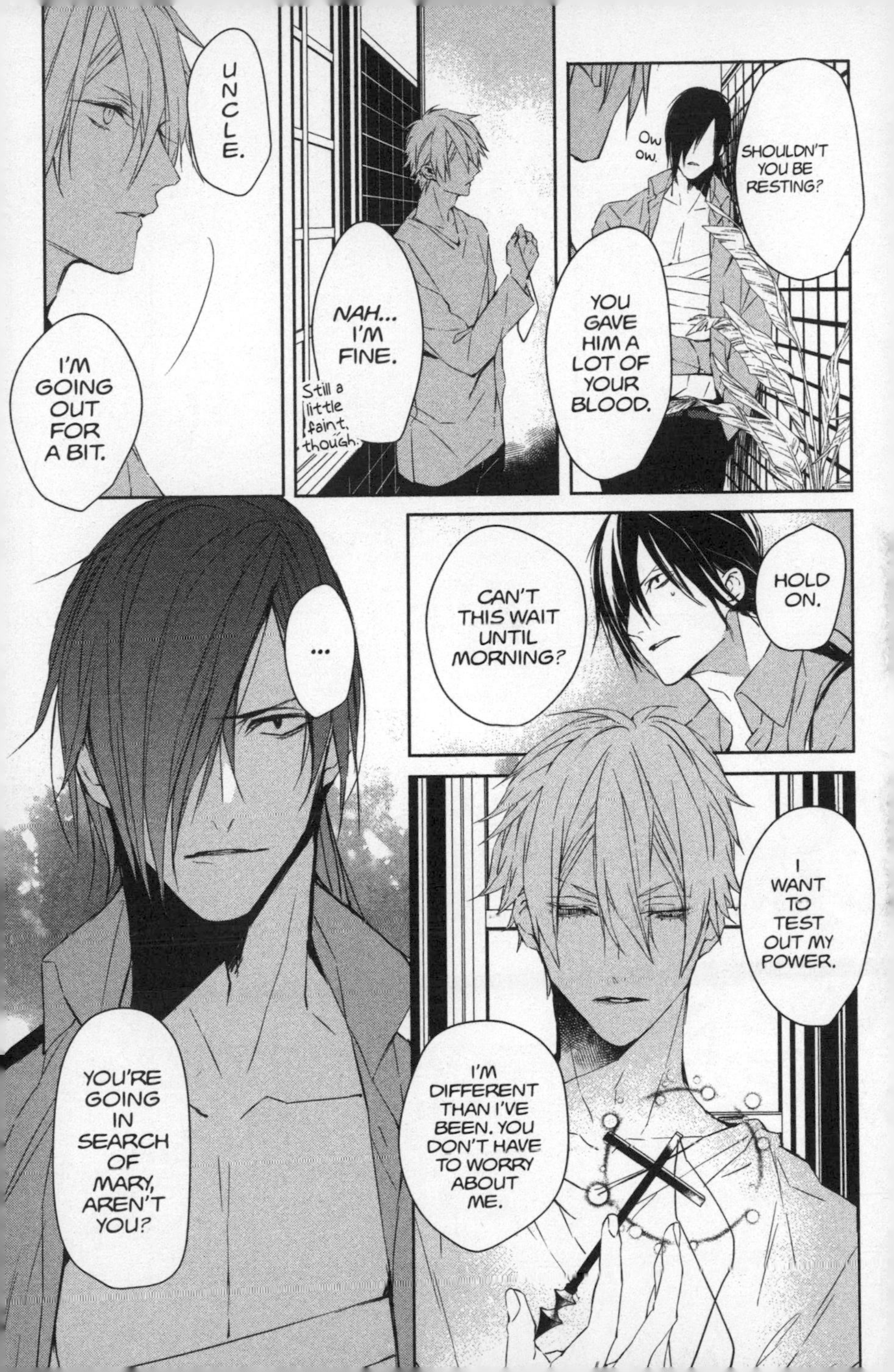
SHOULDN'T YOU BE RESTING?
Ow ow.
YOU GAVE HIM A LOT OF YOUR BLOOD.
NAH... I'M FINE.
Still a little faint, though.
UNCLE.
I'M GOING OUT FOR A BIT.
HOLD ON.
CAN'T THIS WAIT UNTIL MORNING?
I WANT TO TEST OUT MY POWER.
I'M DIFFERENT THAN I'VE BEEN. YOU DON'T HAVE TO WORRY ABOUT ME.
...
YOU'RE GOING IN SEARCH OF MARY, AREN'T YOU?

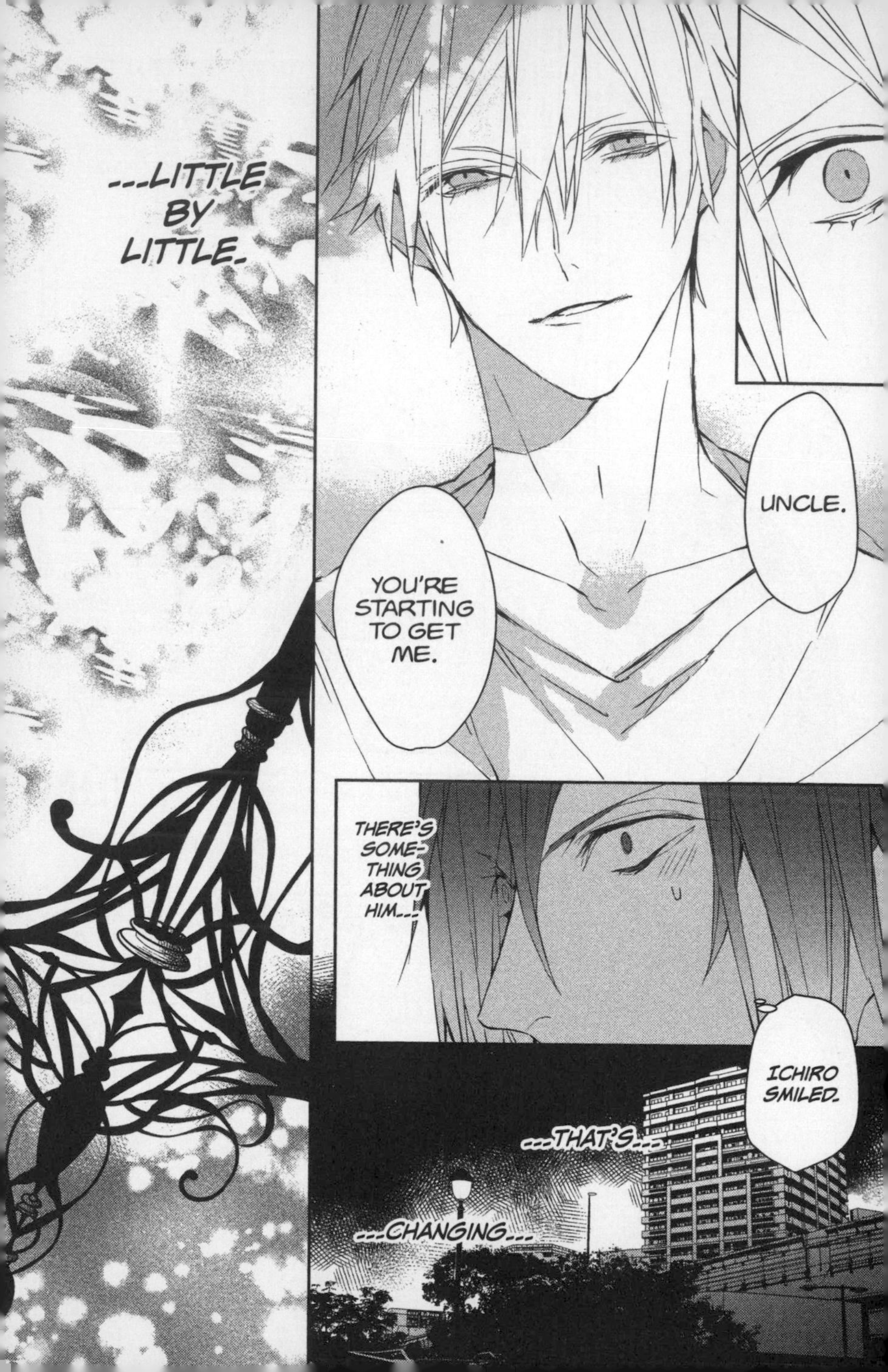
UNCLE.
YOU'RE STARTING TO GET ME.
THERE'S SOME-THING ABOUT HIM...
ICHIRO SMILED.
...THAT'S...
...CHANGING...
...LITTLE BY LITTLE.

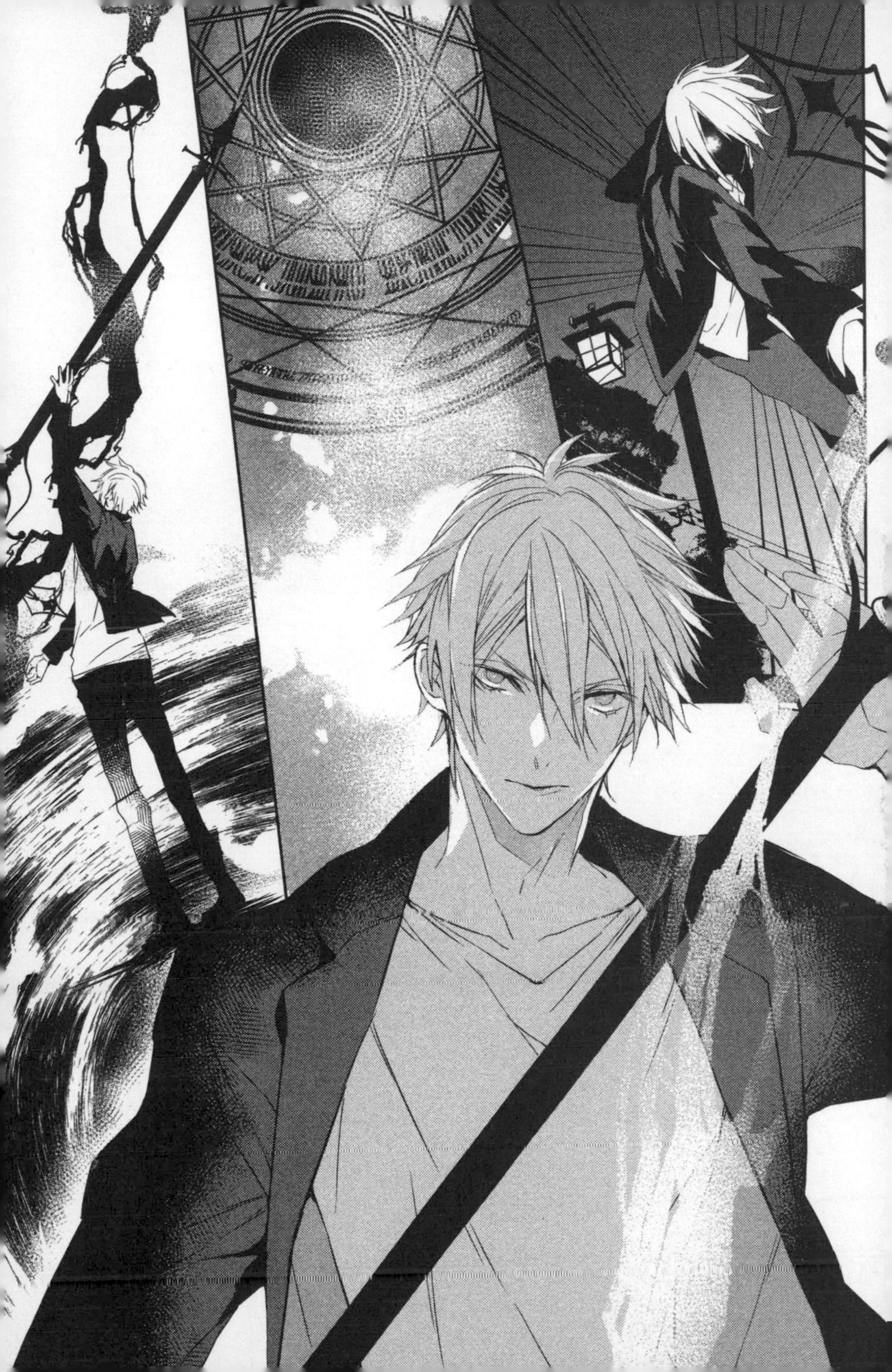

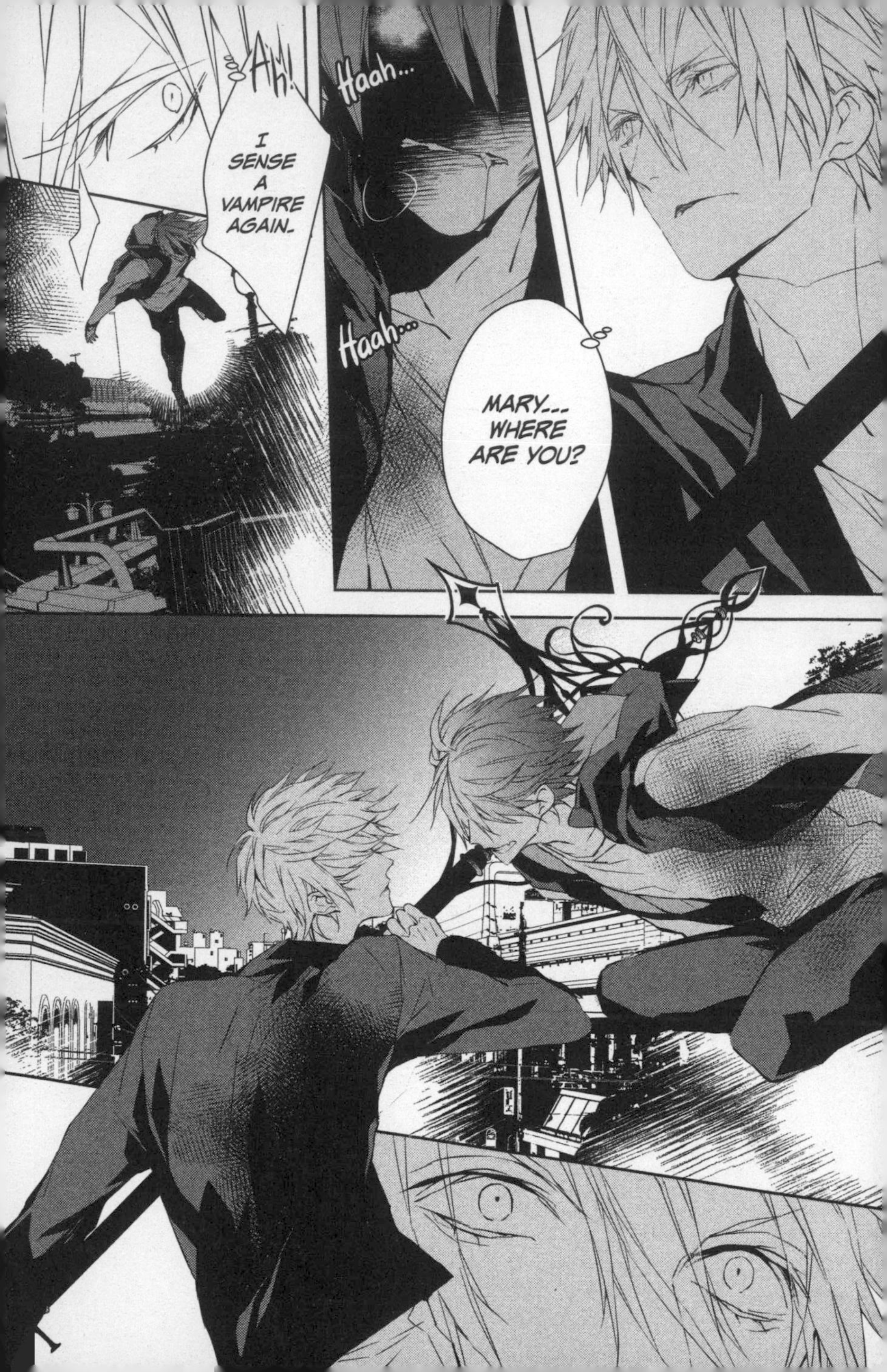
MARY... WHERE ARE YOU?
Haah...
Haah...
Ah!
I SENSE A VAMPIRE AGAIN...

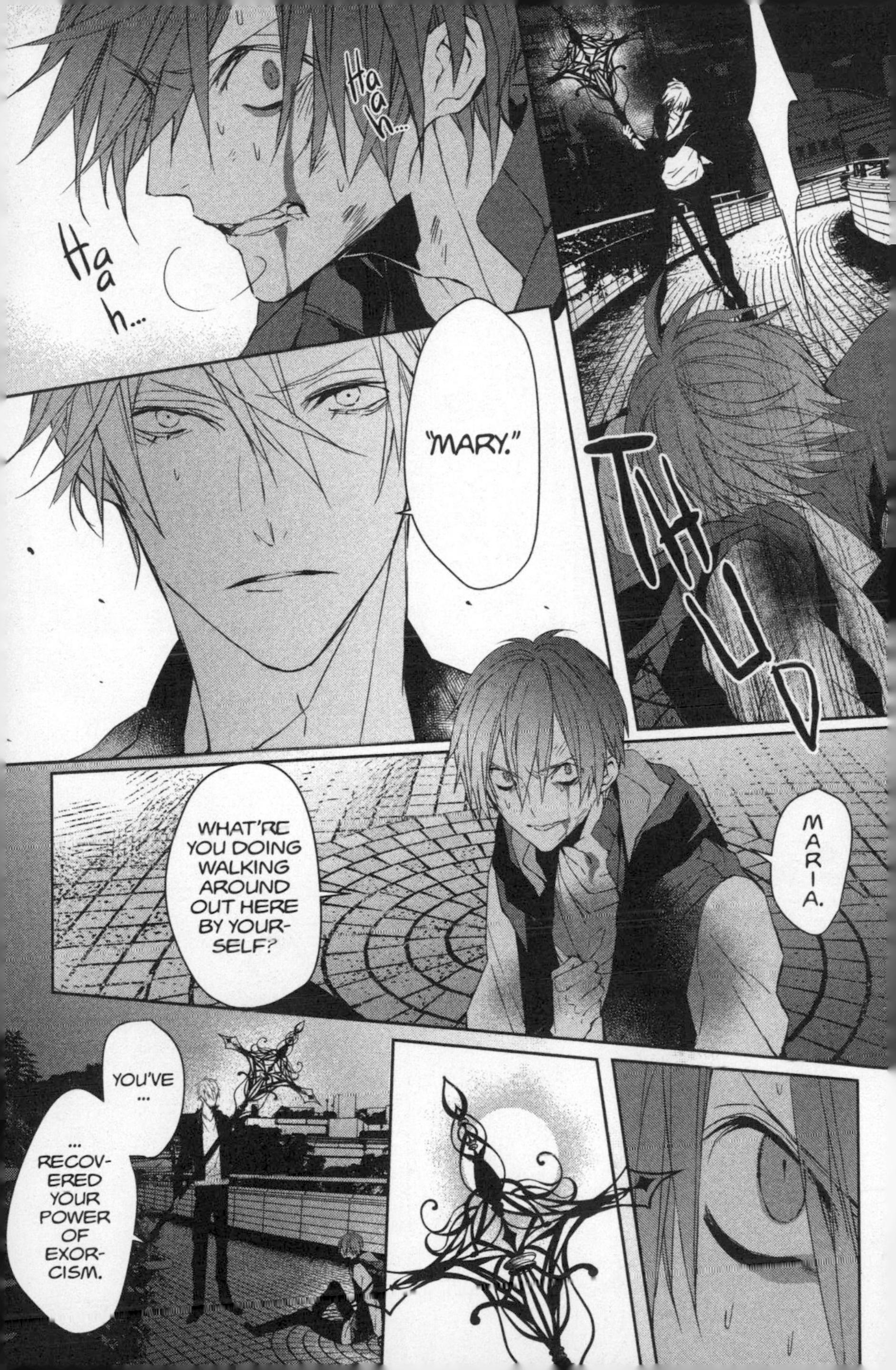
THUD
Haah...
Haah...
"MARY."
MARIA.
WHAT'RE YOU DOING WALKING AROUND OUT HERE BY YOUR-SELF?
YOU'VE ...
... RECOV-ERED YOUR POWER OF EXOR-CISM.

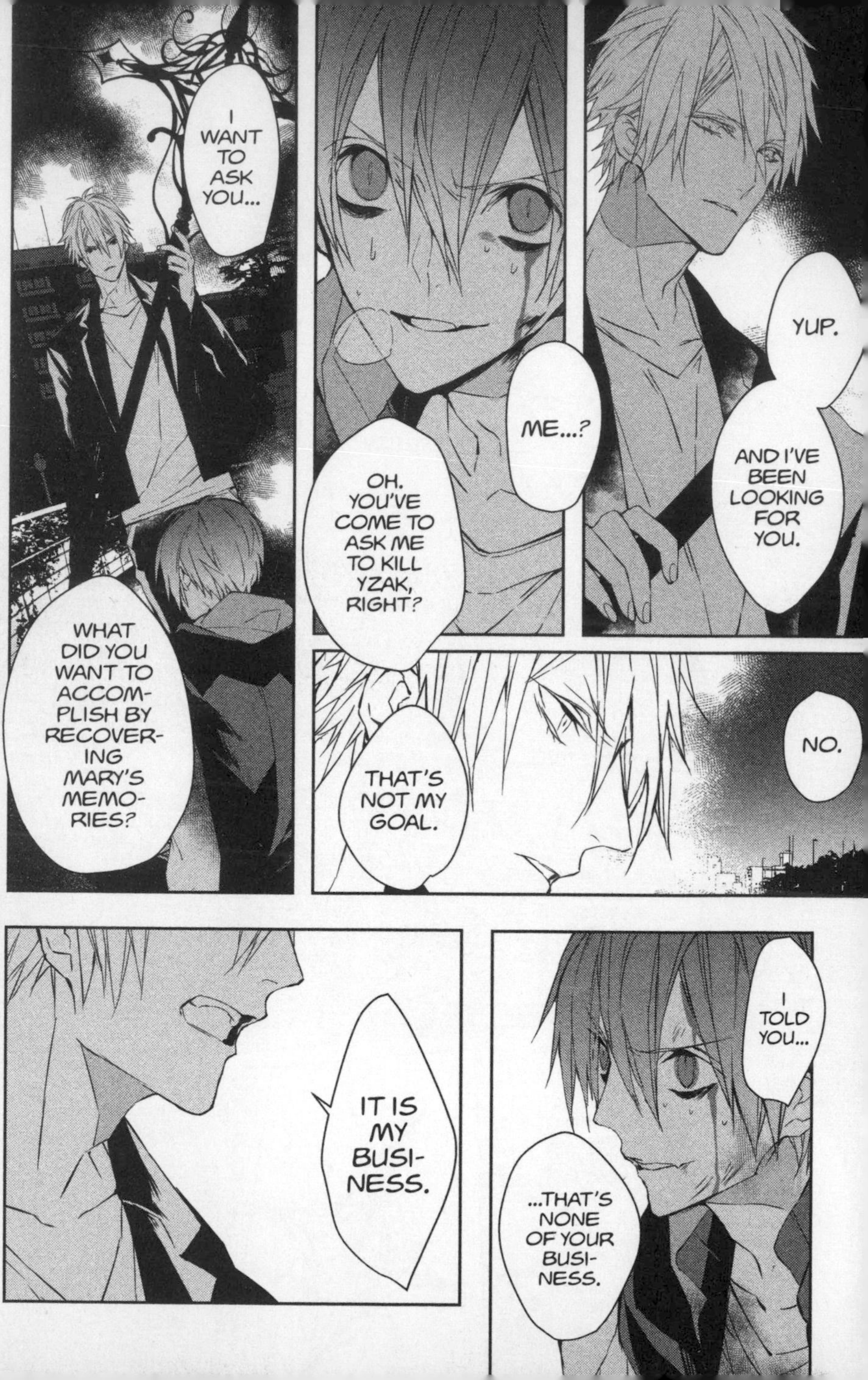
YUP.
AND I'VE BEEN LOOKING FOR YOU.
ME...?
OH. YOU'VE COME TO ASK ME TO KILL YZAK, RIGHT?
NO.
THAT'S NOT MY GOAL.
I WANT TO ASK YOU...
WHAT DID YOU WANT TO ACCOMPLISH BY RECOVERING MARY'S MEMORIES?
I TOLD YOU...
...THAT'S NONE OF YOUR BUSINESS.
IT IS MY BUSINESS.

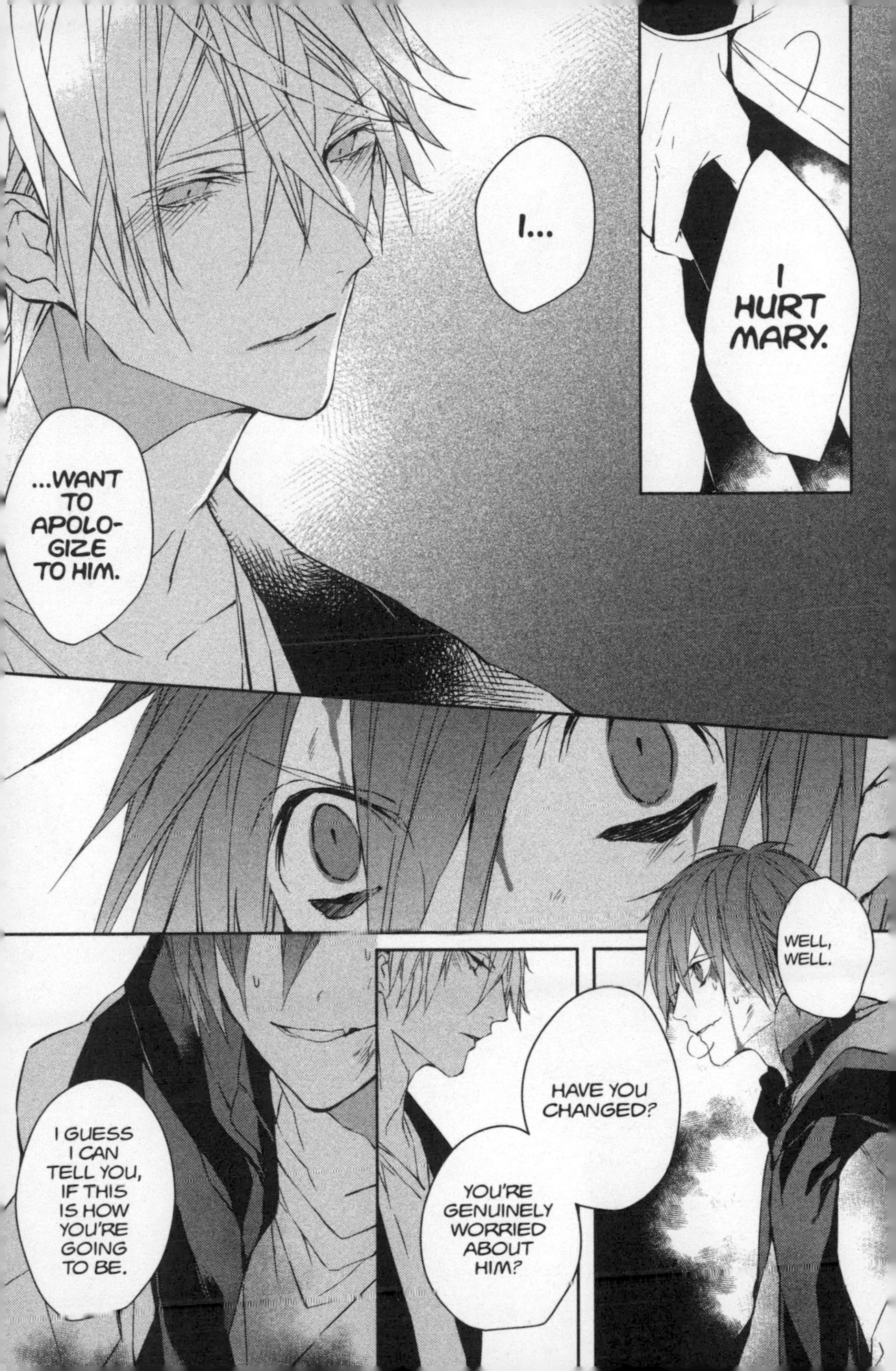
I HURT MARY.
I...
...WANT TO APOLO-GIZE TO HIM.
WELL, WELL.
HAVE YOU CHANGED?
YOU'RE GENUINELY WORRIED ABOUT HIM?
I GUESS I CAN TELL YOU, IF THIS IS HOW YOU'RE GOING TO BE.

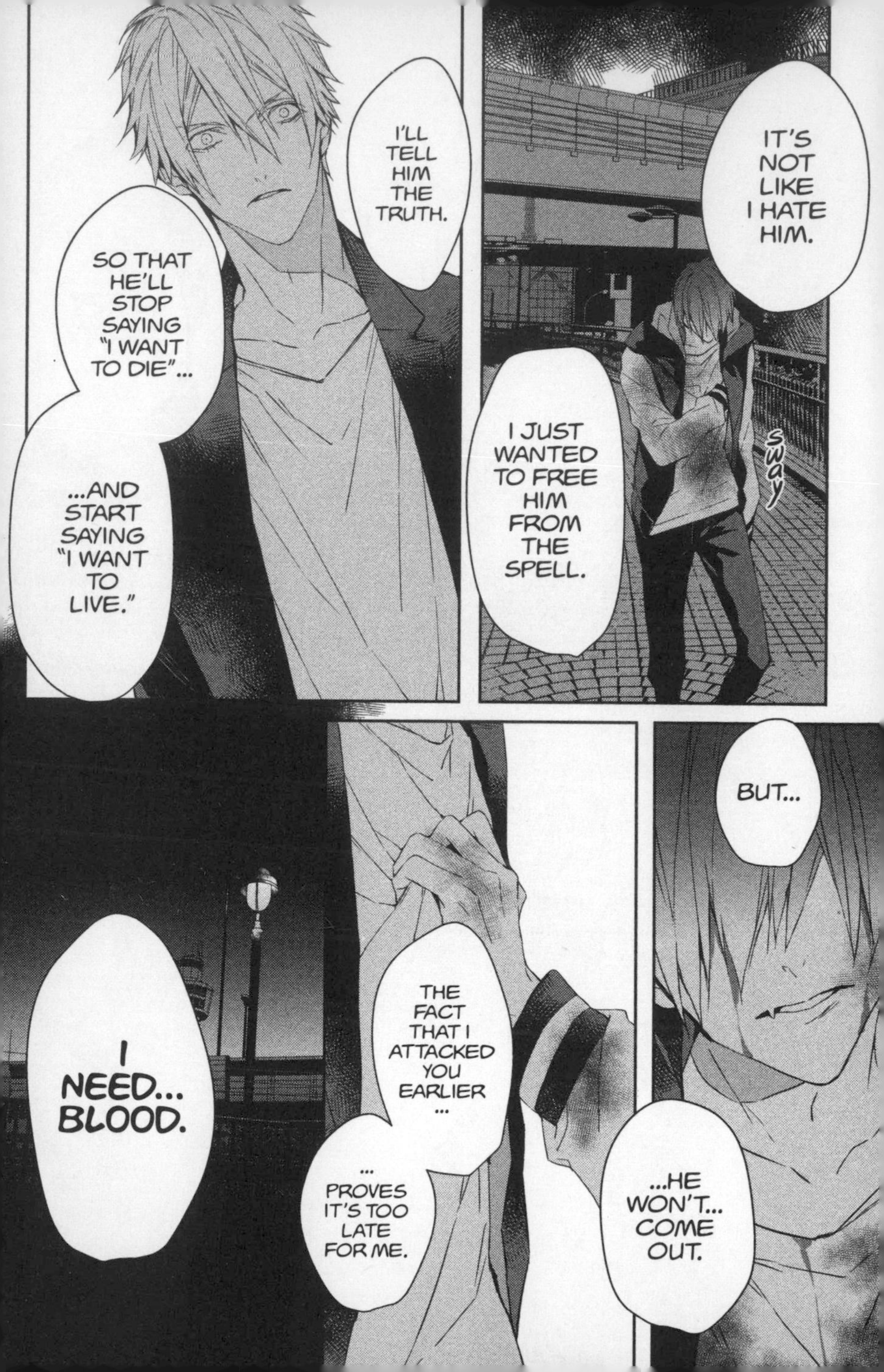
IT'S NOT LIKE I HATE HIM.
I JUST WANTED TO FREE HIM FROM THE SPELL.
SWAY
I'LL TELL HIM THE TRUTH.
SO THAT HE'LL STOP SAYING "I WANT TO DIE"...
...AND START SAYING "I WANT TO LIVE."
BUT...
...HE WON'T... COME OUT.
THE FACT THAT I ATTACKED YOU EARLIER...
...PROVES IT'S TOO LATE FOR ME.
I NEED... BLOOD.

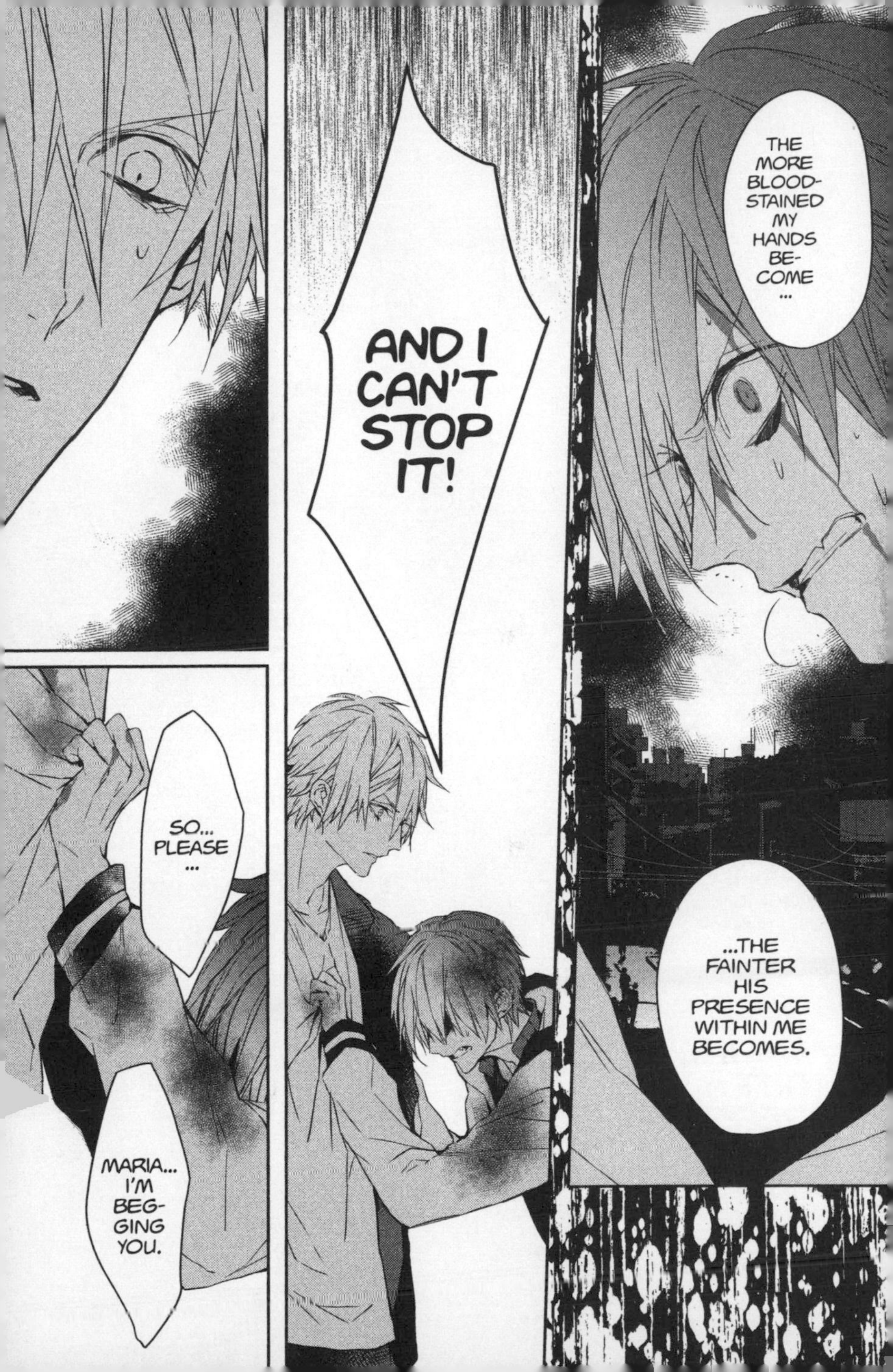
THE MORE BLOOD-STAINED MY HANDS BE-COME...
...THE FAINTER HIS PRESENCE WITHIN ME BECOMES.
AND I CAN'T STOP IT!
SO... PLEASE...
MARIA... I'M BEG-GING YOU.

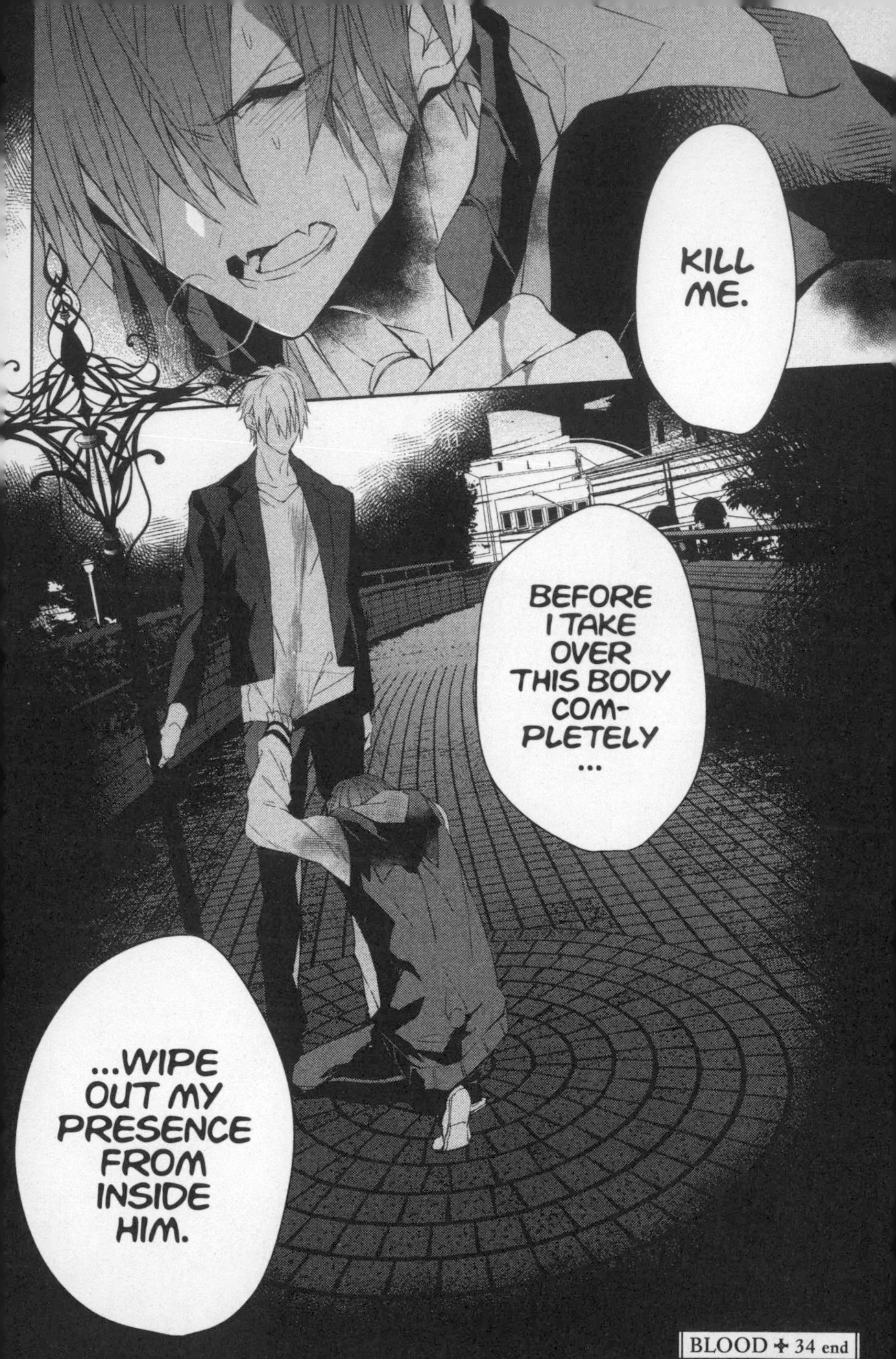
KILL ME.
BEFORE I TAKE OVER THIS BODY COM-PLETELY ...
...WIPE OUT MY PRESENCE FROM INSIDE HIM.
BLOOD ✣ 34 end

This is sudden, but... Since there won't be any opportunity to showcase this later

Fluctuating Sadism Hierarchy!!

✥ Part I ✥

Volume 1

Maria
Takumi

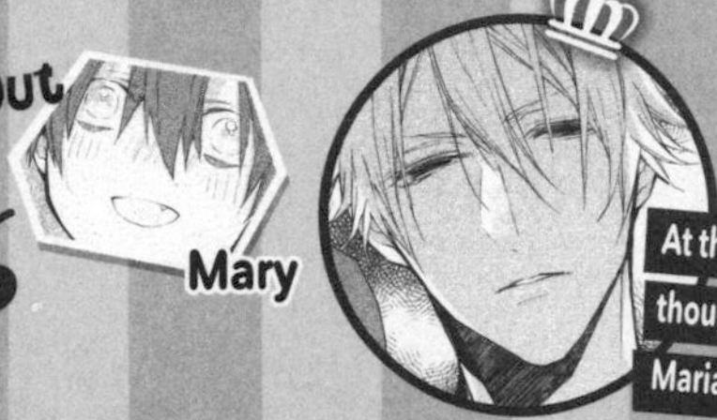
Out
Mary
At the start of the story, we thought nobody could push Maria out as number one.

Volume 2

Yzak
Maria
Takumi

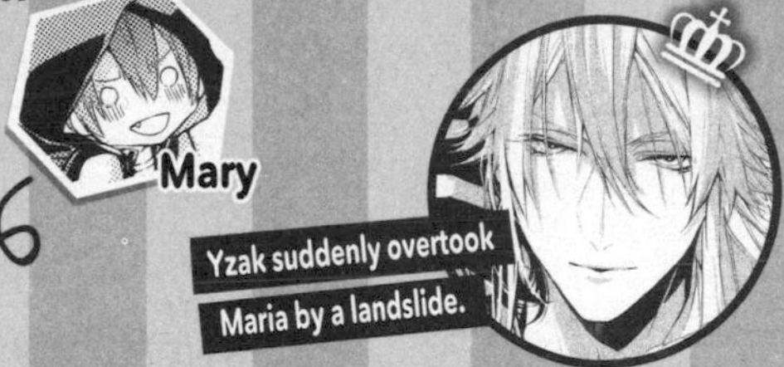
Out of the Rankings
Mary
Yzak suddenly overtook Maria by a landslide.

Volume 3

"Mary"
Gendo
Maria

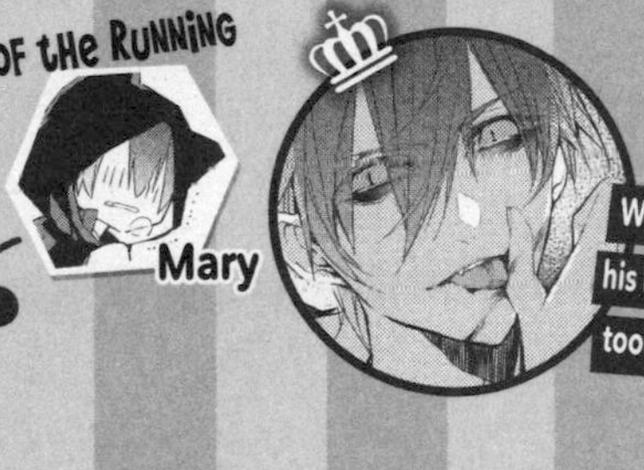
Out of the Running
Mary
When "Mary" drank his blood, Yzak took a tumble!

Volume 4

Gendo
Maria
"Mary"

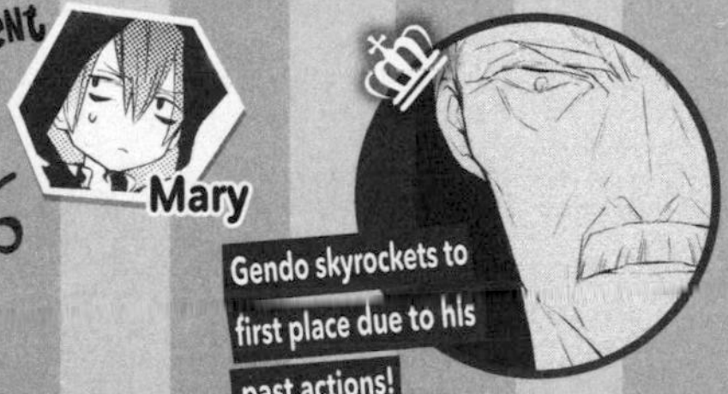
Absent
Mary
Gendo skyrockets to first place due to his past actions!

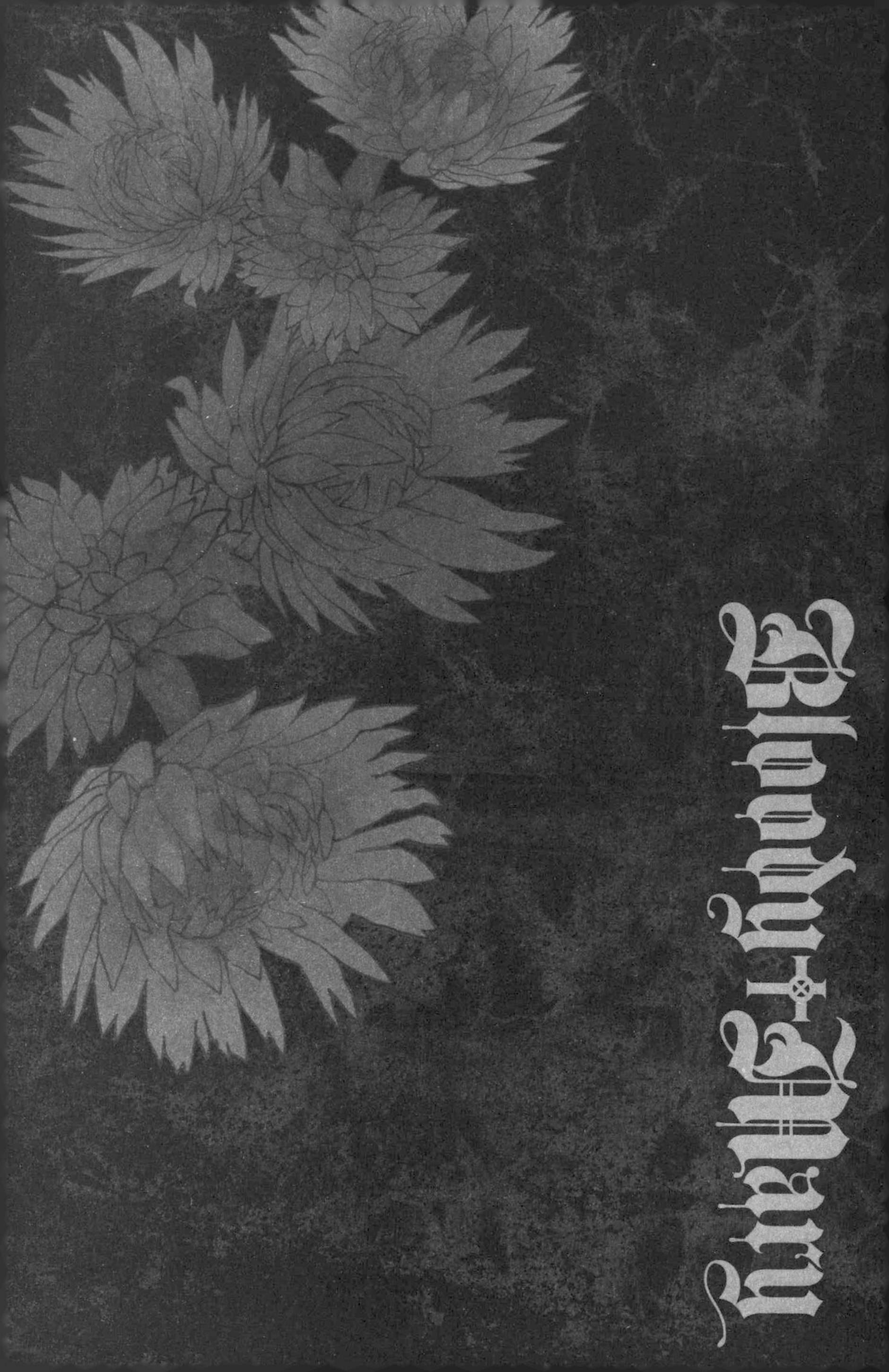
Bloody+Mary

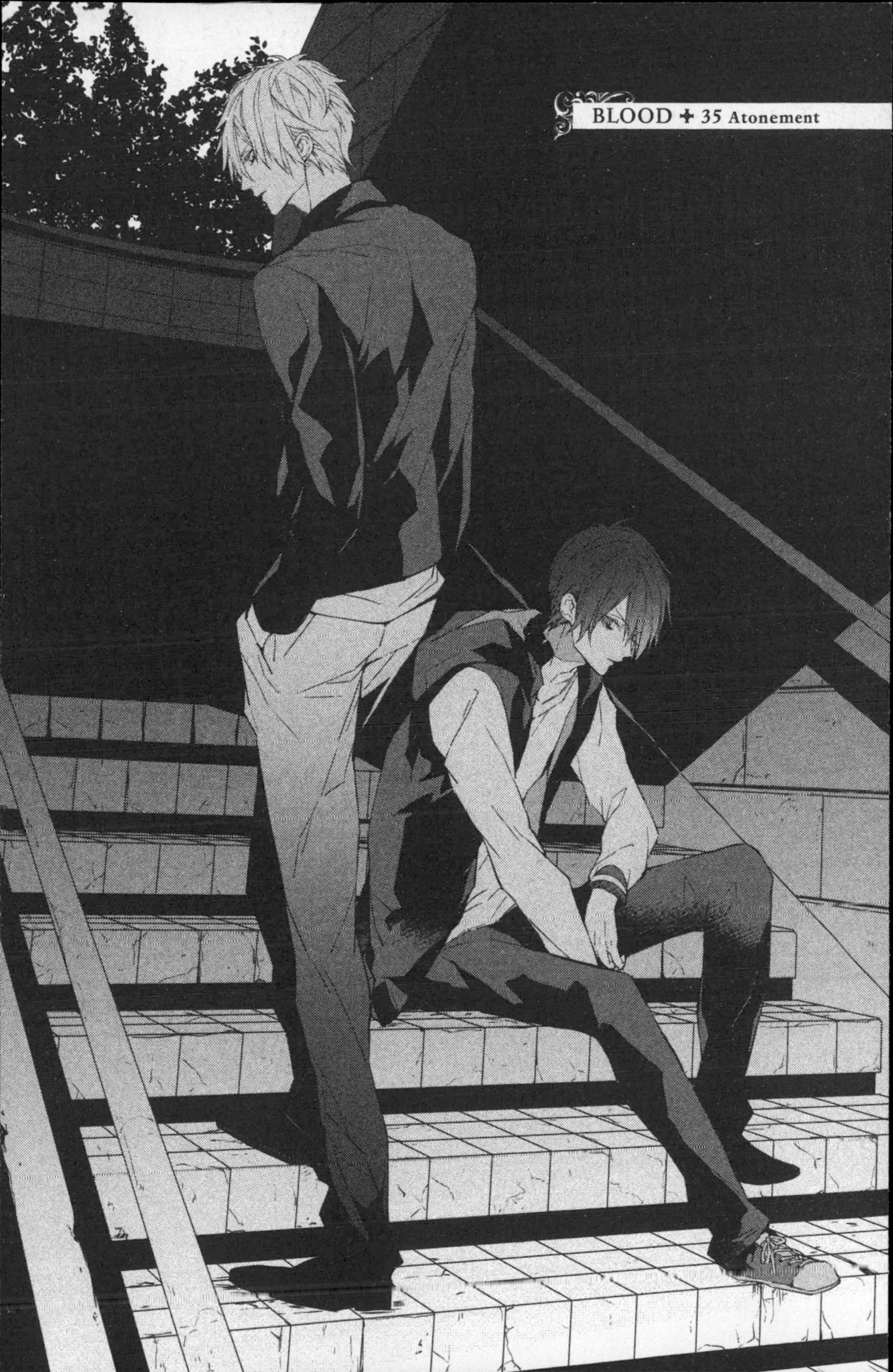
BLOOD ✚ 35 Atonement

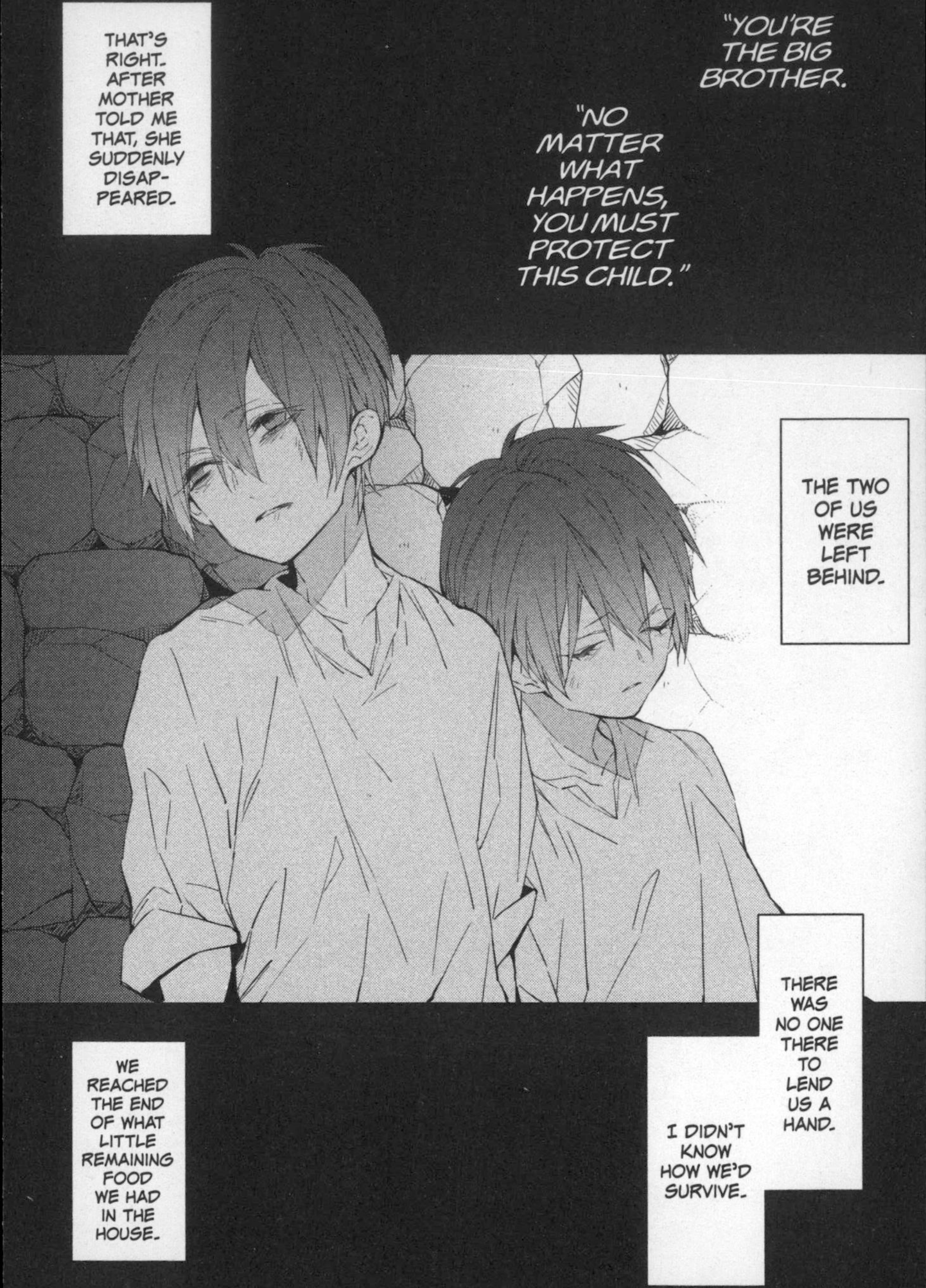
"YOU'RE THE BIG BROTHER.
"NO MATTER WHAT HAPPENS, YOU MUST PROTECT THIS CHILD."
THAT'S RIGHT. AFTER MOTHER TOLD ME THAT, SHE SUDDENLY DISAP- PEARED.
THE TWO OF US WERE LEFT BEHIND.
THERE WAS NO ONE THERE TO LEND US A HAND.
I DIDN'T KNOW HOW WE'D SURVIVE.
WE REACHED THE END OF WHAT LITTLE REMAINING FOOD WE HAD IN THE HOUSE.

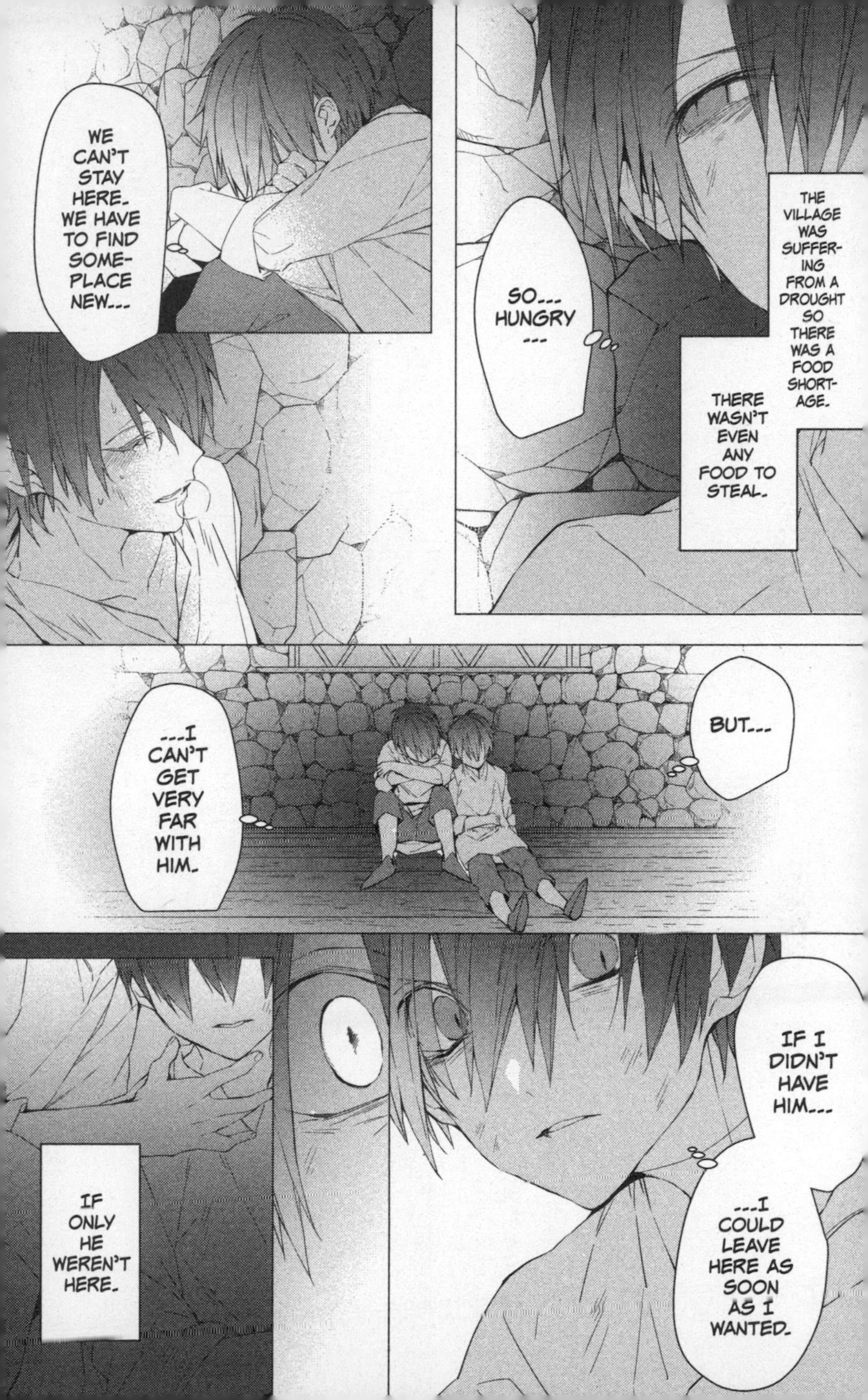
THE VILLAGE WAS SUFFERING FROM A DROUGHT SO THERE WAS A FOOD SHORTAGE.
SO... HUNGRY...
THERE WASN'T EVEN ANY FOOD TO STEAL.
WE CAN'T STAY HERE. WE HAVE TO FIND SOMEPLACE NEW...
BUT...
...I CAN'T GET VERY FAR WITH HIM.
IF I DIDN'T HAVE HIM...
...I COULD LEAVE HERE AS SOON AS I WANTED.
IF ONLY HE WEREN'T HERE.

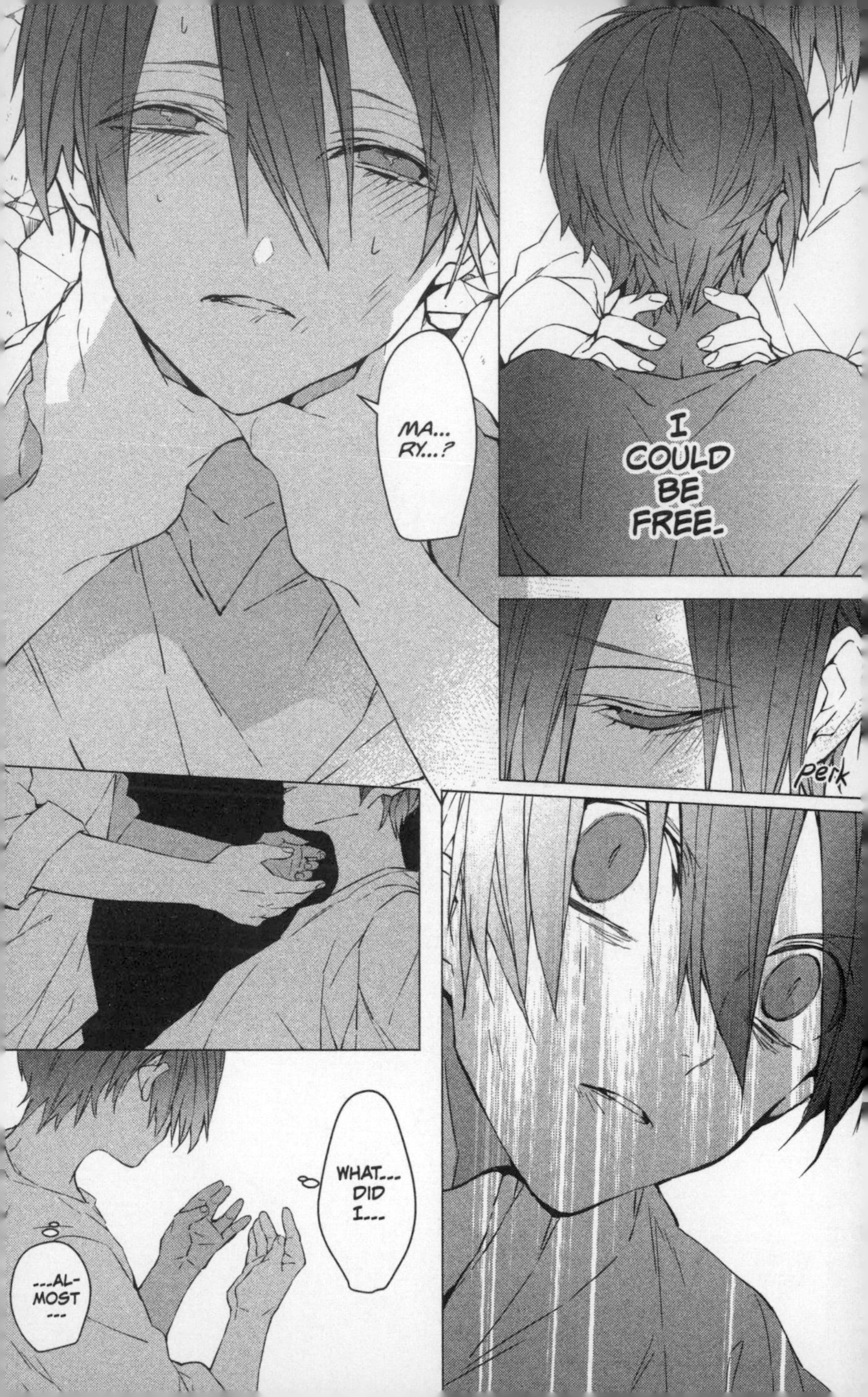
I COULD BE FREE.
Perk
MA... RY...?
WHAT... DID I...
...AL-MOST...

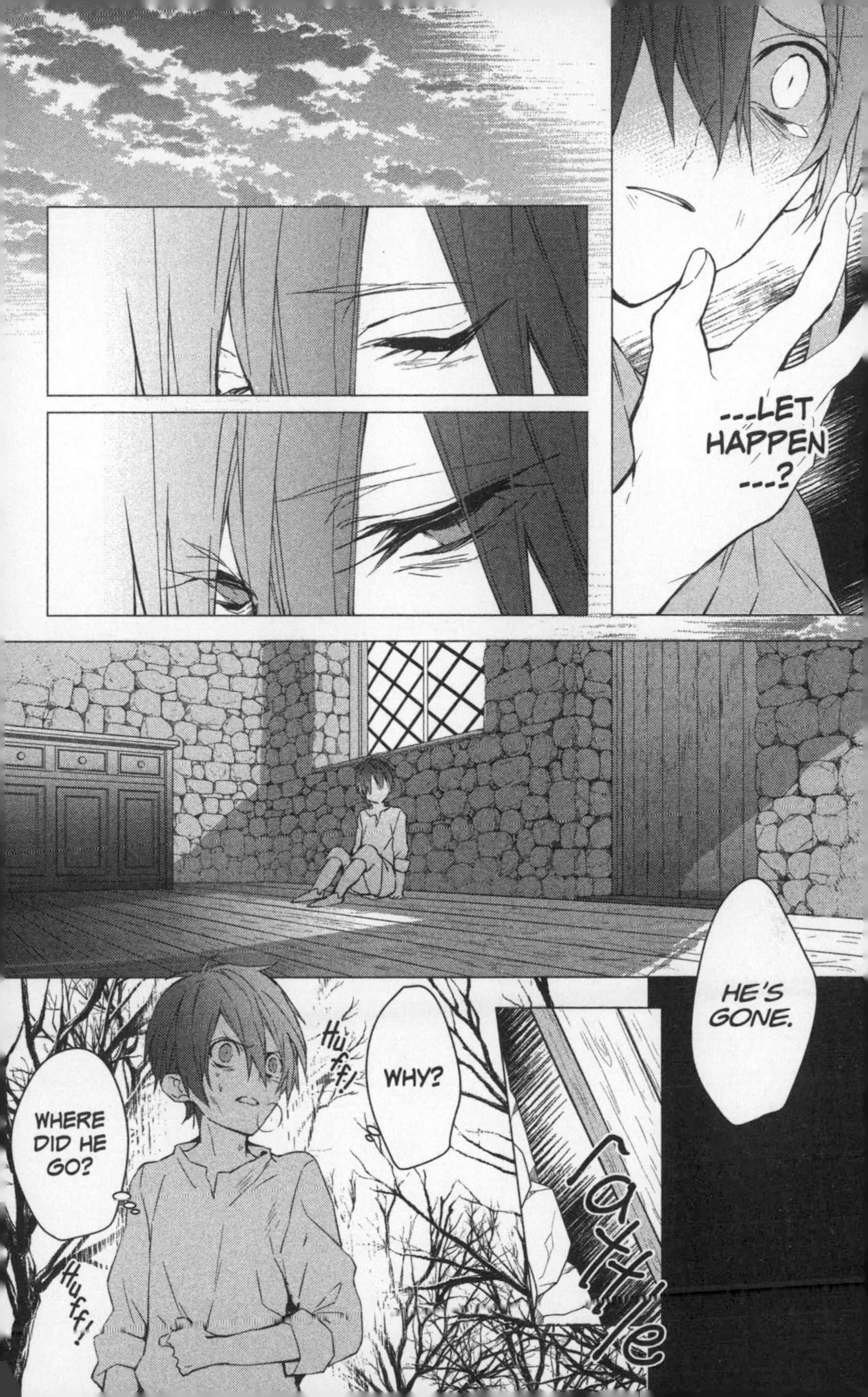
---LET HAPPEN ---?
HE'S GONE.
rattle
Huff!
WHY?
WHERE DID HE GO?
Huff!

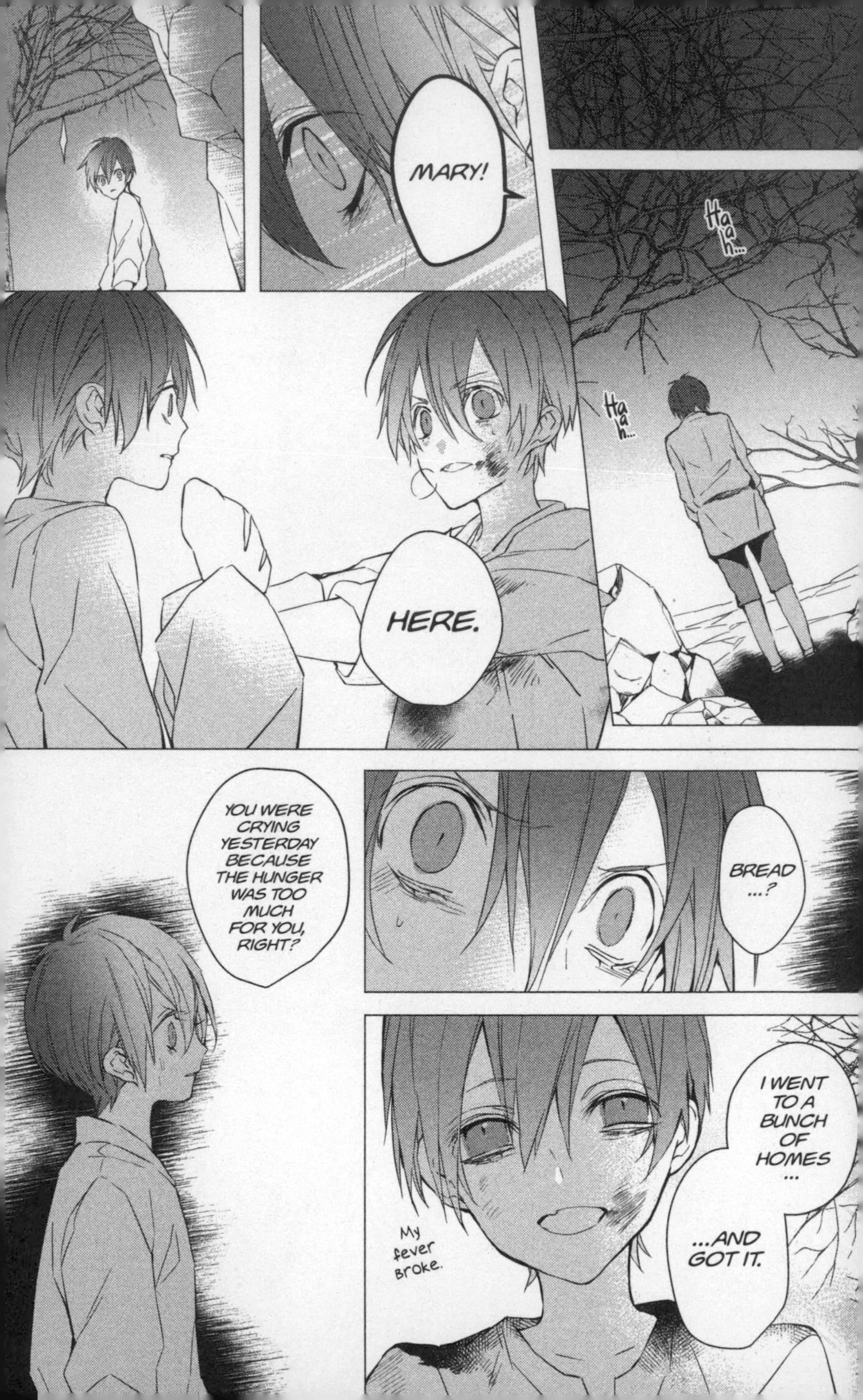
Haah...
Haah...
MARY!
HERE.
BREAD ...?
I WENT TO A BUNCH OF HOMES ...
...AND GOT IT.
My fever broke.
YOU WERE CRYING YESTERDAY BECAUSE THE HUNGER WAS TOO MUCH FOR YOU, RIGHT?

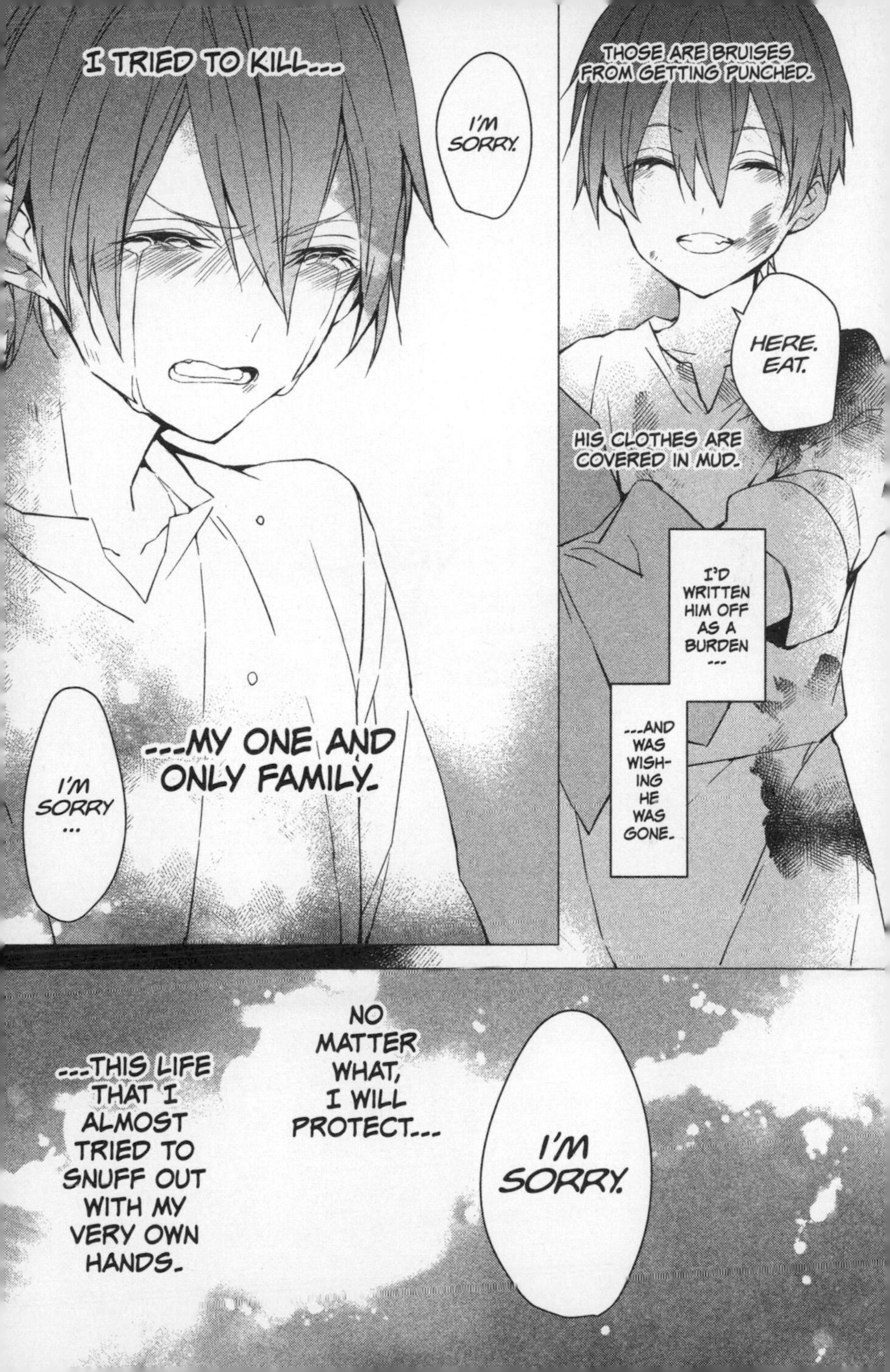

THOSE ARE BRUISES FROM GETTING PUNCHED.
HERE. EAT.
HIS CLOTHES ARE COVERED IN MUD.
I'D WRITTEN HIM OFF AS A BURDEN...
...AND WAS WISH-ING HE WAS GONE.
I'M SORRY.
I TRIED TO KILL...
...MY ONE AND ONLY FAMILY.
I'M SORRY...
I'M SORRY.
NO MATTER WHAT, I WILL PROTECT...
...THIS LIFE THAT I ALMOST TRIED TO SNUFF OUT WITH MY VERY OWN HANDS.

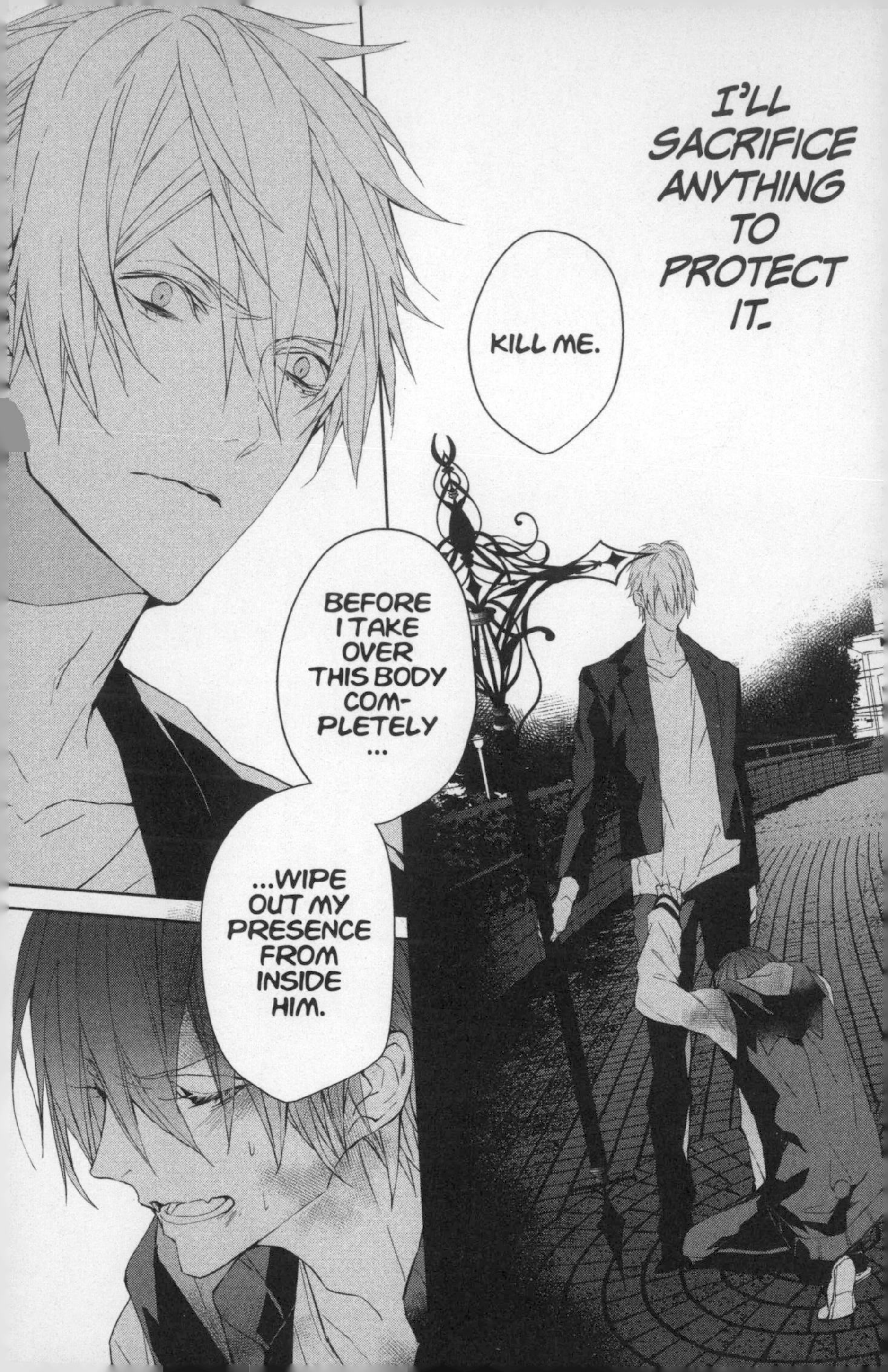
I'LL SACRIFICE ANYTHING TO PROTECT IT...
KILL ME.
BEFORE I TAKE OVER THIS BODY COM- PLETELY ...
...WIPE OUT MY PRESENCE FROM INSIDE HIM.

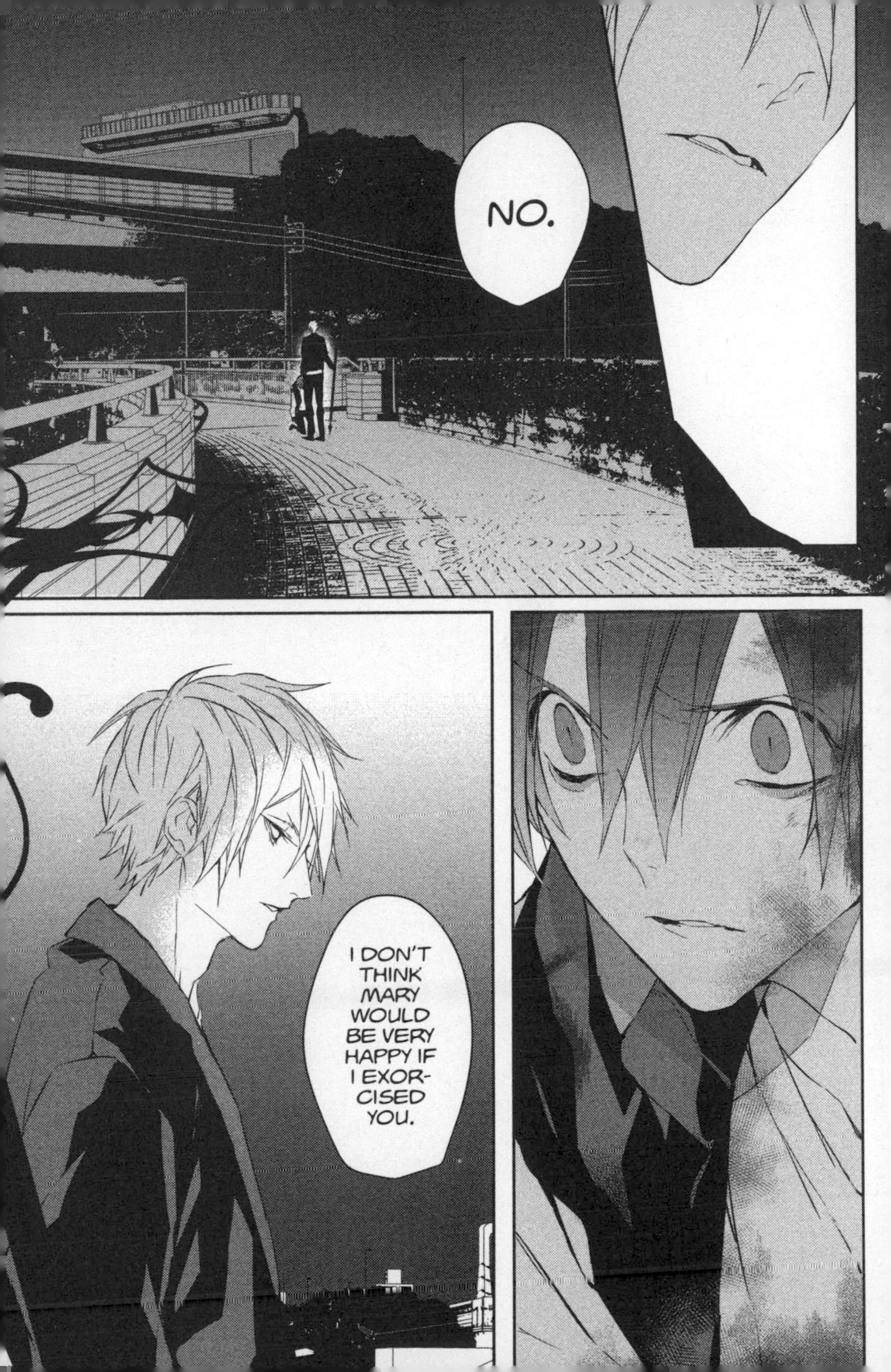
NO.
I DON'T THINK MARY WOULD BE VERY HAPPY IF I EXORCISED YOU.

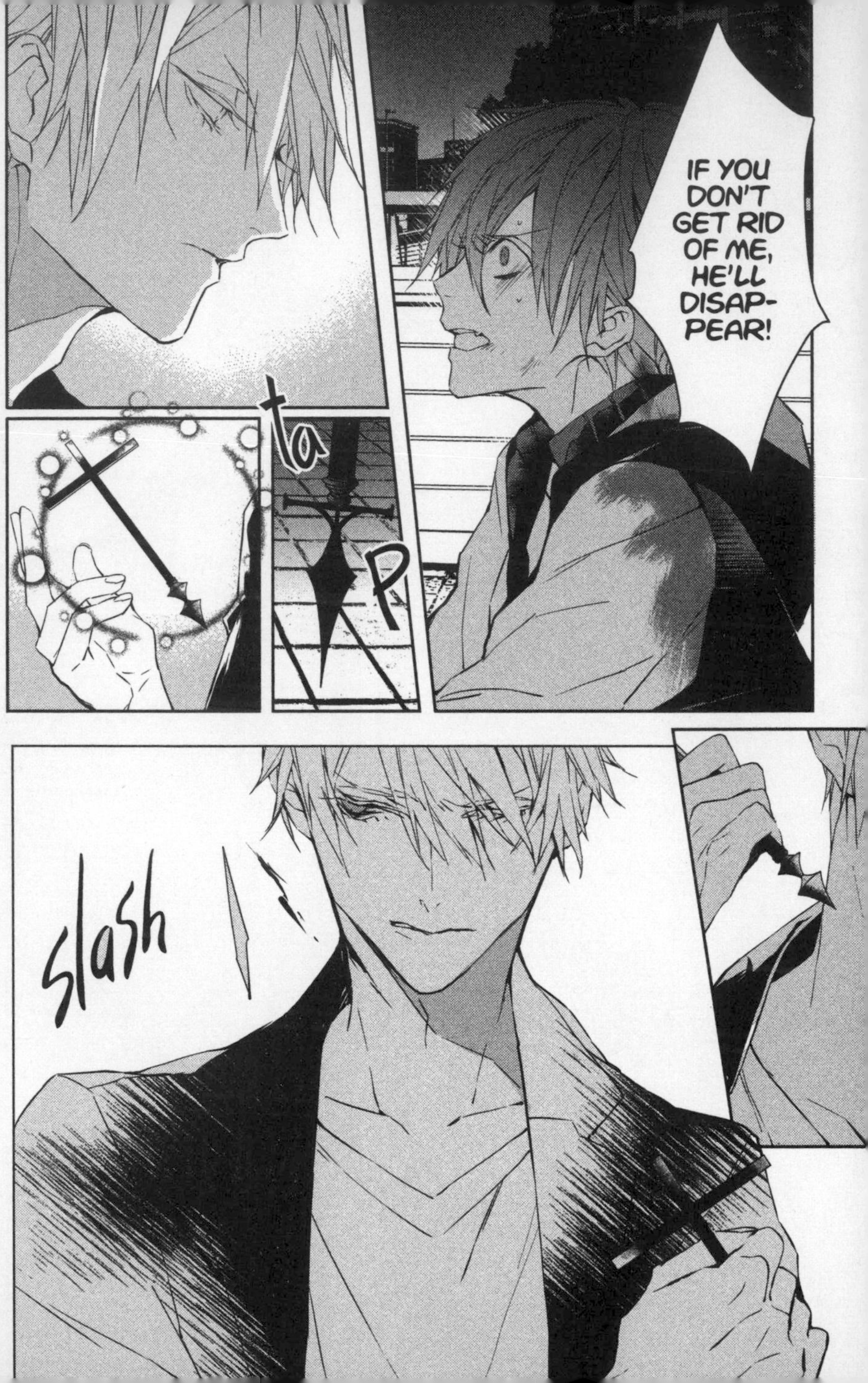
IF YOU DON'T GET RID OF ME, HE'LL DISAP-PEAR!
ta
p
slash

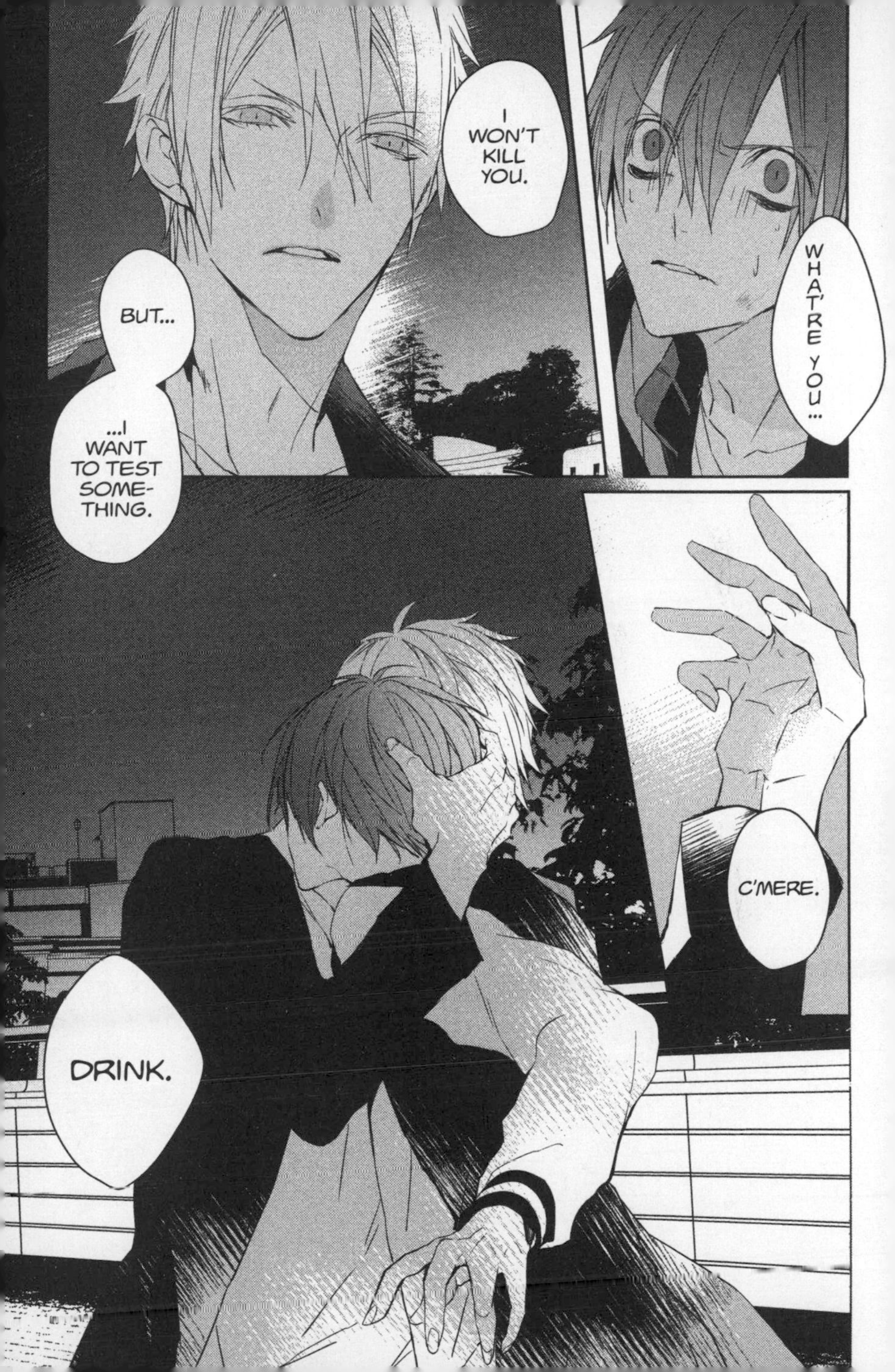
WHAT'RE YOU...
I WON'T KILL YOU.
BUT...
...I WANT TO TEST SOME-THING.
C'MERE.
DRINK.

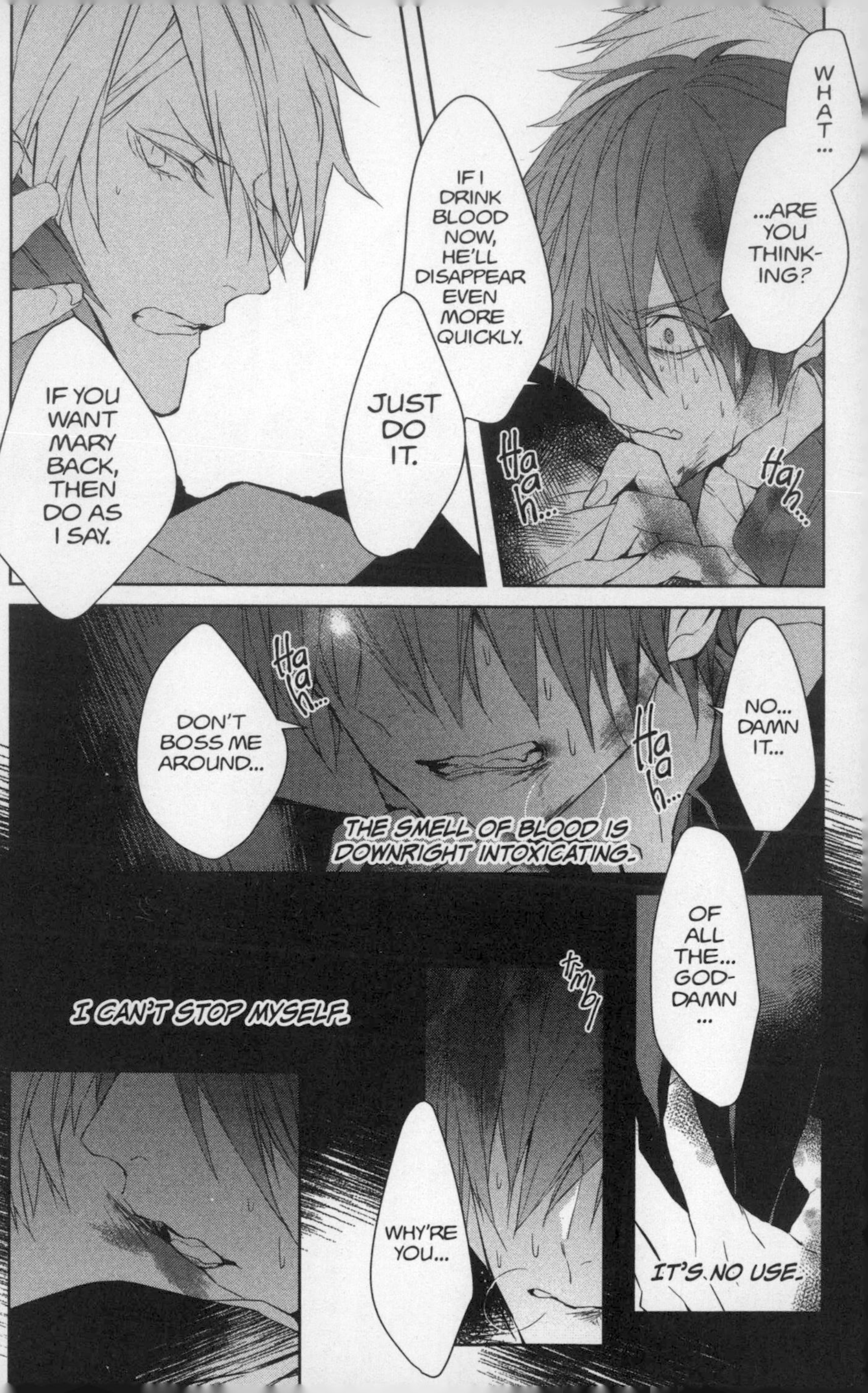
WHAT... ...ARE YOU THINKING?
IF I DRINK BLOOD NOW, HE'LL DISAPPEAR EVEN MORE QUICKLY.
Hah...
Haah...
JUST DO IT.
IF YOU WANT MARY BACK, THEN DO AS I SAY.
NO... DAMN IT...
Haah...
DON'T BOSS ME AROUND...
Haah...
THE SMELL OF BLOOD IS DOWNRIGHT INTOXICATING.
OF ALL THE... GOD-DAMN ...
IT'S NO USE.
trmbl
WHY'RE YOU...
I CAN'T STOP MYSELF.

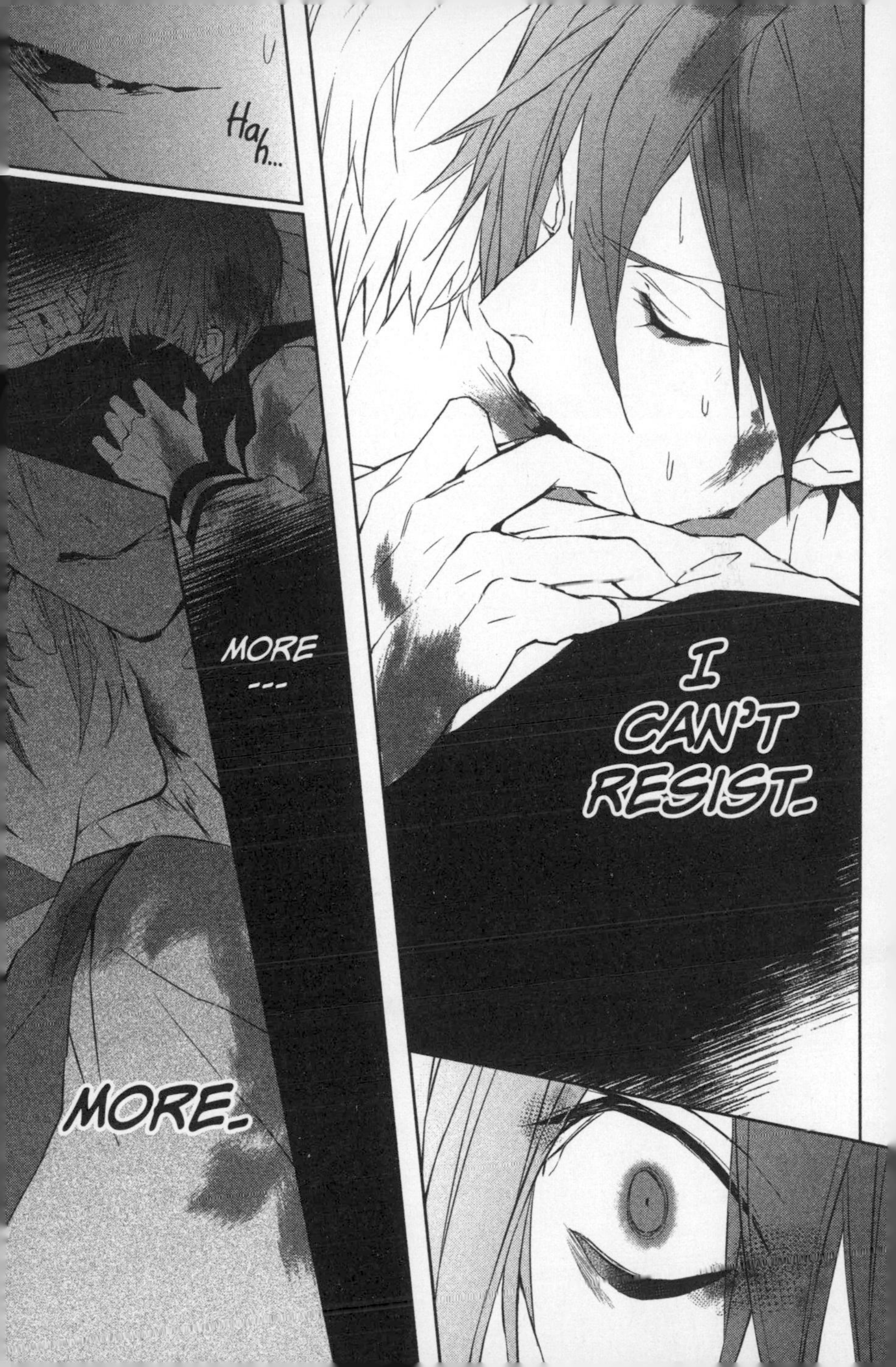
Hah...
I CAN'T RESIST.
MORE---
MORE.

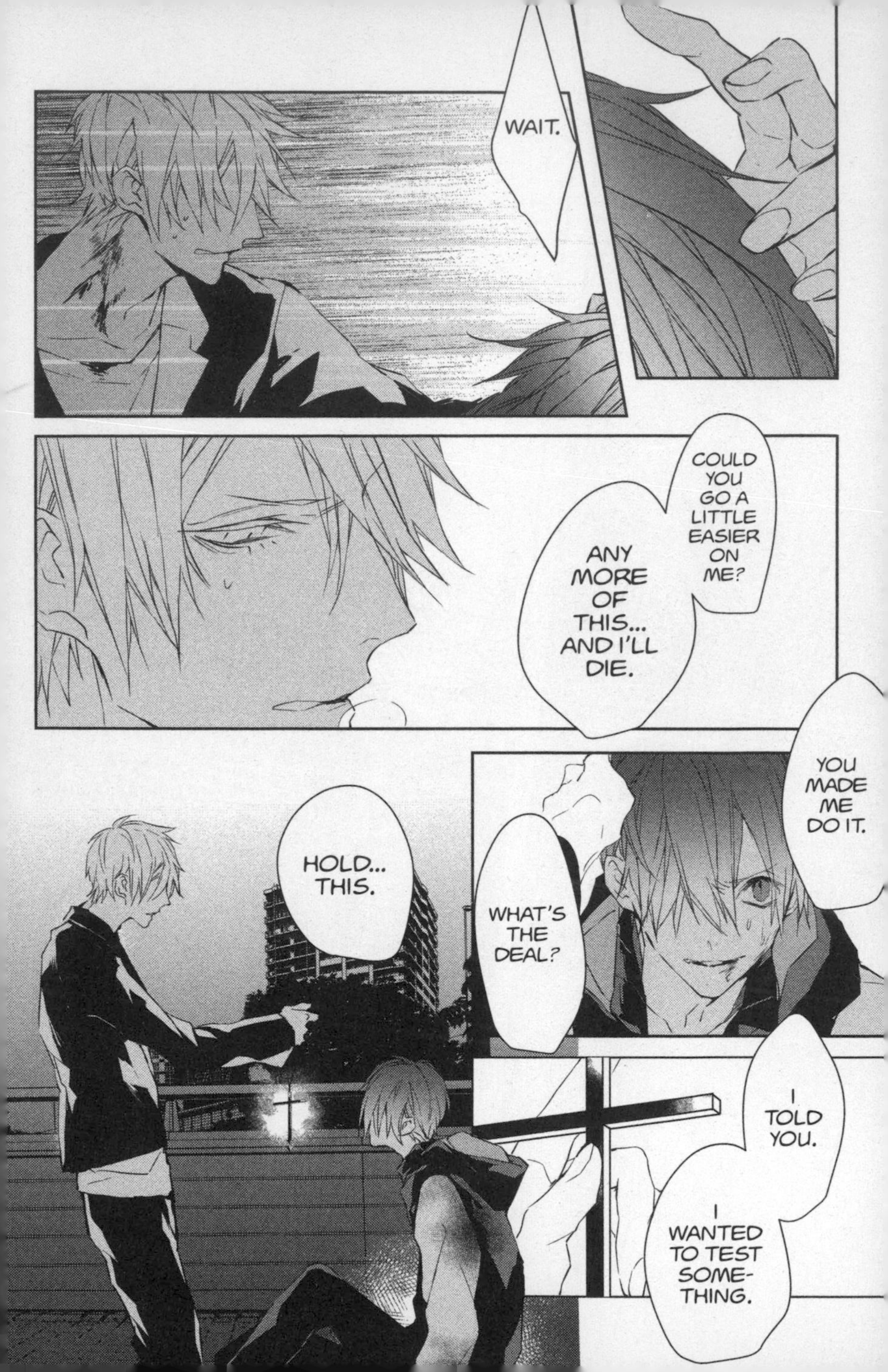
WAIT.
COULD YOU GO A LITTLE EASIER ON ME?
ANY MORE OF THIS... AND I'LL DIE.
YOU MADE ME DO IT.
WHAT'S THE DEAL?
I TOLD YOU.
I WANTED TO TEST SOME-THING.
HOLD... THIS.

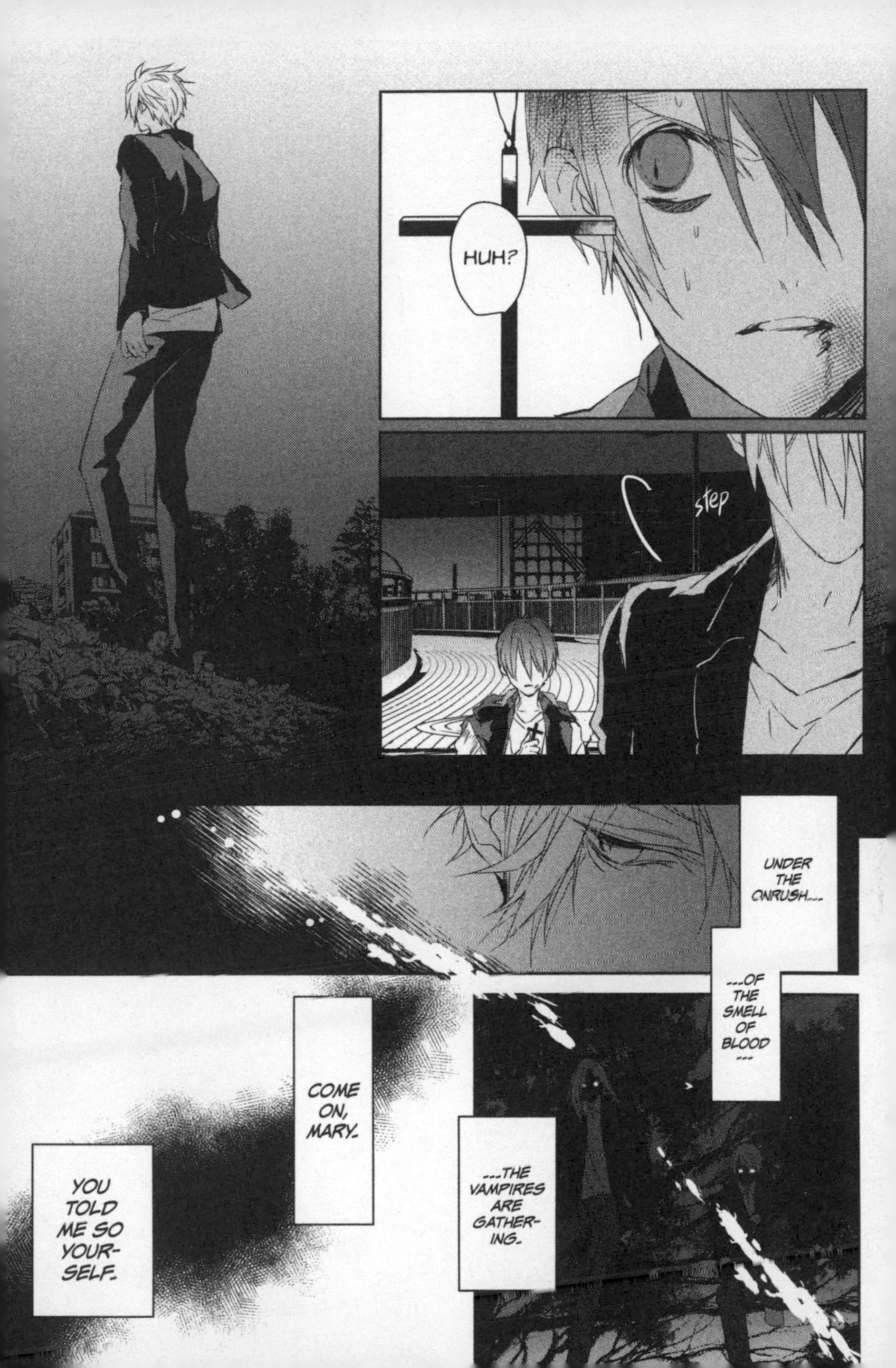
HUH?
step
UNDER THE ONRUSH...
...OF THE SMELL OF BLOOD...
...THE VAMPIRES ARE GATHERING.
COME ON, MARY.
YOU TOLD ME SO YOURSELF.

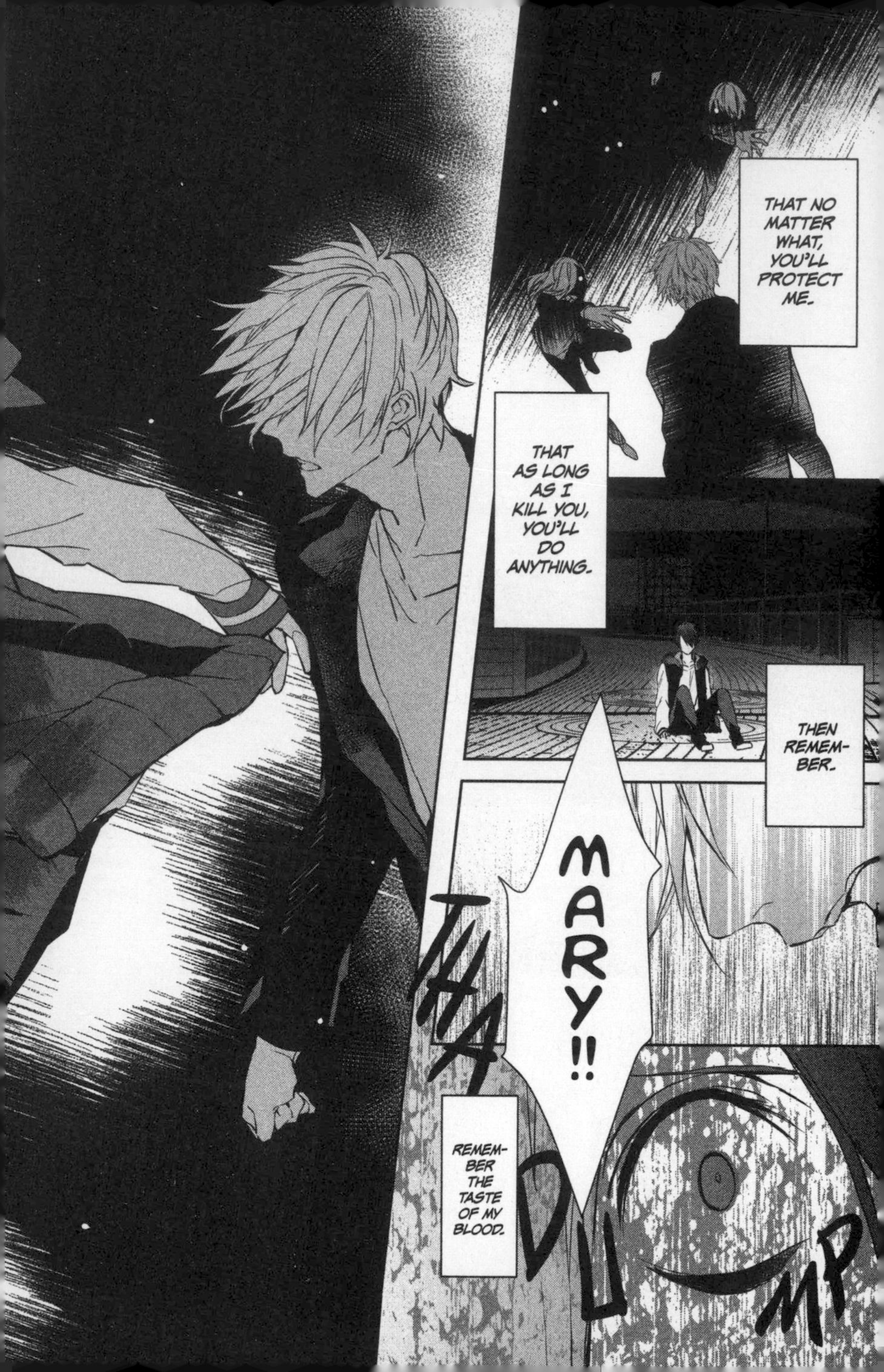
THAT NO MATTER WHAT, YOU'LL PROTECT ME.
THAT AS LONG AS I KILL YOU, YOU'LL DO ANYTHING.
THEN REMEM-BER.
MARY!!
REMEM-BER THE TASTE OF MY BLOOD.
THADUMP

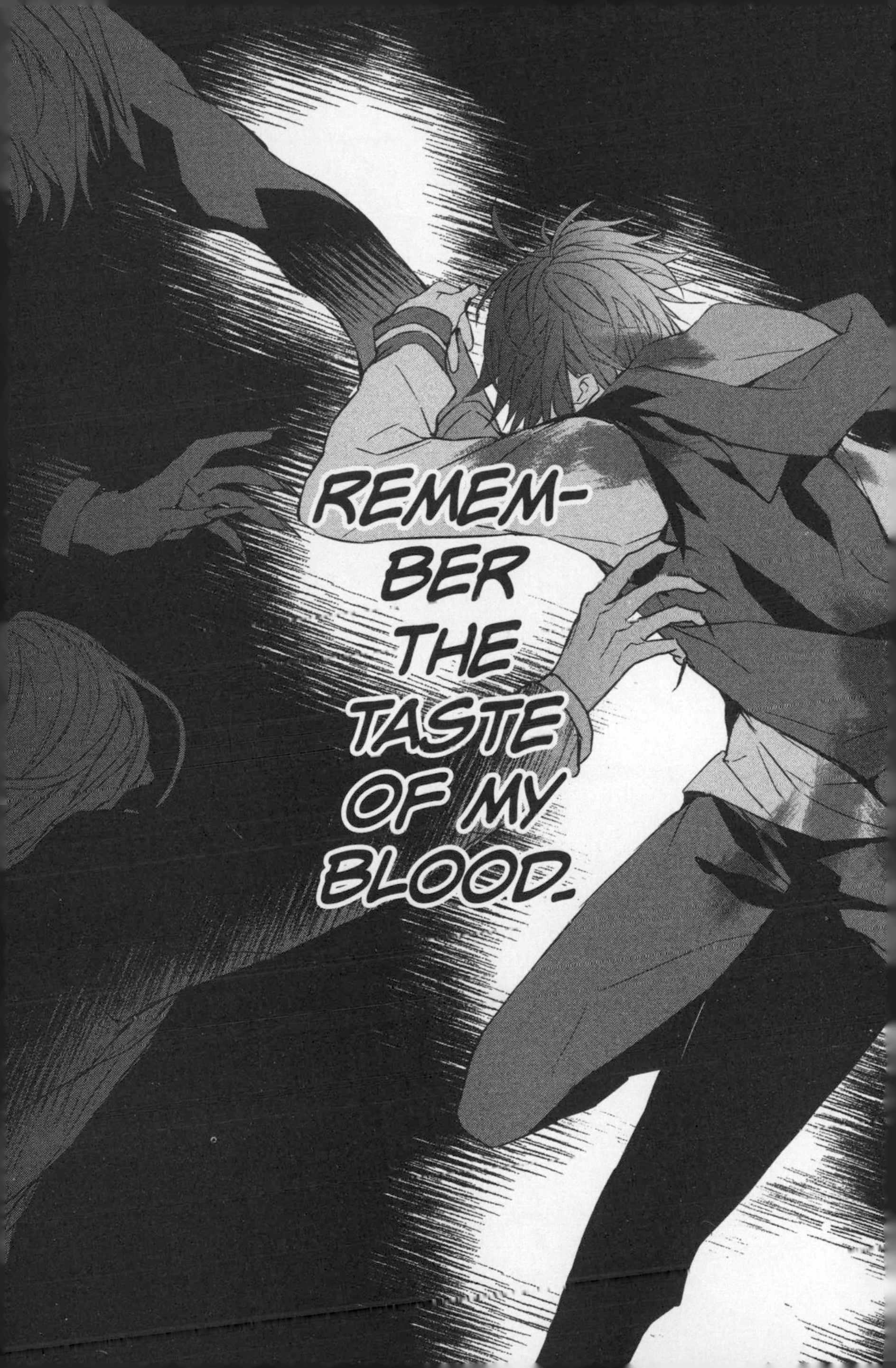
REMEM-
BER
THE
TASTE
OF MY
BLOOD.

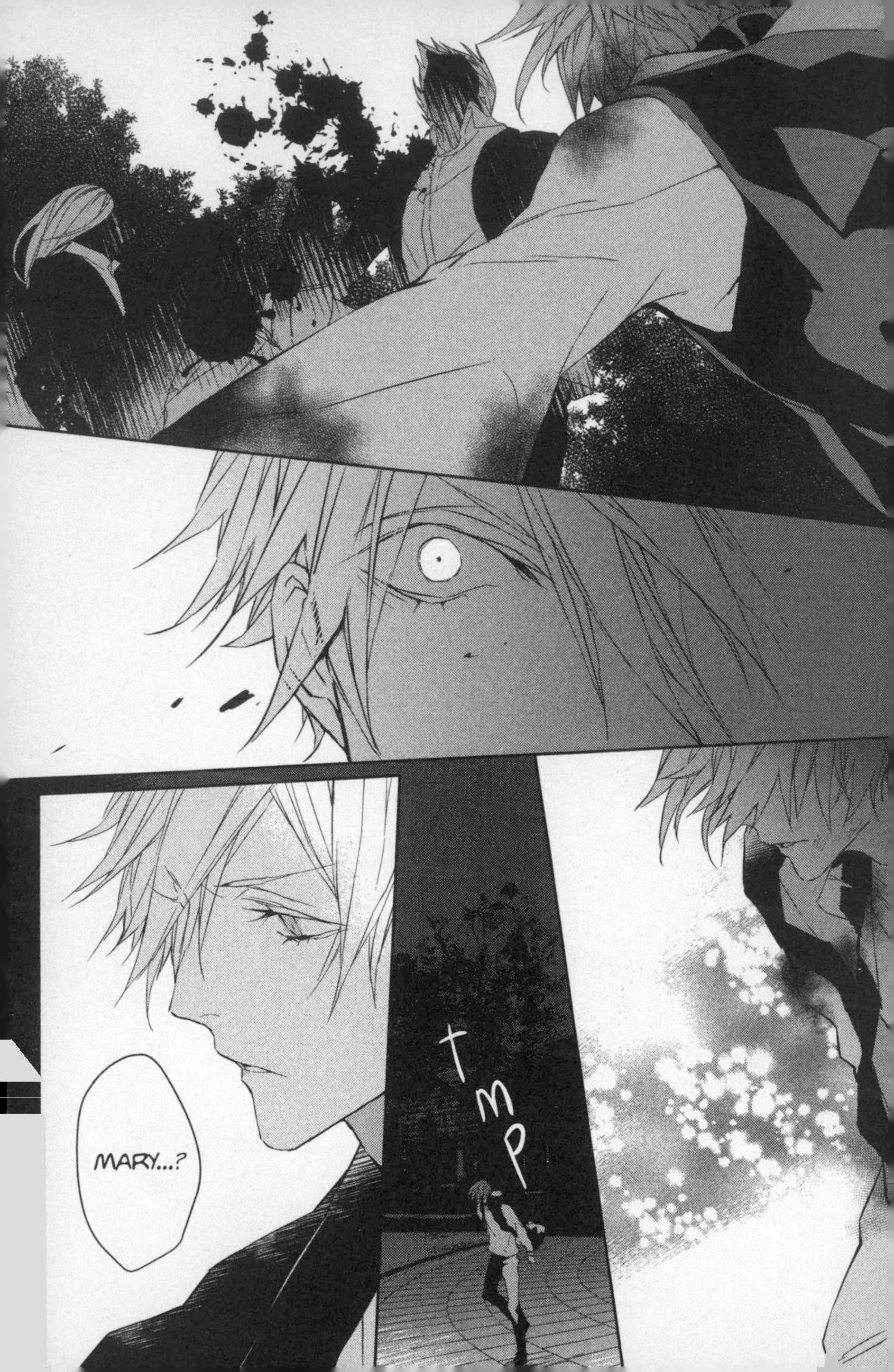
TMP
MARY...?

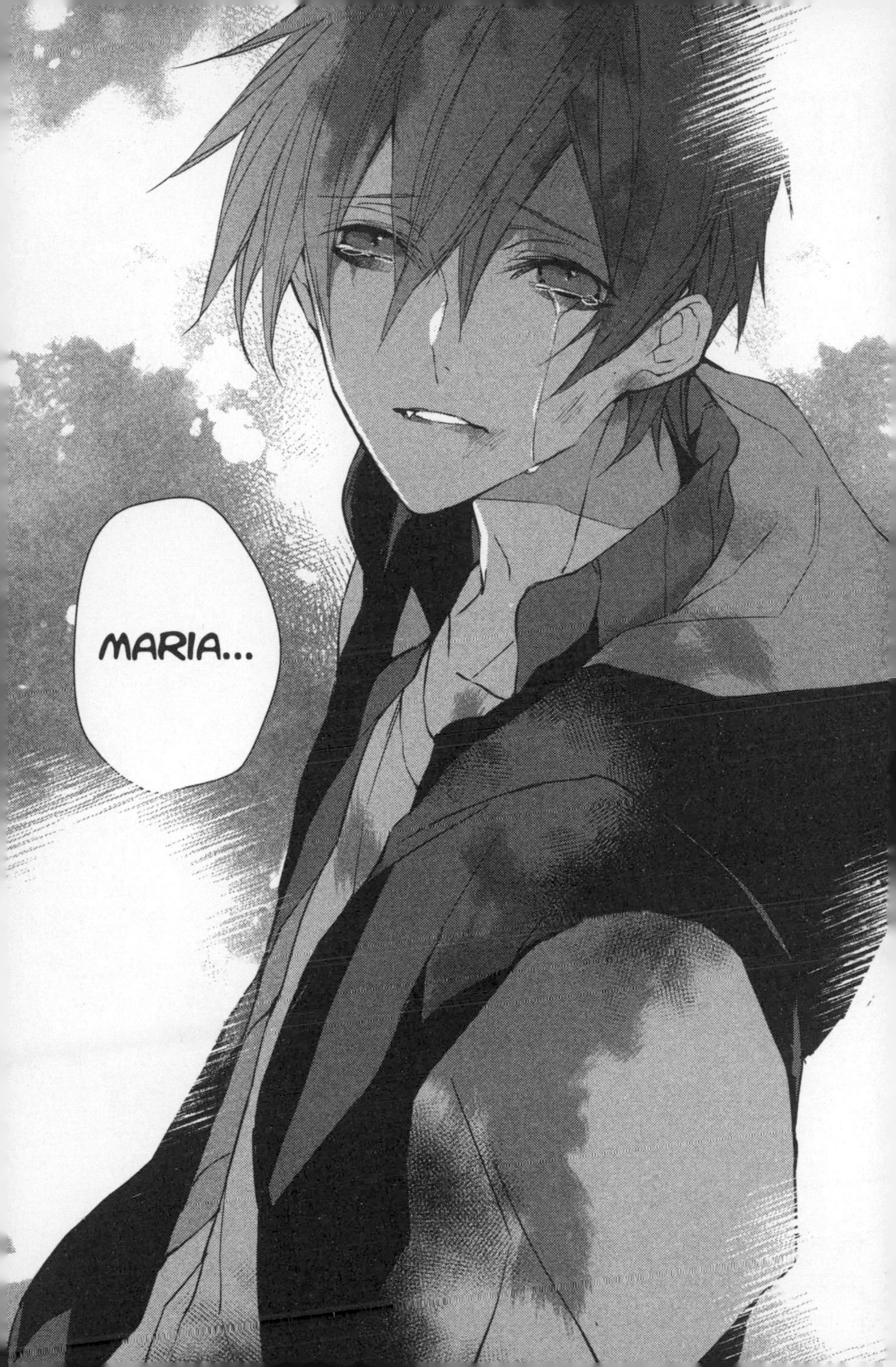
MARIA...

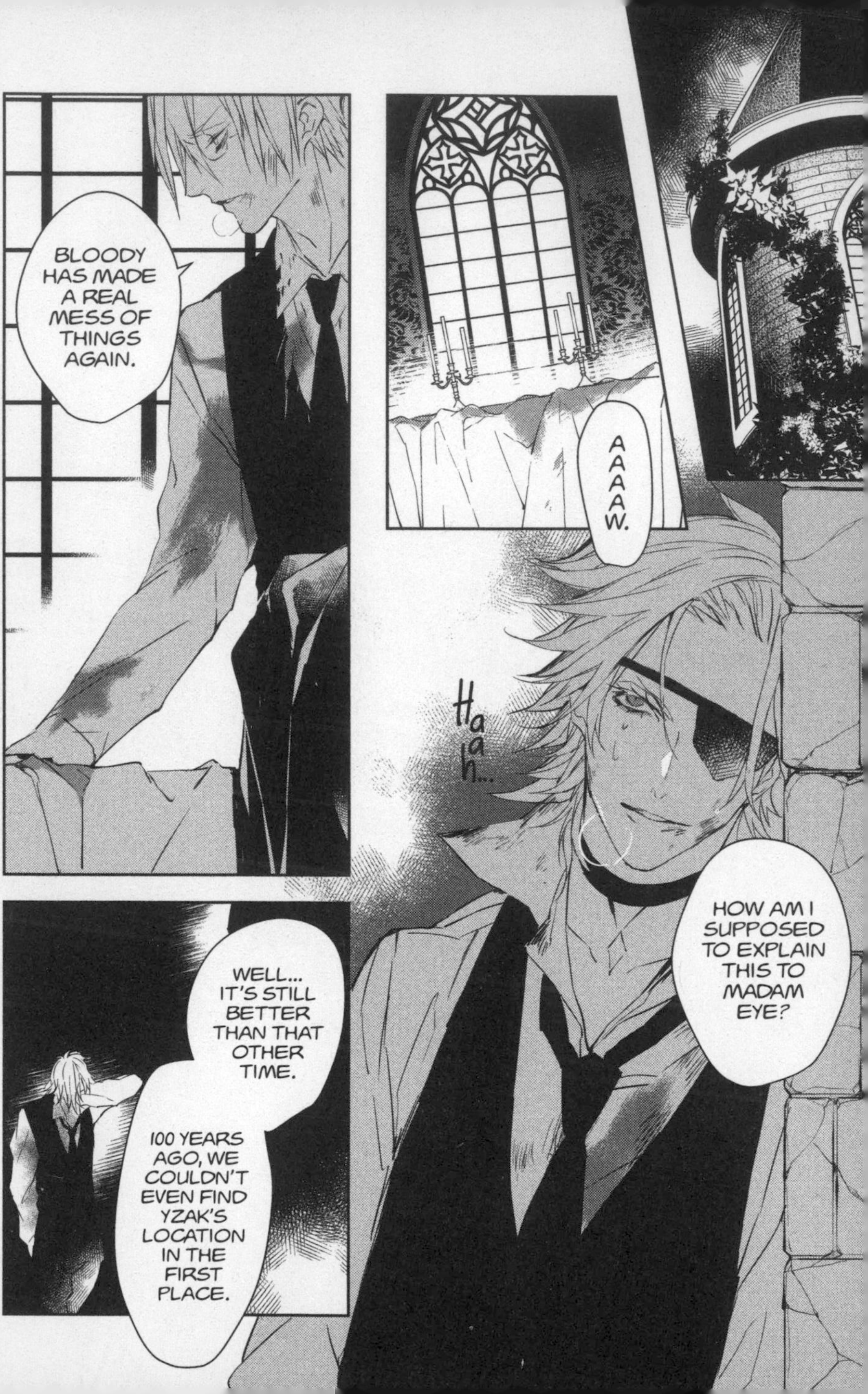
AAAAAW.
Haah...
HOW AM I SUPPOSED TO EXPLAIN THIS TO MADAM EYE?
BLOODY HAS MADE A REAL MESS OF THINGS AGAIN.
WELL... IT'S STILL BETTER THAN THAT OTHER TIME.
100 YEARS AGO, WE COULDN'T EVEN FIND YZAK'S LOCATION IN THE FIRST PLACE.

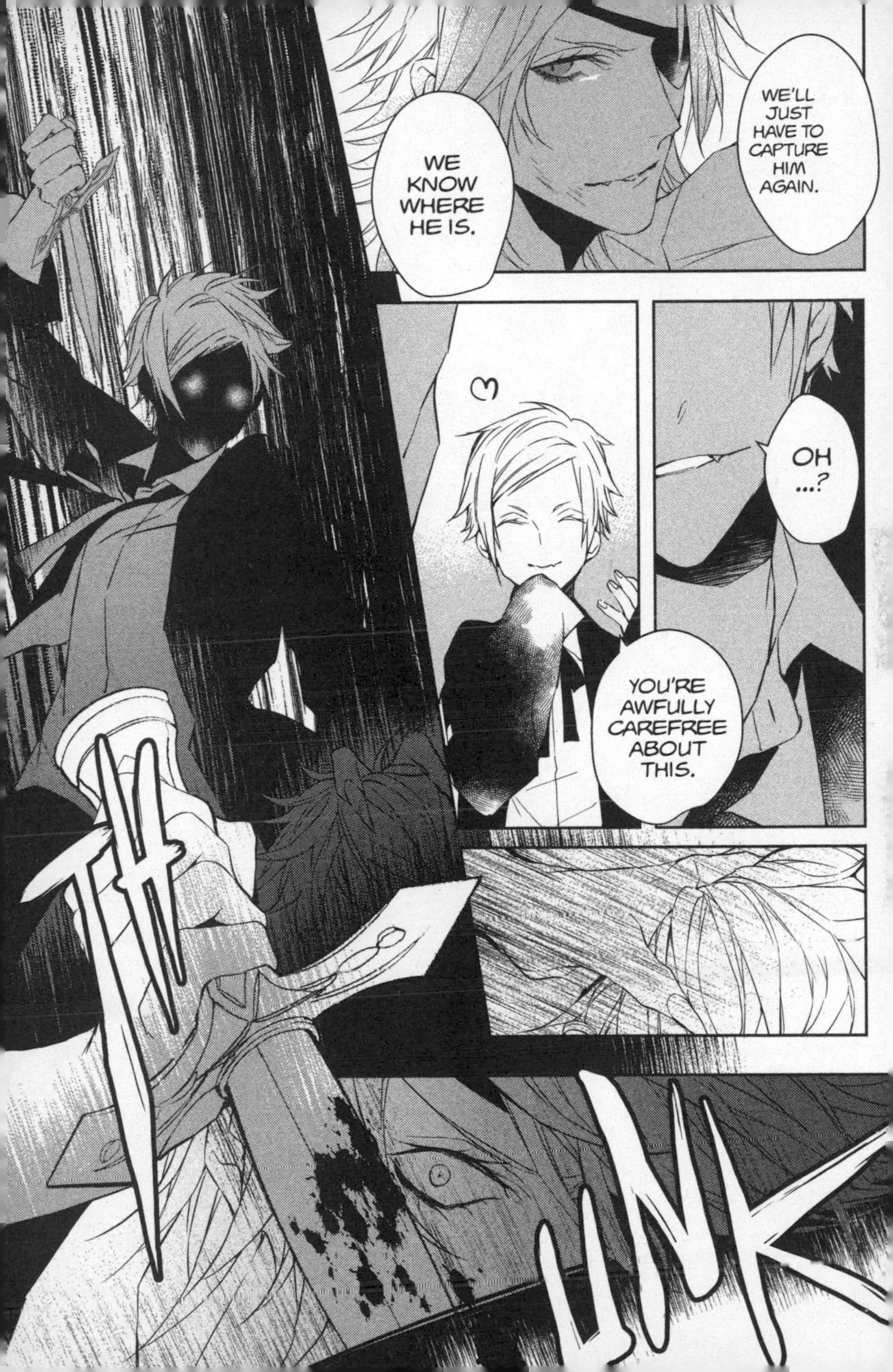
WE'LL JUST HAVE TO CAPTURE HIM AGAIN.
WE KNOW WHERE HE IS.
OH ...?
YOU'RE AWFULLY CAREFREE ABOUT THIS.
TH
UNK

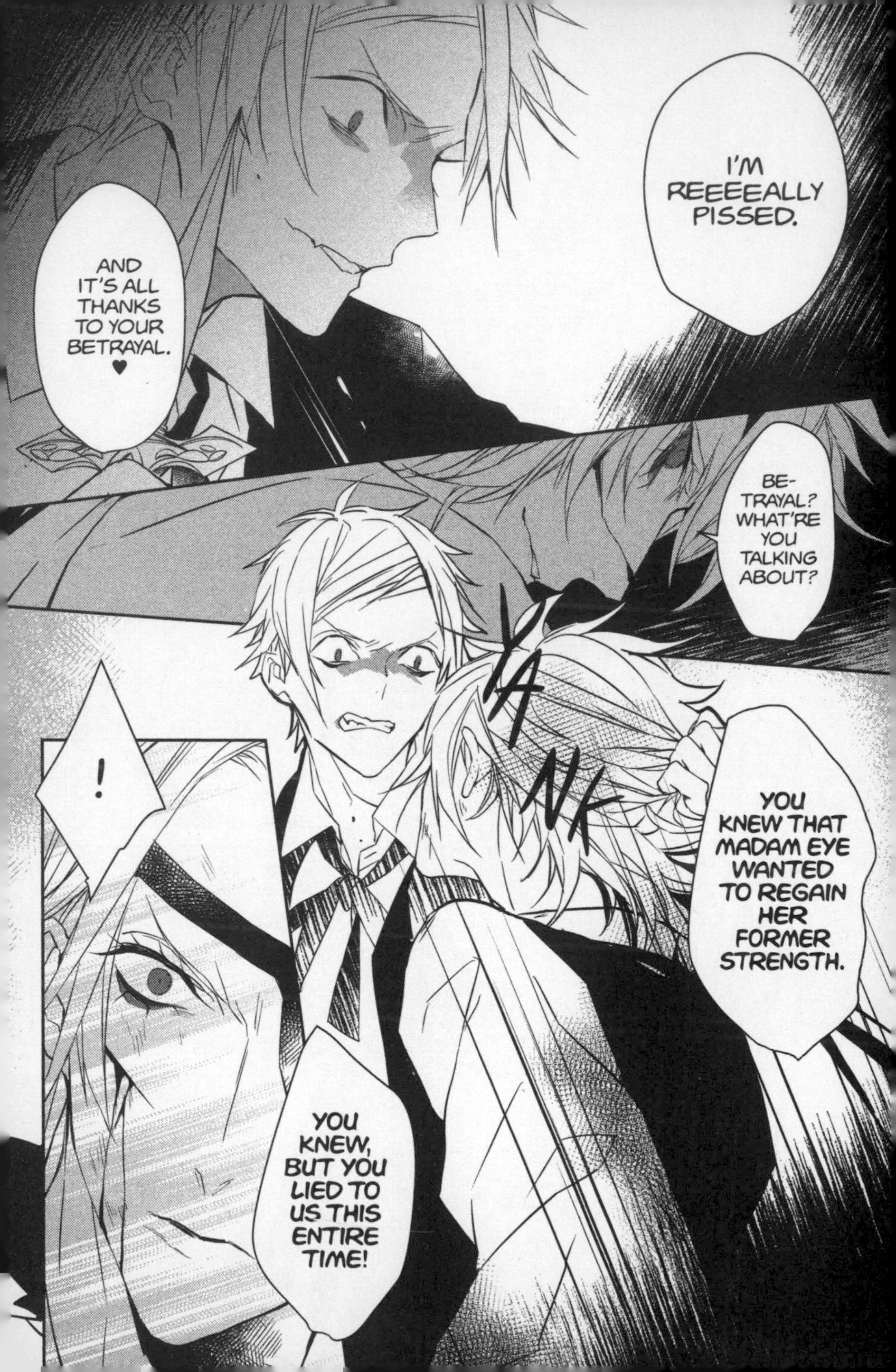
I'M REEEEALLY PISSED.
AND IT'S ALL THANKS TO YOUR BETRAYAL. ♥
BE-TRAYAL? WHAT'RE YOU TALKING ABOUT?
YANK
YOU KNEW THAT MADAM EYE WANTED TO REGAIN HER FORMER STRENGTH.
!
YOU KNEW, BUT YOU LIED TO US THIS ENTIRE TIME!

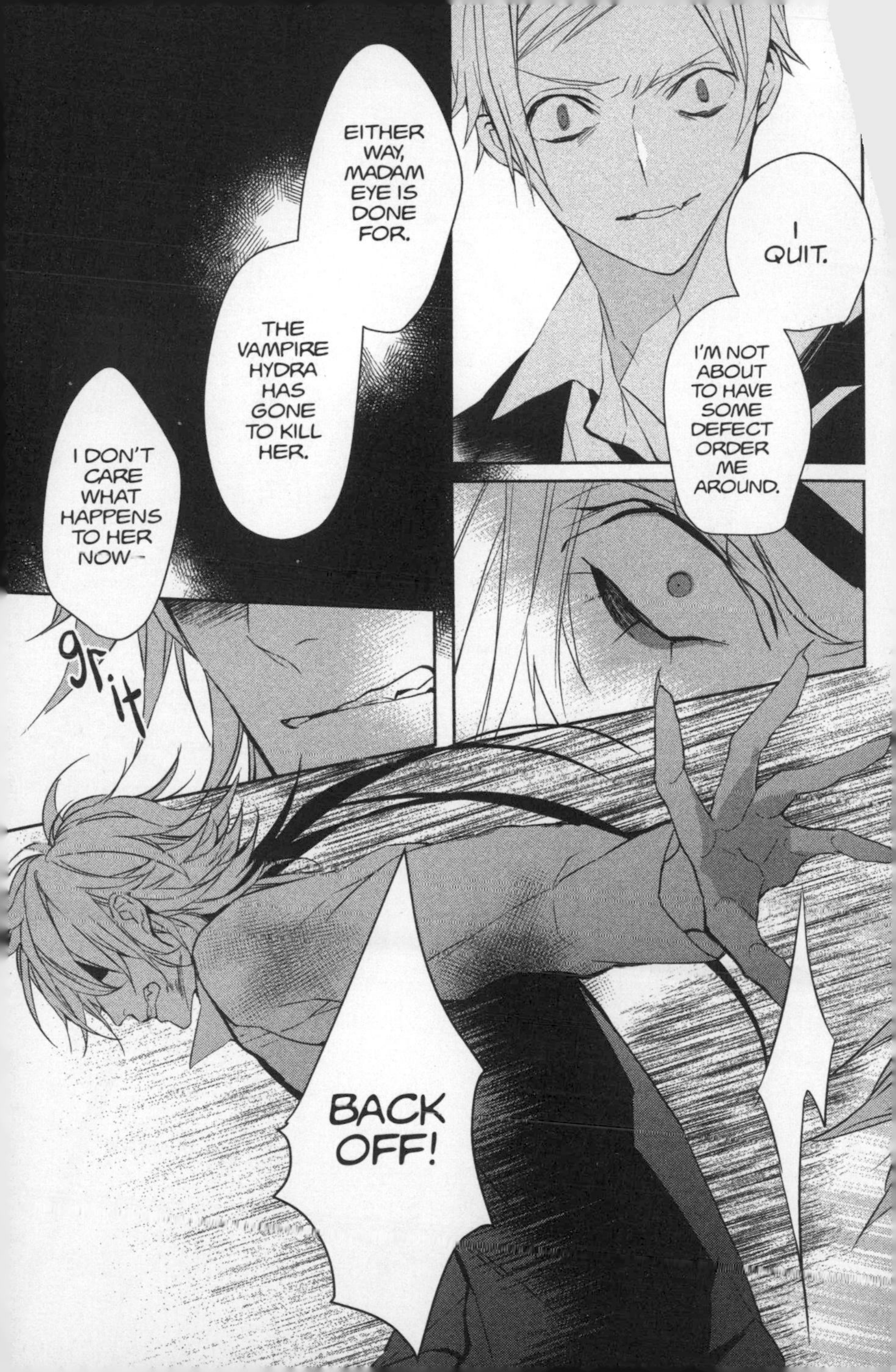
I QUIT.
I'M NOT ABOUT TO HAVE SOME DEFECT ORDER ME AROUND.
EITHER WAY, MADAM EYE IS DONE FOR.
THE VAMPIRE HYDRA HAS GONE TO KILL HER.
I DON'T CARE WHAT HAPPENS TO HER NOW—
gr it
BACK OFF!

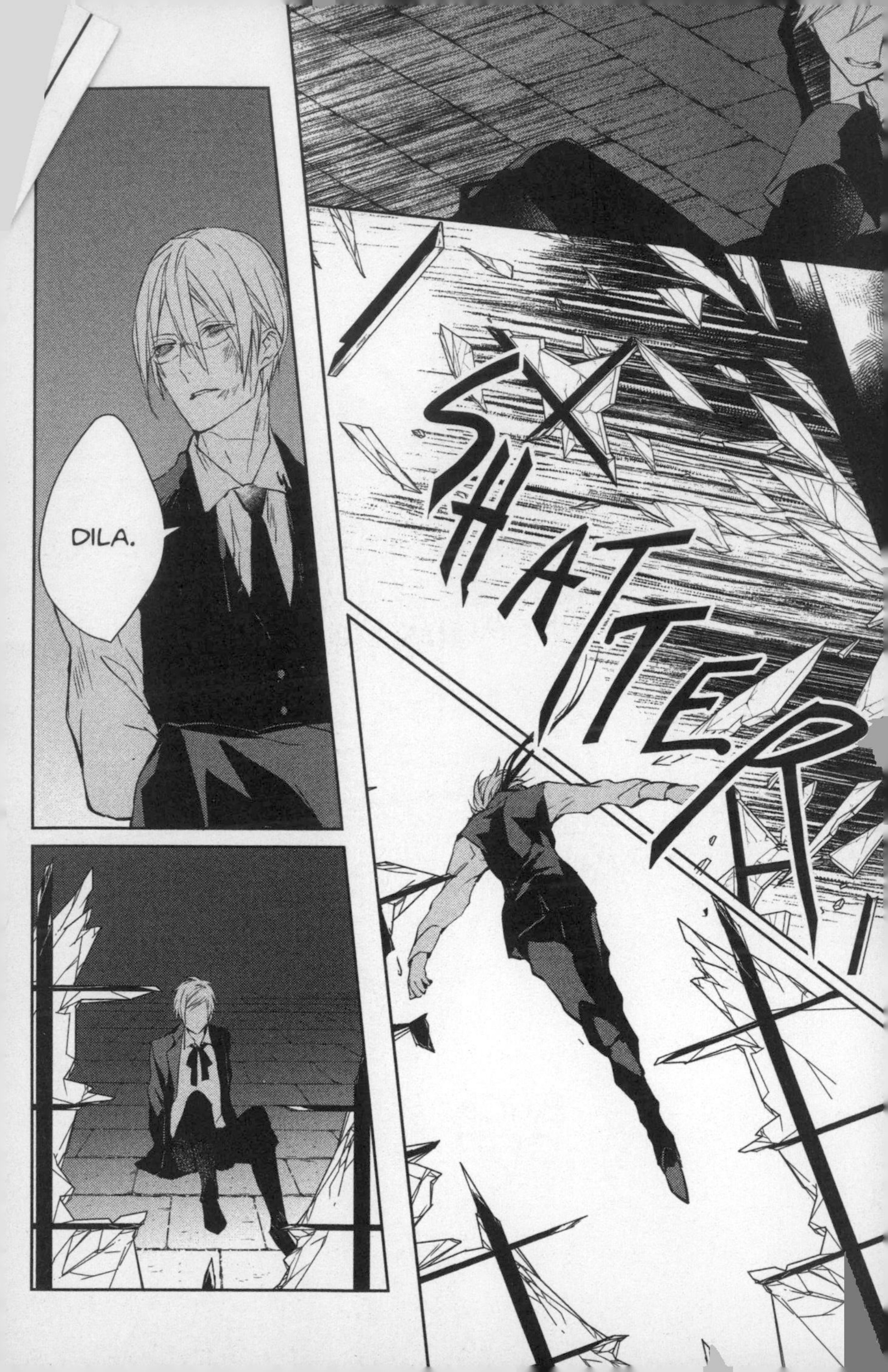
SHATTER
DILA.

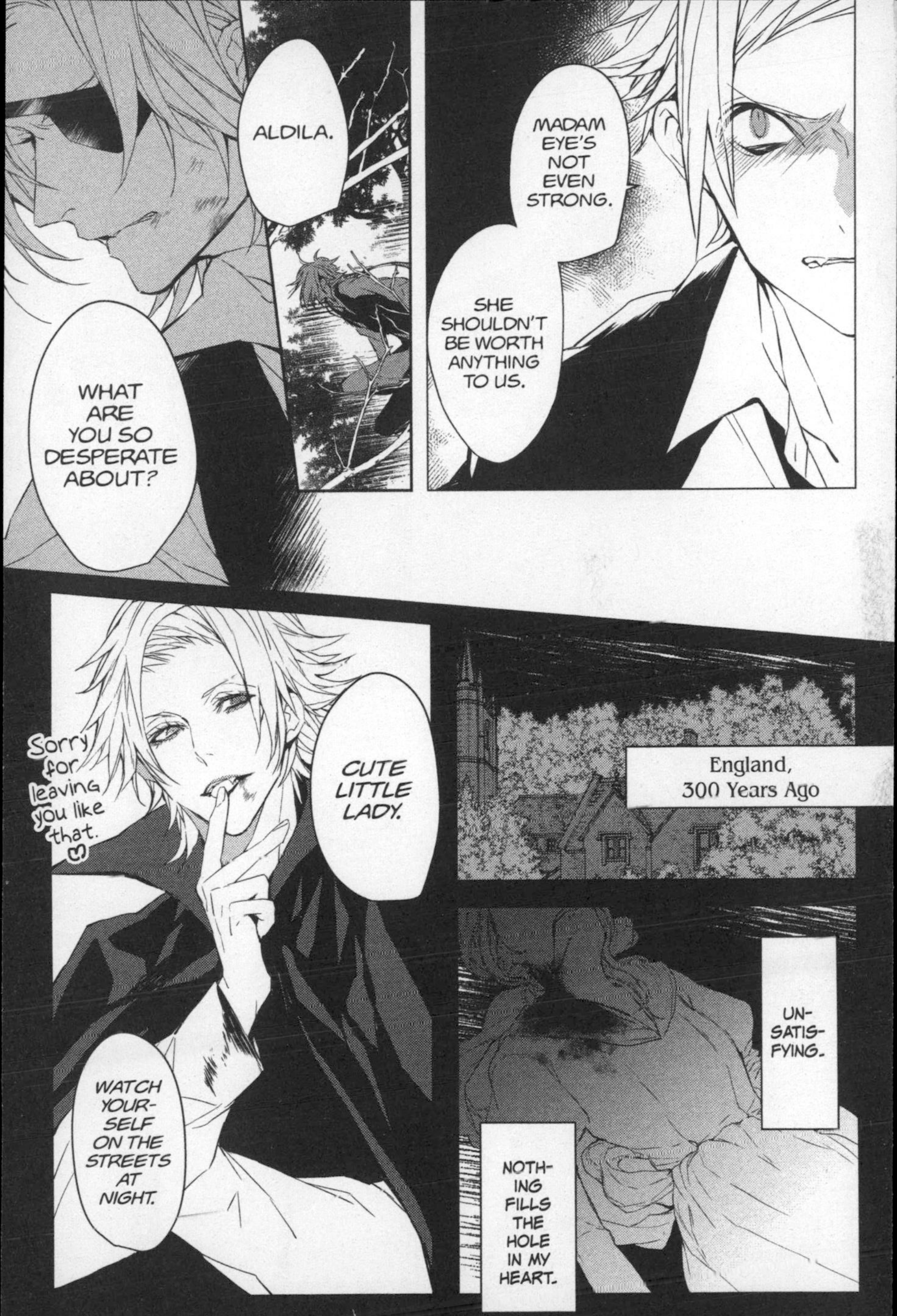
MADAM EYE'S NOT EVEN STRONG.
SHE SHOULDN'T BE WORTH ANYTHING TO US.
ALDILA.
WHAT ARE YOU SO DESPERATE ABOUT?
England, 300 Years Ago
UN-SATIS-FYING.
NOTH-ING FILLS THE HOLE IN MY HEART.
CUTE LITTLE LADY.
Sorry for leaving you like that.
WATCH YOUR-SELF ON THE STREETS AT NIGHT.

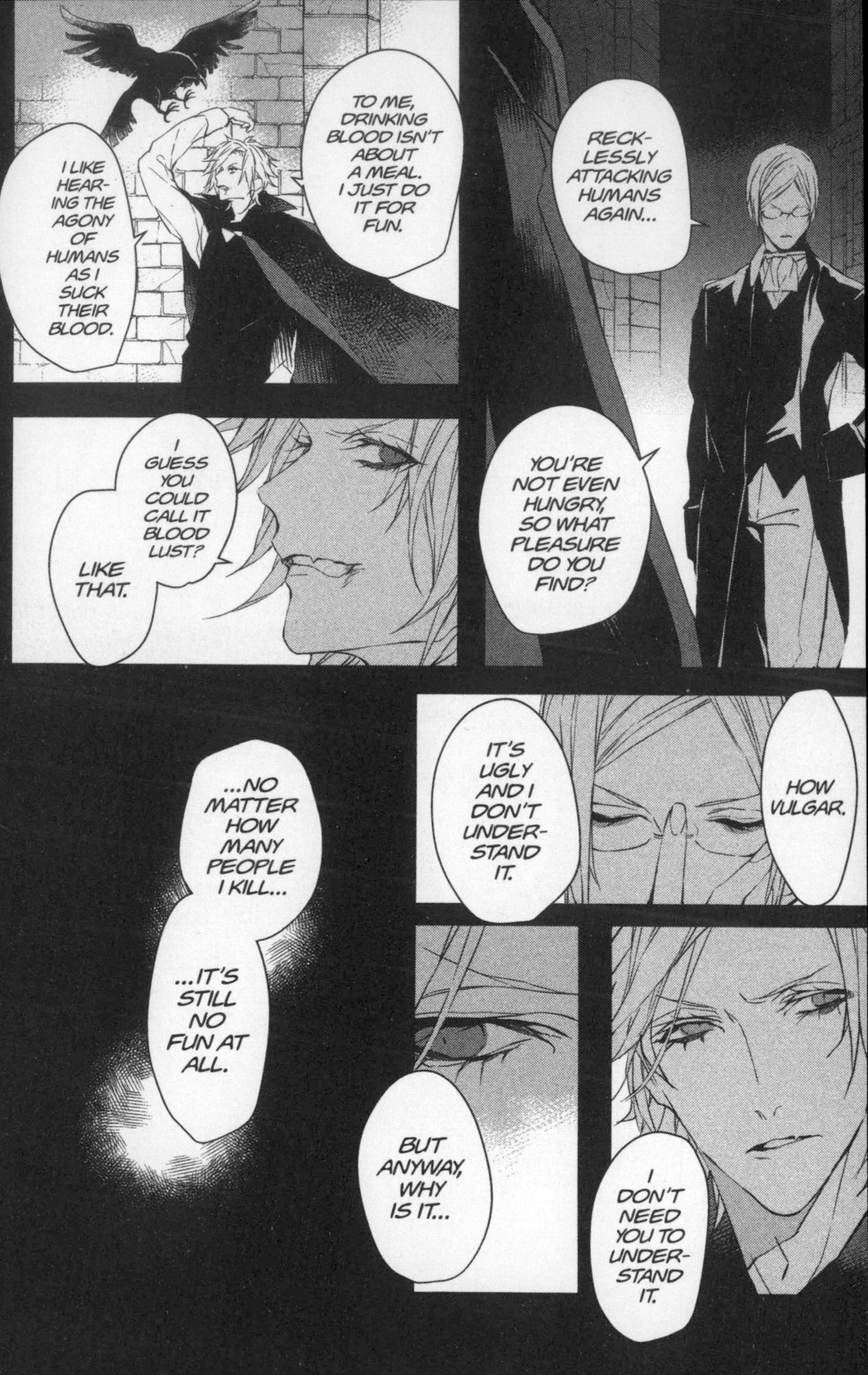
RECK-LESSLY ATTACKING HUMANS AGAIN...
YOU'RE NOT EVEN HUNGRY, SO WHAT PLEASURE DO YOU FIND?
TO ME, DRINKING BLOOD ISN'T ABOUT A MEAL. I JUST DO IT FOR FUN.
I LIKE HEAR-ING THE AGONY OF HUMANS AS I SUCK THEIR BLOOD.
I GUESS YOU COULD CALL IT BLOOD LUST?
LIKE THAT.
HOW VULGAR.
IT'S UGLY AND I DON'T UNDER-STAND IT.
I DON'T NEED YOU TO UNDER-STAND IT.
BUT ANYWAY, WHY IS IT...
...NO MATTER HOW MANY PEOPLE I KILL...
...IT'S STILL NO FUN AT ALL.

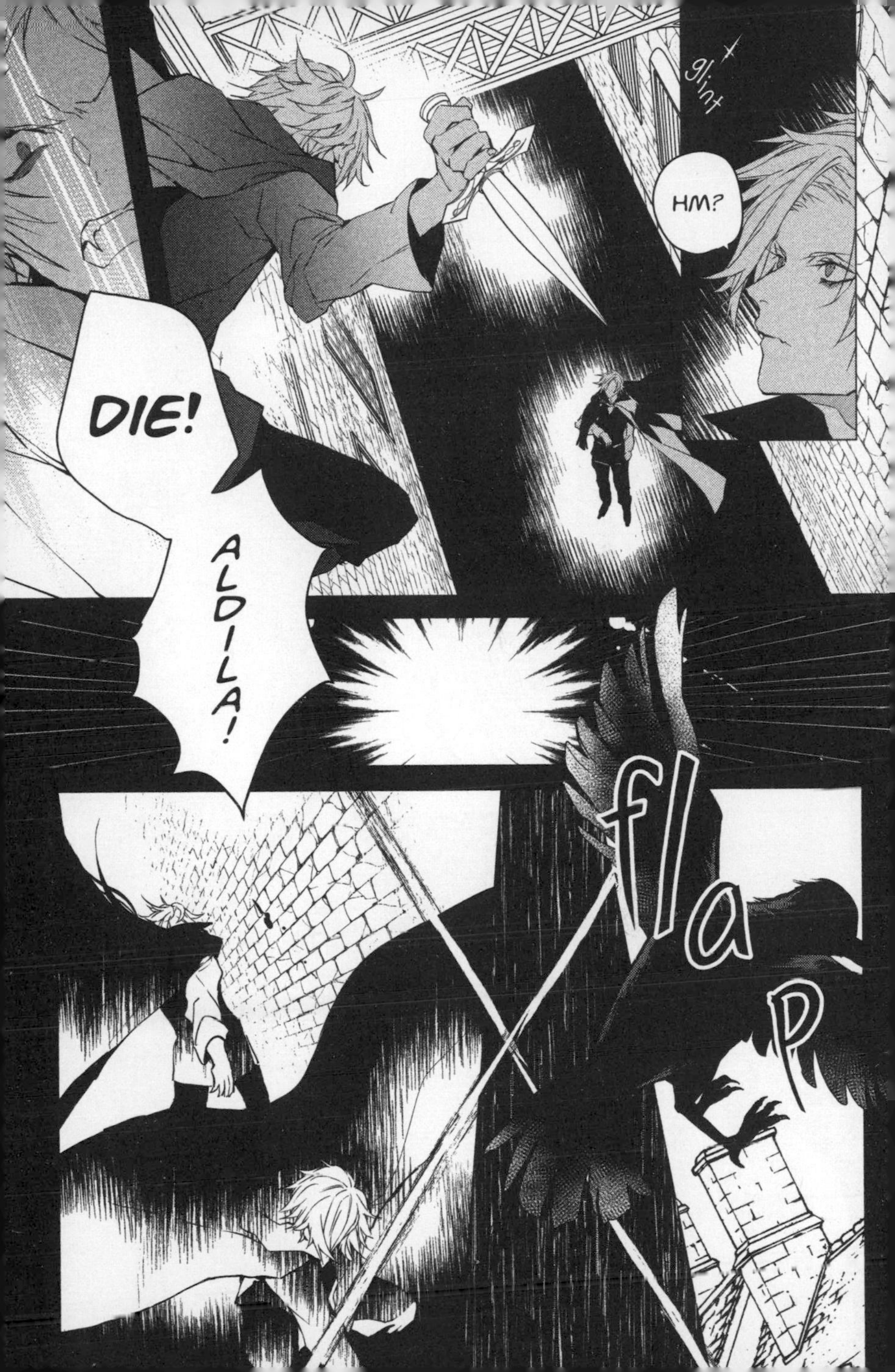
glint
HM?
DIE! ALDILA!
flap

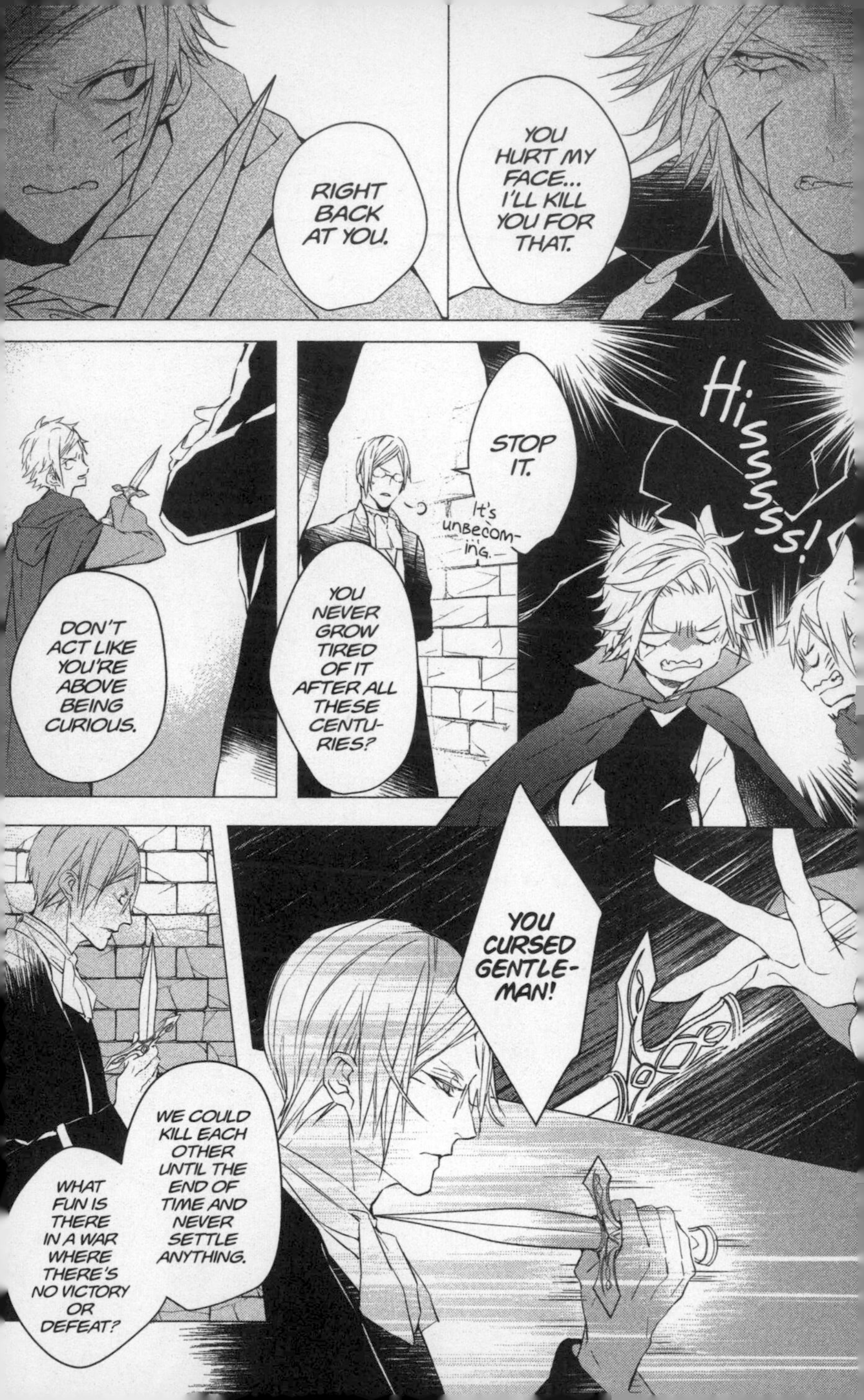
YOU HURT MY FACE... I'LL KILL YOU FOR THAT.
RIGHT BACK AT YOU.
Hissssss!
STOP IT.
It's unbecoming.
YOU NEVER GROW TIRED OF IT AFTER ALL THESE CENTURIES?
DON'T ACT LIKE YOU'RE ABOVE BEING CURIOUS.
YOU CURSED GENTLEMAN!
WE COULD KILL EACH OTHER UNTIL THE END OF TIME AND NEVER SETTLE ANYTHING.
WHAT FUN IS THERE IN A WAR WHERE THERE'S NO VICTORY OR DEFEAT?

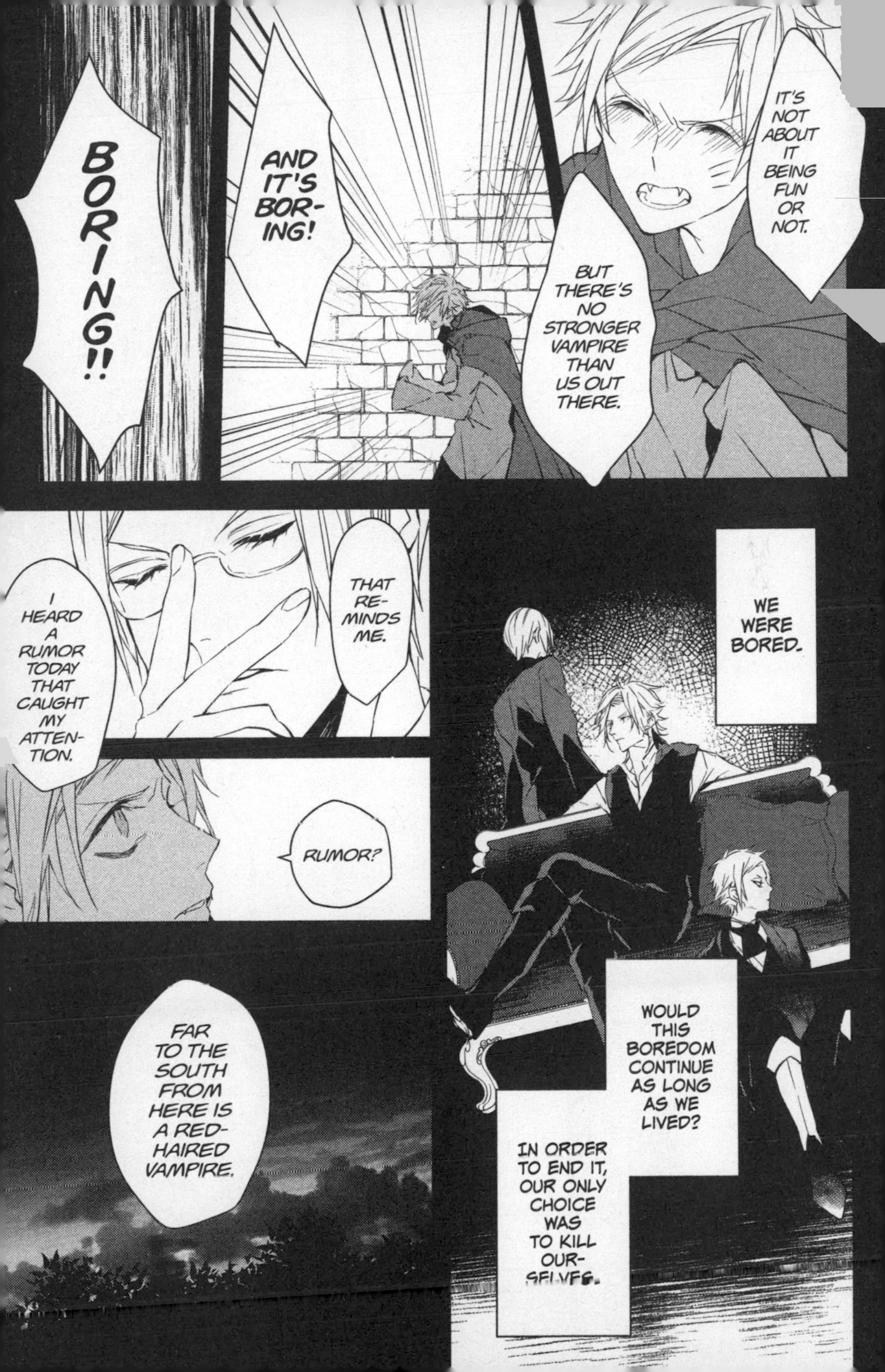
IT'S NOT ABOUT IT BEING FUN OR NOT.
BUT THERE'S NO STRONGER VAMPIRE THAN US OUT THERE.
AND IT'S BOR-ING!
BORING!!
WE WERE BORED.
WOULD THIS BOREDOM CONTINUE AS LONG AS WE LIVED?
IN ORDER TO END IT, OUR ONLY CHOICE WAS TO KILL OUR-SELVES.
THAT RE-MINDS ME.
I HEARD A RUMOR TODAY THAT CAUGHT MY ATTEN-TION.
RUMOR?
FAR TO THE SOUTH FROM HERE IS A RED-HAIRED VAMPIRE.

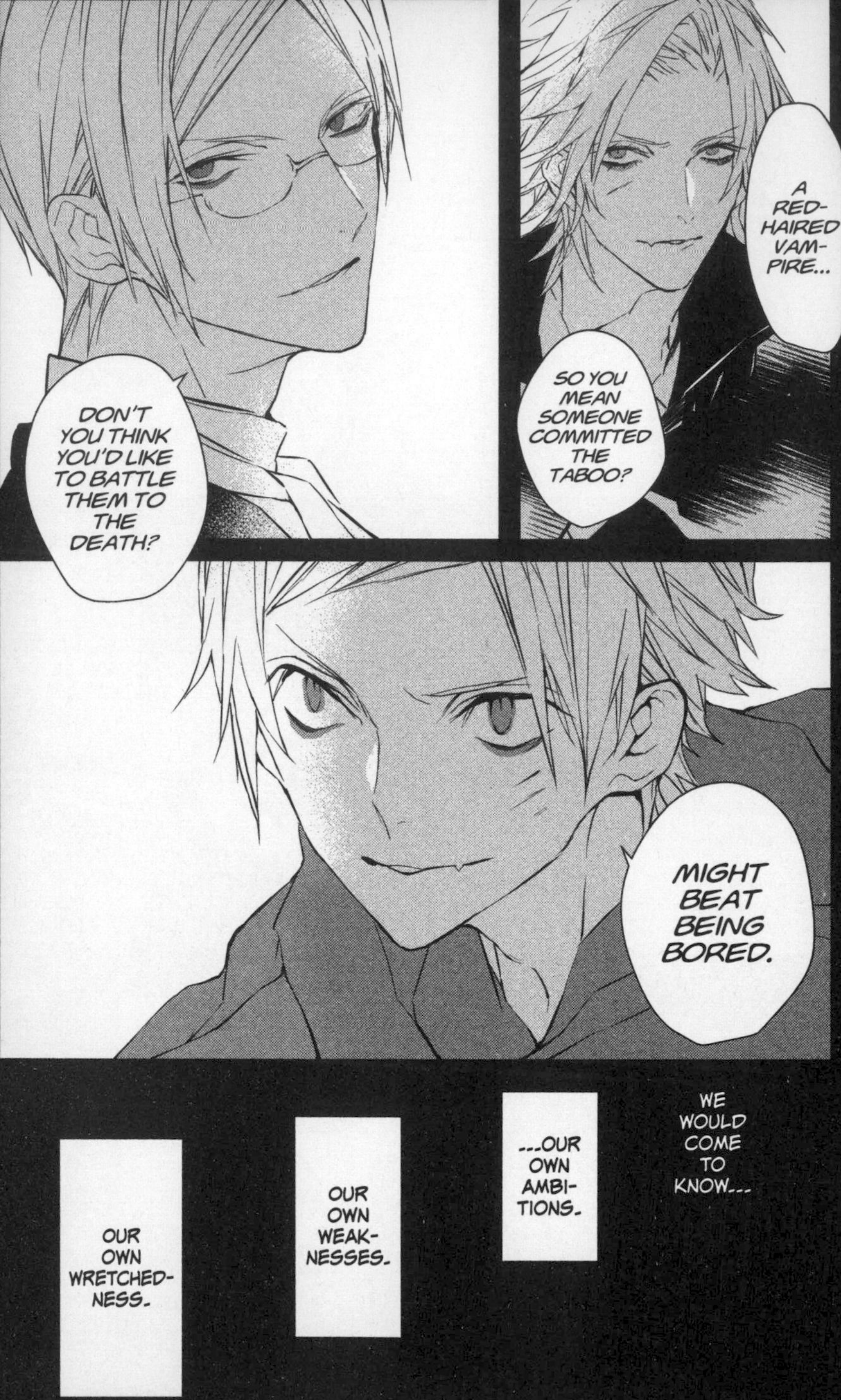
A RED-HAIRED VAMPIRE...
SO YOU MEAN SOMEONE COMMITTED THE TABOO?
DON'T YOU THINK YOU'D LIKE TO BATTLE THEM TO THE DEATH?
MIGHT BEAT BEING BORED.
WE WOULD COME TO KNOW...
...OUR OWN AMBITIONS.
OUR OWN WEAKNESSES.
OUR OWN WRETCHEDNESS.

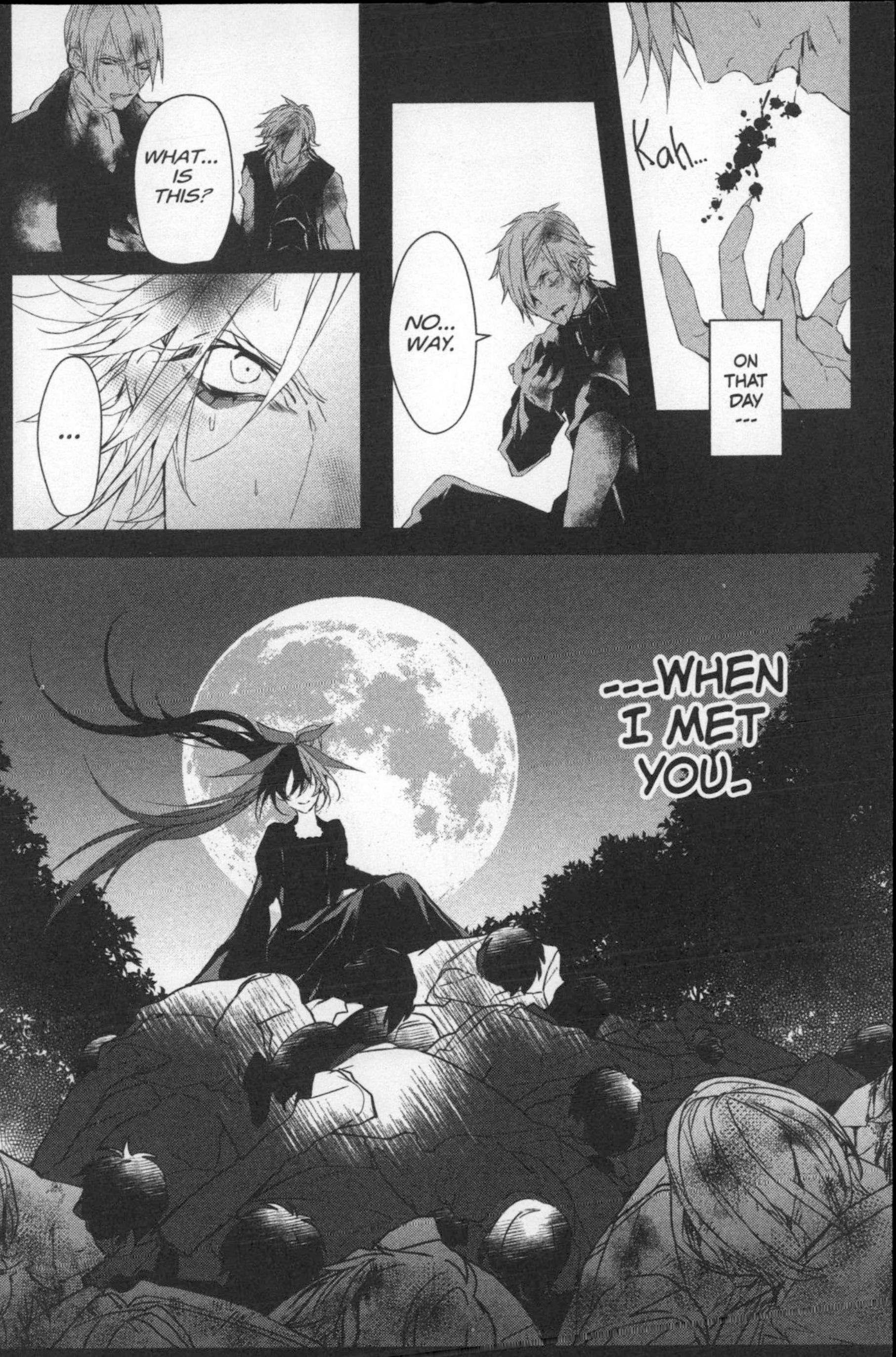
Kah...
ON THAT DAY ---
NO... WAY.
WHAT... IS THIS?
...
---WHEN I MET YOU.

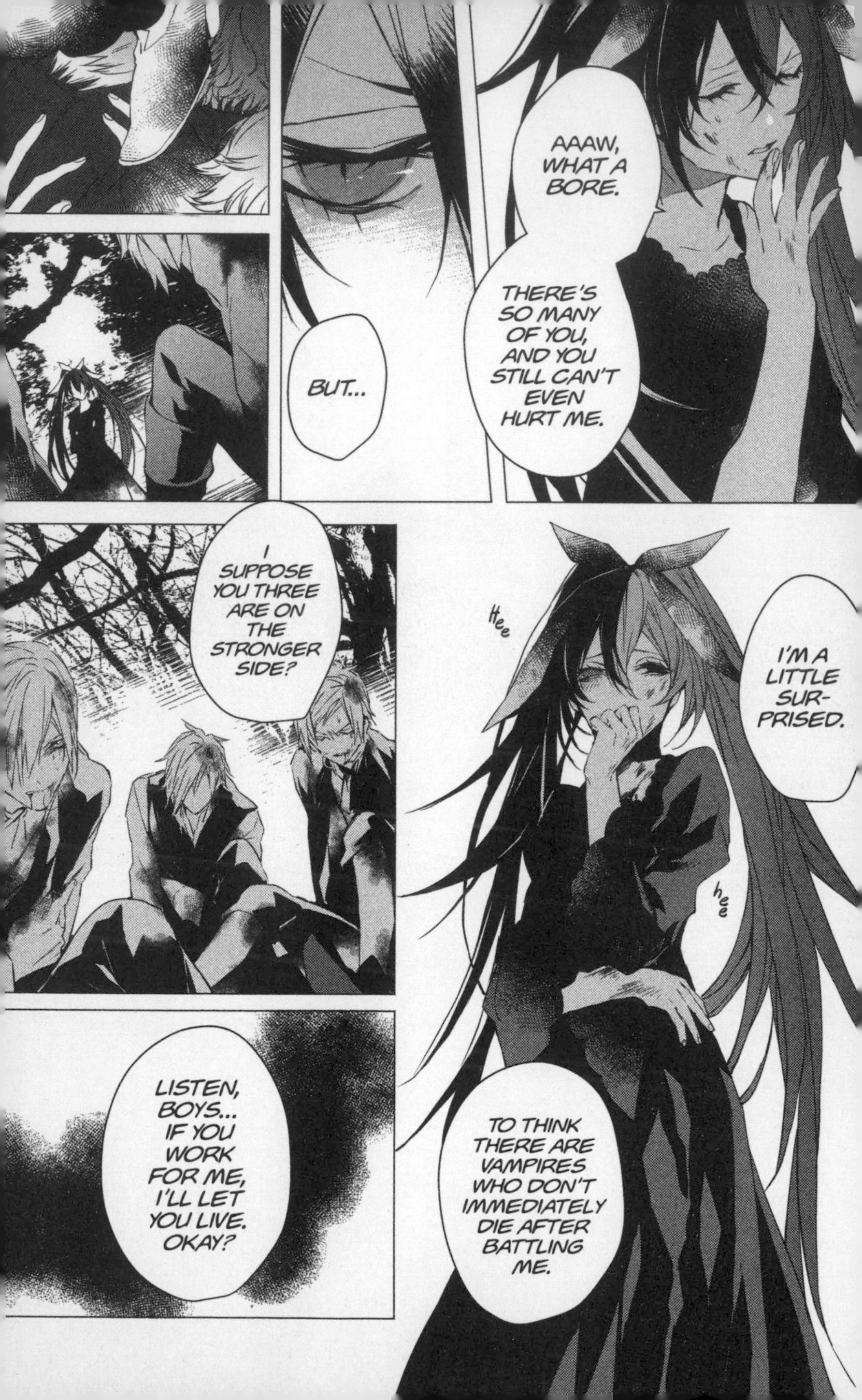
AAAW, WHAT A BORE.
THERE'S SO MANY OF YOU, AND YOU STILL CAN'T EVEN HURT ME.
BUT...
I'M A LITTLE SUR-PRISED.
Hee
hee
TO THINK THERE ARE VAMPIRES WHO DON'T IMMEDIATELY DIE AFTER BATTLING ME.
I SUPPOSE YOU THREE ARE ON THE STRONGER SIDE?
LISTEN, BOYS... IF YOU WORK FOR ME, I'LL LET YOU LIVE. OKAY?

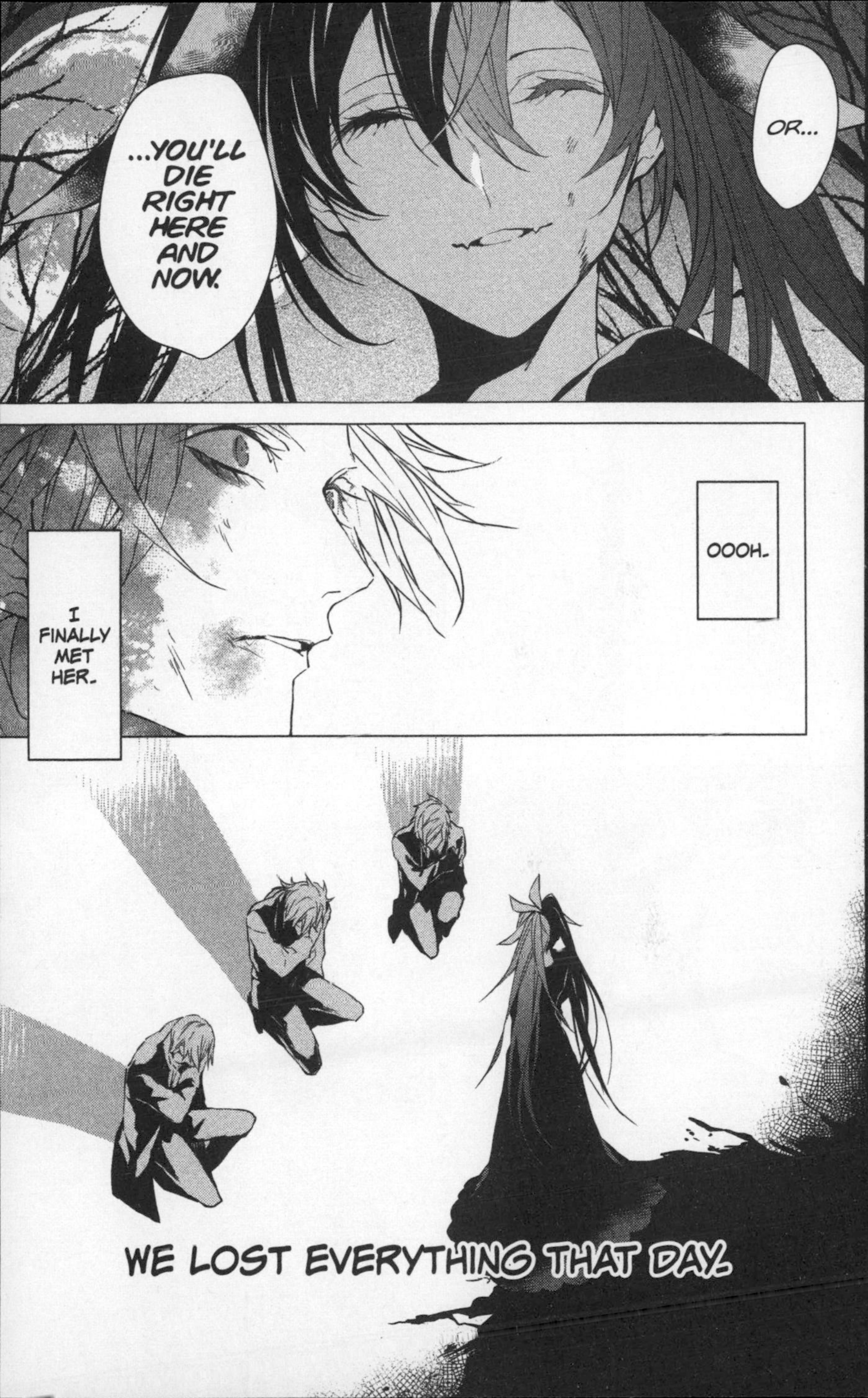
OR...
...YOU'LL DIE RIGHT HERE AND NOW.
OOOH.
I FINALLY MET HER.
WE LOST EVERYTHING THAT DAY.

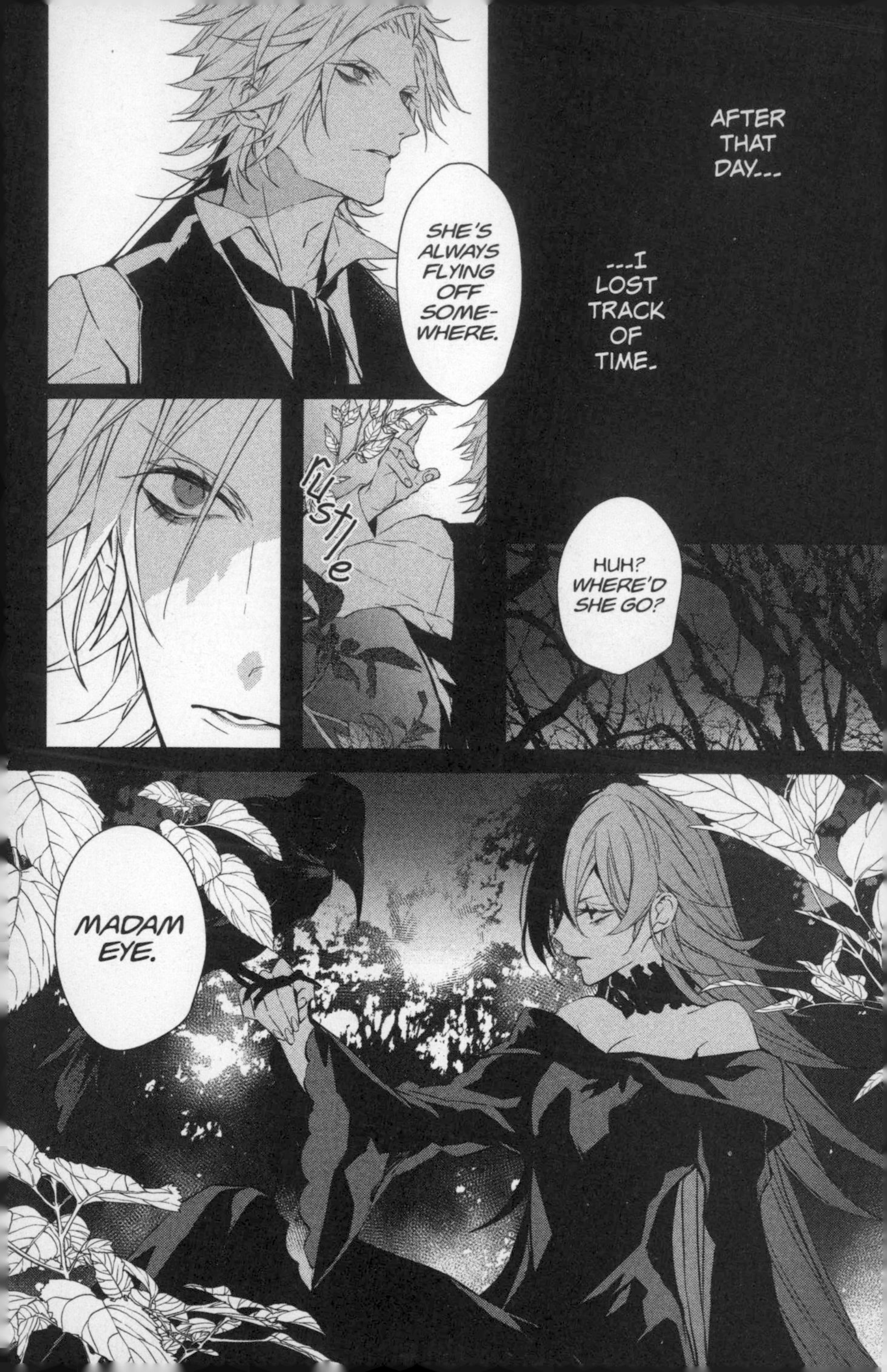
AFTER THAT DAY...
...I LOST TRACK OF TIME.
SHE'S ALWAYS FLYING OFF SOME-WHERE.
HUH? WHERE'D SHE GO?
rustle
MADAM EYE.

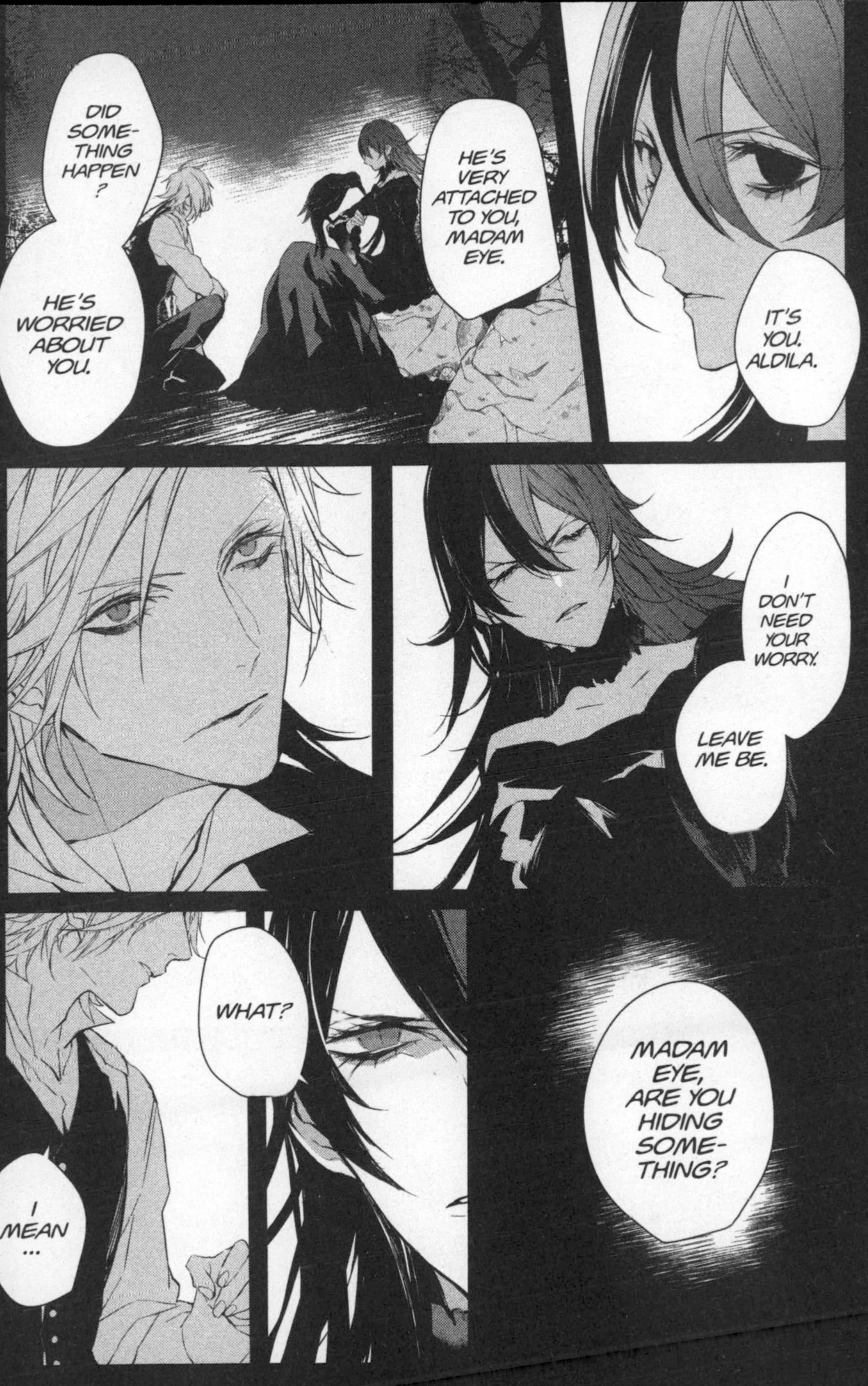
IT'S YOU. ALDILA.
HE'S VERY ATTACHED TO YOU, MADAM EYE.
DID SOMETHING HAPPEN?
HE'S WORRIED ABOUT YOU.
I DON'T NEED YOUR WORRY.
LEAVE ME BE.
MADAM EYE, ARE YOU HIDING SOMETHING?
WHAT?
I MEAN...

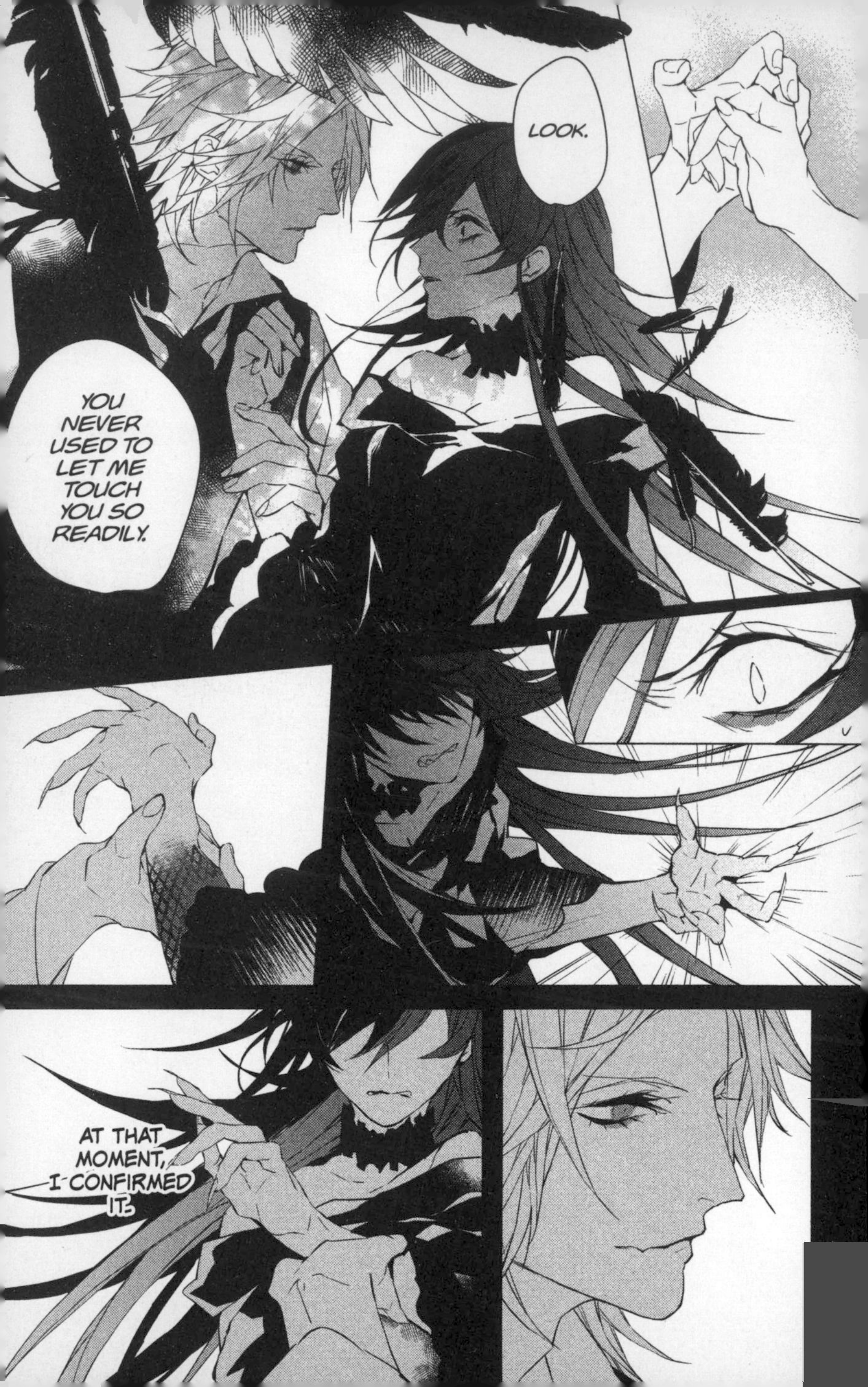
LOOK.
YOU NEVER USED TO LET ME TOUCH YOU SO READILY.
AT THAT MOMENT, I CONFIRMED IT.

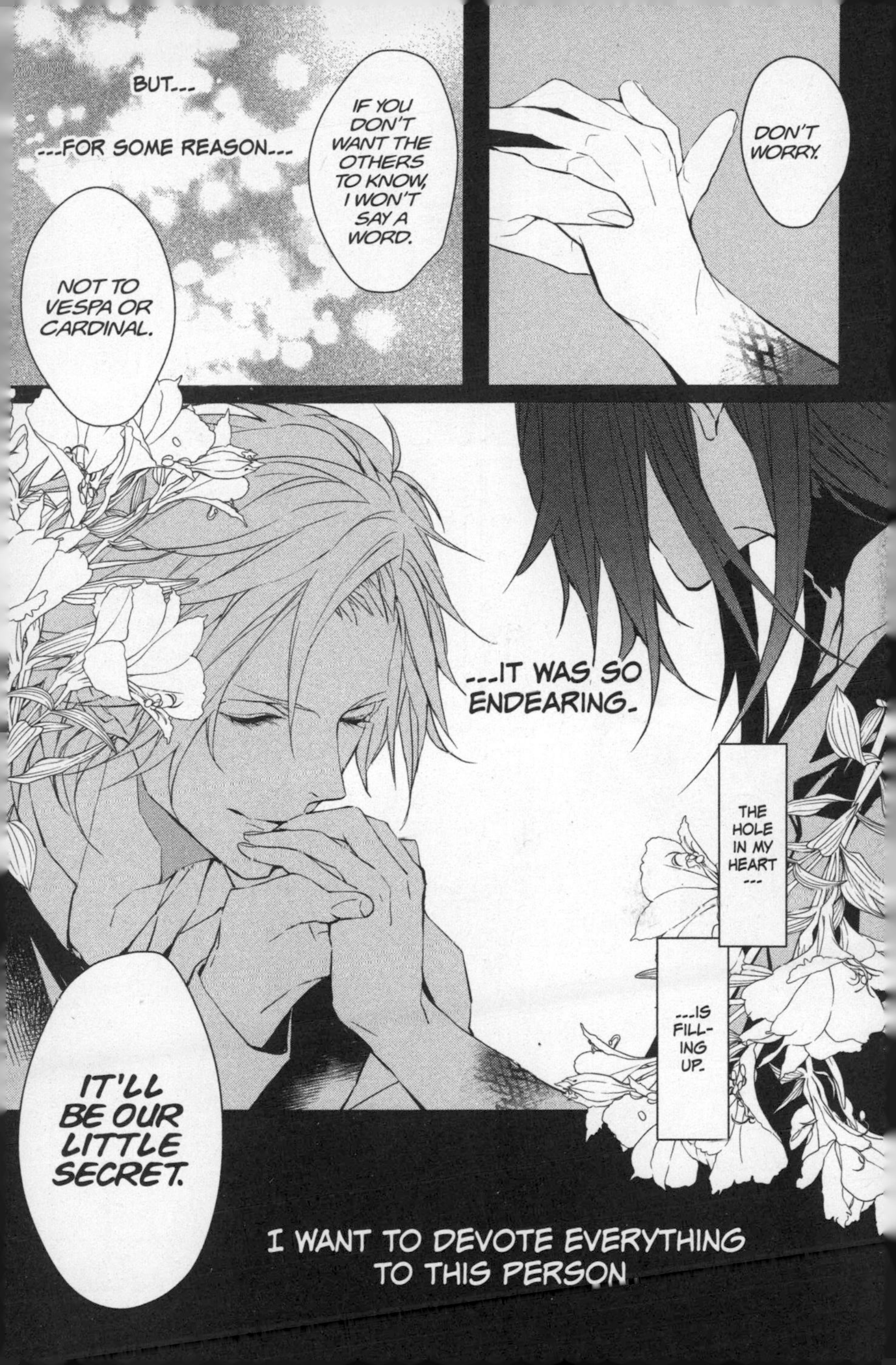
DON'T WORRY.
IF YOU DON'T WANT THE OTHERS TO KNOW, I WON'T SAY A WORD.
NOT TO VESPA OR CARDINAL.
BUT...
...FOR SOME REASON...
...IT WAS SO ENDEARING.
THE HOLE IN MY HEART...
...IS FILLING UP.
IT'LL BE OUR LITTLE SECRET.
I WANT TO DEVOTE EVERYTHING TO THIS PERSON.

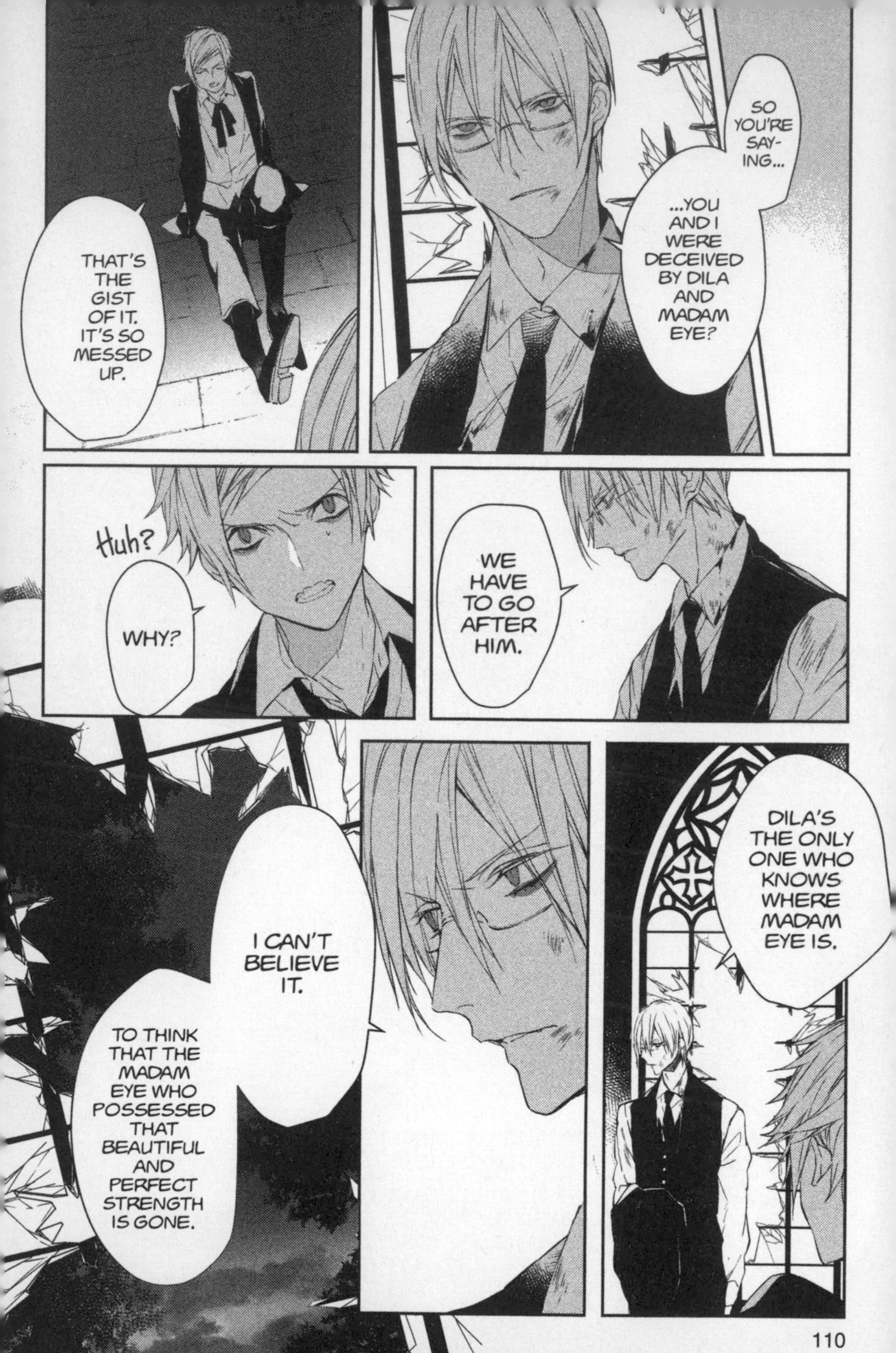
SO YOU'RE SAYING...
...YOU AND I WERE DECEIVED BY DILA AND MADAM EYE?
THAT'S THE GIST OF IT. IT'S SO MESSED UP.
WE HAVE TO GO AFTER HIM.
Huh?
WHY?
DILA'S THE ONLY ONE WHO KNOWS WHERE MADAM EYE IS.
I CAN'T BELIEVE IT.
TO THINK THAT THE MADAM EYE WHO POSSESSED THAT BEAUTIFUL AND PERFECT STRENGTH IS GONE.

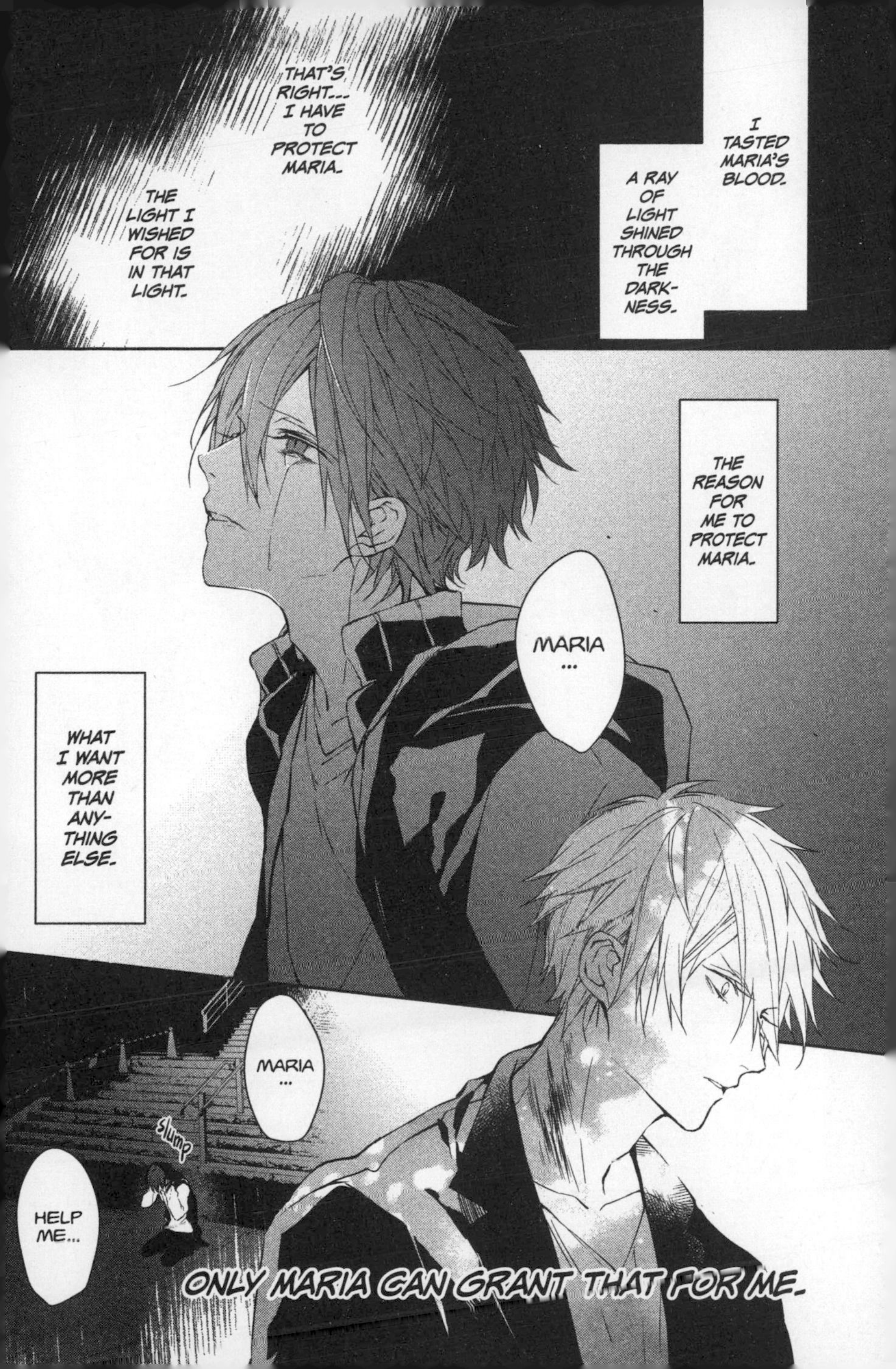
I TASTED MARIA'S BLOOD.
A RAY OF LIGHT SHINED THROUGH THE DARKNESS.
THAT'S RIGHT... I HAVE TO PROTECT MARIA.
THE LIGHT I WISHED FOR IS IN THAT LIGHT.
THE REASON FOR ME TO PROTECT MARIA.
MARIA...
WHAT I WANT MORE THAN ANYTHING ELSE.
MARIA...
slump
HELP ME...
ONLY MARIA CAN GRANT THAT FOR ME.

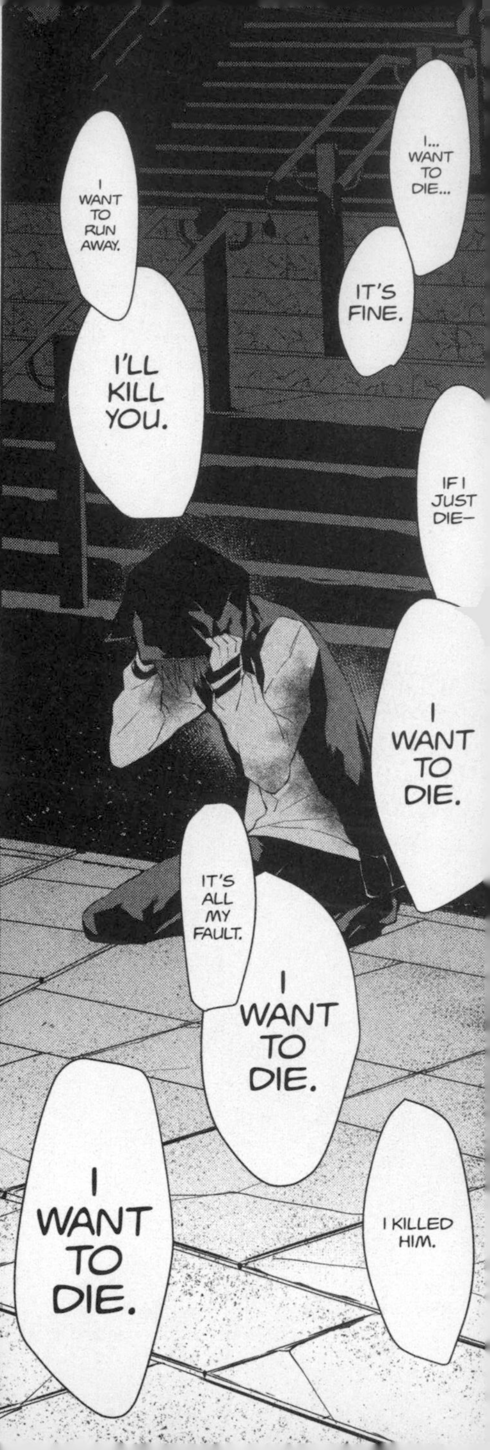
I... WANT TO DIE...
IT'S FINE.
I WANT TO RUN AWAY.
I'LL KILL YOU.
IF I JUST DIE—
I WANT TO DIE.
IT'S ALL MY FAULT.
I WANT TO DIE.
I KILLED HIM.
I WANT TO DIE.
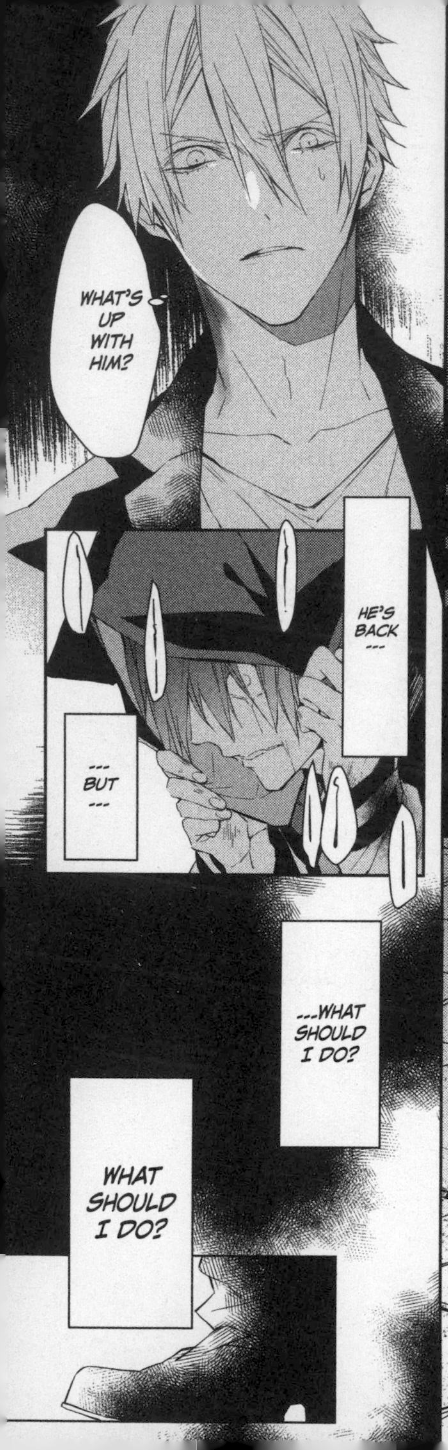
WHAT'S UP WITH HIM?
HE'S BACK ---
--- BUT ---
---WHAT SHOULD I DO?
WHAT SHOULD I DO?

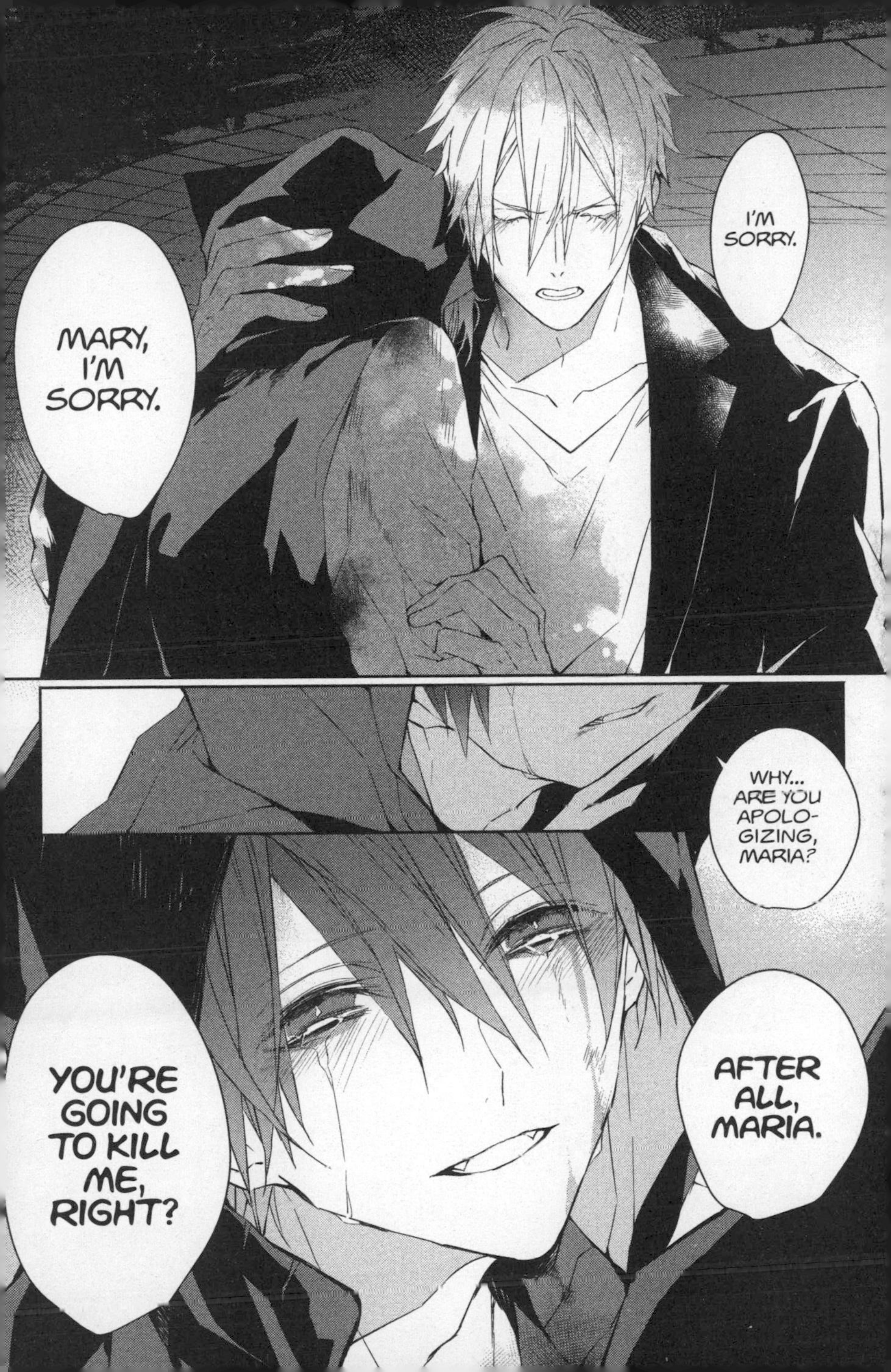
I'M SORRY.
MARY, I'M SORRY.
WHY... ARE YOU APOLOGIZING, MARIA?
AFTER ALL, MARIA.
YOU'RE GOING TO KILL ME, RIGHT?

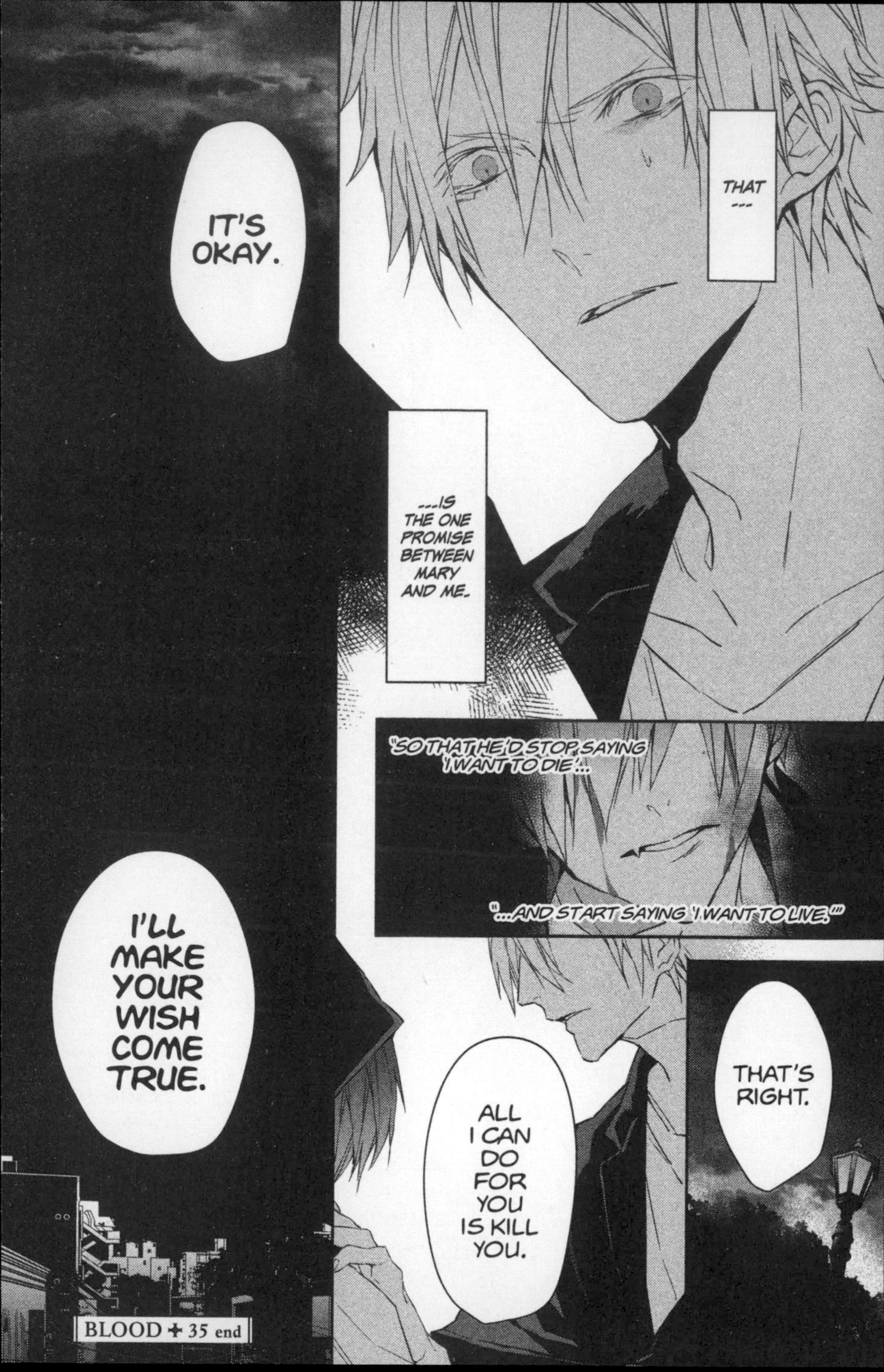
THAT ---
...IS THE ONE PROMISE BETWEEN MARY AND ME.
"SO THAT HE'D STOP SAYING 'I WANT TO DIE'...
"...AND START SAYING 'I WANT TO LIVE.'"
THAT'S RIGHT.
ALL I CAN DO FOR YOU IS KILL YOU.
IT'S OKAY.
I'LL MAKE YOUR WISH COME TRUE.
BLOOD + 35 end

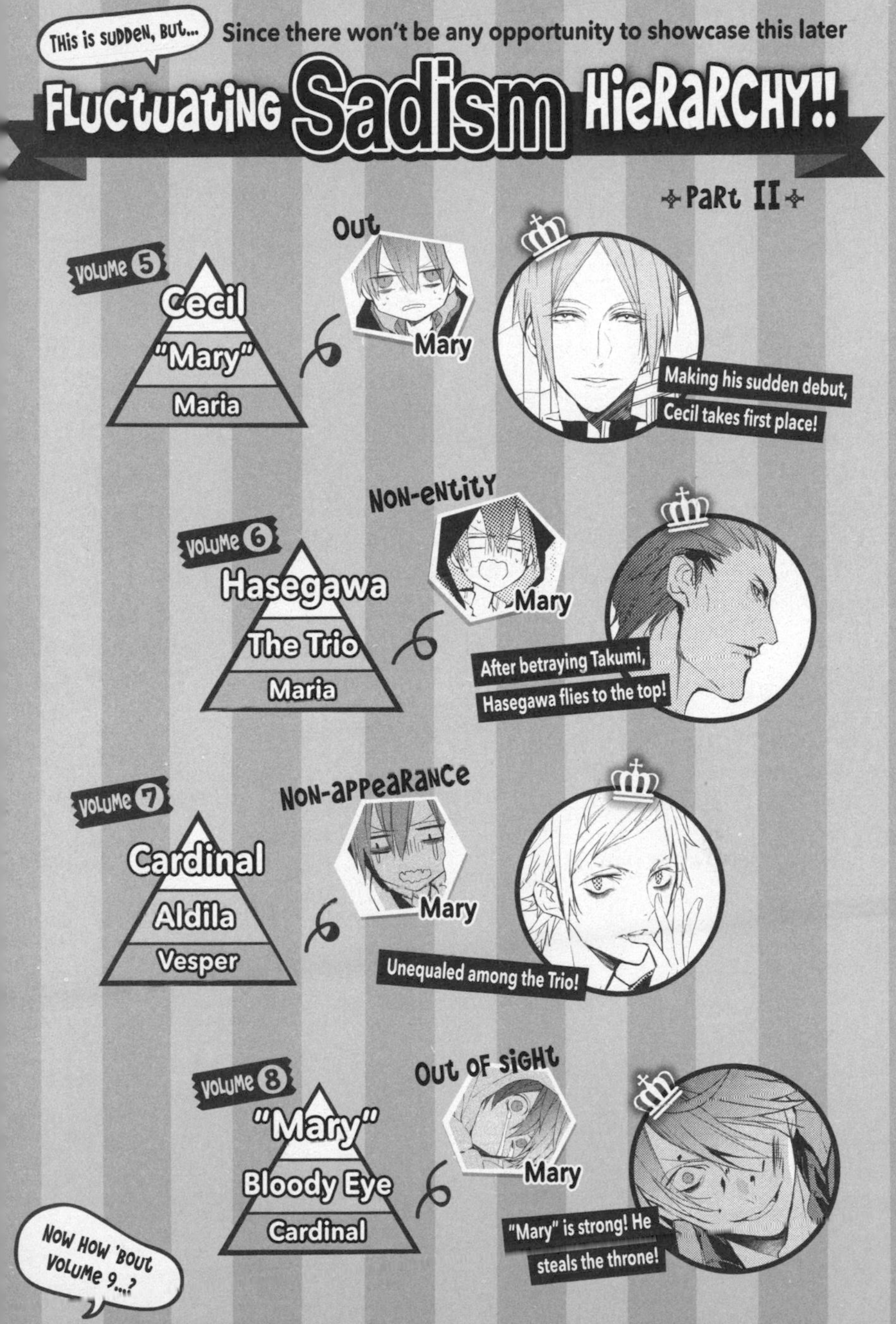

THIS IS SUDDEN, BUT...
Since there won't be any opportunity to showcase this later
FLUCTUATING Sadism HIERARCHY!!
PART II
VOLUME 5
Cecil
"Mary"
Maria
Out
Mary
Making his sudden debut, Cecil takes first place!
VOLUME 6
Hasegawa
The Trio
Maria
NON-ENTITY
Mary
After betraying Takumi, Hasegawa flies to the top!
VOLUME 7
Cardinal
Aldila
Vesper
NON-APPEARANCE
Mary
Unequaled among the Trio!
VOLUME 8
"Mary"
Bloody Eye
Cardinal
OUT OF SIGHT
Mary
"Mary" is strong! He steals the throne!
NOW HOW 'BOUT VOLUME 9...?

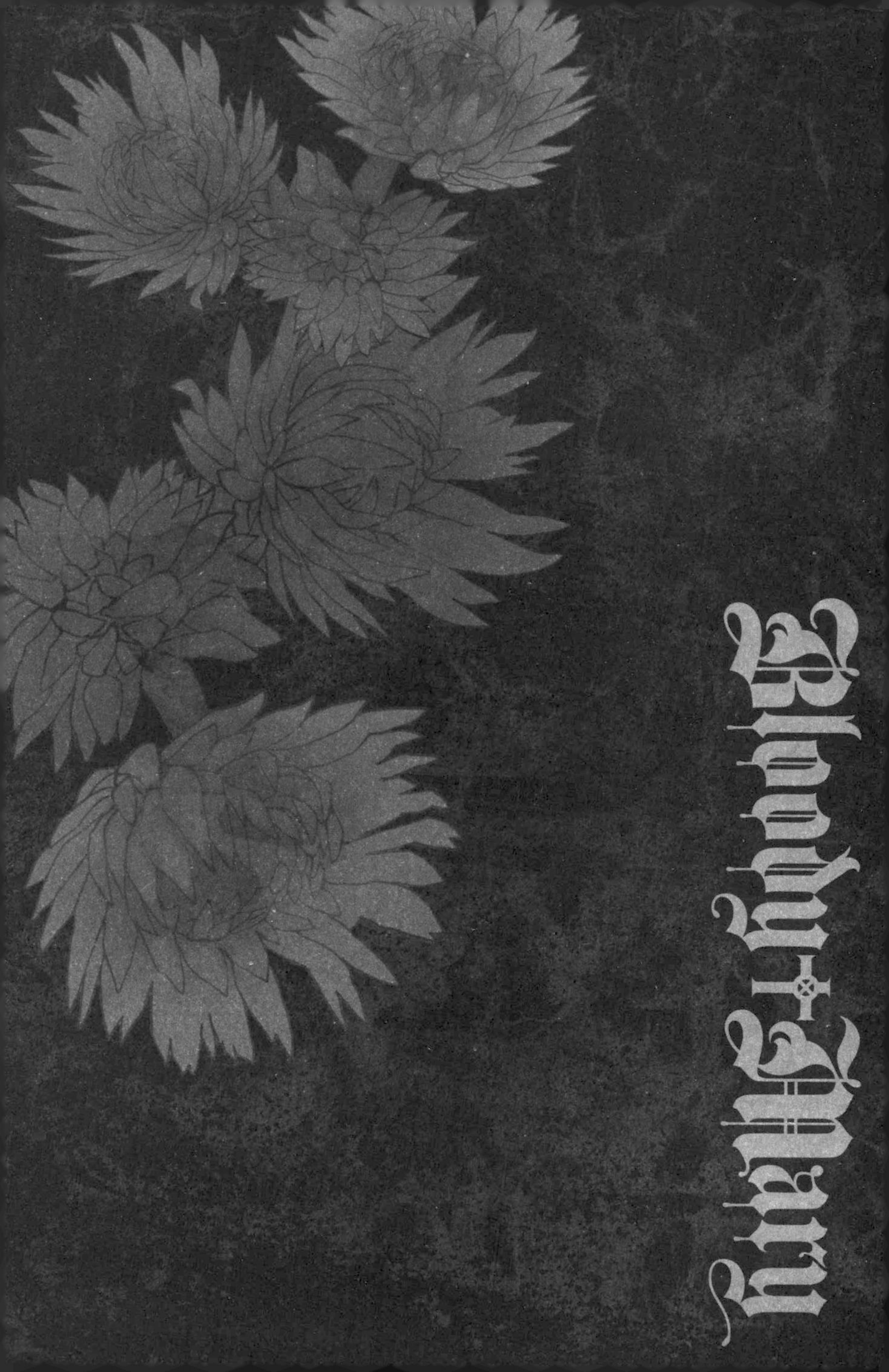
Bloody+Mary

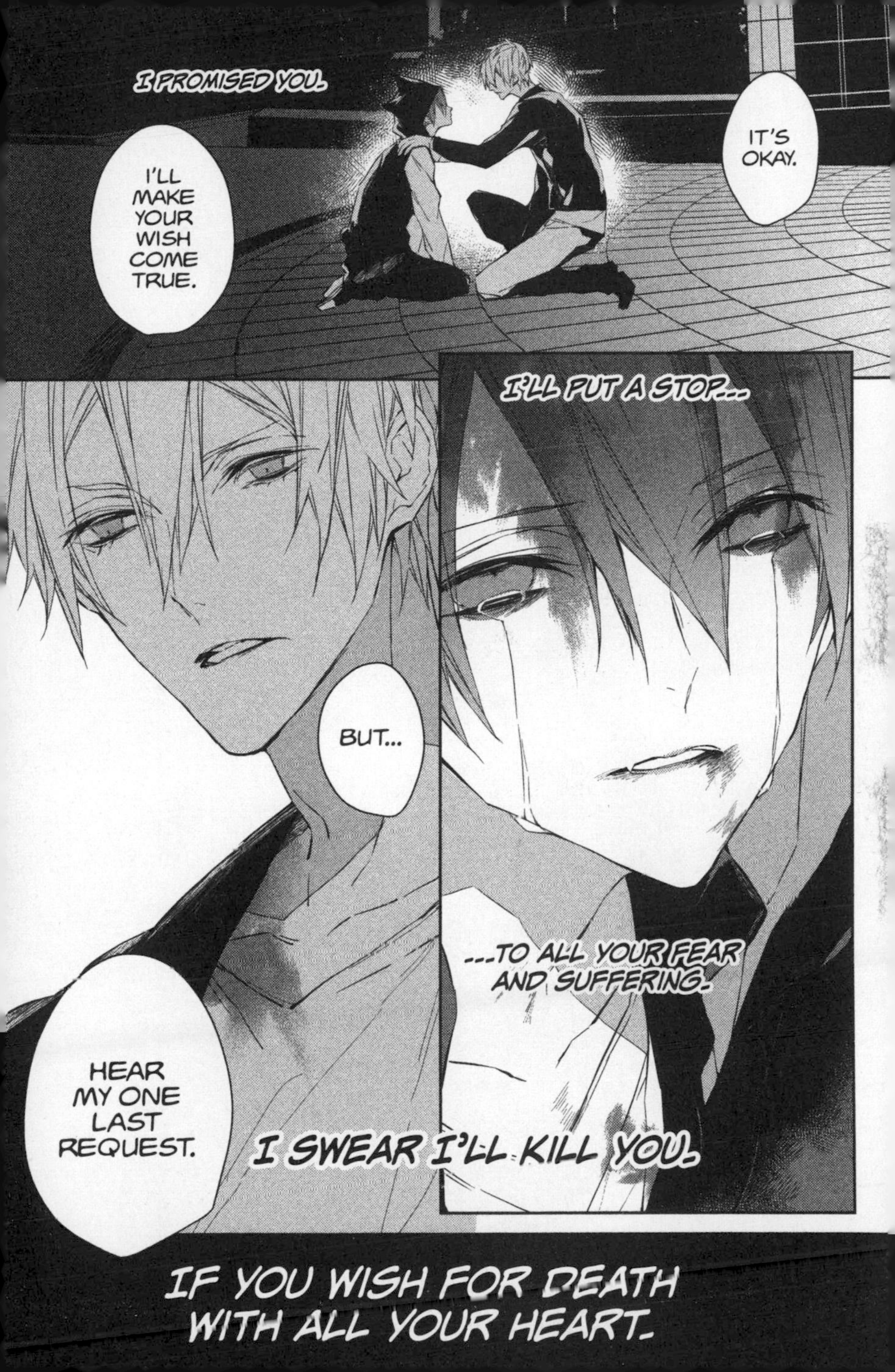
I PROMISED YOU.
IT'S OKAY.
I'LL MAKE YOUR WISH COME TRUE.
I'LL PUT A STOP...
BUT...
...TO ALL YOUR FEAR AND SUFFERING.
HEAR MY ONE LAST REQUEST.
I SWEAR I'LL KILL YOU.
IF YOU WISH FOR DEATH WITH ALL YOUR HEART.

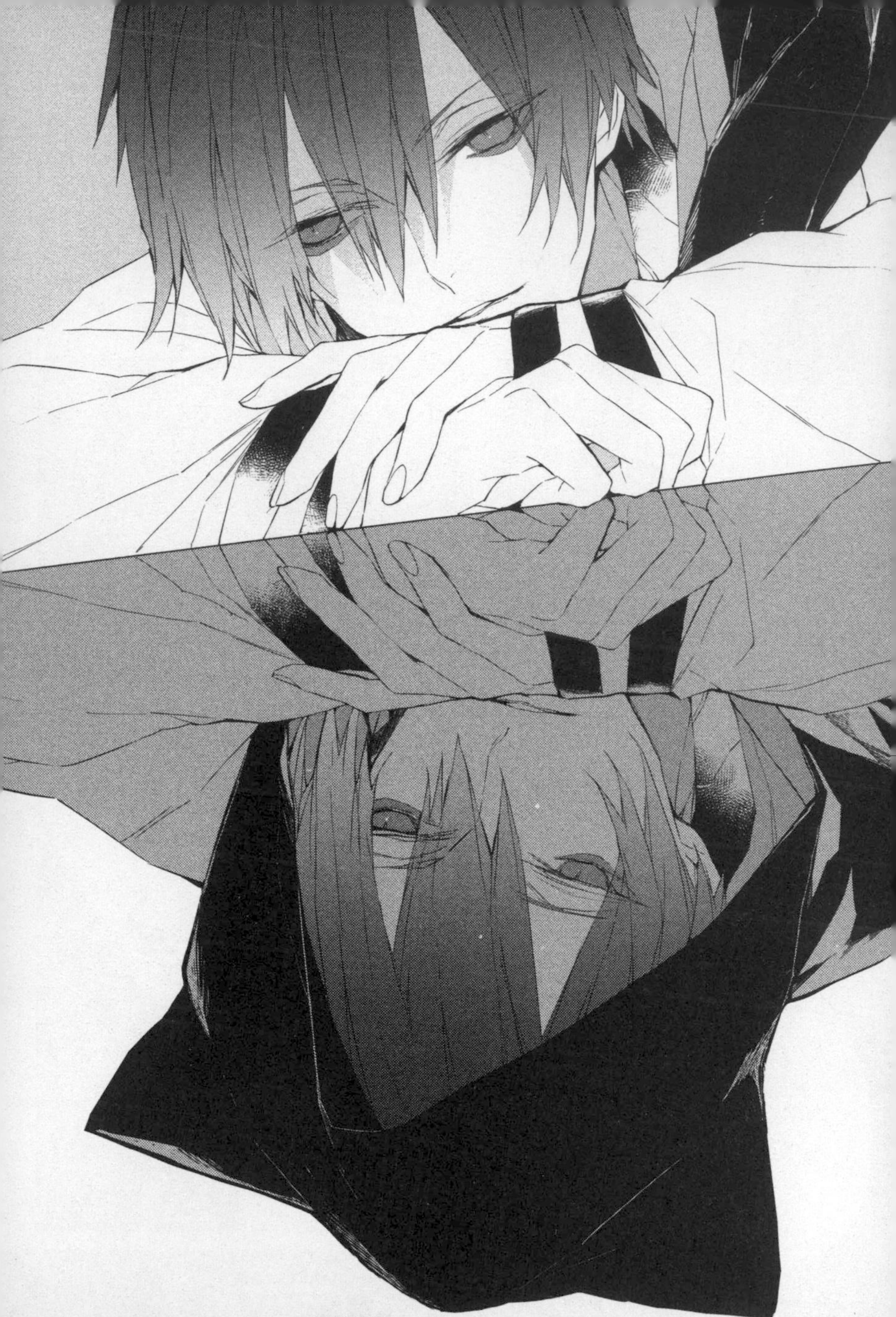

BLOOD ✣ 36 Mary and "Mary"

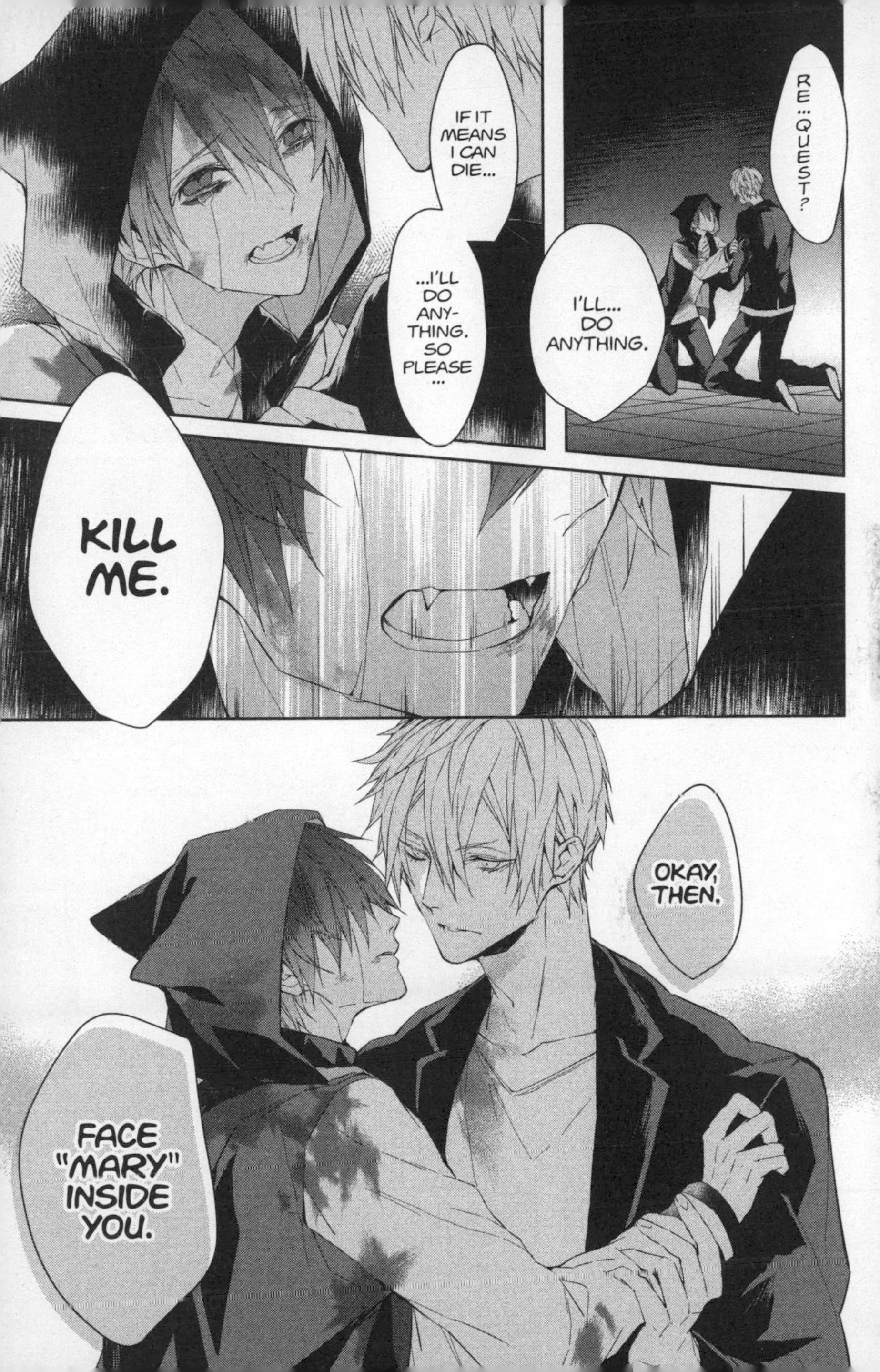
RE...QUEST?
I'LL... DO ANYTHING.
IF IT MEANS I CAN DIE...
...I'LL DO ANYTHING. SO PLEASE...
KILL ME.
OKAY, THEN.
FACE "MARY" INSIDE YOU.

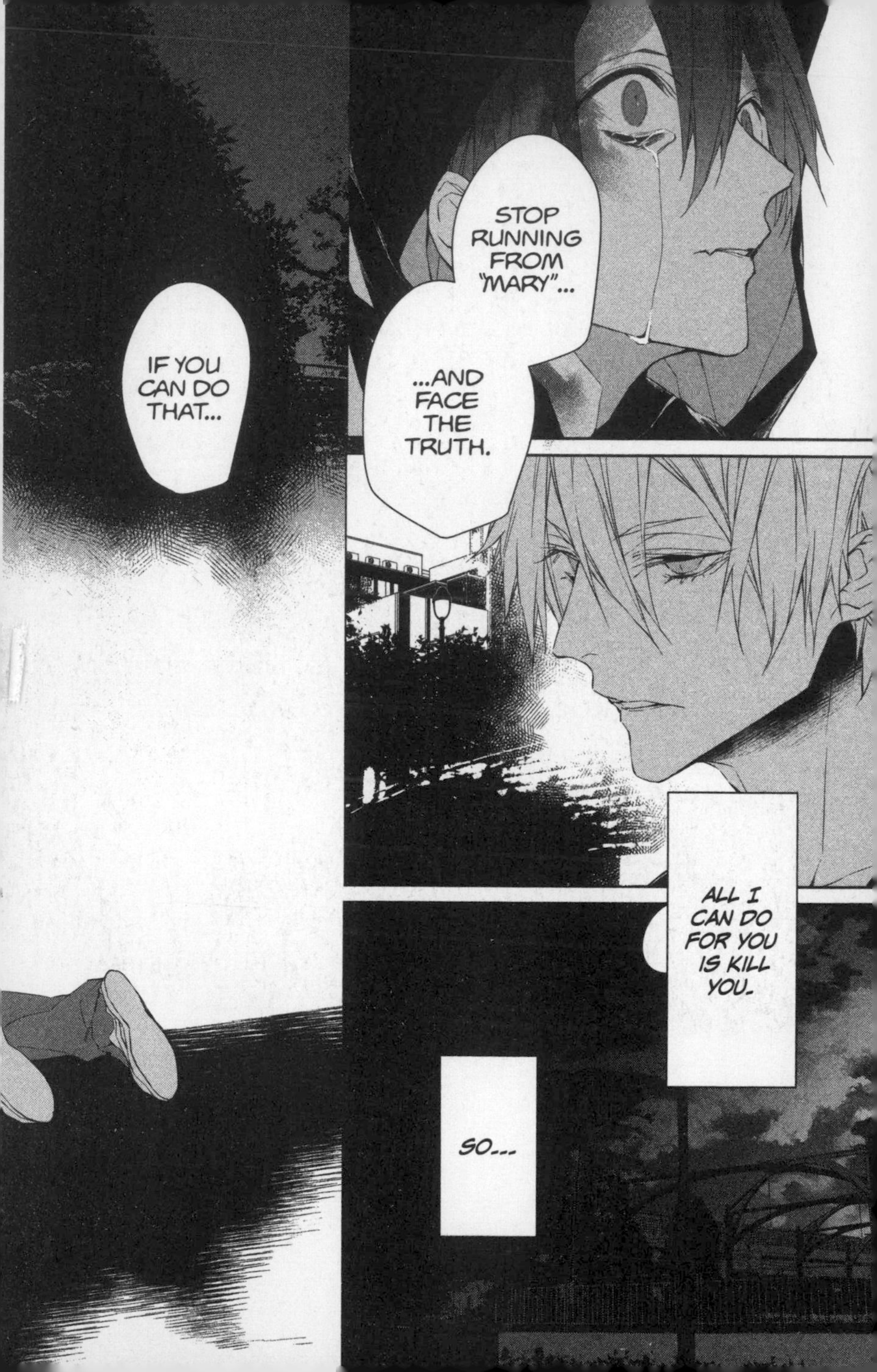
STOP RUNNING FROM "MARY"...
...AND FACE THE TRUTH.
ALL I CAN DO FOR YOU IS KILL YOU.
SO...
IF YOU CAN DO THAT...

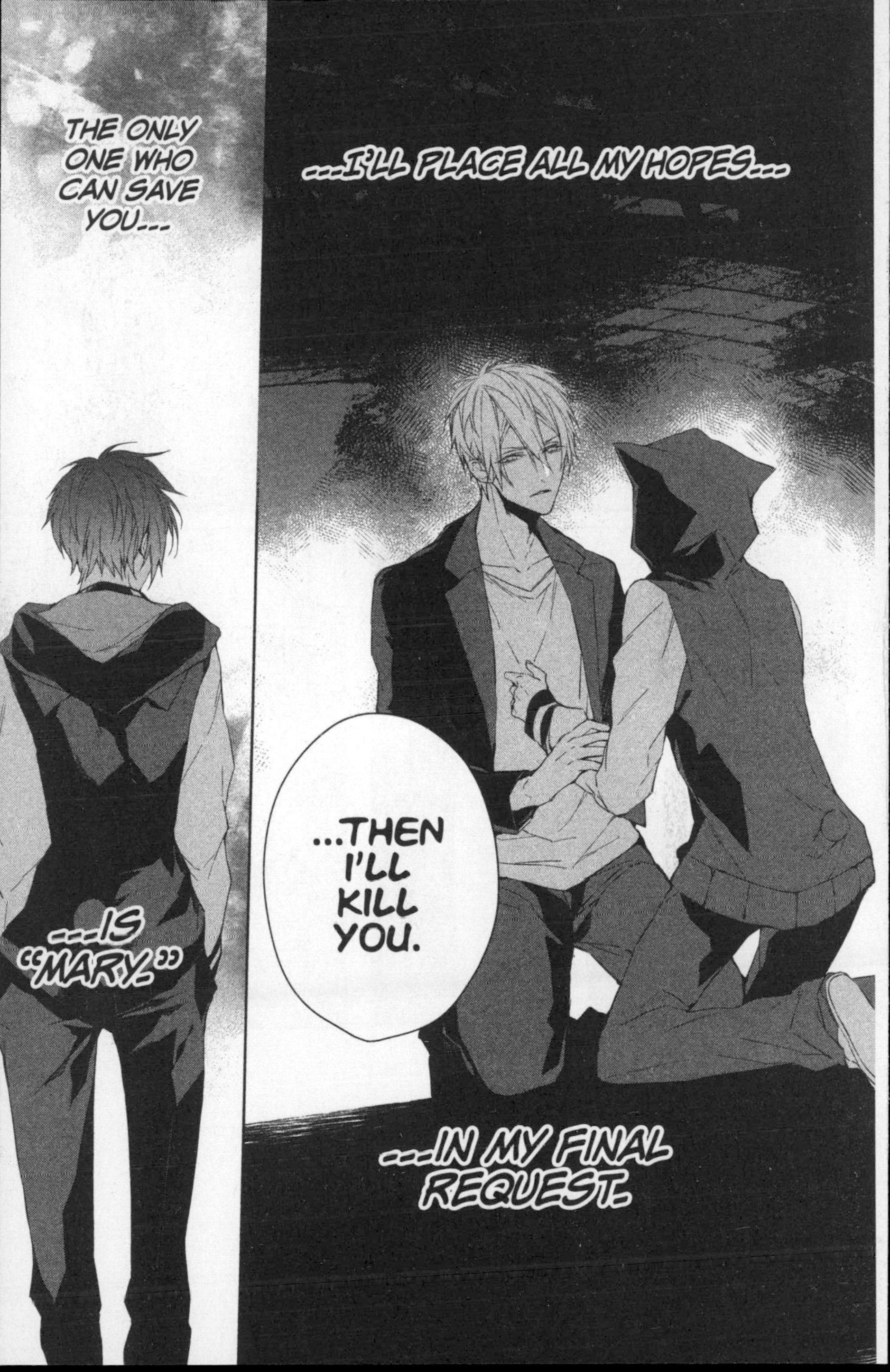
...I'LL PLACE ALL MY HOPES...
...THEN I'LL KILL YOU.
...IN MY FINAL REQUEST.
THE ONLY ONE WHO CAN SAVE YOU...
...IS "MARY."

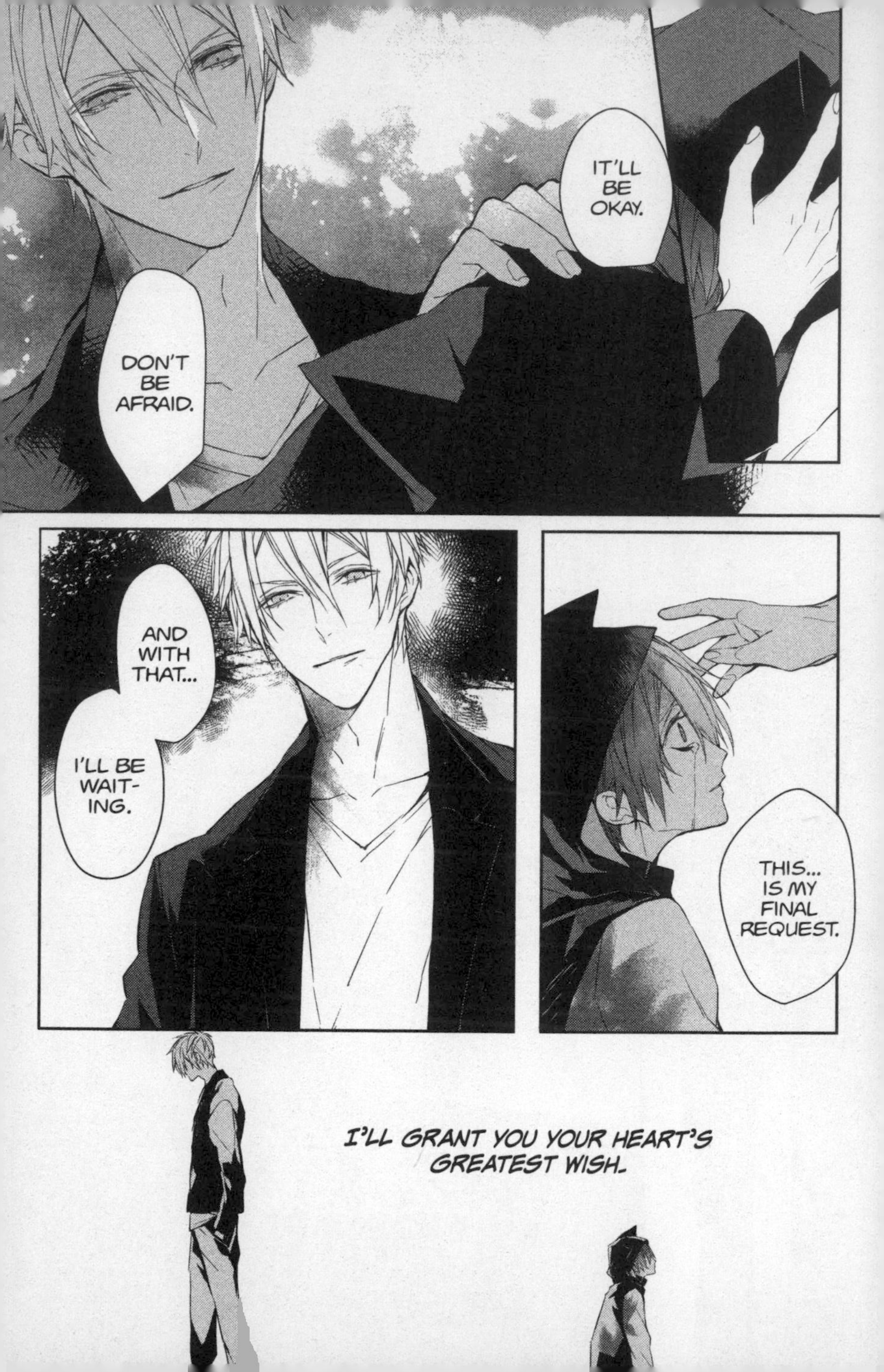
IT'LL BE OKAY.
DON'T BE AFRAID.
THIS... IS MY FINAL REQUEST.
AND WITH THAT...
I'LL BE WAIT-ING.
I'LL GRANT YOU YOUR HEART'S GREATEST WISH.

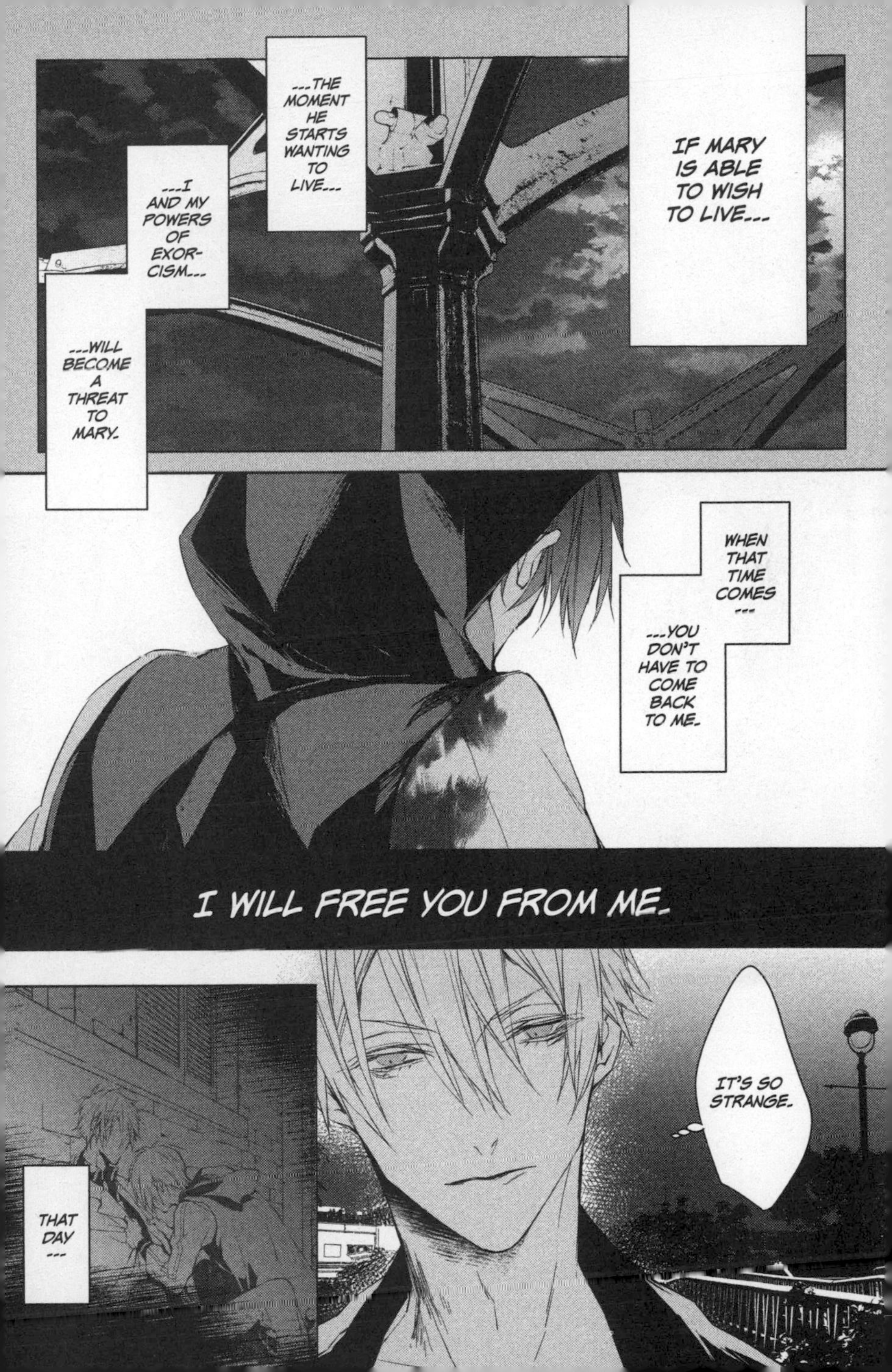
IF MARY IS ABLE TO WISH TO LIVE...
...THE MOMENT HE STARTS WANTING TO LIVE...
...I AND MY POWERS OF EXORCISM...
...WILL BECOME A THREAT TO MARY.
WHEN THAT TIME COMES ---
...YOU DON'T HAVE TO COME BACK TO ME.
I WILL FREE YOU FROM ME.
IT'S SO STRANGE.
THAT DAY ---

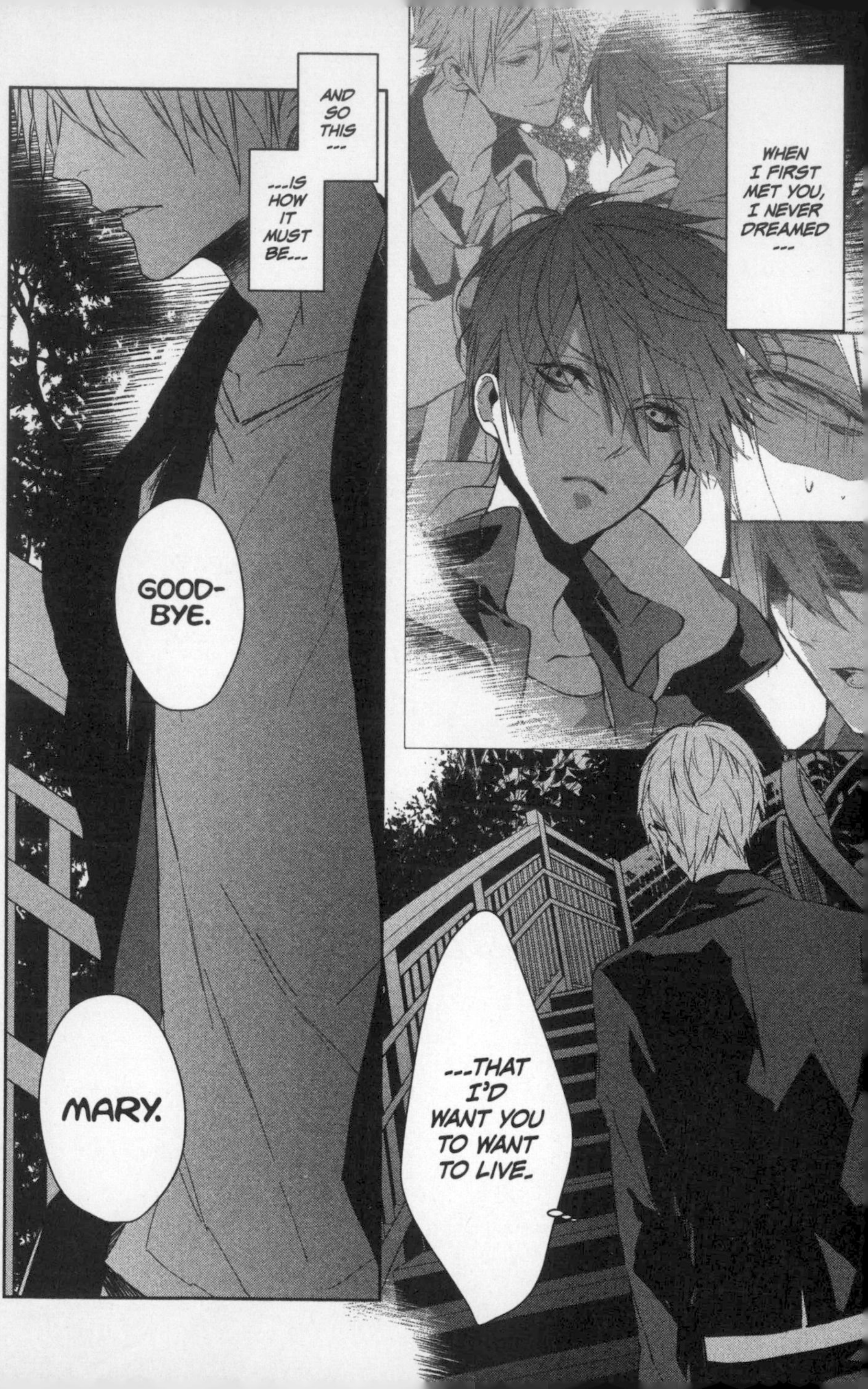
WHEN I FIRST MET YOU, I NEVER DREAMED ---
---THAT I'D WANT YOU TO WANT TO LIVE.
AND SO THIS ---
---IS HOW IT MUST BE...
GOOD-BYE.
MARY.

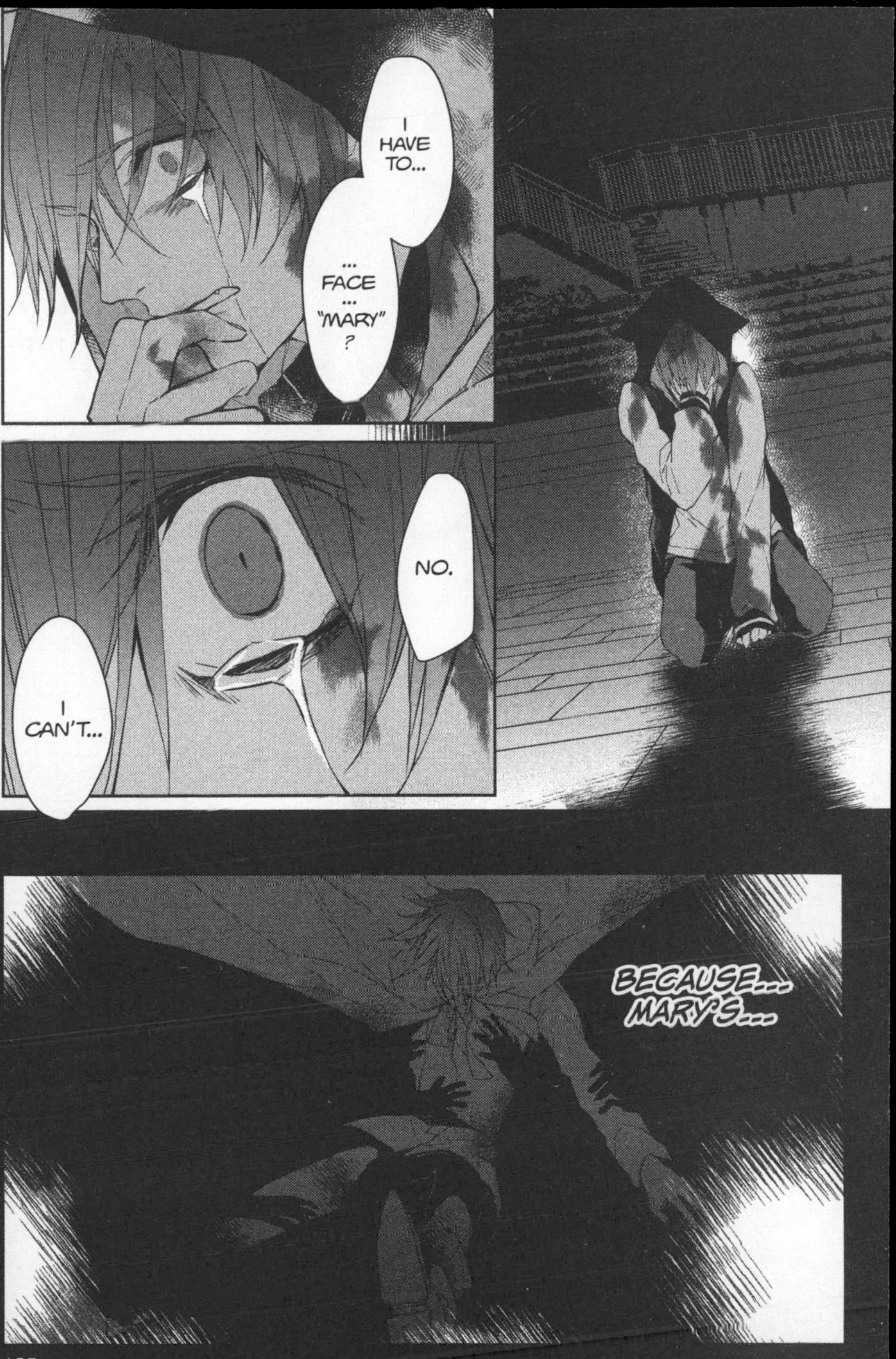
I HAVE TO...
... FACE ... "MARY" ?
NO.
I CAN'T...
BECAUSE... MARY'S...

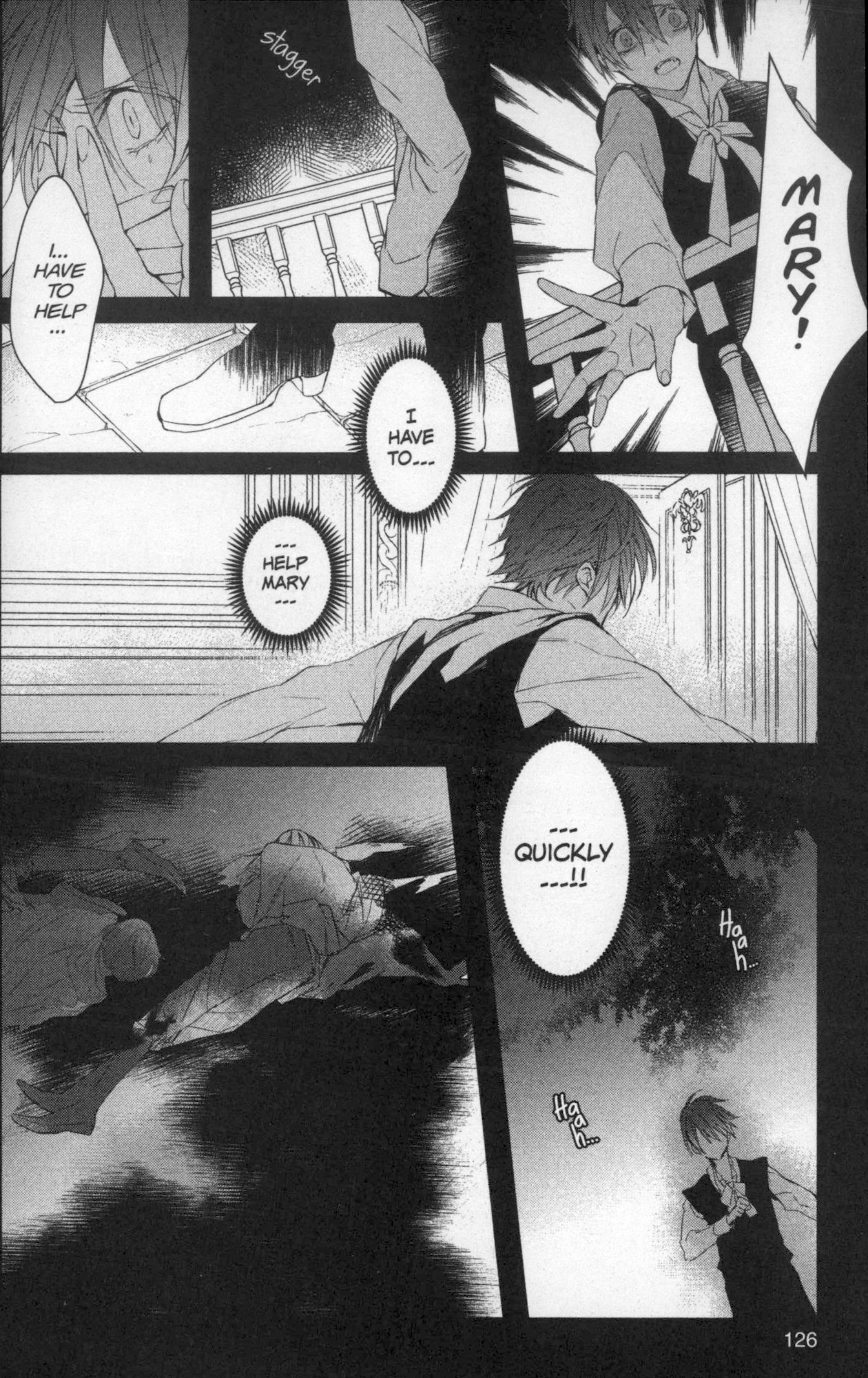
MARY!
stagger
I... HAVE TO HELP...
I HAVE TO---
---HELP MARY---
---QUICKLY---!!
Haah...
Haah...

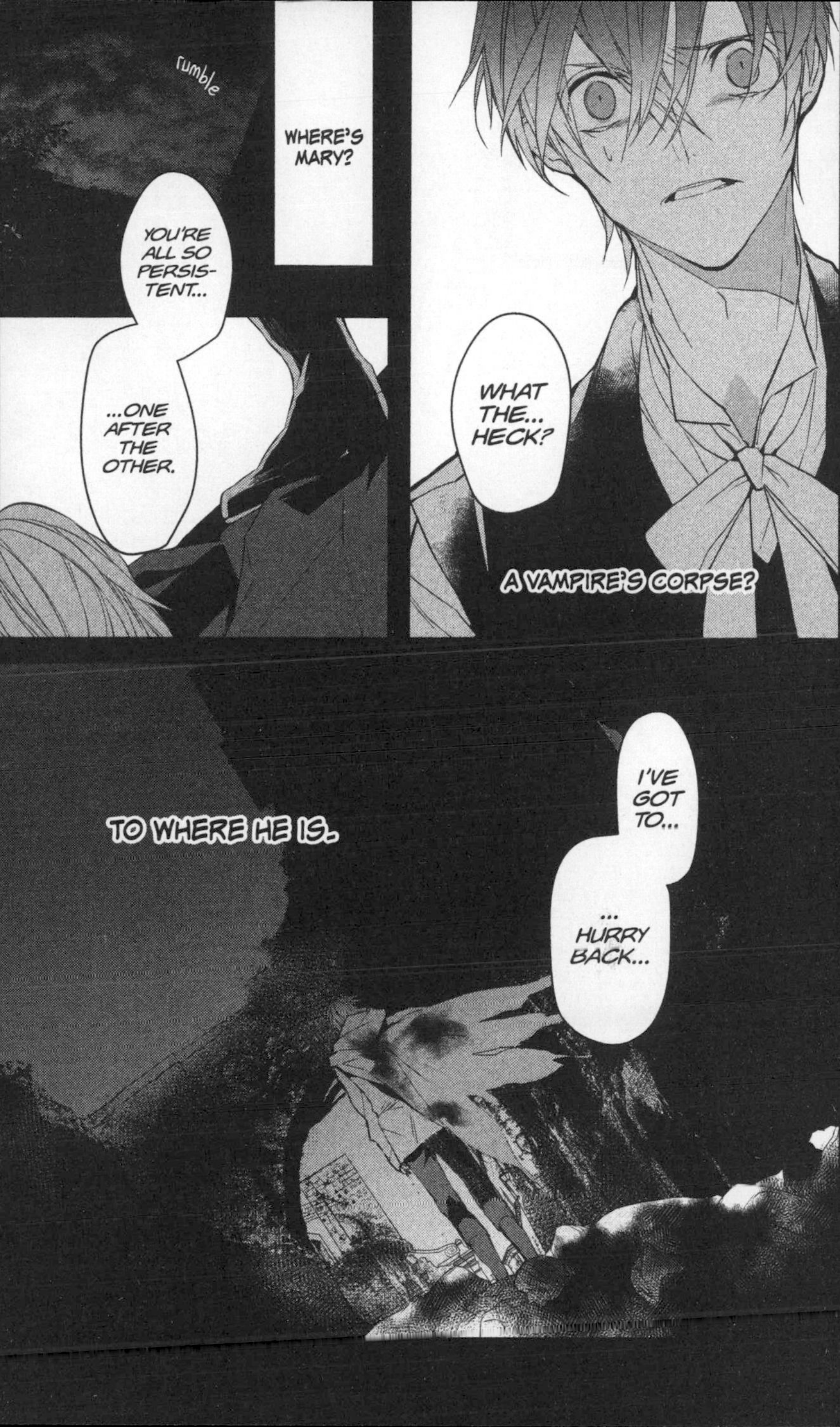
WHAT THE... HECK?
A VAMPIRE'S CORPSE?
rumble
WHERE'S MARY?
YOU'RE ALL SO PERSIS-TENT...
...ONE AFTER THE OTHER.
I'VE GOT TO...
...HURRY BACK...
TO WHERE HE IS.

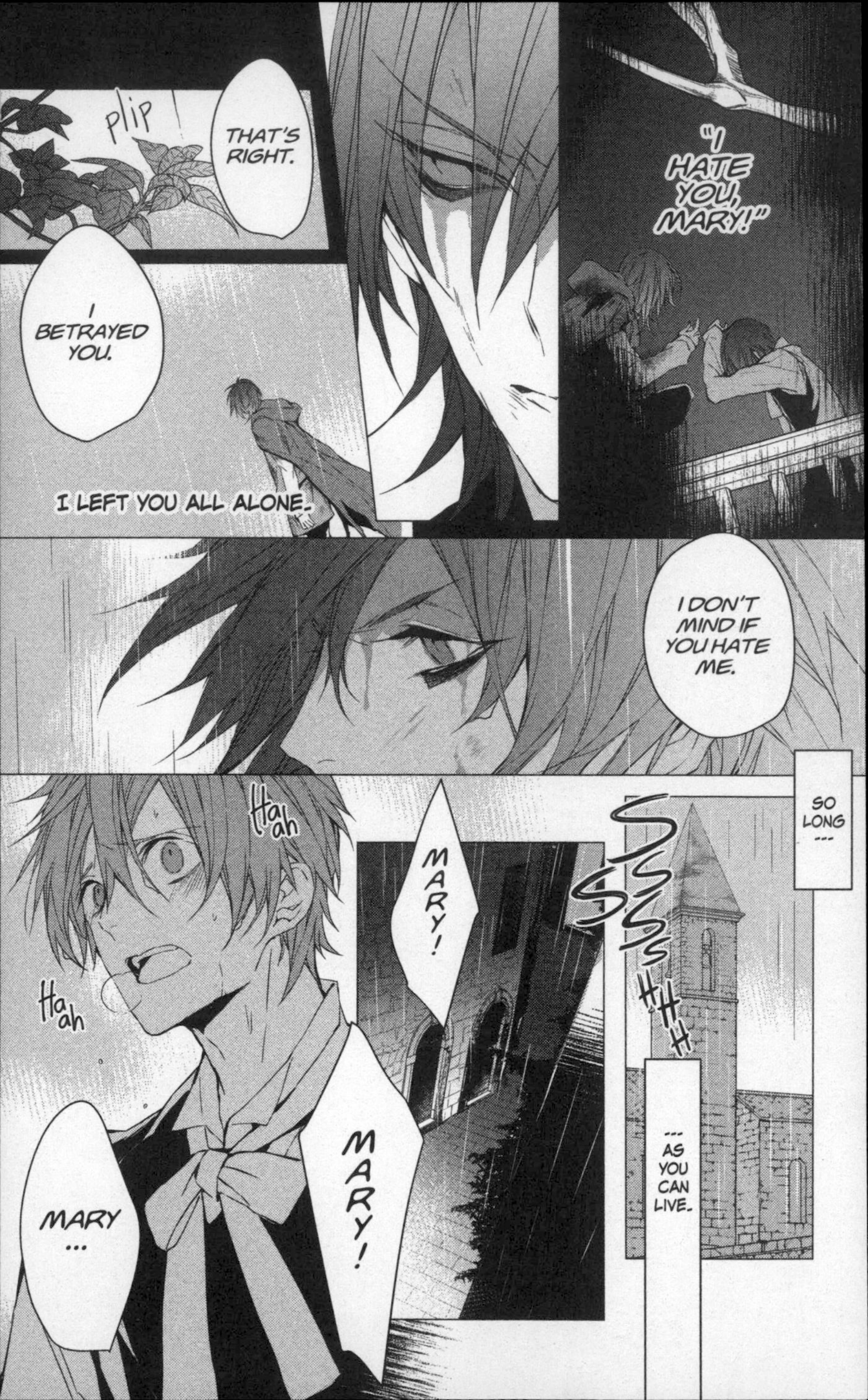
"I HATE YOU, MARY!"
plip
THAT'S RIGHT.
I BETRAYED YOU.
I LEFT YOU ALL ALONE...
I DON'T MIND IF YOU HATE ME.
SO LONG ---
SSSHHH
--- AS YOU CAN LIVE.
MARY!
MARY!
Haah
Haah
MARY ...

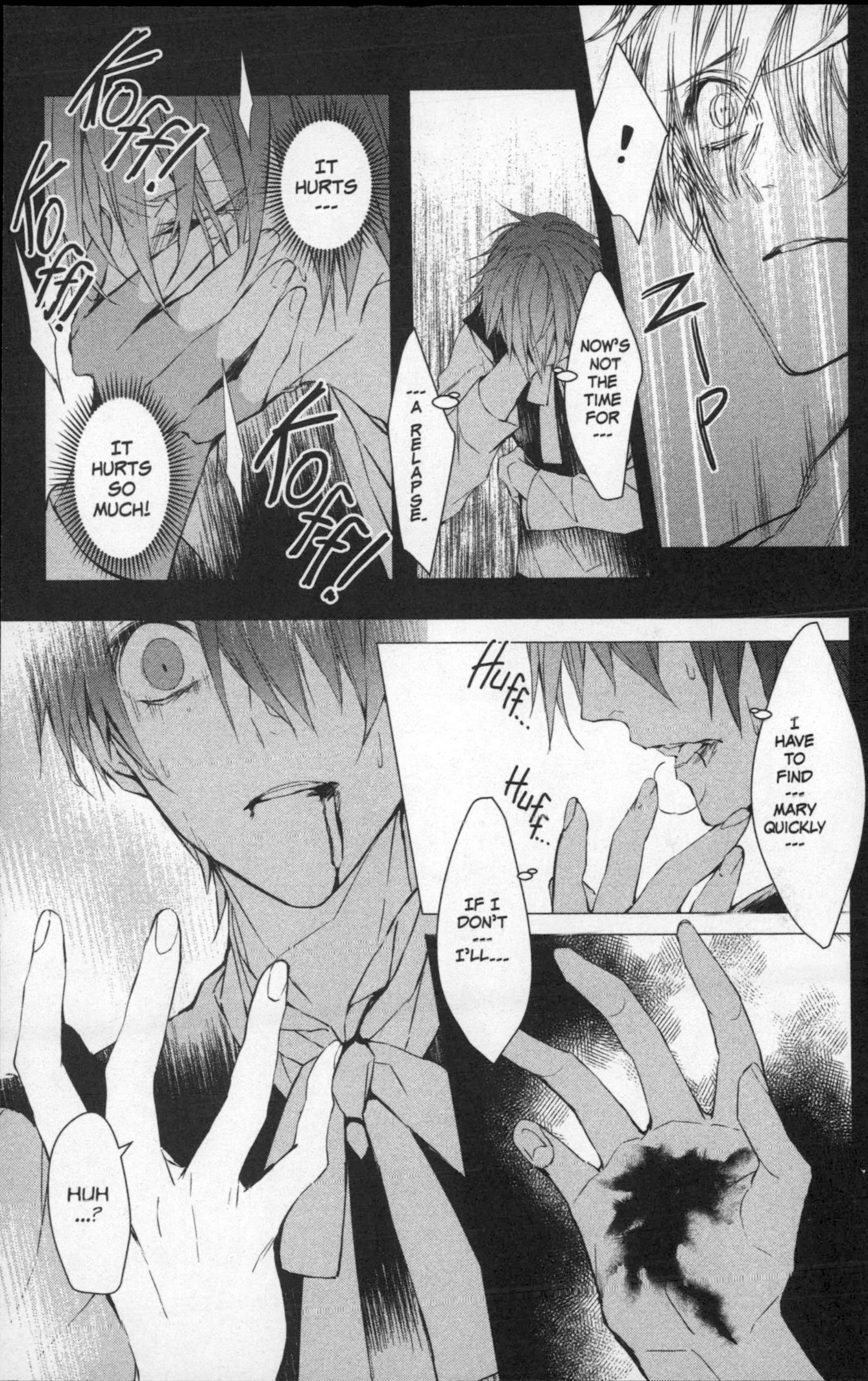
!
ZIP
NOW'S NOT THE TIME FOR ---
--- A RELAPSE.
IT HURTS ---
KOFF! KOFF!
KOFF!
IT HURTS SO MUCH!
I HAVE TO FIND --- MARY QUICKLY ---
HUFF...
HUFF...
IF I DON'T --- I'LL...
HUH ...?

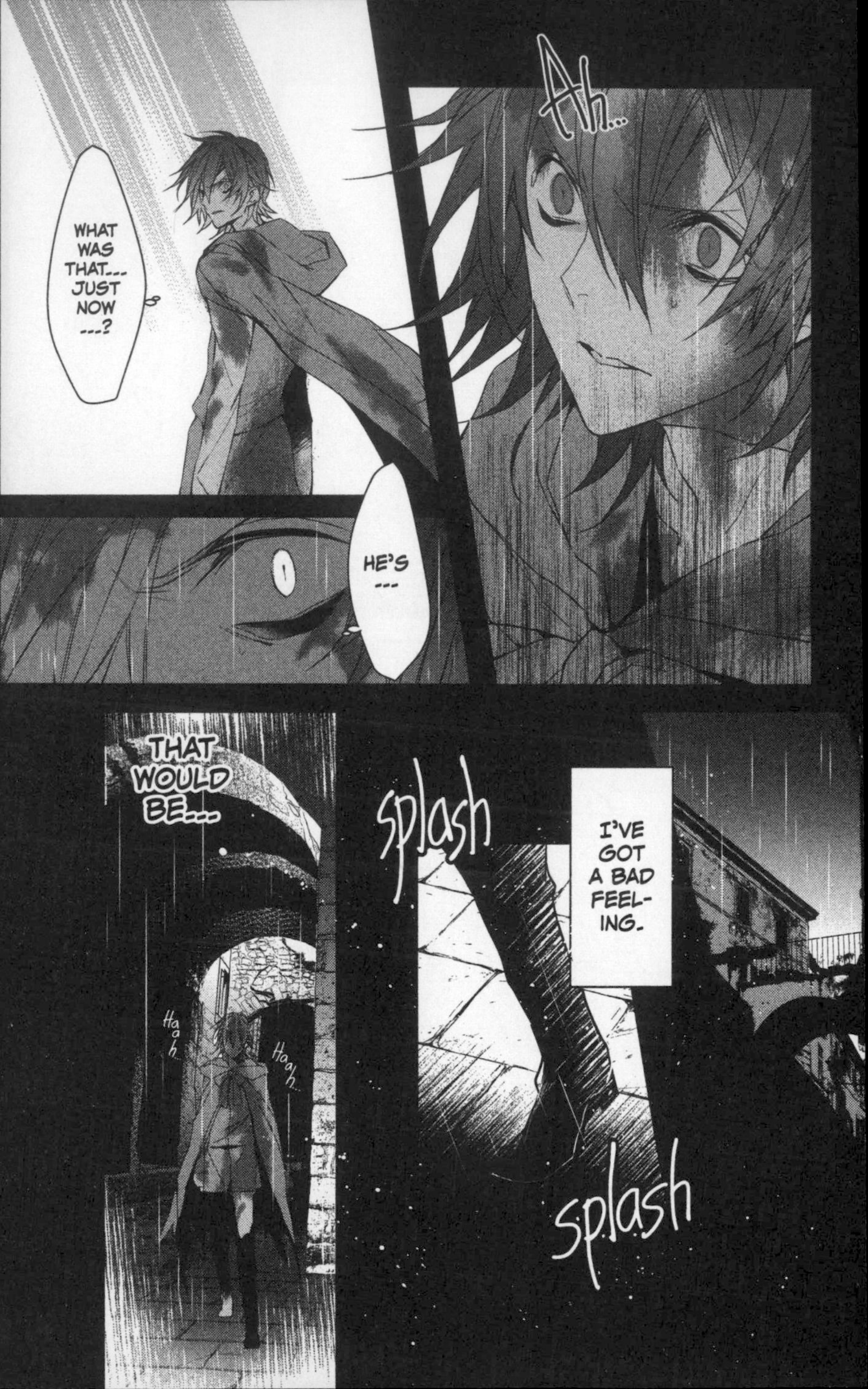
Ah...
WHAT WAS THAT... JUST NOW ...?
HE'S ---
splash
I'VE GOT A BAD FEEL-ING.
splash
THAT WOULD BE...
Haah...
Haah...

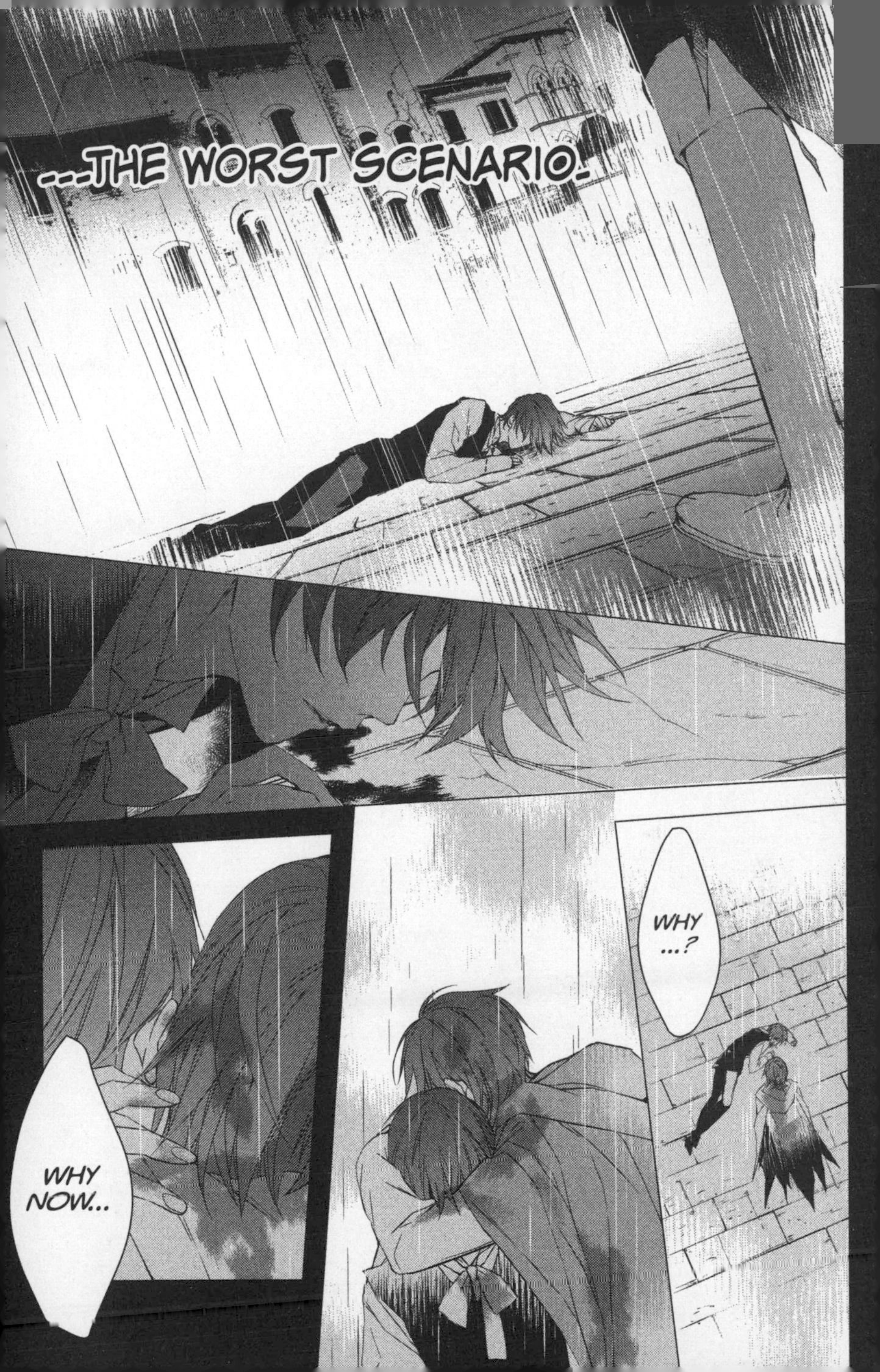
...THE WORST SCENARIO.
WHY ...?
WHY NOW...

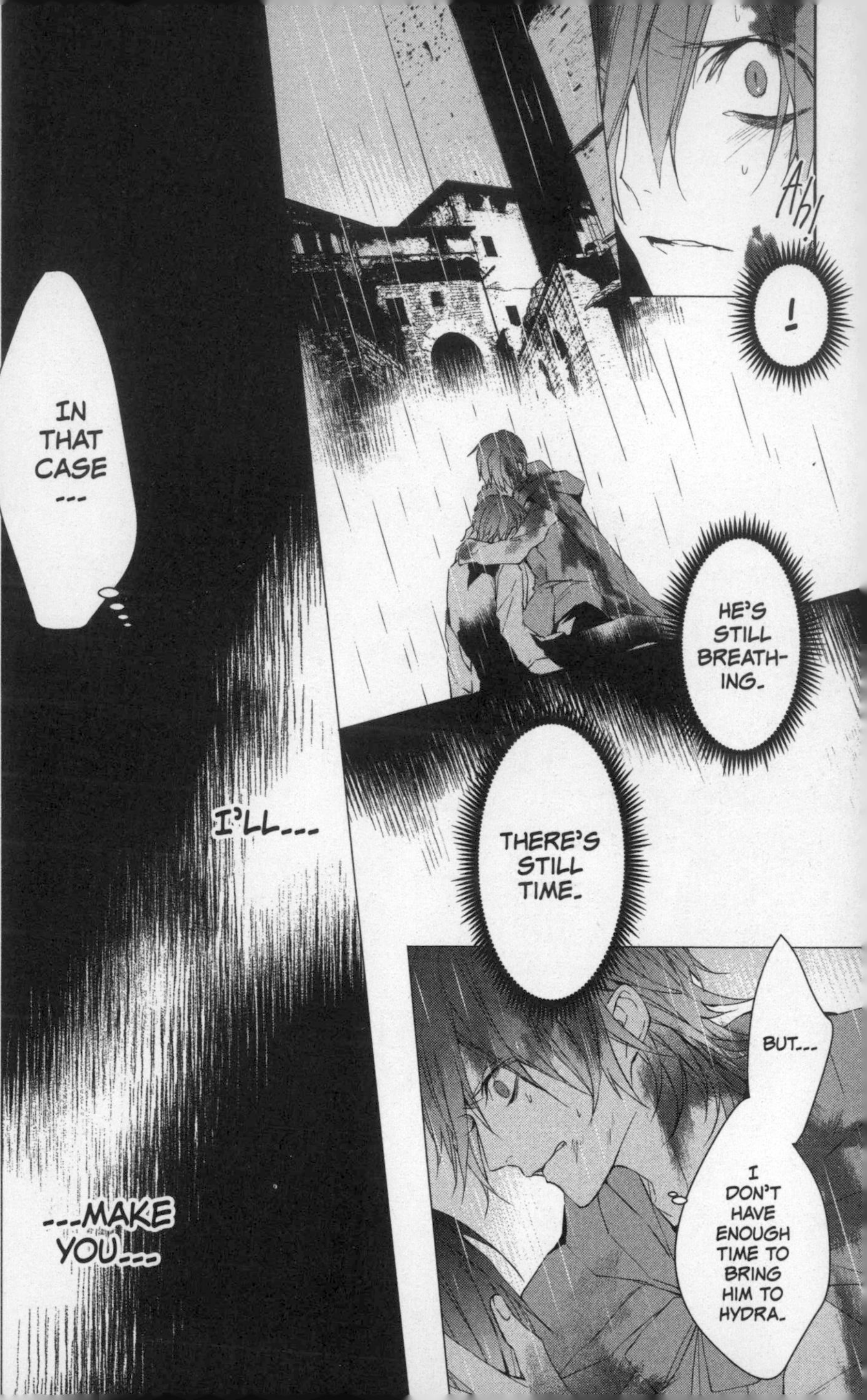
AH!
!
HE'S STILL BREATHING.
THERE'S STILL TIME.
BUT...
I DON'T HAVE ENOUGH TIME TO BRING HIM TO HYDRA.
IN THAT CASE ---
I'LL...
---MAKE YOU...

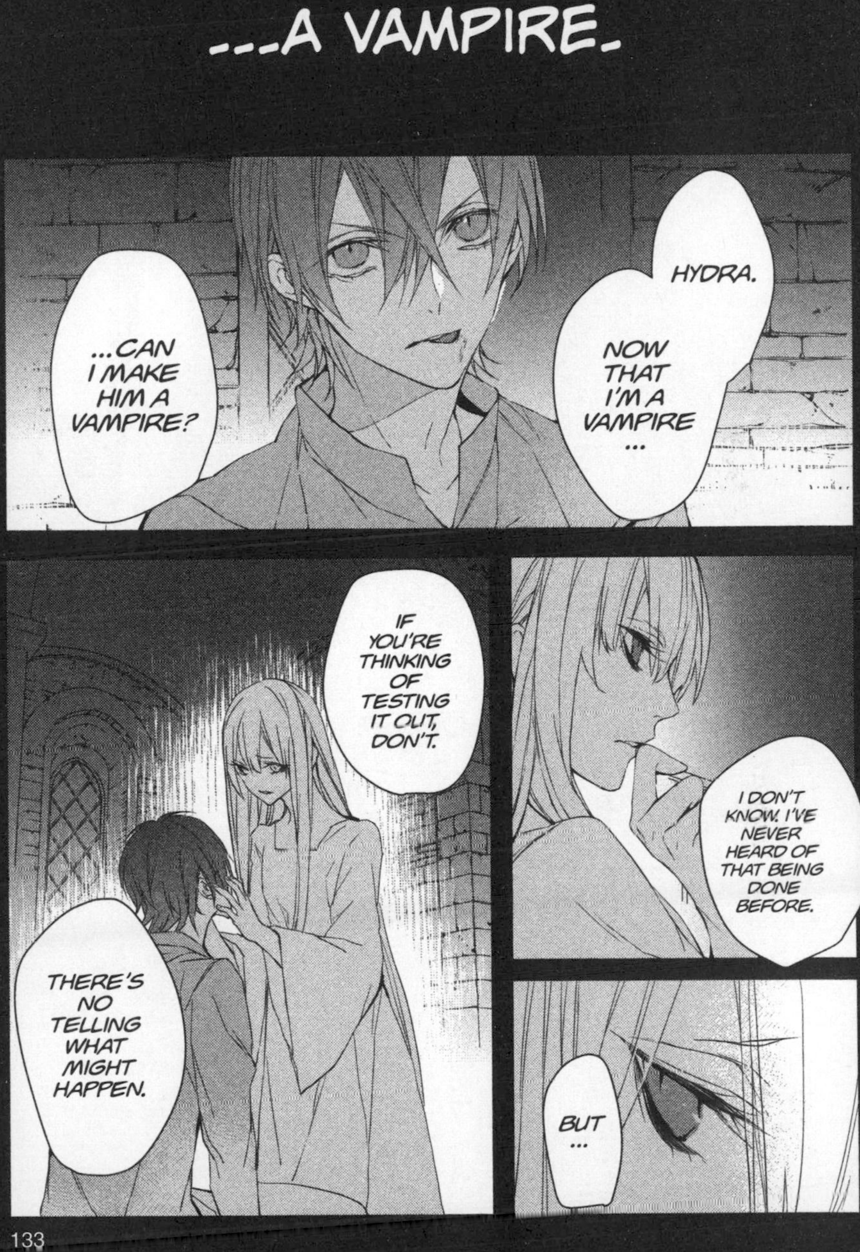

...A VAMPIRE.
HYDRA.
NOW THAT I'M A VAMPIRE...
...CAN I MAKE HIM A VAMPIRE?
I DON'T KNOW. I'VE NEVER HEARD OF THAT BEING DONE BEFORE.
BUT...
IF YOU'RE THINKING OF TESTING IT OUT, DON'T.
THERE'S NO TELLING WHAT MIGHT HAPPEN.

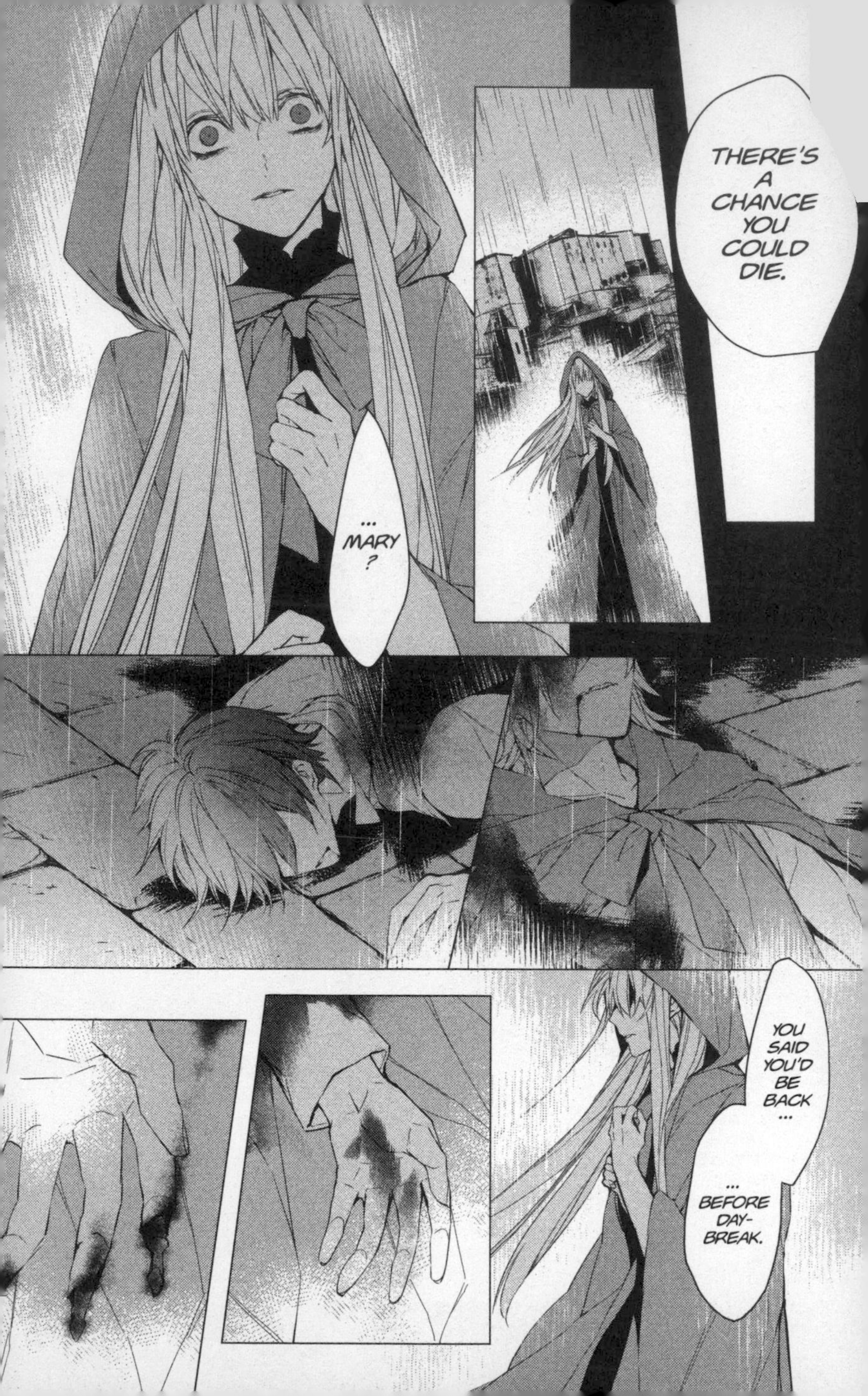
THERE'S A CHANCE YOU COULD DIE.
... MARY?
YOU SAID YOU'D BE BACK...
... BEFORE DAY-BREAK.

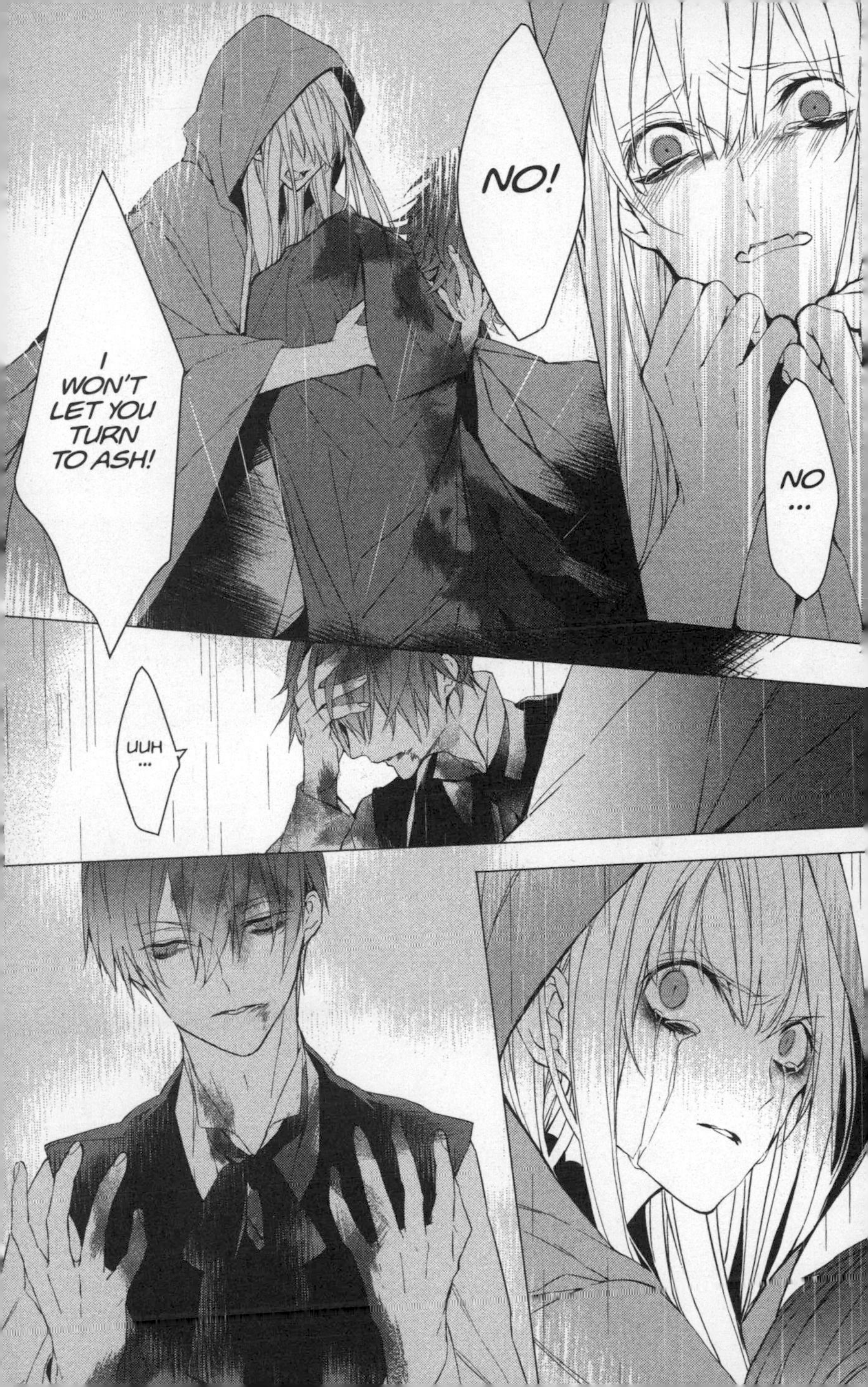
NO!
NO ...
I WON'T LET YOU TURN TO ASH!
UUH ...

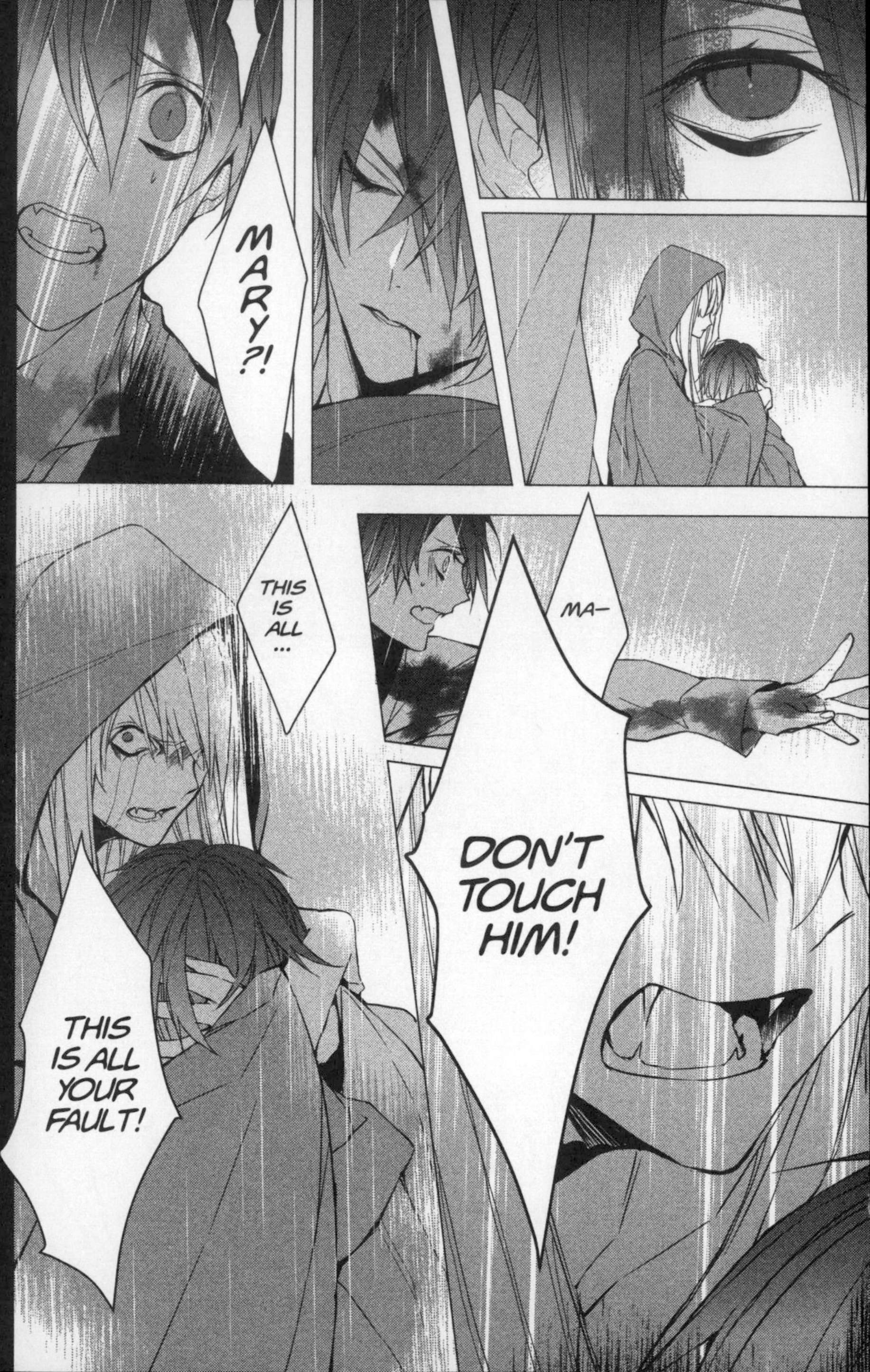
MARY?!
MA—
DON'T TOUCH HIM!
THIS IS ALL...
THIS IS ALL YOUR FAULT!

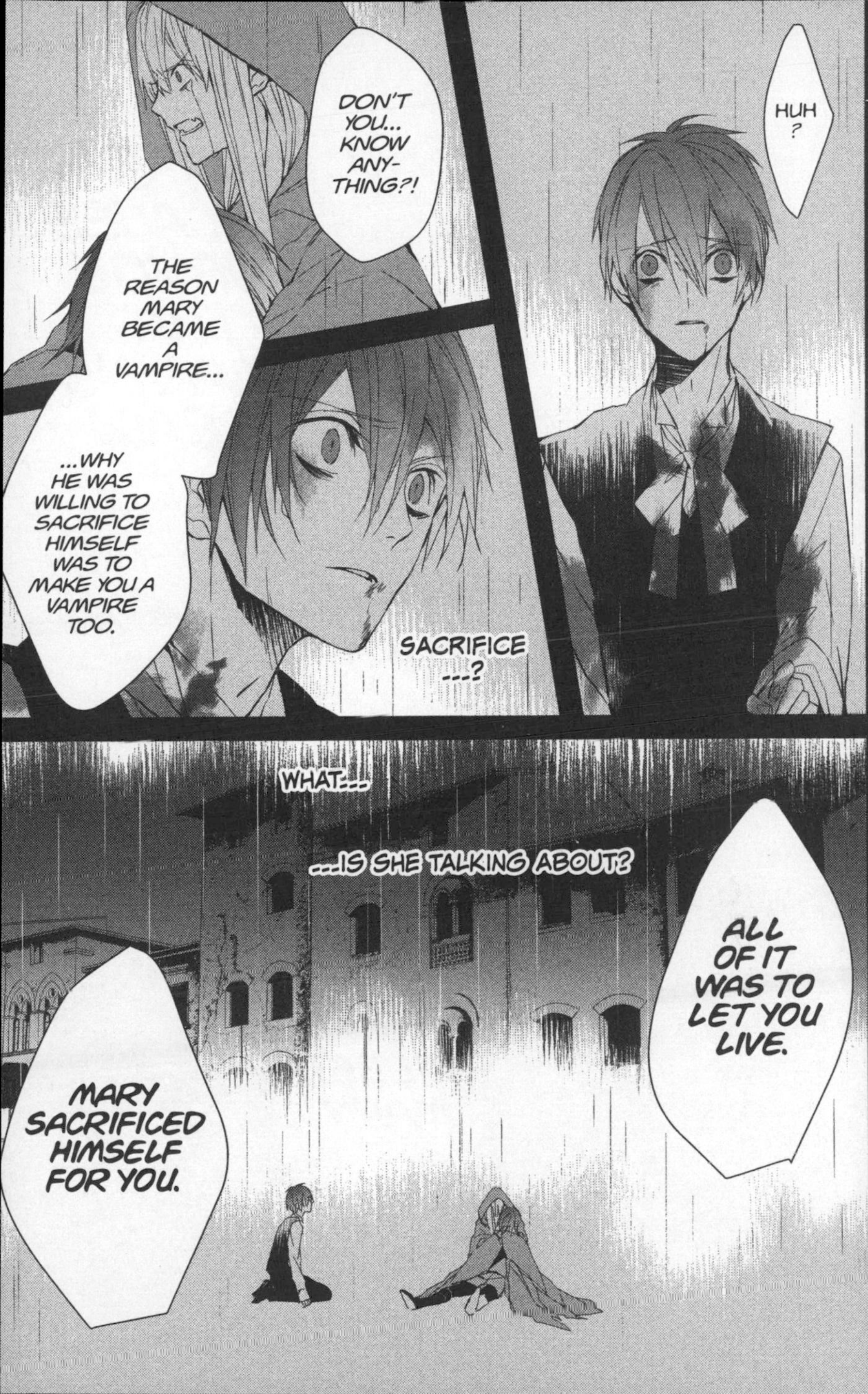
HUH?
DON'T YOU... KNOW ANYTHING?!
THE REASON MARY BECAME A VAMPIRE...
...WHY HE WAS WILLING TO SACRIFICE HIMSELF WAS TO MAKE YOU A VAMPIRE TOO.
SACRIFICE---?
WHAT---
---IS SHE TALKING ABOUT?
ALL OF IT WAS TO LET YOU LIVE.
MARY SACRIFICED HIMSELF FOR YOU.

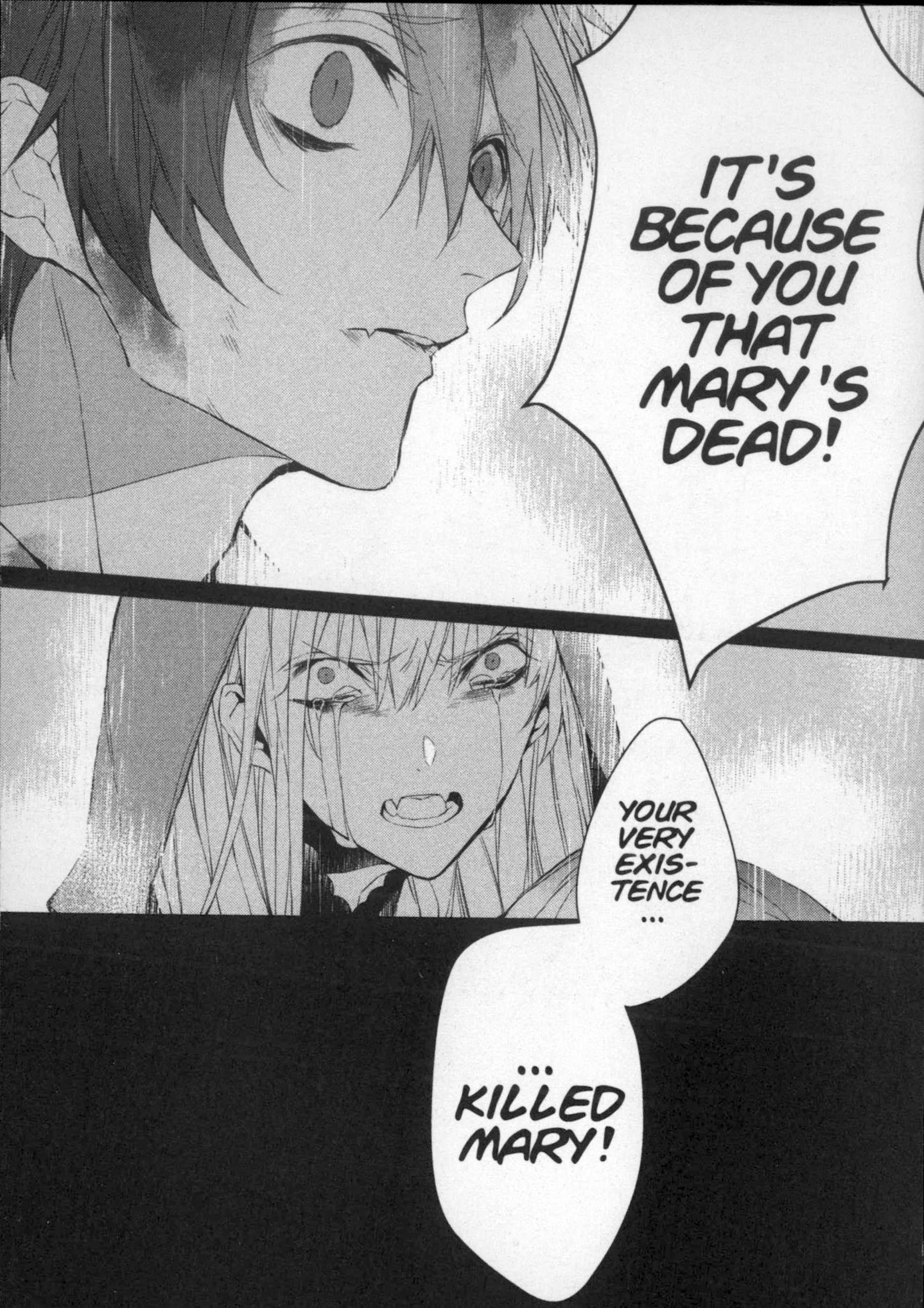
IT'S BECAUSE OF YOU THAT MARY'S DEAD!
YOUR VERY EXIS-TENCE ...
... KILLED MARY!

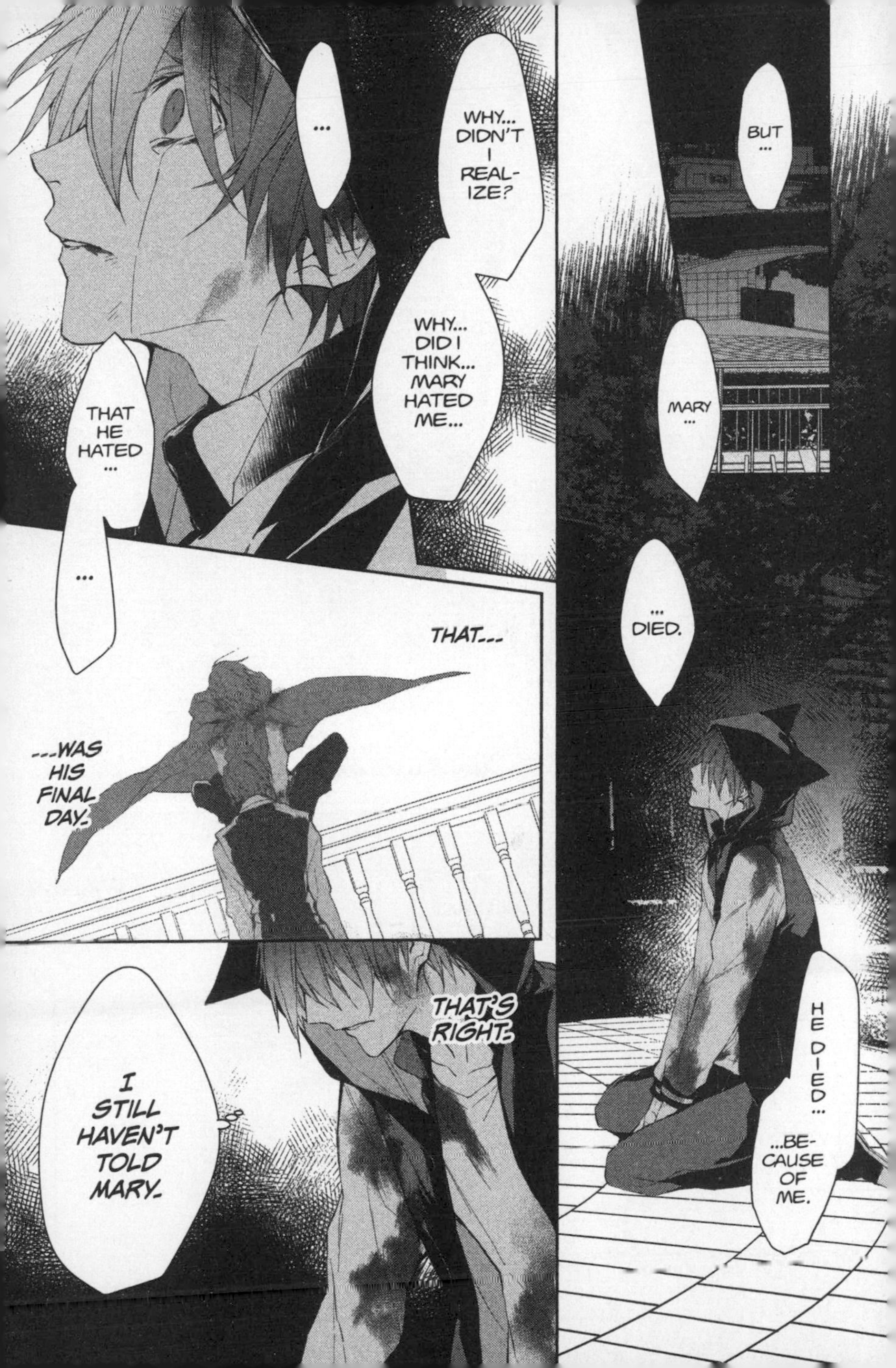
BUT...
MARY...
...DIED.
HE DIED...
...BE-CAUSE OF ME.
WHY... DIDN'T I REAL-IZE?
...
WHY... DID I THINK... MARY HATED ME...
THAT HE HATED...
...
THAT---
---WAS HIS FINAL DAY.
THAT'S RIGHT.
I STILL HAVEN'T TOLD MARY.

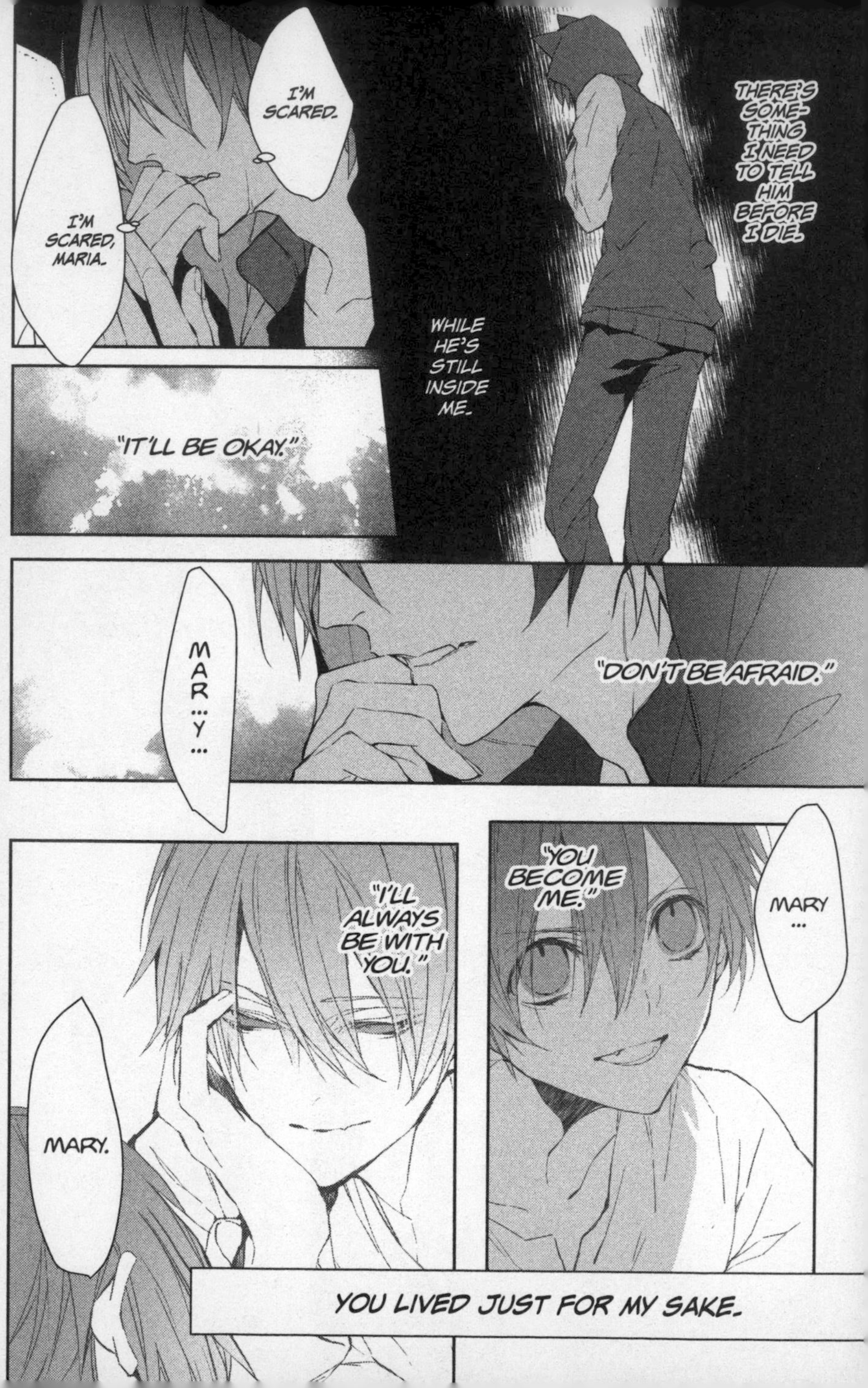
THERE'S SOME-THING I NEED TO TELL HIM BEFORE I DIE.
WHILE HE'S STILL INSIDE ME.
I'M SCARED.
I'M SCARED, MARIA.
"IT'LL BE OKAY."
"DON'T BE AFRAID."
MAR... Y...
MARY...
"YOU BECOME ME."
"I'LL ALWAYS BE WITH YOU."
MARY.
YOU LIVED JUST FOR MY SAKE.

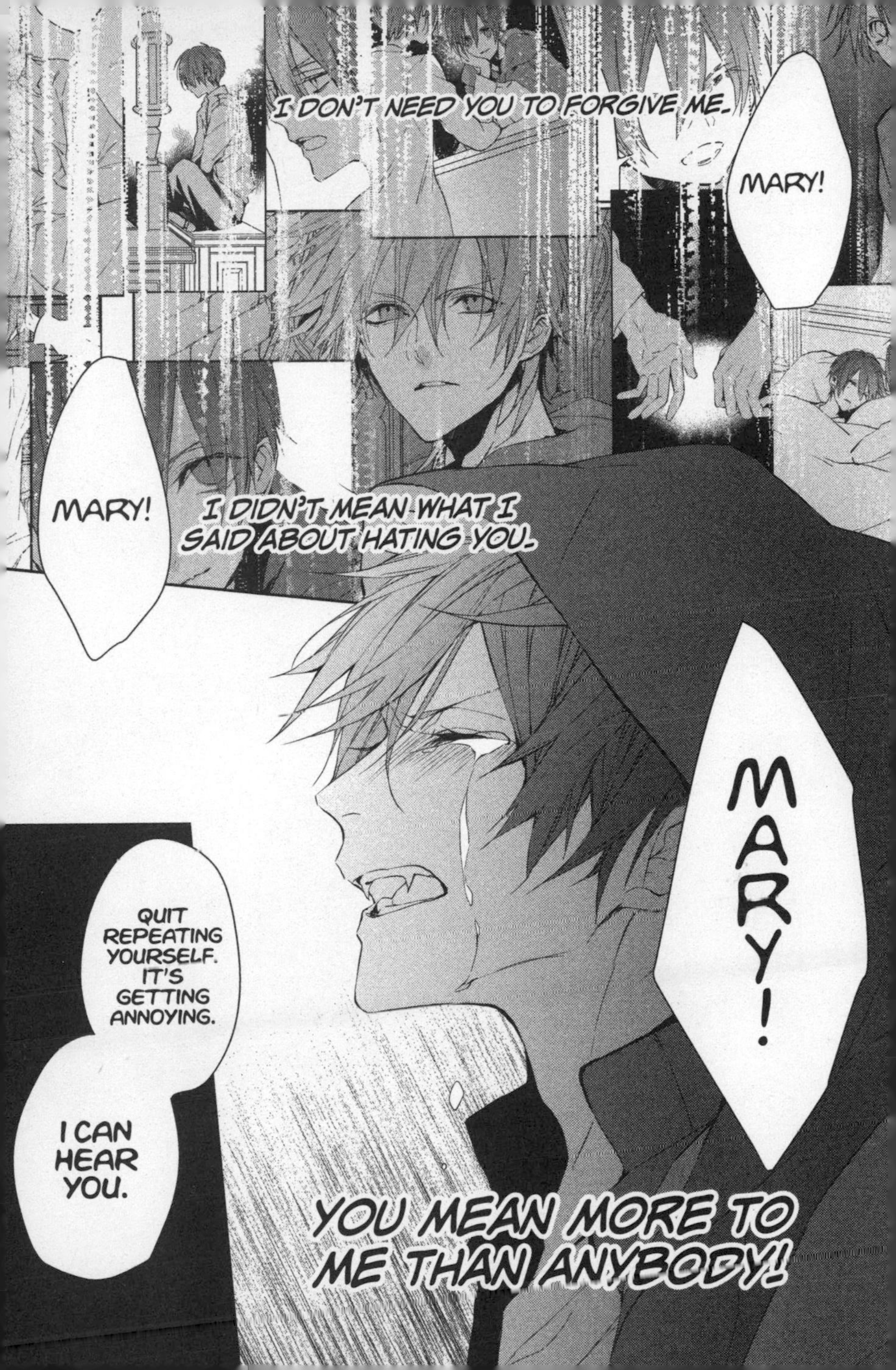
MARY!
I DON'T NEED YOU TO FORGIVE ME.
I DIDN'T MEAN WHAT I SAID ABOUT HATING YOU.
MARY!
MARY!
YOU MEAN MORE TO ME THAN ANYBODY!
QUIT REPEATING YOURSELF. IT'S GETTING ANNOYING.
I CAN HEAR YOU.

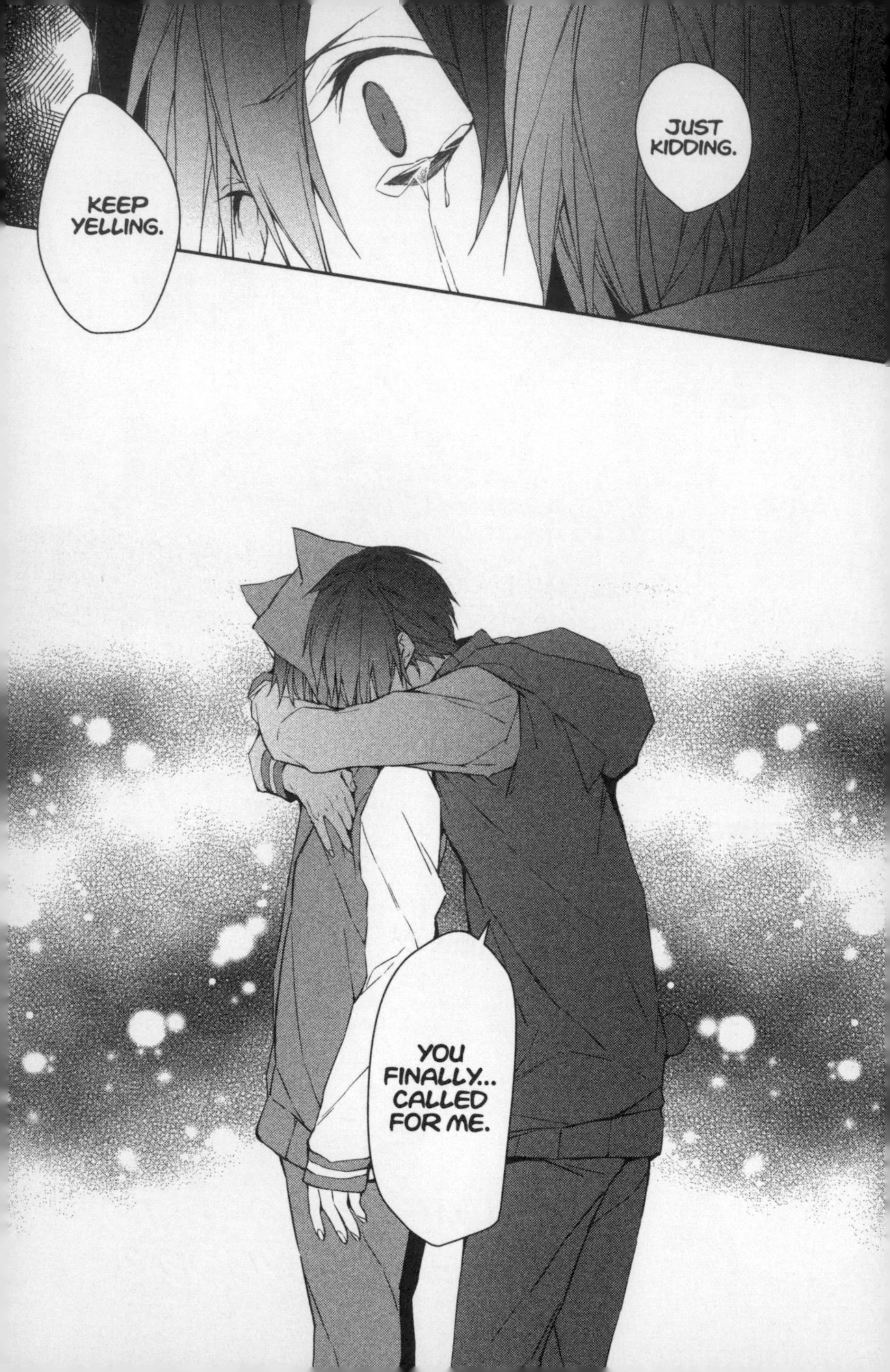
JUST KIDDING.
KEEP YELLING.
YOU FINALLY... CALLED FOR ME.

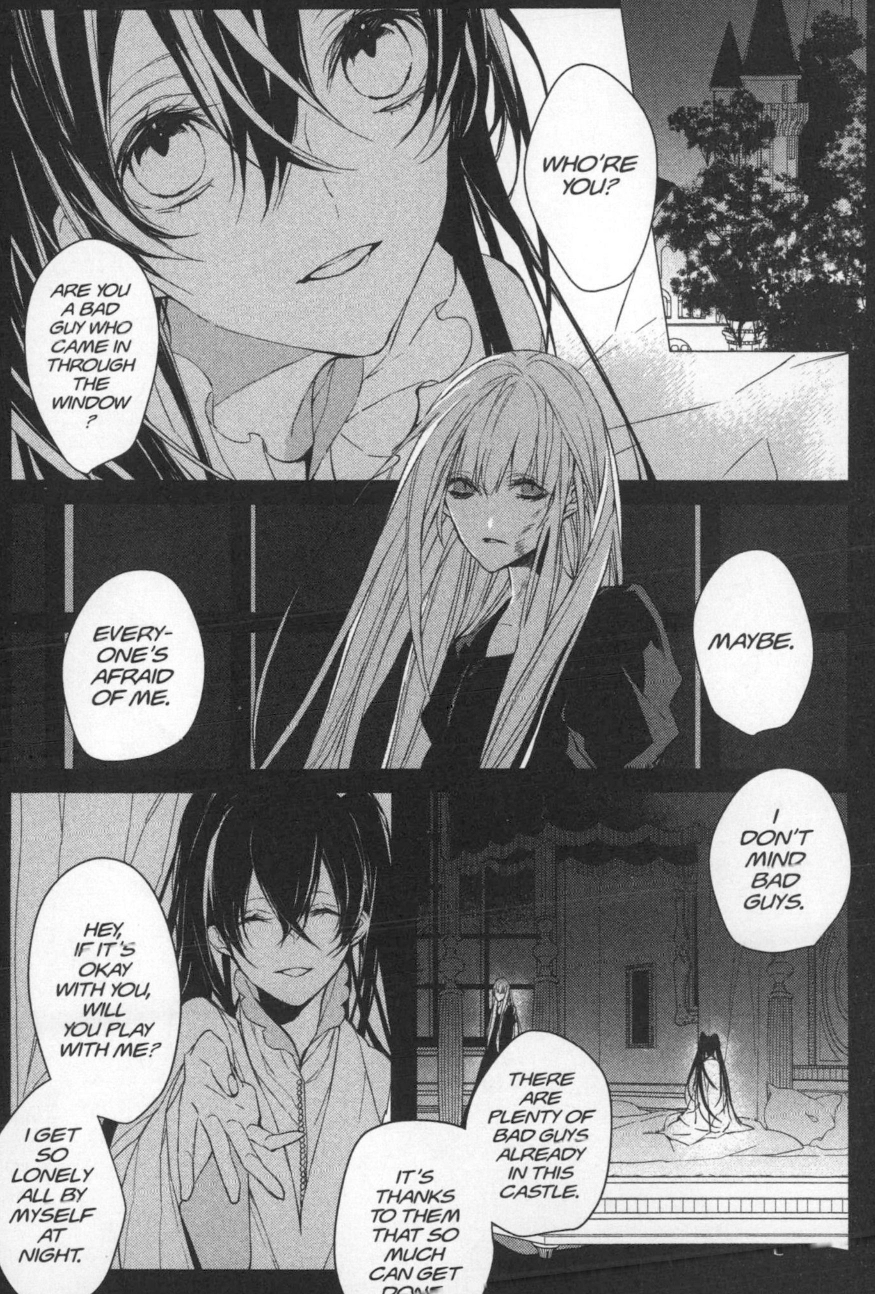
WHO'RE YOU?
ARE YOU A BAD GUY WHO CAME IN THROUGH THE WINDOW?
MAYBE.
EVERY-ONE'S AFRAID OF ME.
I DON'T MIND BAD GUYS.
THERE ARE PLENTY OF BAD GUYS ALREADY IN THIS CASTLE.
IT'S THANKS TO THEM THAT SO MUCH CAN GET DONE.
HEY, IF IT'S OKAY WITH YOU, WILL YOU PLAY WITH ME?
I GET SO LONELY ALL BY MYSELF AT NIGHT.

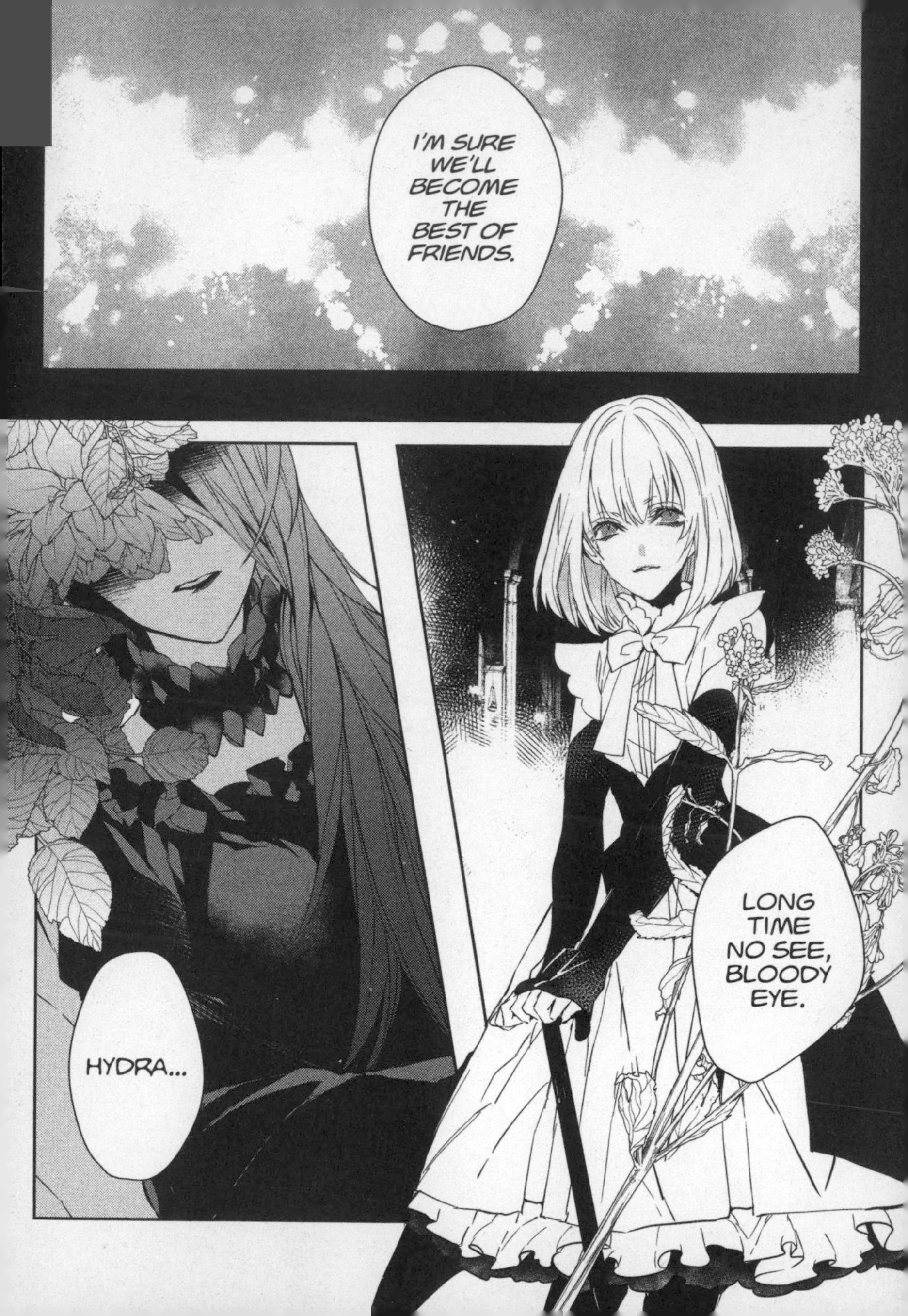
I'M SURE WE'LL BECOME THE BEST OF FRIENDS.
LONG TIME NO SEE, BLOODY EYE.
HYDRA...

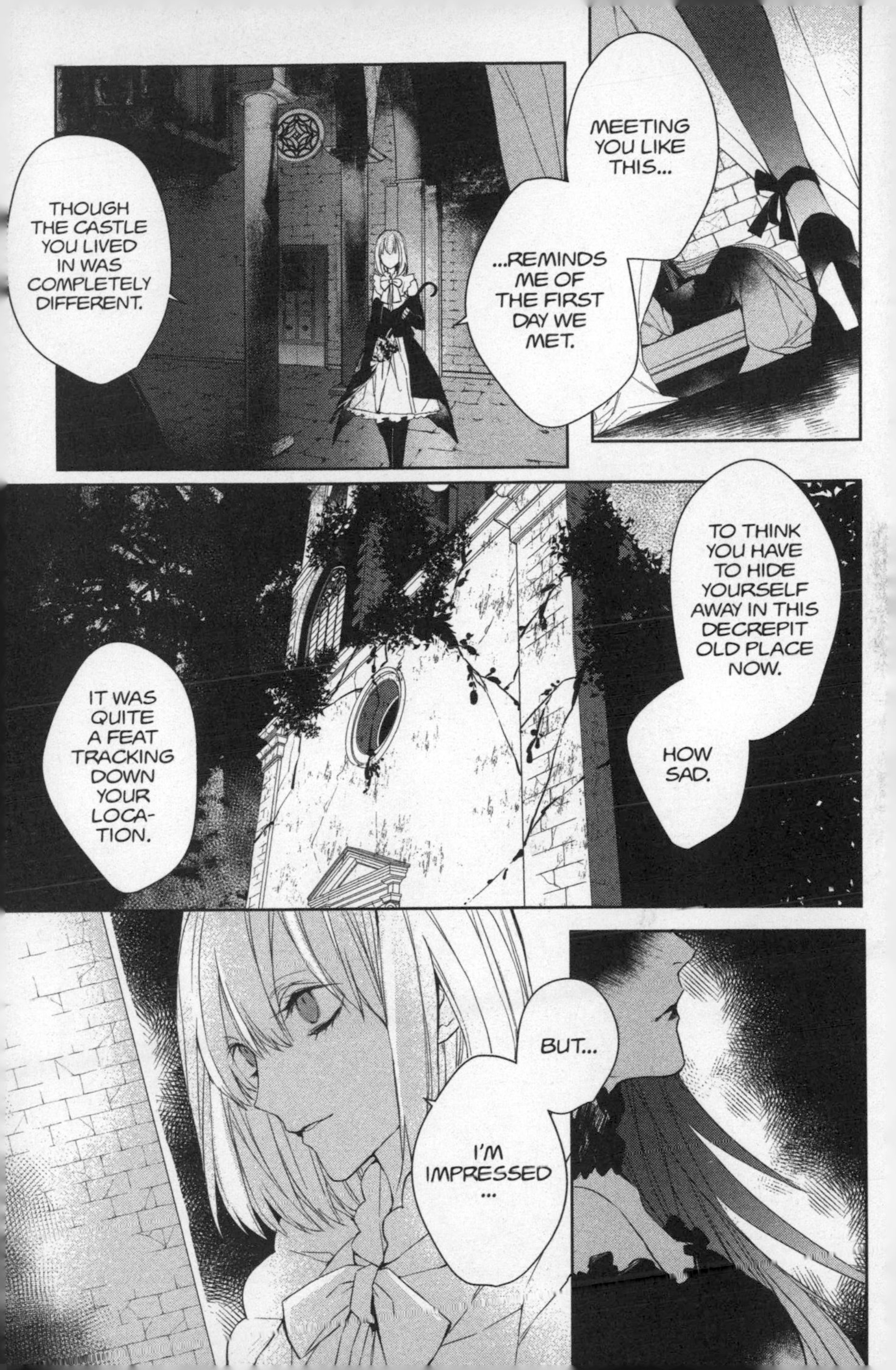
MEETING YOU LIKE THIS...
...REMINDS ME OF THE FIRST DAY WE MET.
THOUGH THE CASTLE YOU LIVED IN WAS COMPLETELY DIFFERENT.
TO THINK YOU HAVE TO HIDE YOURSELF AWAY IN THIS DECREPIT OLD PLACE NOW.
HOW SAD.
IT WAS QUITE A FEAT TRACKING DOWN YOUR LOCA-TION.
BUT...
I'M IMPRESSED...

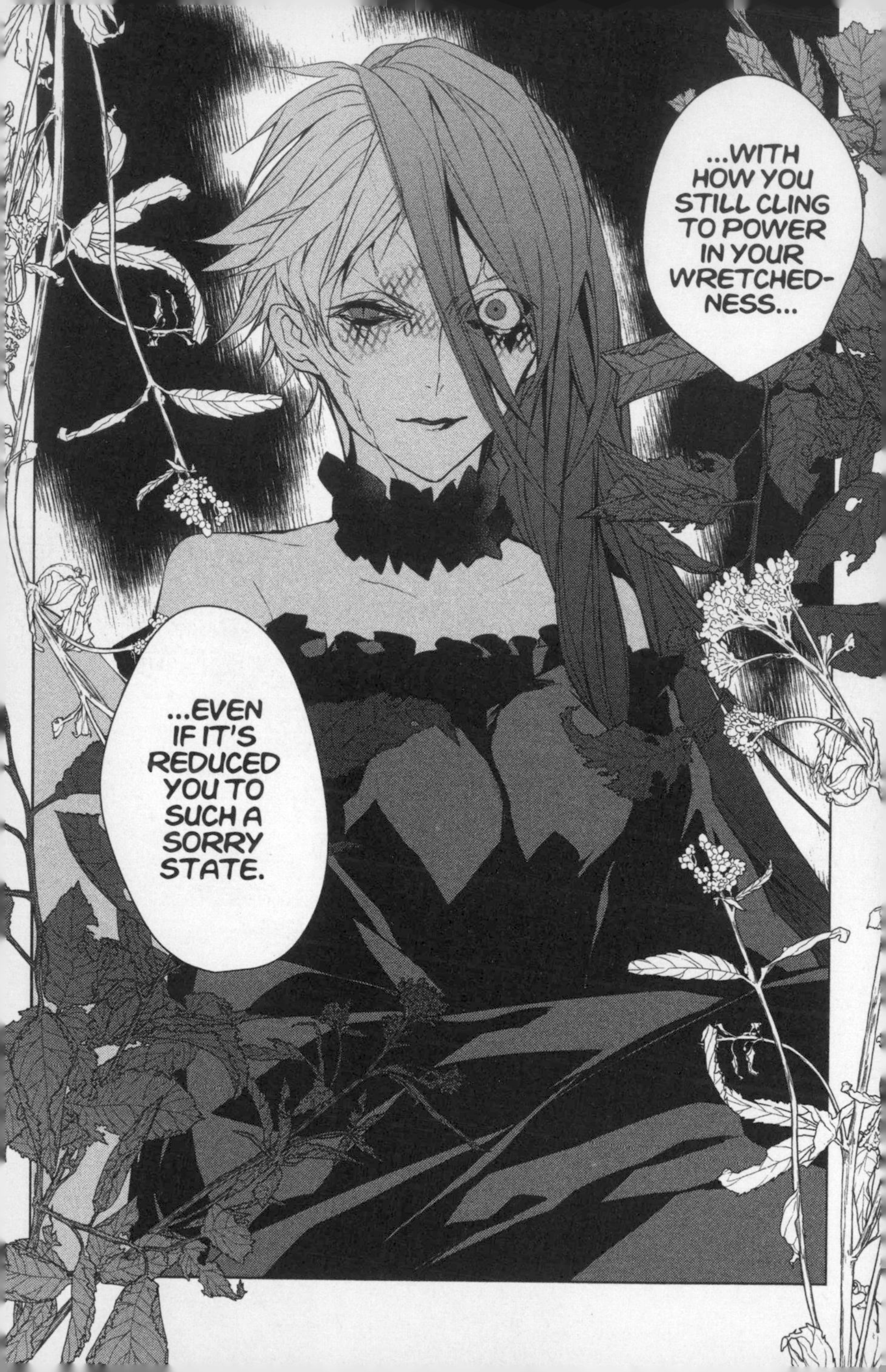
...WITH HOW YOU STILL CLING TO POWER IN YOUR WRETCHED-NESS...
...EVEN IF IT'S REDUCED YOU TO SUCH A SORRY STATE.

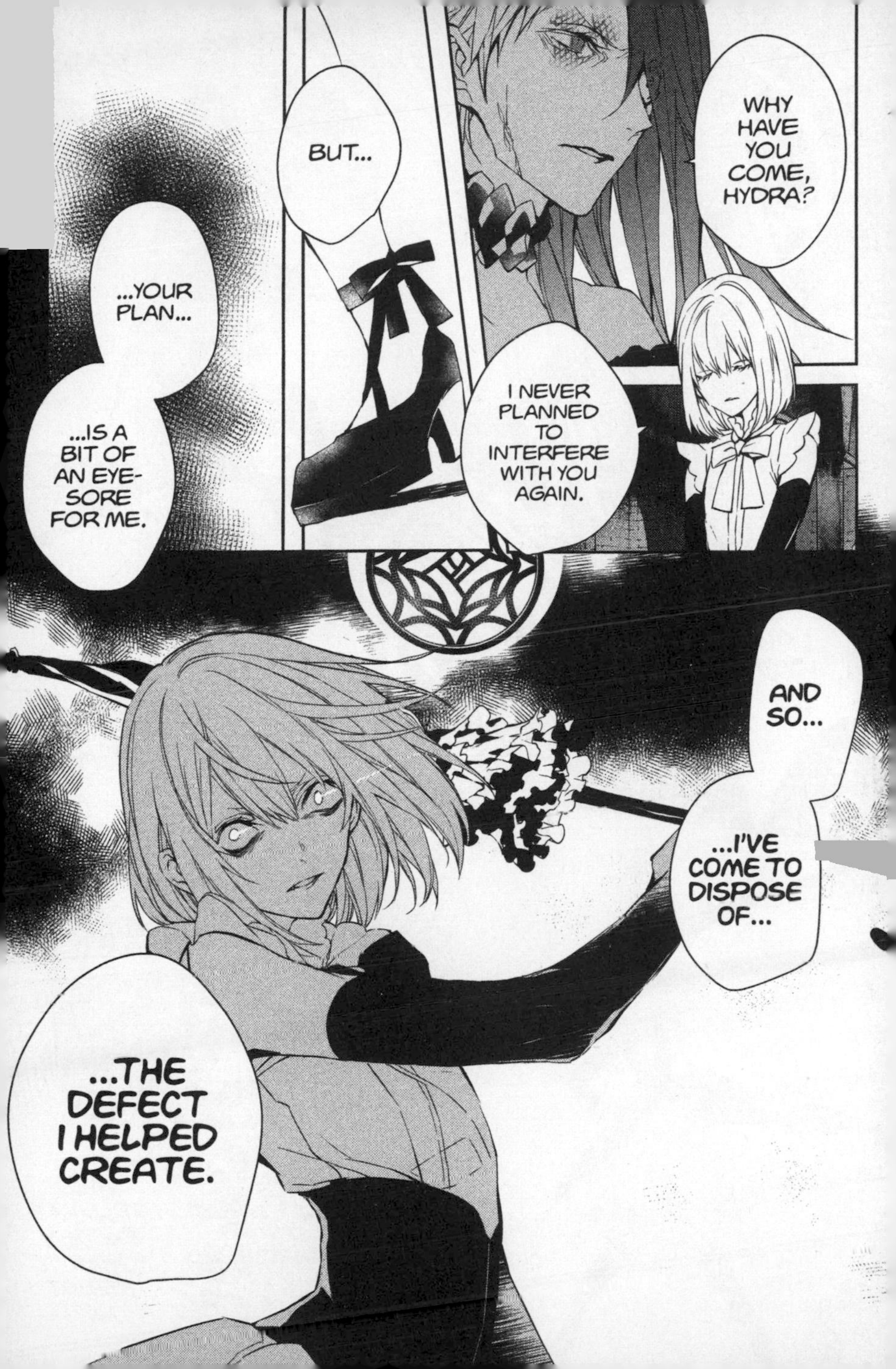
WHY HAVE YOU COME, HYDRA?
I NEVER PLANNED TO INTERFERE WITH YOU AGAIN.
BUT...
...YOUR PLAN...
...IS A BIT OF AN EYE-SORE FOR ME.
AND SO...
...I'VE COME TO DISPOSE OF...
...THE DEFECT I HELPED CREATE.

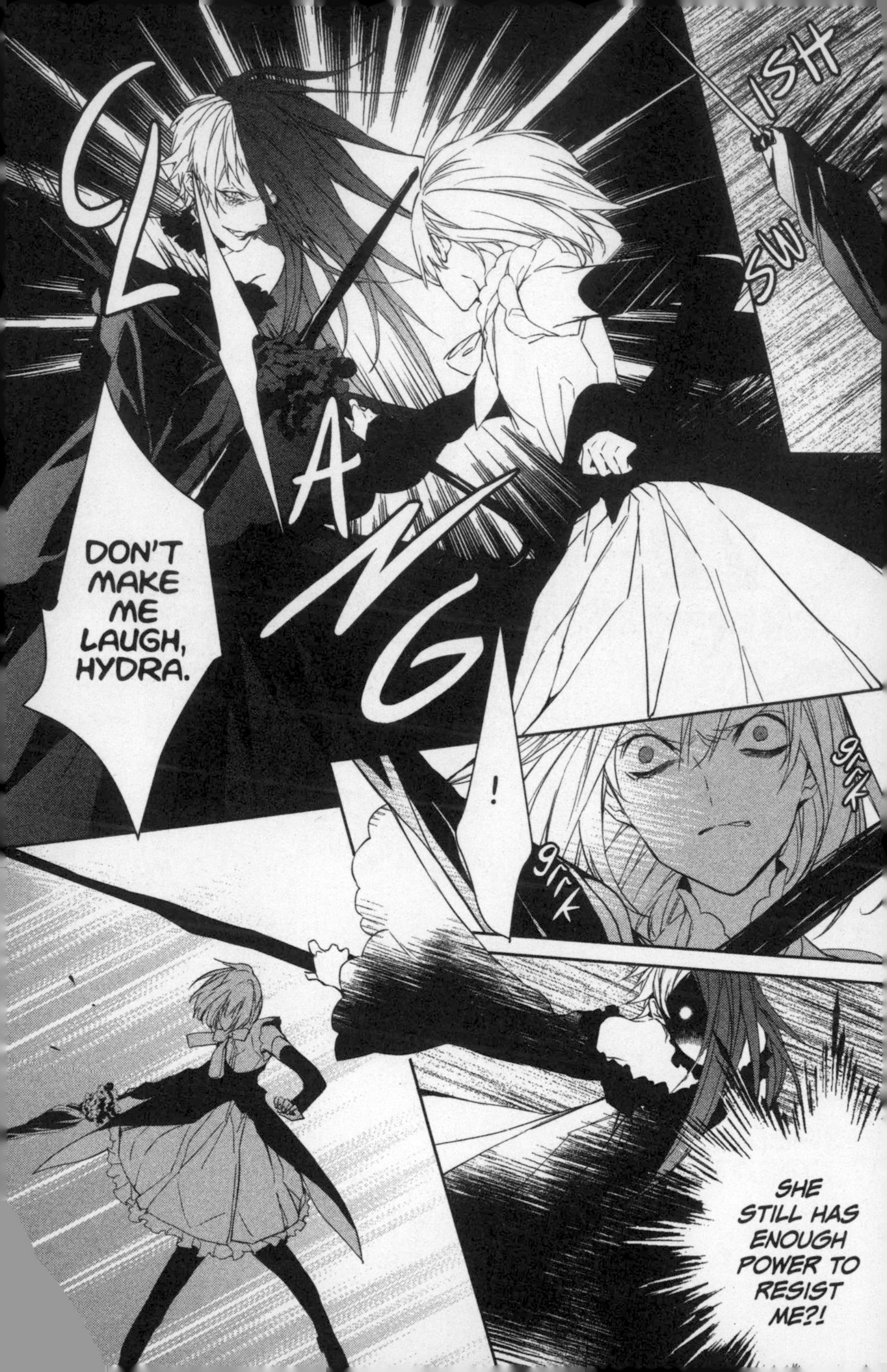
SWISH
CLANG
DON'T MAKE ME LAUGH, HYDRA.
!
grrk
grrk
SHE STILL HAS ENOUGH POWER TO RESIST ME?!

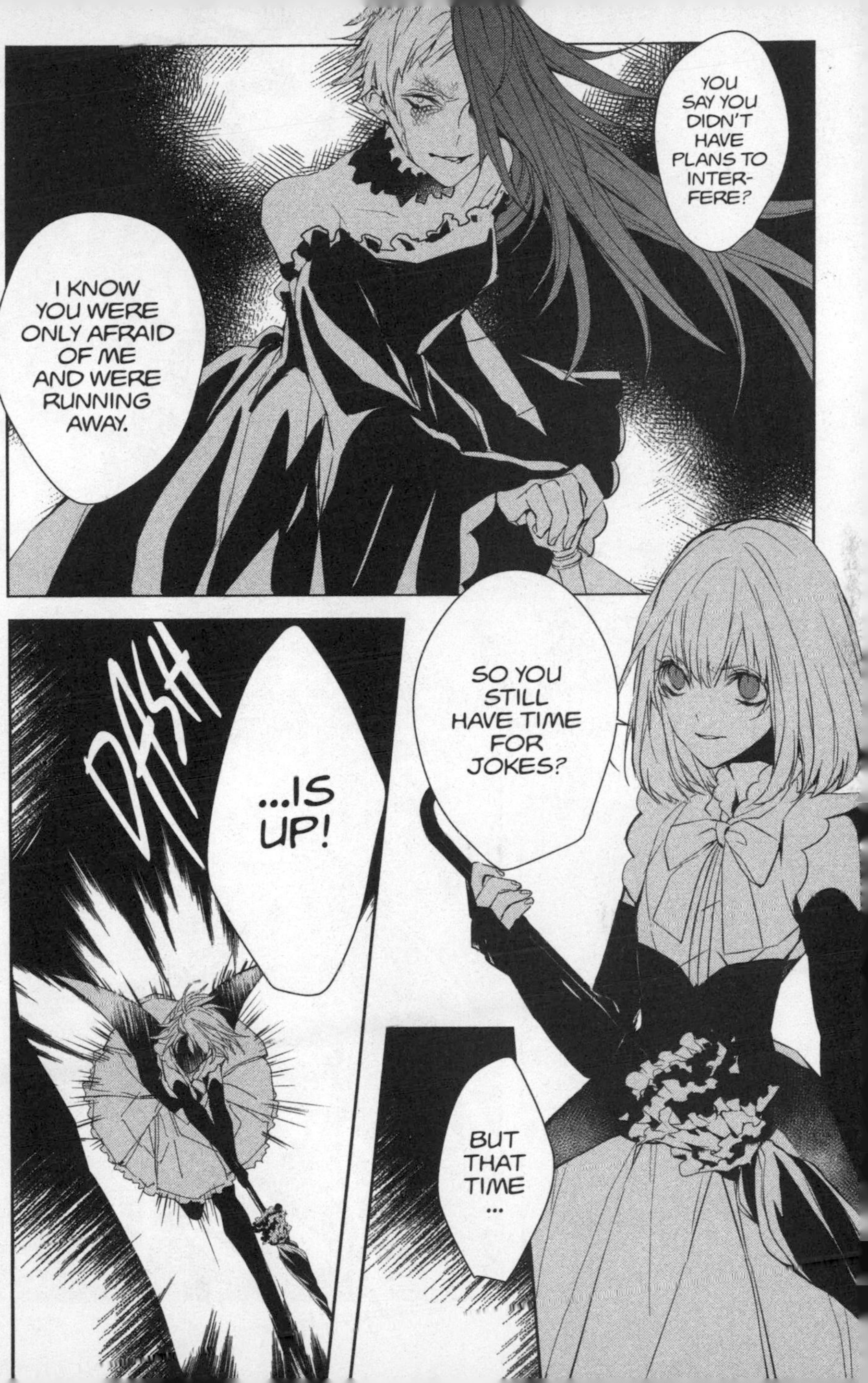
YOU SAY YOU DIDN'T HAVE PLANS TO INTER-FERE?
I KNOW YOU WERE ONLY AFRAID OF ME AND WERE RUNNING AWAY.
SO YOU STILL HAVE TIME FOR JOKES?
BUT THAT TIME ...
...IS UP!
DASH

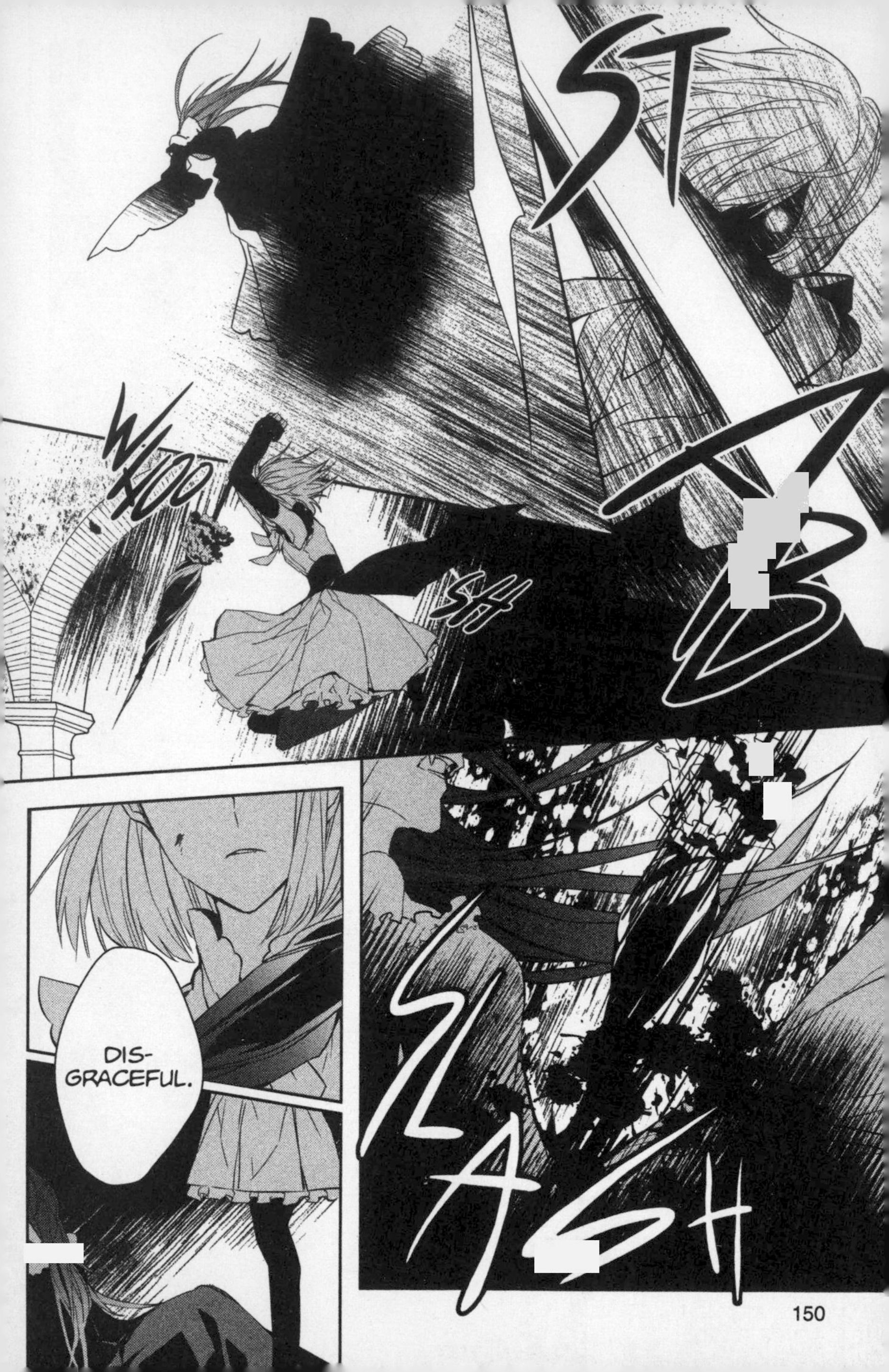
STAB
WHOO
SH
SLASH
DIS-
GRACEFUL.

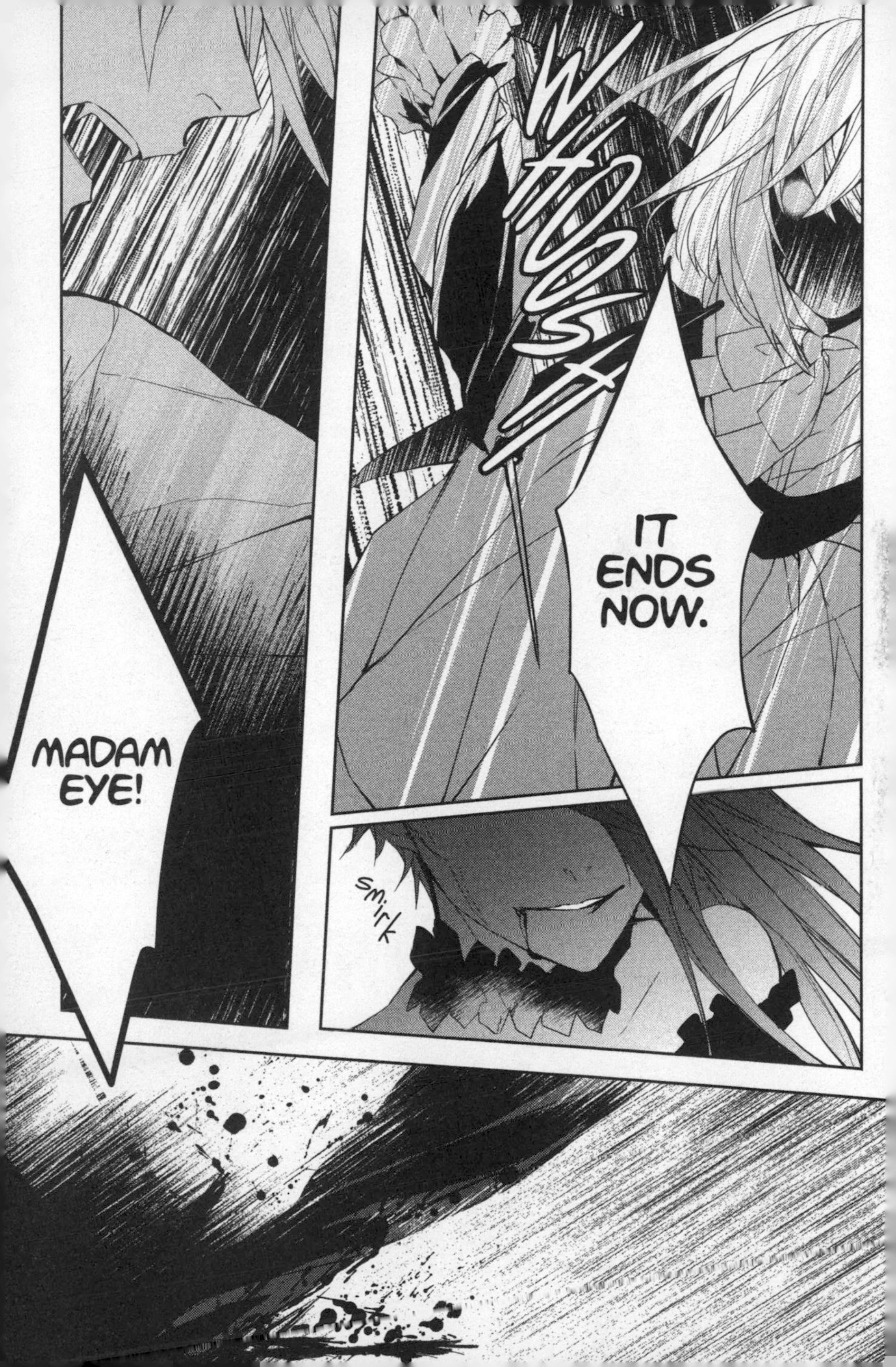
WHOOSH
IT ENDS NOW.
smirk
MADAM EYE!

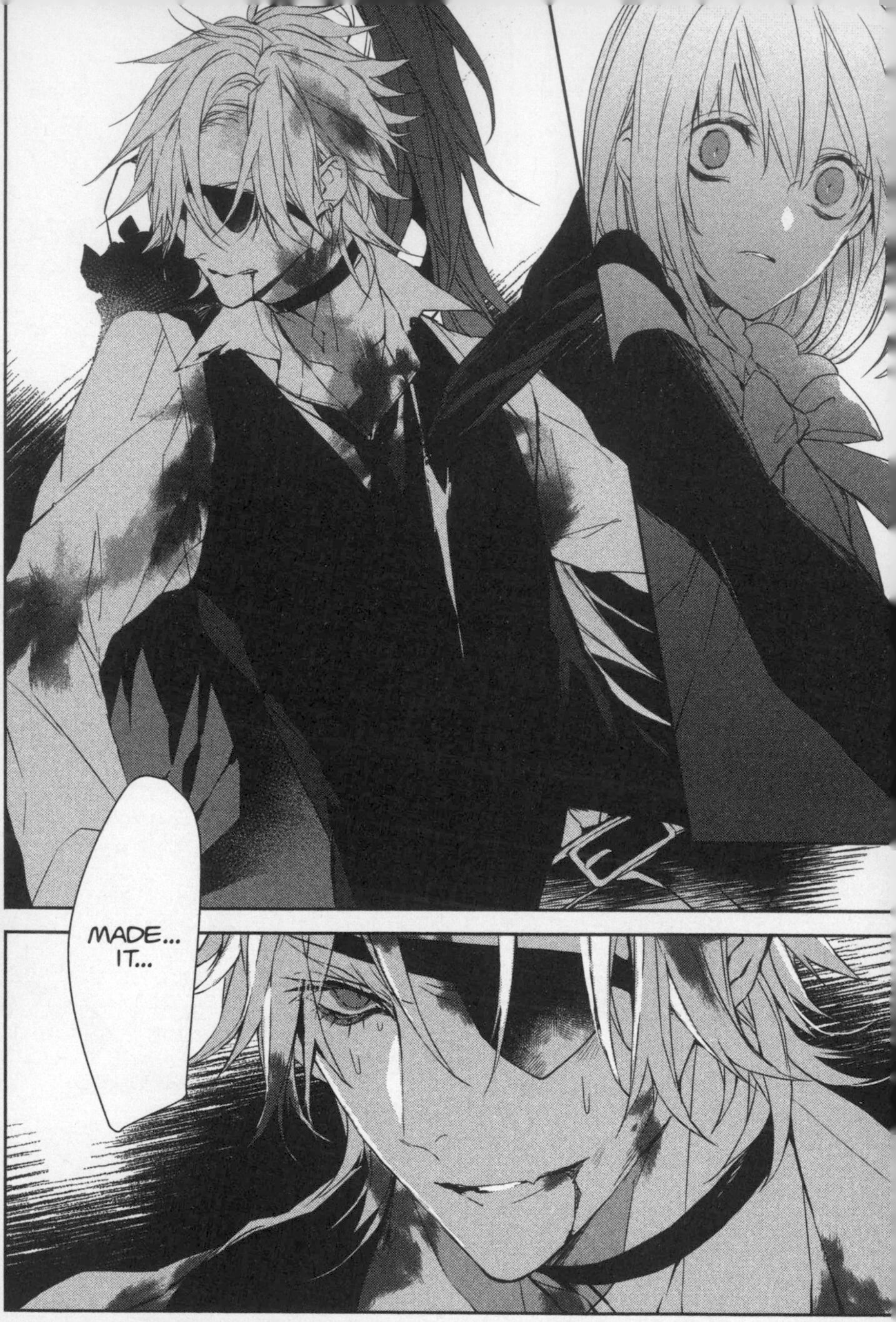
MADE... IT...

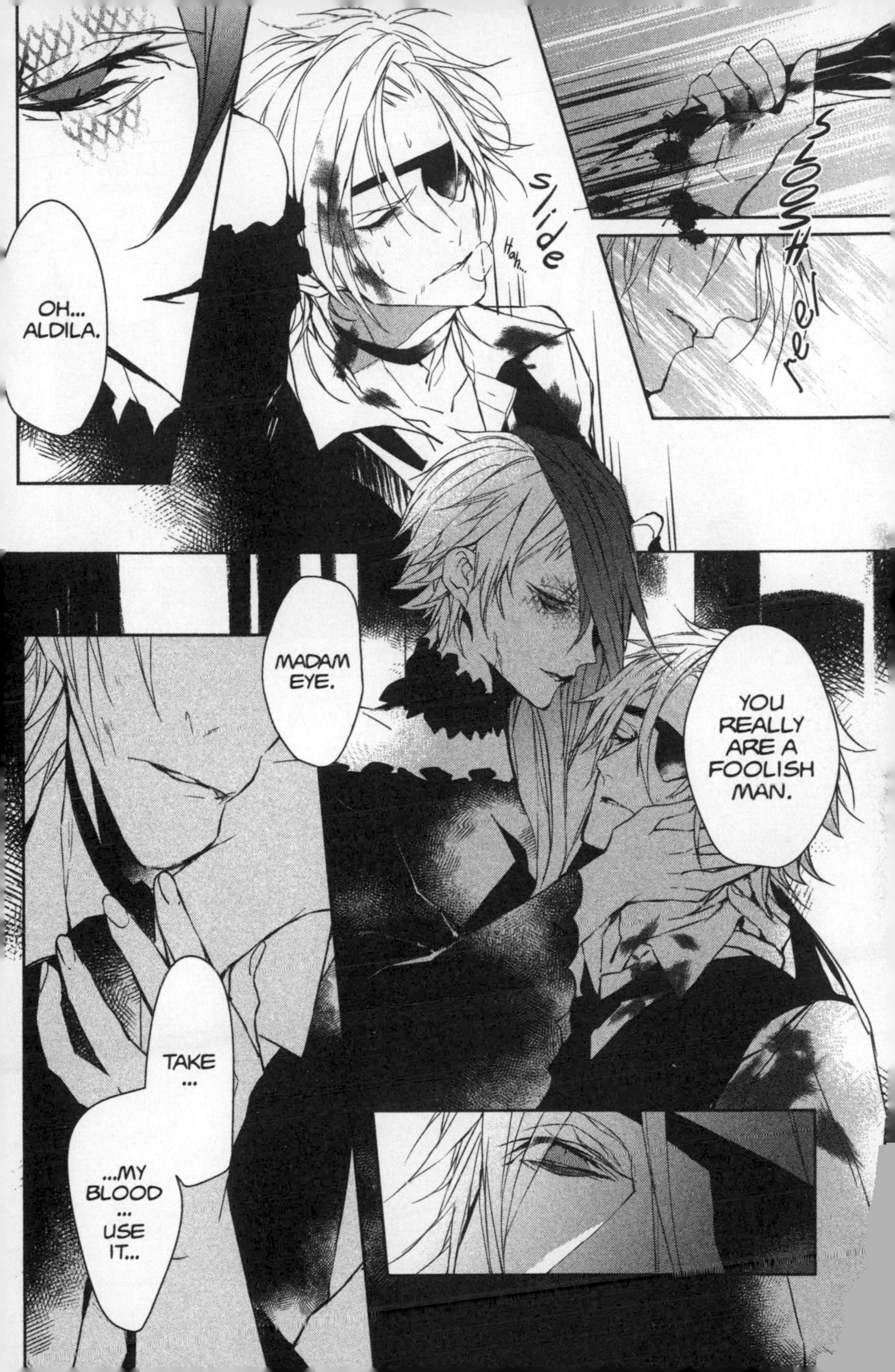
SLOOSH
reel
slide
Hah...
OH... ALDILA.
MADAM EYE.
YOU REALLY ARE A FOOLISH MAN.
TAKE ...
...MY BLOOD ... USE IT...

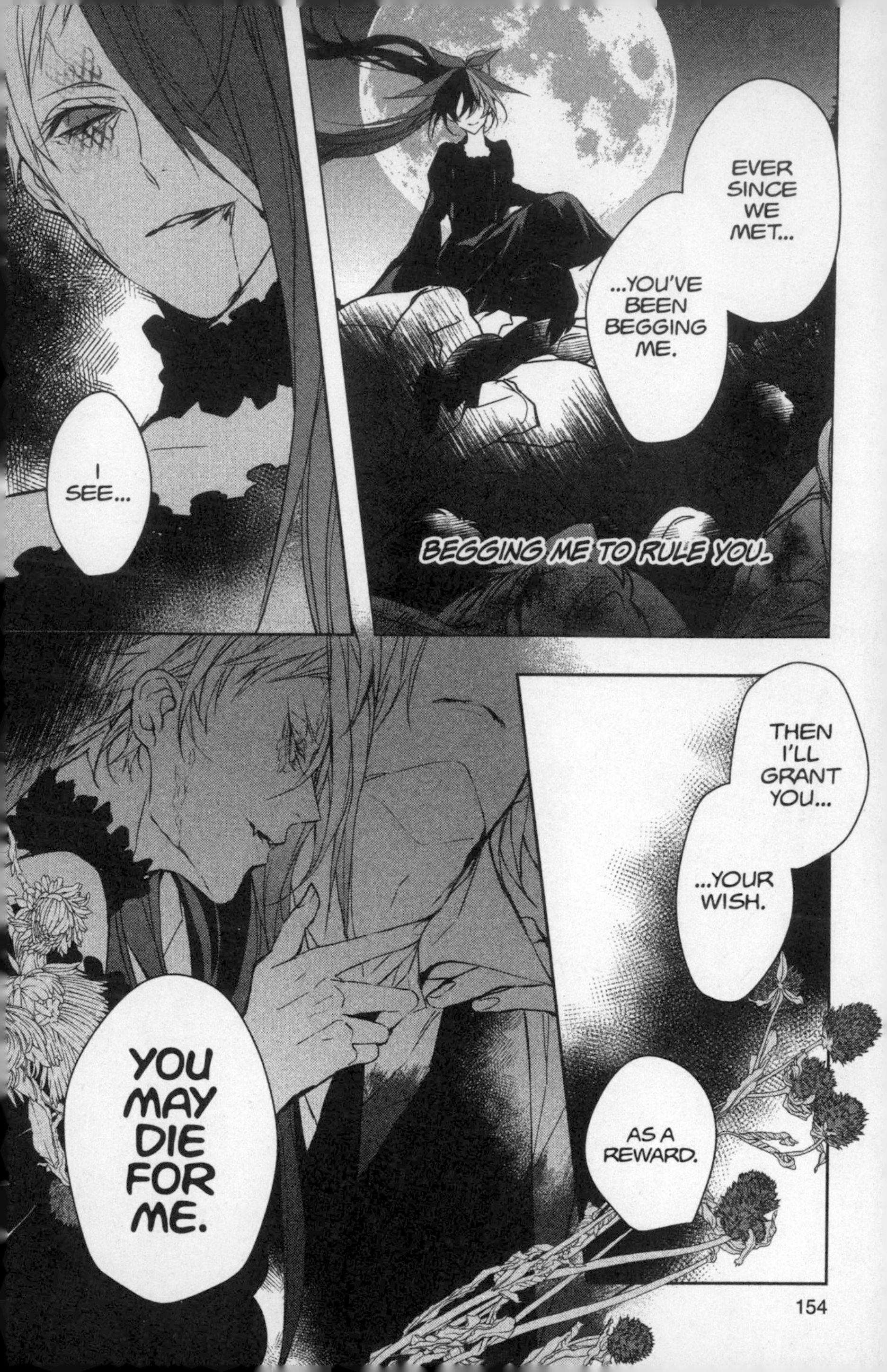
EVER SINCE WE MET...
...YOU'VE BEEN BEGGING ME.
BEGGING ME TO RULE YOU.
I SEE...
THEN I'LL GRANT YOU...
...YOUR WISH.
AS A REWARD.
YOU MAY DIE FOR ME.

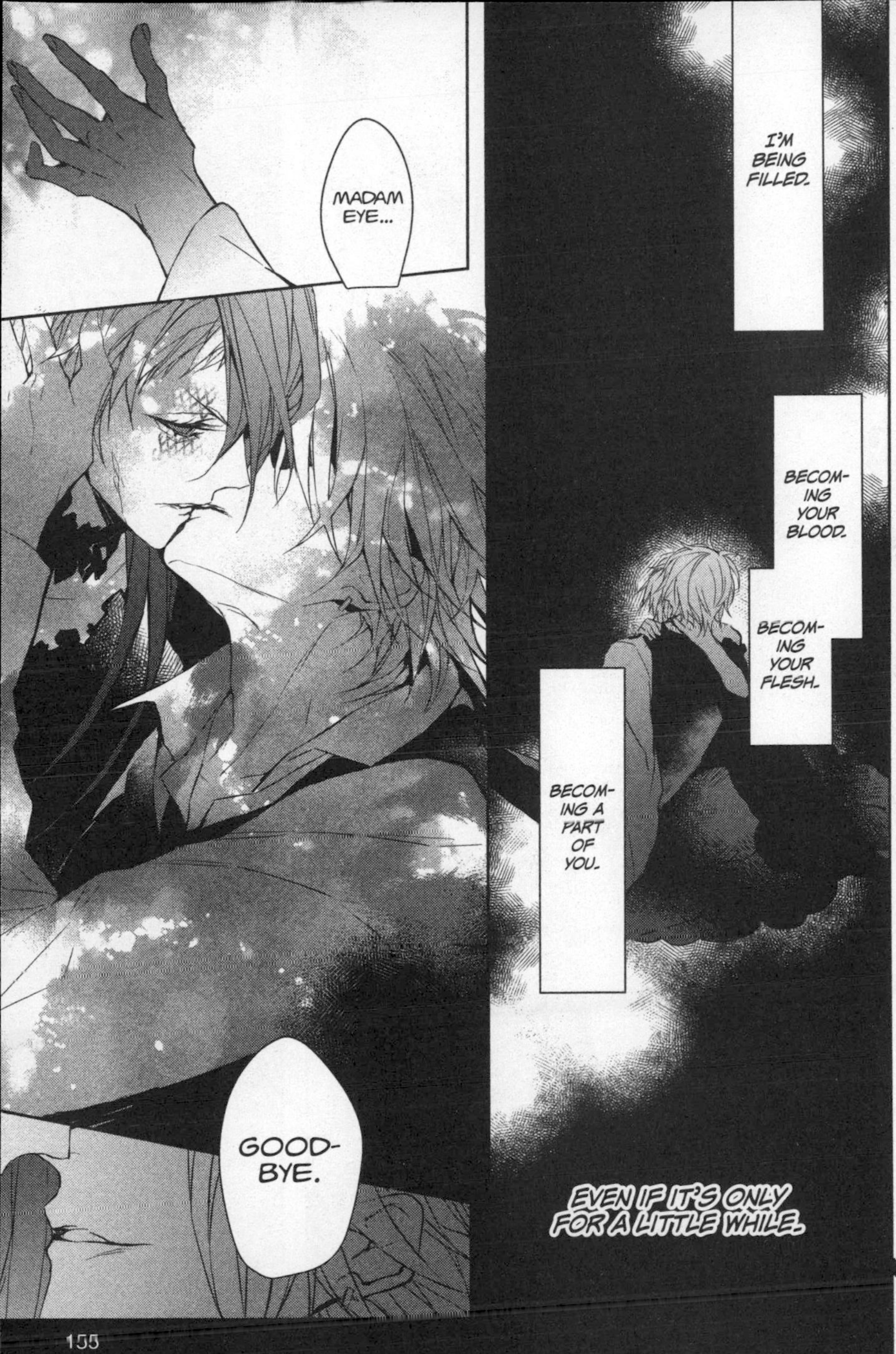
I'M BEING FILLED.
BECOMING YOUR BLOOD.
BECOMING YOUR FLESH.
BECOMING A PART OF YOU.
EVEN IF IT'S ONLY FOR A LITTLE WHILE.
MADAM EYE...
GOOD-BYE.

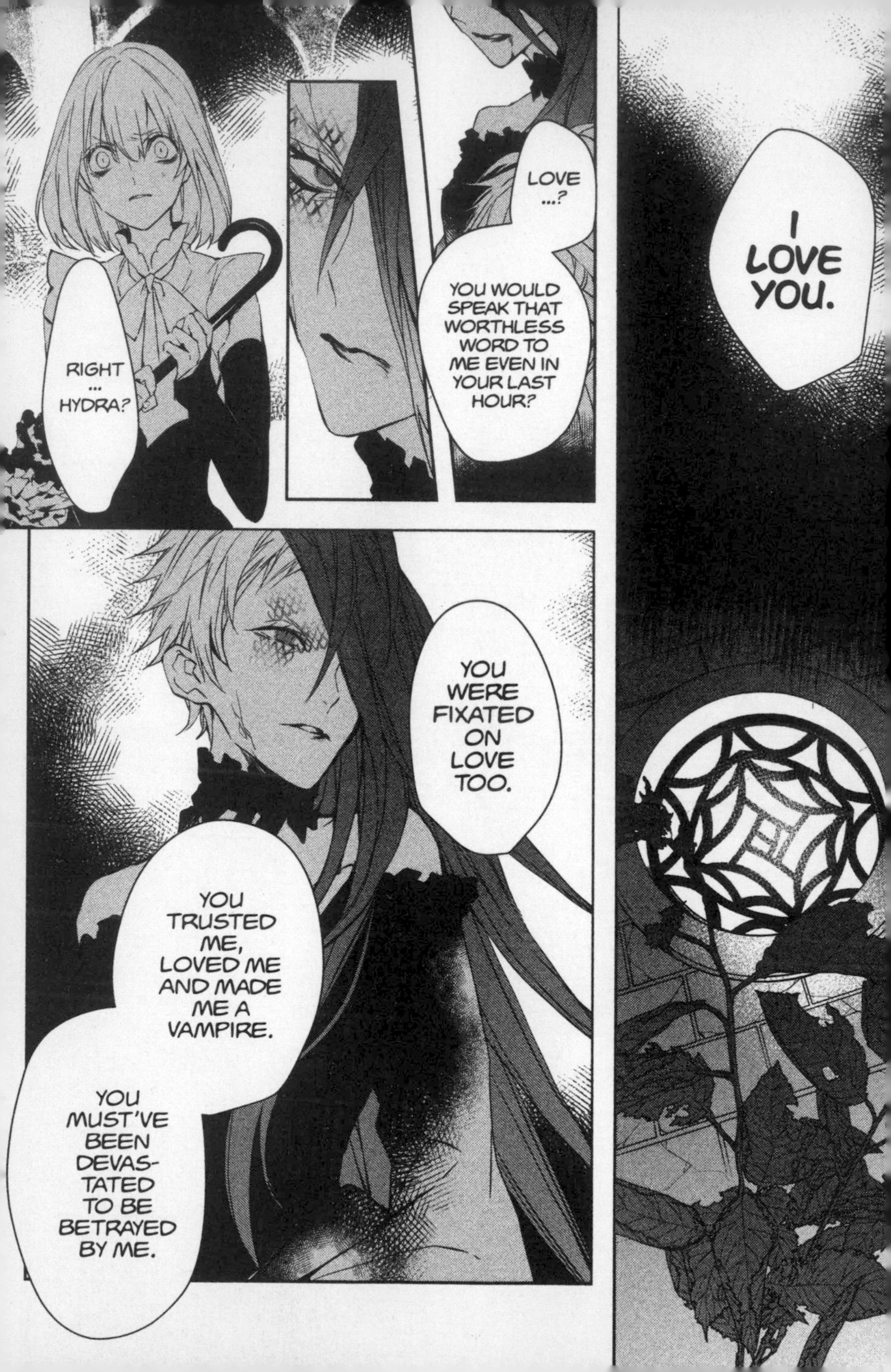
I LOVE YOU.
LOVE ...?
YOU WOULD SPEAK THAT WORTHLESS WORD TO ME EVEN IN YOUR LAST HOUR?
RIGHT ... HYDRA?
YOU WERE FIXATED ON LOVE TOO.
YOU TRUSTED ME, LOVED ME AND MADE ME A VAMPIRE.
YOU MUST'VE BEEN DEVAS-TATED TO BE BETRAYED BY ME.

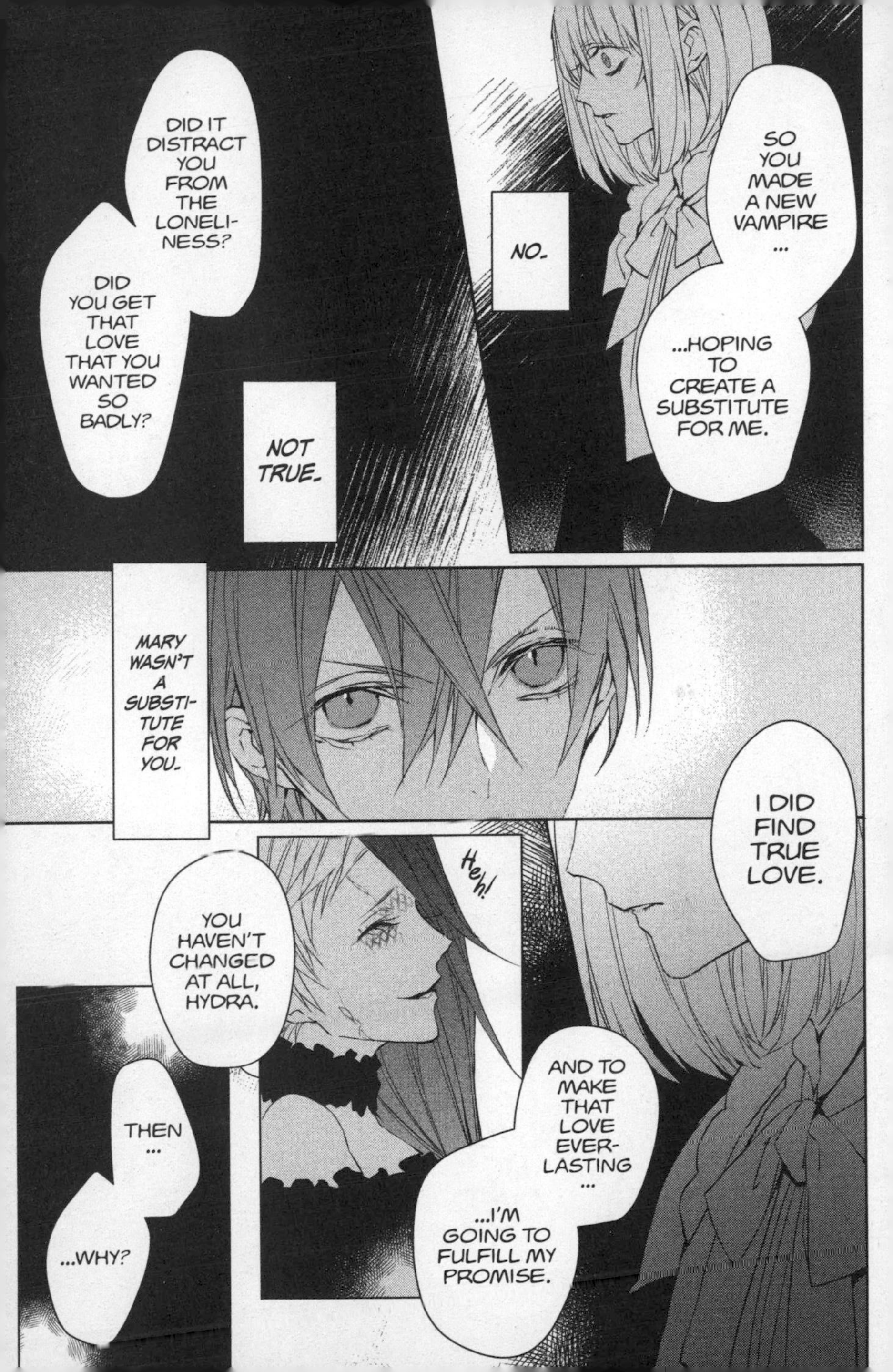
SO YOU MADE A NEW VAMPIRE ...
...HOPING TO CREATE A SUBSTITUTE FOR ME.
NO.
DID IT DISTRACT YOU FROM THE LONELINESS?
DID YOU GET THAT LOVE THAT YOU WANTED SO BADLY?
NOT TRUE.
MARY WASN'T A SUBSTITUTE FOR YOU.
I DID FIND TRUE LOVE.
Heh!
YOU HAVEN'T CHANGED AT ALL, HYDRA.
AND TO MAKE THAT LOVE EVERLASTING ...
...I'M GOING TO FULFILL MY PROMISE.
THEN ...
...WHY?

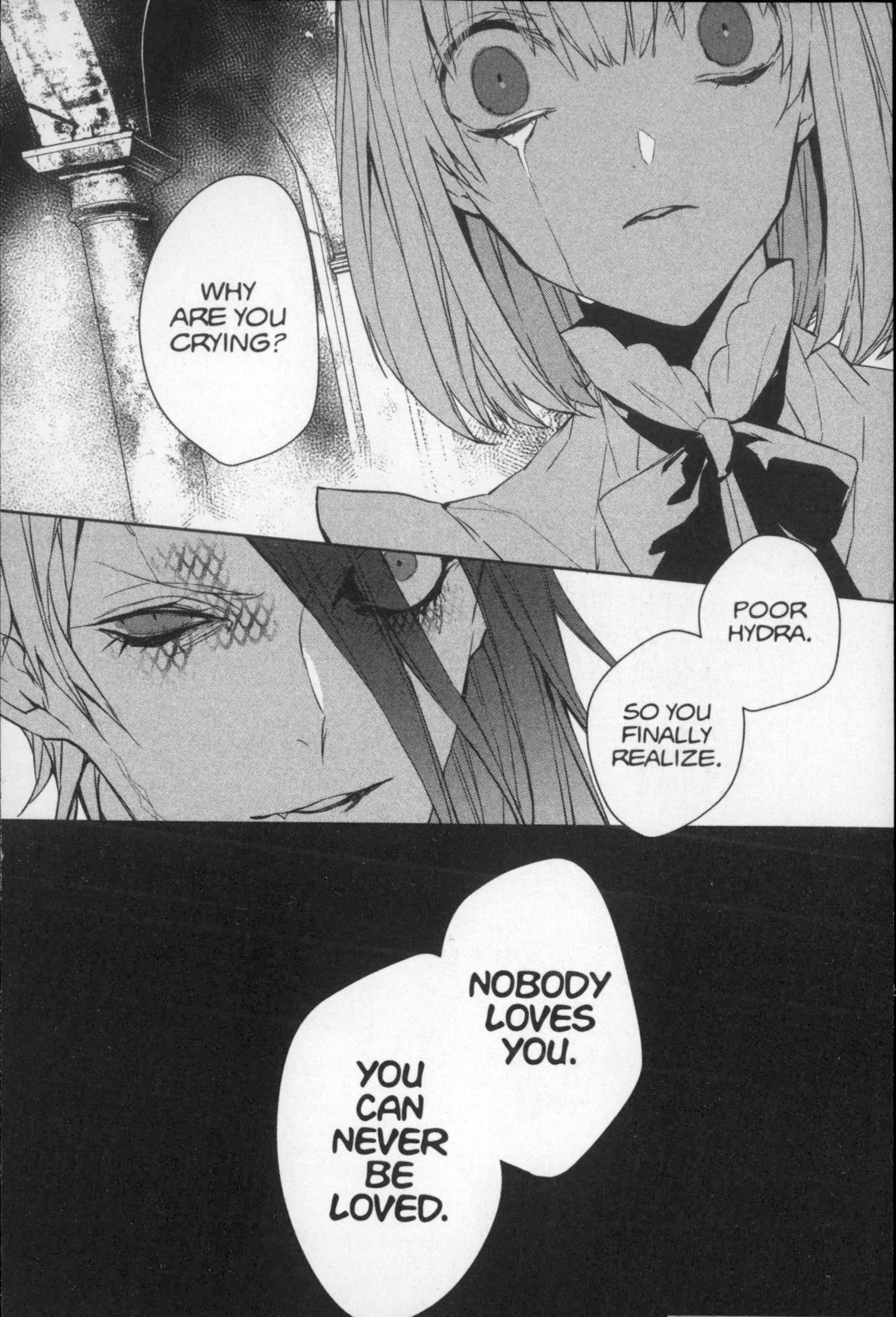
WHY ARE YOU CRYING?
POOR HYDRA.
SO YOU FINALLY REALIZE.
NOBODY LOVES YOU.
YOU CAN NEVER BE LOVED.

BLOOD ✦ 36 end

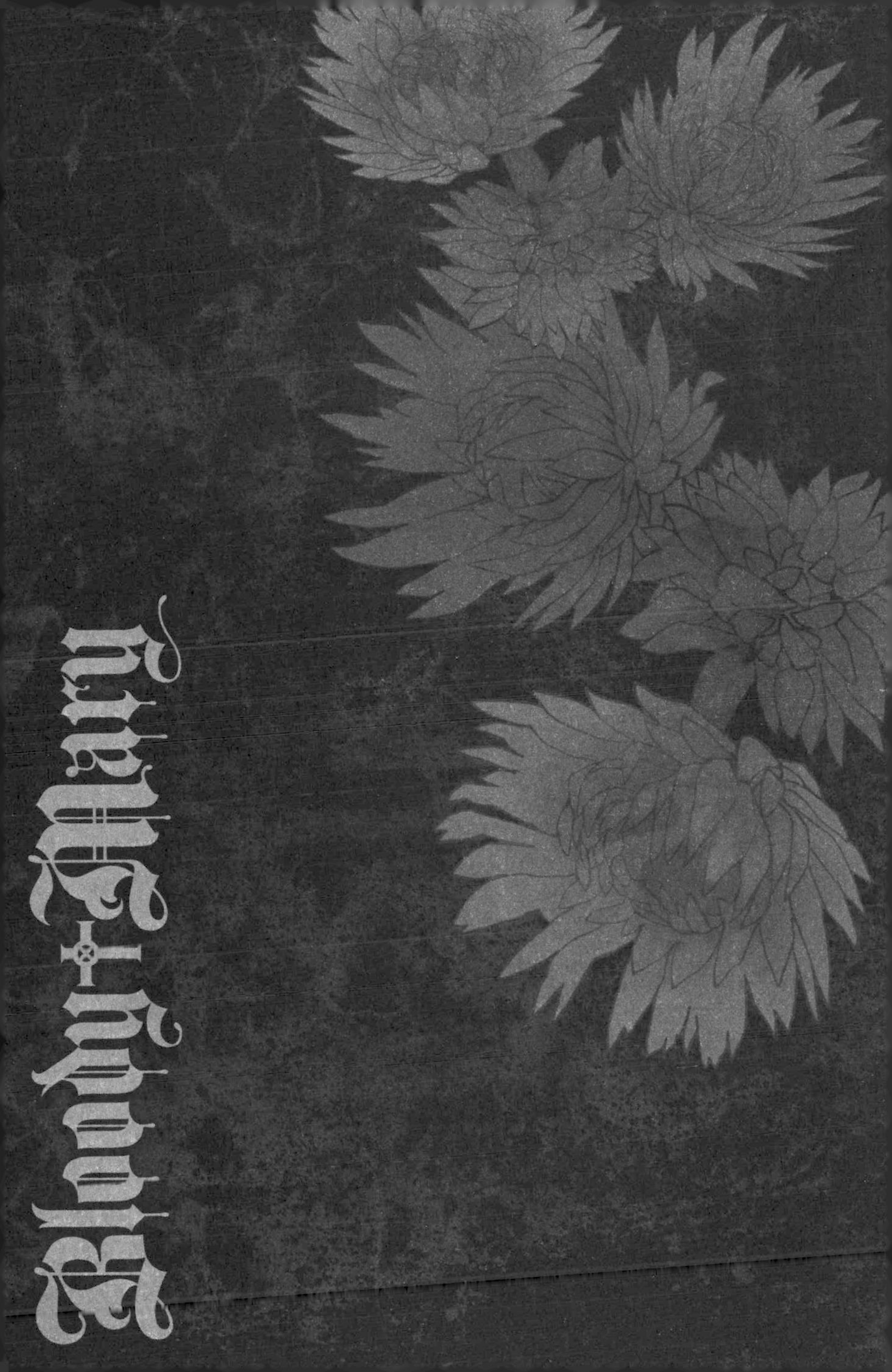
Bloody Mary

A Colloquy on the Bedroom: Follow-Up

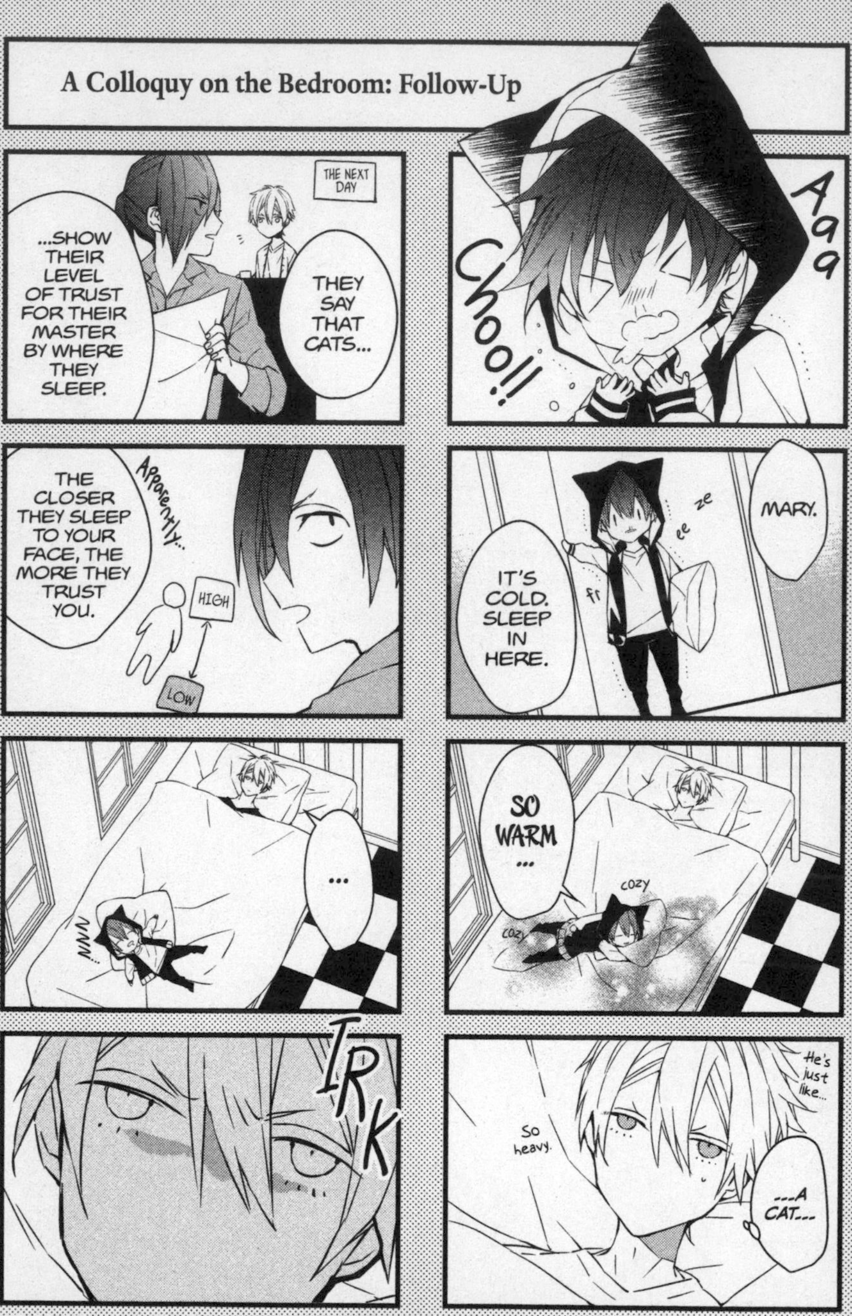
Aaa
Choo!!
THE NEXT DAY
THEY SAY THAT CATS...
...SHOW THEIR LEVEL OF TRUST FOR THEIR MASTER BY WHERE THEY SLEEP.
MARY.
eeze
IT'S COLD. SLEEP IN HERE.
fr
Apparently...
THE CLOSER THEY SLEEP TO YOUR FACE, THE MORE THEY TRUST YOU.
HIGH
LOW
SO WARM ...
cozy
cozy
...
NNN...
He's just like...
...A CAT...
So heavy.
IRK

AND IT'S EVEN WORSE THAN THE PREVIOUS DAY.

Postscript

Thank you very much for picking up volume 9 of Bloody Mary!
You may have noticed the release of volume 9 is exactly three years
after the start of the serialization.
It's thanks to your support throughout all this time.
Thank you so much.
Bloody Mary will be reaching the climax of the story soon.
I hope you watch over the characters for the little remaining time
we have left with them!

SPECIAL THANKS

Mihoru / M-fuchi / H-gawa / T-mizu-sama / T-ko-sama

Production Team/Support
Haruo / Sumida / M-ika

Editor S / Designer
Everyone involved /
And everyone who read this

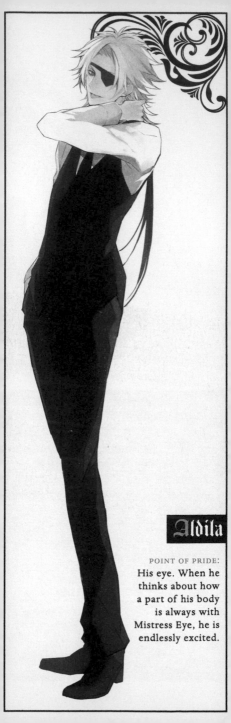

Aldila

POINT OF PRIDE:
His eye. When he thinks about how a part of his body is always with Mistress Eye, he is endlessly excited.

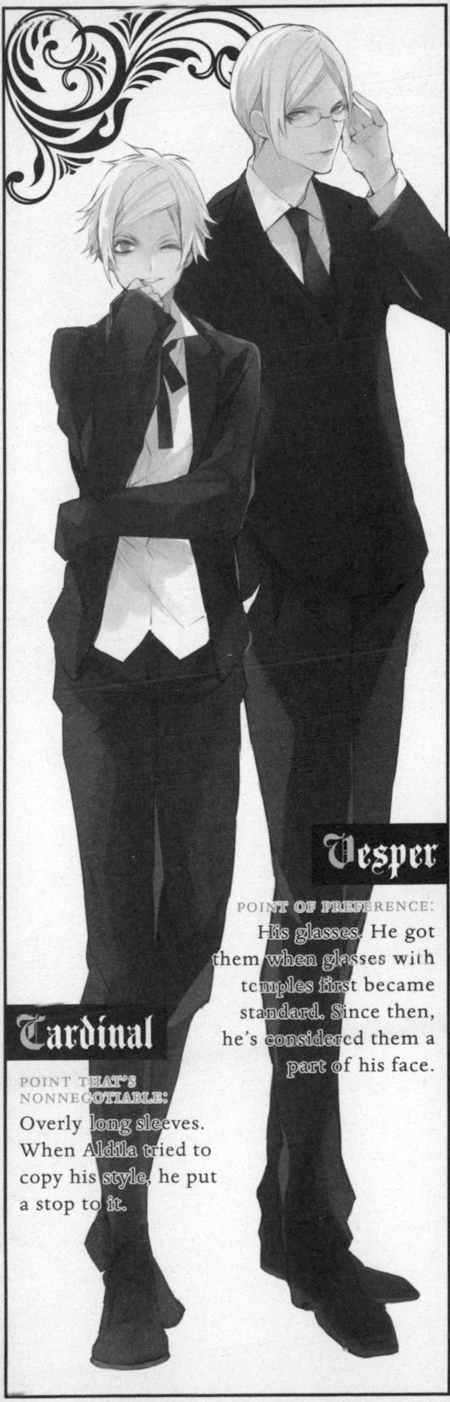
Vesper
POINT OF PREFERENCE:
His glasses. He got them when glasses with temples first became standard. Since then, he's considered them a part of his face.
Cardinal
POINT THAT'S NONNEGOTIABLE:
Overly long sleeves. When Aldila tried to copy his style, he put a stop to it.

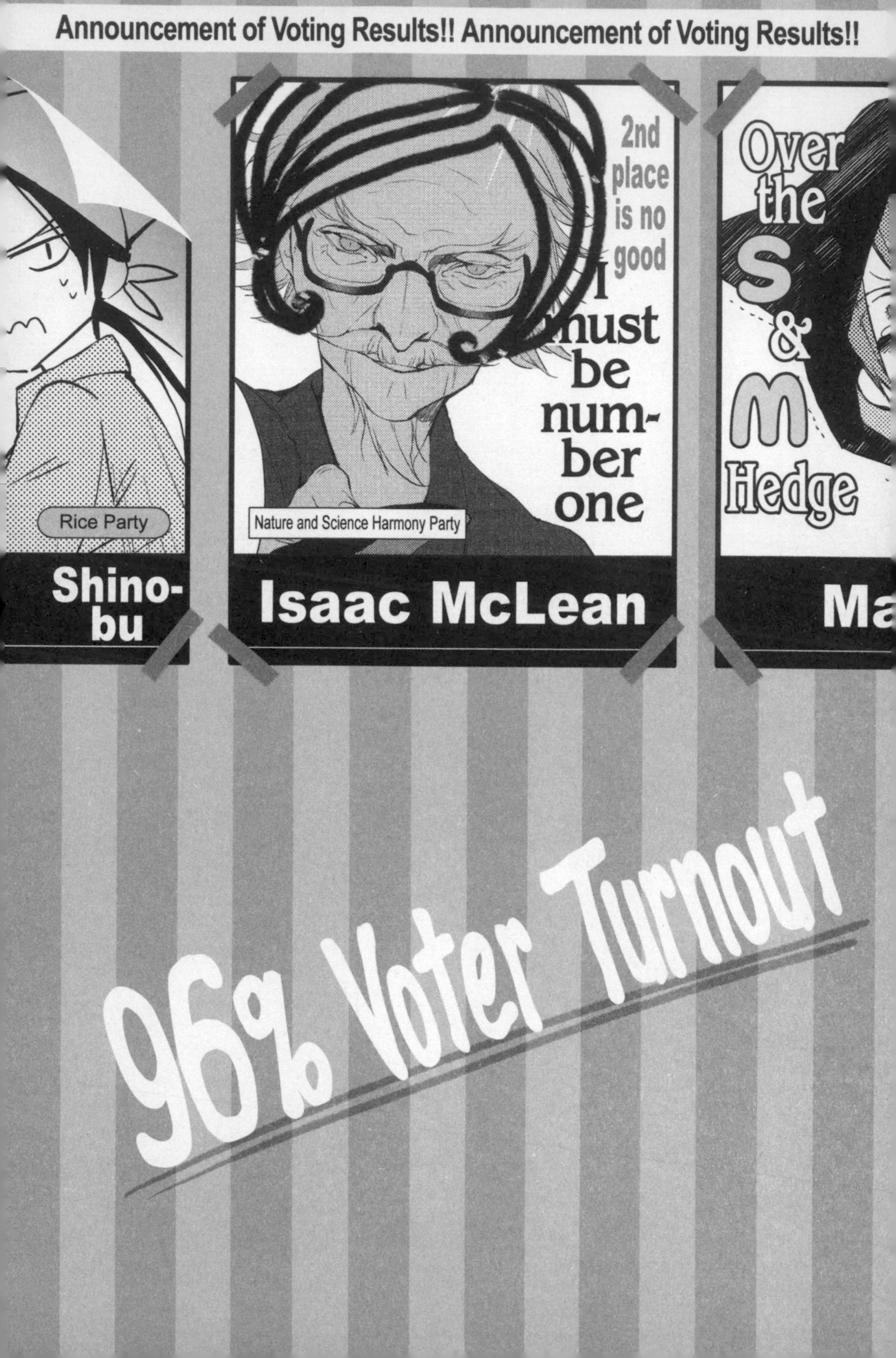
Announcement of Voting Results!! Announcement of Voting Results!!
Over the S & M Hedge
Ma
2nd place is no good
I must be number one
Nature and Science Harmony Party
Isaac McLean
Rice Party
Shinobu
96% Voter Turnout

Announcement of Voting Results!! Announcement of Voting Results!!
Yuki
An Ally to
HOUSE-WIFE
NOT JUST HOUSE-WIVES!!
Rosario di Maria
Con-grats!
I will devote myself to You-know-who
Until my last dying breath
Rice Party
inal
Two-Tone Party

Bloody+Mary

Akaza Samamiya

akaza samamiya

Born November 7, Scorpio, blood type B.
I got a customized pillow made, and I
sleep even more soundly than before.

Bloody Mary
Volume 9
Shojo Beat Edition

story and art by Akaza Samamiya

translation Katherine Schilling
touch-up art & lettering Sabrina Heep
design Shawn Carrico
editor Erica Yee

BLOODY MARY Volume 9
© Akaza SAMAMIYA 2016
First published in Japan in 2016 by KADOKAWA
CORPORATION, Tokyo.
English translation rights arranged with KADOKAWA
CORPORATION, Tokyo.

The stories, characters and incidents mentioned
in this publication are entirely fictional.

Printed in the U.S.A.

Published by VIZ Media, LLC
P.O. Box 77010
San Francisco, CA 94107

10 9 8 7 6 5 4 3 2 1
First printing, December 2017

www.viz.com
www.shojobeat.com

PARENTAL ADVISORY
BLOODY MARY is rated T for Teen and
is recommended for ages 13 and up.
This volume includes fantasy violence.
ratings.viz.com

stop

YOU MAY BE READING THE
wrong way

IT'S TRUE: In keeping with the original Japanese comic format, this book reads from right to left—so action, sound effects and word balloons are completely reversed. This preserves the orientation of the original artwork—plus, it's fun! Check out the diagram shown here to get the hang of things, and then turn to the other side of the book to get started!

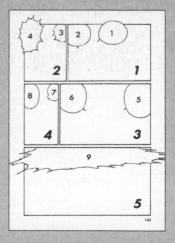